WIDE NEIGHBORHOODS

Wide

Neighborhoods

A Story of the
Frontier Nursing Service

Mary Breckinridge

THE UNIVERSITY PRESS OF KENTUCKY

Frontispiece photo of Mary Breckinridge
by Caufield & Shook, Louisville

The Frontier Nursing Service expresses its
appreciation to those special friends who made
this edition possible by supporting its publication.

ISBN: 0-8131-1453-5 cloth; -0149-2 paper
Library of Congress Catalog Card number: 81-50181

Copyright© 1981 by The University Press of Kentucky

Scholarly publisher for the Commonwealth,
serving Berea College, Centre College of Kentucky,
Eastern Kentucky University, The Filson Club,
Georgetown College, Kentucky Historical Society,
Kentucky State University, Morehead State University,
Murray State University, Northern Kentucky University,
Transylvania University, University of Kentucky,
University of Louisville, and Western Kentucky University.

Editorial and Sales Offices: Lexington, Kentucky 40506.

CONTENTS

ciation by the American press—Courtesies of the American press—Magazine articles, feature stories, and the like, plus photographers, and the trouble they bring—Facts as opposed to theories.

FOREWORD

By Marvin Breckinridge Patterson

Wide Neighborhoods is the story of a woman of vision with sound practical sense. Nothing in Mary Breckinridge's origins or upbringing would have led one to guess that she would become one of the great nurses in history, to follow in the footsteps of Florence Nightingale and Clara Barton. Her great achievements lay in introducing into the United States the concept of the trained nurse-midwife, modeled on those of the British Isles, and in establishing a demonstration project of complete family health care in a remote rural area through the organization which she founded in 1925 and directed until her death in 1965—the Frontier Nursing Service.

I was fortunate enough to know Mary Breckinridge and to work with her in the formative years of the Frontier Nursing Service. She was my father's first cousin, and I remember her staying with my family when I was a school girl, first in France and later in New York. During those visits she told us of her plans to establish a nursing service primarily for mothers and babies in the remote mountains of Eastern Kentucky. When the FNS became a reality, I wanted to help in her work, to live as frontier Americans had lived a century earlier, to share in the adventure, and at the same time to be of service to the public. So in 1928, a year after graduating from Vassar College, I went to Hyden, Kentucky, as the FNS's first girl "courier"—as the volunteers were and are called. I lived mostly at Wendover, the two-story log house which Mrs. Breckinridge had had built with her own money.

My duties at Wendover were mainly in transportation, as they are for today's couriers, but in those days it was all done on horseback, for there were no roads for automobiles. One of Mrs. Breckinridge's duties was to make monthly "rounds," which meant riding half a day to an outpost center, reviewing the records and problems for half a day with the nurses, and then proceeding to the next center. It took almost a week to cover the six centers then open. I vividly remember one such occasion when I accompanied her. It was winter and the weather was bitterly cold, but we were dressed properly—she in her gray-blue riding uniform and I in riding breeches and boots, both of us with yellow slickers over all. The horses had to splash through several creeks, after cautiously tapping the sheet of ice at the edge, and their manes, tails, and fetlocks were soon covered with ice. After several hours we reached the hospital, the end of our journey, and I found, to my embarrassment, that my hands were too cold to perform part of my job, removing the bridles. But willing, warm hands came out to help. When we entered the nurses' living room, other hands unfastened the slickers, which stood straight up on the floor, stiff with ice!

Couriers did all sorts of tasks, usually on horseback, besides taking care of the horses. We met visitors at the railway station in Hazard, twenty-five miles away, and explained the work to them. We guided doctors to remote cabins, through the fords in the Middle Fork of the Kentucky River and up rocky creekbeds, to visit sick children. We also did a lot of odd jobs to save the nurses' valuable time, and sometimes we accompanied a nurse-midwife to a nighttime delivery, where the courier would make a fire, boil water, and hold a flashlight. There was no electricity in the entire area except at the Hyden Hospital and one nursing center.

It was an exciting time for me, full of rich learning experiences, and a far cry from my New York life. I learned a great deal about humanity and compassion from Mary Breckinridge. The following year she wrote and asked me to study professional film-making so I could return and make a 35 mm film to help raise funds for the Service. This resulted in "The Forgotten Frontier," made in 1930. I travelled over six hundred miles on horseback while filming it.

I was glad to be back working at Wendover. The dog-trot had been enclosed to make a dining room for the fourteen women of the staff—nurses, supervisors, secretaries, clerks, and couriers. Mrs. Breckinridge presided at the head of the table and said grace before meals. Since the diners were young, they deferred politely to their older leader, who sometimes wished for a happy little argument. As a cousin, I had a little more leeway. I remember one argument I had with her when I wanted her, as the most important person, to appear in my film, and she thought that it would be embarrassing to stand up before an audience and show a film in which she herself appeared. She did not want to play the role of heroine. After a couple of days I finally persuaded her, appealing to her great sense of hospitality and courtesy, to be filmed receiving guests on the terrace in front of Wendover. She said I was like a kitten—you put it out one door and it came in the other.

Receiving guests from this country and abroad was one of Mary Breckinridge's pleasures, for they brought news of the world outside and often prompted lively discussions. Despite her inner grief at the loss of her two children, she was able to laugh aloud and to entertain others from her own full, rich life. A doctor from Madras wrote of her: "She had in her the elegance of past ages, the gracious daily life, and the courage to ride a spacecraft. I must thank the State Department for giving me the unique opportunity and the pleasure of enjoying for a few days her hospitality, her youthful spirit in spite of age, her sense of humor, her joyous laughter and homely chats by the fireside. In her presence one felt elated and confident, and from her one imbibed the urge to make life better for our fellow men. I shall cherish her memory."

Mary Breckinridge was a small woman with big blue eyes that opened wide. She was an eager listener, sitting with face thrust forward. After a riding accident in 1931 that broke her back, she wore a brace, which made her slightly hunch-backed. Her hair was straight and brown until it grayed in later years, and she wore it as short as boys did then, with no special haircut. She had no vanity—she thought that her work, her kinfolk, her friends, and books were far more important than her looks. She cared nothing for fashion, either, but abhorred a spot or a hole in anything. She bought good clothes and wore them again and again. I tried to persuade her to dress smartly when addressing chic city women, as she frequently did for the FNS committees she had formed in a dozen cities to help raise funds. I thought she should show them that, although she was happy to live in the wilderness and ride horseback through mud and water to work with the sick, she belonged to their group, too. My argument made no impression whatever.

Whenever she started out on a speaking tour, her female cousins would tell her, "Mary, you *must* get a new hat." Ladies always wore hats in public in those days, but she hated them, and after being introduced to an audience she would tear off her hat with a sweeping gesture and face the audience with her styleless haircut. Once when I was a young girl in New York she asked me to go with her to buy a new hat, as the cousins had told her to do. She took me to Knox Hatters and asked for a classic felt hat, with brim down in front and up in back and a feather in the hatband. She asked me how I liked it, and I replied, "Cousin Mary, it looks just like your old one!" That was what she wanted. When she turned seventy she said she would not wear a hat again—and she didn't. (She disliked being in her sixties because she did not like the word sexagenarian, but how she loved to roll out septuagenarian—every syllable of it!)

She had trouble with corsages, too. It was customary to present one to the speaker, yet she struggled between her annoyance at having to wear one and her great sense of courtesy. She was wont to say, "Gratitude is an aristocratic virtue." She also disliked microphones and would banish them whenever she could.

An excellent speaker, she took after her grandfather, John C. Breckinridge, who had been vice president of the United States under James Buchanan. Her manner was lively, her talks informative and laced with heartwarming anecdotes. She tried to make life on the frontier vivid to her city-bred audiences. At one conservative woman's club, when she noted a few elderly ladies starting to doze off, she described the round worms that infested the children, told of how many came from one child, and held up her hands to show how long they were—maybe eight or ten inches. The dozing ladies woke up with a start, horrified, and listened attentively thereafter. The female cousins said, "Mary, you shouldn't talk about things like that," but she knew what she was doing.

Another subject considered taboo in the 1930s was birth control. She did not include it in her speeches, but she always hoped someone would ask a question about it, and if necessary she planted a question to give her a good reason for mentioning the delicate subject. On the survey which she made alone on horseback in 1923, she discovered many families with ten or twelve children, living in extreme poverty. The people were hospitable and would invite her to "take the night." One woman, in answer to her question about how many children she had, said, "Eight are here and four are better-off," meaning "in the next world."

In her later years, because of her broken back, Mrs. Breckinridge spent much of her day in bed. The night watchman, on guard against fires, would bring her coffee at four in the morning and light her open coal fire. Then she worked in bed until the daily conference with three or four senior staff members began at eight. She would dress just before lunch at noon, and afterwards go out to feed her chickens, which were both hobby and exercise and provided fresh eggs for all at Wendover. Then she returned to work again until four, when all would gather around the tea table near the window overlooking the river. On the day before she died, she was busy editing material for the FNS *Quarterly Bulletin*.

One of Mrs. Breckinridge's sayings was, "The easiest thing is to do, the next easiest is to write, and the hardest is to think." She did all three, though not in that order. Having decided that what she wanted to do with the last half of her life was to provide quality health care for families in a remote area, as a model for the rest of the world, she set to her task with intelligence and careful preparation. Inwardly she was guided by a deep spiritual feeling, and influenced by the anchoress who appears in these pages. An FNS trustee wrote: "What she hid closest in her heart was her deep religious faith. Of this she spoke little, but it was at the back of all she accomplished. Each morning was begun with her own special arrangement of prayer and devotional reading, and while she could, she always led Sunday Evensong at Wendover Chapel. Her innate truthfulness required that whatever she expressed spiritually must be real, must be acted on daily and tested by life." It is appropriate that banners in memory of Mary Breckinridge hang in the Washington Cathedral.

Mrs. Breckinridge took a two-year leave of absence to write *Wide Neighborhoods*. She delighted in great English literature, which she read widely until her eyesight failed. She would quote from it aptly to spice her conversation. Her love of books gave her a sense of style, and her autobiography holds the interest of the reader effortlessly, as its wide sales attest. Its reappearance, after being out of print for many years, is a welcome event.

Since *Wide Neighborhoods* was written, many changes have come to the FNS. Its service area has grown from 700 square miles to 1,000 square miles, almost the size of Rhode Island, and the inhabitants now number over 20,000. An excellent highway comes within two miles of Hyden, the seat of Leslie County, and paved roads reach all the nursing centers. There are no more horses in use—the nurses use jeeps to reach outlying houses over rocky roads and up creekbeds. Easier and quicker transportation has meant that some outpost centers could be combined, yet the patients can still reach the nurses. At the same time, new centers are being established on the periphery of the area to treat those who could not be served before.

The people of the area no longer suffer severe economic hardship, thanks in part to government welfare programs, and they now take a more active part in planning and supporting their nursing centers. A women's auxiliary of local residents has been formed to work in the hospital and to raise funds for needed equipment. In 1952 all but two members of the board of governors were from Kentucky but none from the mountains. Now they come from seven states and five are local residents.

In the years covered by this book, most of the 9,000 babies delivered by the FNS nurse-midwives were born in their cabins. Now almost all are born in the FNS hospital at Hyden. It is a matter of pride that in fifty-five years and nearly 19,000 deliveries, the FNS has lost only eleven mothers, two of whom were cardiac victims, and since 1951 not a single mother has died in childbirth. Even in the early years the infant mortality rate was under three percent. In 1979 the rate was zero.

Preventive health care has always been a major objective of the FNS. In the early years the nurses, in addition to regular clinics held at the outpost centers, made many house visits. While treating a patient they also evaluated the living conditions and taught the family how to live a healthier life by building sanitary privies to eliminate such diseases as typhoid fever. To cut down the incidence of pellagra they encouraged the mountain families to balance their diet of corn, pork, and sometimes chicken by adding local fruits and greens, such as poke which grows wild on the hillsides. And they taught child care, especially the care of infants. In addition, over half a million immunizations against smallpox, typhoid fever, diphtheria, whooping cough, tetanus, and later measles were given in the schools. This program is still being carried on, for prevention of illness not only reduces human suffering but also cuts the costs of health care.

In 1958, when Dr. John Rock's famous Pill was introduced, the FNS region was one of the first areas where it was used. Since then a broad family planning program has been started which has been highly successful.

The volunteer program has been extended in recent years, and a few young men have been added, as well as some medical, nursing, dental, and other health care students. Some of the couriers work as aides in clinics, on the oral history project, and in research, with audio-visuals, and in public relations. Transportation of patients, supplies, and guests is still an important part of the courier's job, but whereas in 1952 this was done with twenty horses, one mule, fourteen jeeps, and one station-wagon, there are no longer any animals and all is mechanized.

During its first complete year, the Service's expenses amounted to just under $26,000. These were met by private donations except for small fees of a dollar or two per family per year and five dollars for complete care of a maternity case. In 1979, expenses were over $4,000,000. Payments from Medicare, Medicaid, and insurance companies now supply part of the FNS income, but contributions are still needed to balance the budget. Mary Breckinridge said proudly that she never asked for money, though she raised over six million dollars. She said she just told people about the conditions and the need, and if their hearts were touched they would open their checkbooks. Out of her own small fortune she saved only enough to spare the Service any expense if she should become incapacitated; the rest she gave to the FNS.

Mary Breckinridge was a woman of extraordinary vision. In her last chapter she writes about the future of the Service. She foresaw many visits by health professionals to share their knowledge and to study this model of rural health care in order to adapt the plan to their own needs. Thousands have come from sixty countries on six continents, sent by the World Health Organization, the Department of State, the Department of Health, Education and Welfare, and the Agency for International Development.

Mrs. Breckinridge foresaw the formal academic training needed to prepare the family nurse, a concept which she put into practice in 1925. In 1970 a course in family nursing was added to the Graduate School of Midwifery which she founded in 1939. That school is the oldest such school still in operation in the United States. It was preceded only by the Maternity Center in New York, whose school was started in 1932 by an FNS nurse-midwife.

Mrs. Breckinridge foresaw the need for a new and larger hospital for both patient care and teaching. The forty-bed Mary Breckinridge Hospital, opened in 1975, is a modern unit which has extended its facilities to include not only medical and surgical care but also dental, pharmaceutical, and mental health services and social work.

She foresaw the need for a chapel as a place to worship and to provide religious inspiration. St. Christopher's Chapel, built largely through local private donations, now stands on the hill next to the old hospital.

Mary Breckinridge planned and established a new concept of health care for rural areas, and her dreams have been carried out. Her efforts have benefitted not only the people who live in a section of the Kentucky mountains, but also those in far-flung areas of the world through the visits of health professionals and the services of FNS trainees who work and teach others in many countries. Truly Mary Breckinridge carried out her intention, expressed in the title of this book: ". . . like the banyan tree of the forest, yielding shade and fruit to wide neighborhoods of men."

Marvin Breckinridge Patterson (Mrs. Jefferson Patterson), Chairman of the Board of Governors, 1960-1975, is now Honorary Chairman of the Frontier Nursing Service.

This book is dedicated to you
who read it and like parts of it.
To you who read and like it all—
it is dedicated with fervor.

AUTHOR'S ACKNOWLEDGMENTS

This book has no preface, no footnotes, no appendix, and no apologies. I do, however, want to acknowledge the help I have received in its preparation. I am grateful to the following people for the following things:

To my kinsman Church Ford, United States District Judge for the Eastern District of Kentucky, for reading the section on the prohibition era in the Kentucky mountains, and giving me advice, which I took—To Mr. W. E. Hedges, Forester, Regional Office U. S. Forest Service, Philadelphia, and to Mr. H. L. Borden, Forest Supervisor, Cumberland National Forest, for their help in the preparation of the forestry section—To Mr. J. F. Blackerby, Director of the Division of Vital Statistics of the Kentucky State Department of Health, for reading the story of our survey of Leslie County, and checking the figures on births and deaths—To Mrs. Myrtle C. Applegate and Miss Jessie Greathouse of our National Nursing Council for giving their approval to the section on the training of nurses—To Mr. Howard G. Brunsman, Chief of the Population and Housing Division of the Bureau of the Census, for sending me the Bureau's rural-farm household figures and writing me that a valid comparison could be made between them and the average number of related persons in the Frontier Nursing Service households—To our statistician, Kay MacMillan, for supplying the Frontier Nursing Service figures—To the Research Director of the Frontier Nursing Service, Ella Woodyard, for permission to use, in advance of their publication elsewhere, her Intelligence Quotient figures for 810 children, age 35 to 40 months.

For reading the manuscript of this book, in its entirety, on her three visits to Wendover, and for her suggestions, I tender my special thanks to our national chairman, Mrs. Morris B. Belknap of Louisville—And to our vice-chairman, Mrs. Henry B. Joy of Detroit, for reading a large part of it on her two visits to Wendover—And to my friends, Margaret Gage and Gerald Heard, who followed the progress of the book from its inception, read and advised on the story—in batches—and sustained me by their encouragement.

I am indebted to Helen E. Browne, Agnes Lewis, and Ella Woodyard of our Wendover staff for their study of each chapter as it was written—To Mary Jo Clark and Mary Ann Quarles for information on social service—To my cousin Anne Steele (Mrs. Waring Wilson) for her help with the family sections—To Leona and Gillous Morgan of Hyden for looking up data for me—To Ruth Morgan, my book secretary, for her skill and hardihood, and to Peggy Elmore, who coped with me during the month in which Ruth got married—To my personal secretary, Lucille Knechtly, who carried the weight of my correspondence almost without me—To many others, including members of our Hyden Hospital staff, who advised me on bits of the book.

Although I know it is unusual to do so, I want to thank Miss Elizabeth Lawrence of the editorial staff of Harper & Brothers for her courtesy and patience, and for the high quality of her suggestions—From the depth of a grateful heart, I thank our committees of Hyden, Wendover, Beech Fork, Bowlingtown, Brutus, Confluence, Flat Creek, and Red Bird for meeting with me and listening to parts of the book on which I wanted their advice—In like manner, I thank those in our committees beyond the mountains, chairmen and members, who not only left me free to spend long months in writing, but carried their work for the Frontier Nursing Service with abiding loyalty.

The lines from "The Death of St. Christopher" by Laurence Housman are taken from Housman's *Selected Poems* published in 1908 by Sidgwick and Jackson, Ltd., of London.

Since there is no other place where I can give the information, I might as well say here that the royalties from the sale of this book go direct to the Frontier Nursing Service. In its behalf, I have executed an irrevocable deed of conveyance to all rights in *Wide Neighborhoods*.

MARY BRECKINRIDGE

Wendover, Kentucky
January 12, 1952

Chapter 1

I

IN looking back over the years of my childhood to find things that had a bearing on what came to be the Frontier Nursing Service, there is one event that stands out in my memory above all others and that is the birth of my younger brother in Russia in the early nineties. My father was the American Minister in Cleveland's second administration and we were living in what was then St. Petersburg. We had not had a baby in the family for ten years. I was fourteen years old. We had spent the summer in a *dacha* at Terijoki on the Gulf of Finland but went back to Petersburg early because of the baby that was to come in September. If it had been my own, I could not have taken a larger interest in the preparations. Aside from that, anything that led to an escape from my governess was always welcome. The dainty things made by nuns in a convent were a compromise between what American babies wore and the fashions of Russian babies. The Russians were swaddled and bound to little mattresses. My mother was afraid to discard the mattress altogether, since nurses never held the babies in their arms without them. So baby, unswaddled, was to go on a mattress encased by a piqué coverlet. There was a rubber mattress for his bath.

Russian women of rank did not nurse their babies; wet nurses were provided for them from the country. These women wore picturesque costumes of red for boys and blue for girls. They were always attended by responsible women, in dark clothes, who looked after their habits and their health. One often met them taking an airing on the streets. We did not have one of these gorgeous creatures and her attendant because my mother had made up her mind to nurse her baby herself. In this departure from custom, she had the example of the young Empress, whose first baby, the Grand Duchess Olga, was expected at about the same time as ours. To a shocked court the young Empress announced that she was going to nurse her baby herself.

Now to come to the event in this setting that made an early impression on my young mind and was to lead long afterward to my realization of the kind of nurse we needed for the Frontier Nursing Service—a nurse who was also a midwife. My mother had engaged two doctors for her confinement. One was our family physician, Dr. Duncan, a Russian subject with a Scottish father and a Russian mother. We were, all of us, fond of him and he was in and out of the place constantly. The other was one of the outstanding obstetricians in Petersburg. The Russian midwife, Madame Kouchnova, whom the doctors engaged to attend my mother, was chosen because she spoke a little French. Afterward, my mother told me that when the baby was born the two doctors stood by in their white coats while Madame Kouchnova did the delivery. It was a normal delivery and there was no reason why they should interfere. I recalled this often. Apparently, there were women called midwives who were trained to do normal deliveries for the doctors.

Of Madame Kouchnova herself, I remember vividly her waking me up in the night with the exclamation: *"Horosho malchik!"* which is the Russian for "beautiful boy." My mother had another recollection of which she told me afterward. She knew the Russian love of tea. All classes drank it at all hours. On the streets men walked along with samovars on their backs. Any thirsty person could get his tea for a copper coin. In their homes the Russians drank it in glasses in metal holders, but it was always made with a samovar. Knowing that tea was indispensable, my mother had arranged to have a footman wait up on the night of her confinement to make fresh tea for the doctors and midwife whenever they pulled the bell rope in the bedroom.

Early in my mother's labor, Madame Kouchnova came to her and asked for the samovar. My mother told her that if she wanted tea she had only to pull the bell cord and it would be brought in, freshly made. But Madame Kouchnova shook her head and said that she wanted a samovar on a table right at hand. She explained, in her broken French, that she was accustomed to tea whenever she wanted it without waiting for bell cords and footmen. To this my mother replied, "I have no samovar." Here Madame Kouchnova threw up her hands and wailed aloud, "Many babies have I seen born, but never one without a samovar!" Since this was my mother's fourth child, she told Madame Kouchnova that she knew, from experience, that babies could be born without samovars.

At the time of my mother's first two confinements in the South, there was no such thing as antisepsis, to say nothing of asepsis. My older brother was born in 1877 and I was born in 1881. My mother went back both times to stay with her mother in Memphis, Tennessee; and that is how it happens that we were born there in a place of many friends but no kindred and no ancestral ties. When I was at school in Switzerland, the principal, Madame Eytel-Hubbé, asked me where I was born. When I said Memphis, she exclaimed, "How did your mother happen to be wandering among those old ruins?" My mother and her mother belonged no more in Memphis, Tennessee, than in Memphis, Egypt, but there was a reason why my grandmother had gone there. The plantations in Mississippi were too disturbed in Reconstruction days for my mother's brothers to be willing to keep their mother and sister in the country. These uncles were young. Although three of them had been in the Confederate Army, the oldest wasn't twenty-one at the end of the Civil War. They could bear the brunt of Reconstruction on the plantations, but they did not want to risk their beloved women. It was not until after my birth that the Memphis house was sold and, afterward, torn down to make way for the city's growth.

Old Dr. Maurey, the leading physician in Memphis in the late seventies and the early eighties, took care of my mother when we were born. There were no trained nurses then. Mammy Sally, a darling old colored woman, nursed Dr. Maurey's patients. With no asepsis, nor antisepsis even, it was natural enough for women to have what was called childbed fever. My mother had it after I was born, and I was raised on a colored wet nurse and a goat. Mammy Sally's daughter, Victoria, had a baby named Jeannetta. Victoria came morning and evening to nurse me; in between I had the goat. Members of my family have been known to say that my intense interest in breast feeding dates back to those days.

My mother's third child, my sister Lees, was born in Washington, D.C. By that time and in that place, asepsis was known. There were also beginning to be such things as trained nurses, and my mother had one. This was the confinement my mother remembered as a happy time in which everything had been normal. It will be seen that when she told Madame Kouchnova that samovars were not needed in order to give birth to children, she was speaking from a varied experience.

II

The place where my mind was first drawn to the Kentucky mountains was called Hazelwood. This was a large stone rambling country house, near High Bridge, New York, where we stayed every summer until we went to Europe when I was thirteen. It was the home of my great aunt, Mrs. James Lees, whom we children called grandmother. Her only sister was my real grandmother on my mother's side, but she died while we were small. Grandmother Lees's husband had been a

3

banker in New York and long ago they built this house in what was then open country on the Ridge above the Harlem River. There were cow pastures, where I played with my cousins, through which ran a stream called the Minnie Dale. There were wide lawns and many flowers, including a greenhouse full of them. My cousin, Susanna Lees, used to let me help her arrange them when the gardener brought them in for the house. There were wonderful trees to climb and plenty of books to take up into the trees to read. It was a paradise for a city child such as I was then, for in the winter we lived in Washington.

Hazelwood had associations with my mother's young years. She was born on a plantation in Louisiana, called Airlie, which she fondly remembered as the home of her childhood. After the end of the Civil War, when she was twelve years old, her widowed mother brought her to Hazelwood. She stayed there for four years with her aunt, my Grandmother Lees, and with three other little Confederate kinsmen. This meant that we, the children of the little Confederates, were the second generation to play in the cow pastures and climb the trees.

All of this may seem a far cry from the Kentucky mountains but it is not. My Grandmother Lees was a wealthy and charitable woman, a Kentuckian by birth and a Confederate in her allegiance. She spent a large part of her fortune in the education of Southern children and especially Kentucky children. Such is the unity of all Kentuckians, even when divided by Civil War, that it never mattered to my Grandmother Lees whether a child in Kentucky was of Federal or Confederate stock. The majority of the mountaineers had been Unionists. Most of them in those days lacked any opportunities for education. My Grandmother Lees put hundreds of them through school and college. I doubt if she ever refused to help any Kentucky mountain child of whose need she knew. At Hazelwood, I delighted in sitting at her feet and listening to the letters she read aloud from her boys. I suppose there were girls who wrote too, but I seem to remember only the letters from boys. I do know that it was from these letters I first became interested in the Kentucky mountains. Nearly a lifetime later, when I was living on money that had come from my Grandmother Lees (my share of my mother's share), it seemed altogether right to use this money to start the Frontier Nursing Service in the Kentucky mountains.

III

It would be hard to imagine an education less suited to the work I was to do than mine. In fact, in the American sense, I had no education. My older brother, James Carson, whom we called by his middle name,

4

was sent to first-class schools in Washington, but my sister Lees and I had governesses. That had been my mother's own education and it was the kind she wanted for her little girls. I seem to remember a year of kindergarten, and then, from about the age of six, a daily German governess who gave us lessons in the afternoons. Although we liked her, I have no recollection of learning much under her. In the morning we played out of doors near the house, while Nurse Mary sat in the areaway to keep an eye on us.

During all the years in Washington, my mother read aloud to us in the late afternoons, or in the evenings until our bedtime, when she did not have engagements. These books included not only the children's classics of that day, from *Uncle Remus* to *Alice in Wonderland*, but almost all of Dickens' novels, and several of Scott's and Thackeray's.

One winter we spent at Pine Bluff in Arkansas, where my mother not only read to us but taught my sister and me herself. My brother was tutored. We stayed in a rented house with a big fenced-in yard where we had two pets. One was a collie dog named Shep, who went everywhere with us, even to Russia two years later. Another was a mockingbird that fell out of a nest. My mother gave it the French name of Douce, on the assumption that it was a girl bird. We never knew, because it died before it was fully grown. It stayed close by us, even hopping on our pillows in the morning to wake us up. In a copy of a New Testament I owned as a child, I still have one of Douce's feathers and a lock of Shep's hair.

One summer we took a camping trip up to the Nipigon in the Far North in Canada before our annual visit at Hazelwood. My father was a great fisherman. He had been up there the summer before with men, but he was a domestic person and could not rest until he had taken his family with him on a second trip. We outfitted at a Hudson Bay post station (with supplies and Indian guides) for a trek of six weeks' duration. Even there, living in tents and canoes, I can remember my mother reading aloud to us from *Dombey and Son.* She kept a journal of this trip. In it I find the first reference anywhere to my lifelong custom of telling stories to children, making them up as I go along. Here in the Kentucky mountains at our rallies, I tell stories to the children while they sit around me cross-legged on the ground. In her Nipigon journal my mother wrote she overheard me say to my little sister, "He came in on his smiling legs and sat down by the man with the proud and haughty stomach." I was nine years old that summer and Lees had a fifth birthday on the Nipigon trip.

My brother Carson and I invented a story that lasted us for years about a creature called Mean Juice. It was not a boy nor a girl, nor an animal either, and its adventures were fantastic. We would make up stories about Mean Juice on our long journeys by slow trains that traveled wearily down to the Far South. The Pullmans were primitive (with oil lamps) and we lived in them for hours and days.

I must explain why we happened to travel frequently between Washington and Arkansas, and why we were not brought up in Kentucky. My father, who was born and raised near Lexington, Kentucky, became a Confederate soldier at fifteen and a midshipman in what was left of the Confederate Navy in his eighteenth year. When the Civil War was over, he was sent to Washington College at Lexington, Virginia, because General Lee had taken the presidency of it. General Lee told his Confederate soldier-students to stay with the South. Since Reconstruction did not hit Kentucky in the way it hit the Far South, because of the ties of kindred between Kentuckians who had followed the Confederacy and those who had stayed with the Union, my father decided to move to Louisiana. He was in the cotton commission business there, and to New Orleans he took my mother as a bride. He and his older brother, Cabell, became interested in plantations in eastern Arkansas and went there to live as cotton planters. As soon as Reconstruction was over, and Confederate soldiers could vote again, my father was sent to Congress. This is not the place in which to write of his public life, but it will explain why so much of our childhood seems to have been spent on trains.

The brother-sister tie in my mother's family was an unbreakable bond. She adored her four brothers and usually managed to stop off to see the three of them who lived in the South, on our way to or from Arkansas. My uncles Joseph and James Carson lived on Oasis plantation in the Delta country of the Mississippi. Uncle Jimmy died unmarried and young. Oasis, in my childhood and girlhood, was dearer to me than any other place in the world. I can remember now the welcoming sound of the frogs in the swamps on the seven-mile drive at night to the plantation from Friar's Point, where we landed from a Mississippi River steamboat. One thing I did learn on the plantation that was to be of use to me in the Frontier Nursing Service, and that was to ride. My Uncle Joe insisted that children learn to ride bareback. I don't recall when I first fell off a horse, because I was always falling off them. I think I began to ride, not only bareback but probably barelegged as well, seated astride behind my brother.

Oasis plantation was the last of my Grandfather Carson's lands left in the family. His people came from the Natchez neighborhood in Mississippi. He had been raised on a plantation there. An only son of an only son, he had inherited not only large lands but many servants, something like three hundred slaves. After his marriage to Catherine Waller, he went to Philadelphia long enough to take training as a physician, because it was his intention to free his slaves and he wanted a profession. There was one, I recall, whom he did free and send

6

to Liberia. But the lot of freed Negroes in the South was a destitute and unhappy one, so that my grandfather decided it was his duty to care for those he had inherited. He often told his wife that the heaviest thing on his heart was the thought of leaving this responsibility to his children. It was because he had so many slaves that he bought Airlie plantation in Louisiana and, shortly before the Civil War, Oasis plantation in the Delta country. When all of the other lands were gone, the Oasis plantation remained because it was a wilderness then, and not taxed under Reconstruction too heavily to hold.

On a three-acre Indian mound at Oasis, my uncles built a long, low house with a gallery running its full length. Great oak and pecan trees shaded this house. About a half-mile behind it were the Negro quarters. Most of these colored people had belonged to the family and had followed their young masters from Airlie to Oasis. The older ones were taken care of as long as they lived. From among the younger ones came the house servants that I knew and loved as a child. Quasher, Aunt Susan's son, ran the cotton gin. Pompey, who had been Uncle Joe's body servant during the Civil War, lived at the quarters with his wife, Alice, who was one of the house servants. For Pompey, Uncle Joe would do almost anything. Although times were hard on plantations in my childhood, for money could not be borrowed at less than twenty per cent interest, so that improvements were difficult to come by, there always seemed to be an abundance of things to eat. In addition to sheep, hogs, chickens, and vegetables raised on the place, there was game in the forests and fish in the streams.

Even though I had no formal education in the modern sense, I learned to read so young that I don't remember at what age. I do recall reading *Little Women* aloud to Nurse Mary while she brushed my hair and my feeling of chagrin at her lack of interest in the story. My favorite books were those of adventure, of which the best-loved was *The Young Marooners* by Goulding. At about eleven, I adored Mayne Reid's *Afloat in the Forest* and things like that. At thirteen, in London, I found *The Jungle Book* in a shop and got my father to give it to me. I also loved poetry and memorized, for fun, pages of it. A favorite book of mine, because I was an ardent young Confederate, was a collection of verse called *The Southern Amaranth*, a great deal of which I knew by heart.

We never had a home of our own in Washington nor, indeed, anywhere else in our childhood. My mother had the money to make a down payment on a house, and she often told my father that we could buy one for the money we spent year after year in rent. Whenever a desirable place that was within her means came on the market, the same conversation would take place. My father would remind her that his father had bought a Washington house, when he was Vice-

President, and that it had been confiscated by the Federal Government when he went with the Confederacy. My mother would reply that times were different now and the Federal Government would not confiscate our house if we bought one. At this, my father would shake his head and say that Washington real estate wasn't safe. I don't remember his ever refusing my mother anything she wanted that lay within our narrow means, except the thing she wanted most, which was a home of her own. The result of all this was that we continued to live, like St. Paul, in a hired house. For years it was the same building, a three-story house in a row near the Capitol grounds. Before the last winter in Washington, we must have overextended ourselves because we moved to a smaller two-story house that winter.

During the years of our childhood on North Capitol Street, we had a winter visit from my Grandmother Breckinridge, whom we loved dearly. Our family is much given to the writing of private memoirs, so that I have one of my Grandmother Breckinridge, written by one of her daughters, my Aunt Jane. From this I learned more than my grandmother ever told us of the years in which she followed the fortunes of the Confederacy with her husband, and her years of exile with him in Europe and in Canada. The memoir also brings out that aspect of my Grandmother Breckinridge that we knew best, her intense love of home and flowers. She had a faculty, wherever she was, of creating a look of home and of sharing, always of sharing, what she had with others.

As my mind dwells on the memories of my Washington childhood, I realize that, aside from books, of which we had thousands, such education as I received came from people. My father was a free trader and what became known as a Cleveland Gold Democrat. He was an ardent believer in a free competitive form of society, universal, with no hampering restrictions on trade. I often heard him say that if we entered the free trade area of the British Empire, we could, together, keep the peace of the world. I think it would have worked had it been tried; that a Pax Britannica-Americana could have prevented the First World War. All of this has a real bearing on the Frontier Nursing Service. When I went to London to take my training as a midwife, I did not feel as though I were in an alien country. After we started the Frontier Nursing Service, it seemed natural to me to use British nurse-midwives, and our British and American staff have always been as one family.

Chapter 2

I

ALTHOUGH the Russian capital was named St. Petersburg in the days when I lived there, it was usually called Petersburg, after Peter the Great who was no saint. In my second year there, when I was fourteen, I started a journal, which has a bearing on this book because that is how I learned to write and to spell. Nobody taught me English grammar, which I don't know down to this day. Unfortunately, I had no aptitude for arithmetic and no liking for it. Since my governesses, too, knew nothing much about arithmetic, and cared less, that is a subject on which I am probably more ill-informed than any other woman who moves in educated circles today. I agree with Sir Walter Scott's "Pet Marjory" that the multiplication tables are something that even Nature herself can't endure.

My brother Carson, who was with us the first year in Petersburg, had a tutor with whom I read history in English. Lees and I had a French governess. The second year, when Carson went away to school, we gave up the tutor and Fraulein joined our household. She not only kept up our German but handled some of the sewing, and took turnabout with Mademoiselle when we went walking or skating. Although my sister Lees and I and the two governesses were often together, we hadn't a language in common. They both spoke Russian; Lees and I both spoke English. The German one didn't speak French and the French one didn't speak German. When we were all four together, it was a madhouse of constant translating. It had this advantage, that they could say things about us in Russian and we could talk about them in English.

After my baby brother was born we had as his nurse an old Finnish woman named Ieda, with the accent on the "e," who was devotion itself to him during his first two years of life. She was lame and she used to rock him by moving back and forth from the short leg to the long leg. Ieda spoke German, as did nearly all the upper servants in

Russia. This made it possible for us to talk with them. Our maître d'hôtel, a sort of steward for the whole household, spoke French as well as German and, indeed, Turkish and modern Greek, which were of no use to us. His name was André, and I recall one unforgettable kindness of his. When our beloved collie dog, Shep, died during our second year in Russia, André let us bury the body in the garden of a cottage he owned in the suburbs.

The Reverend Alexander Francis was the Scottish minister of the British and American Church at Petersburg. He spoke Russian fluently and had an entrée everywhere, from the Winter Palace on down to the lowest slum. Even the police were not close-lipped with him. We attended his church, which was Independent and Congregational in type, and were so deeply attached to him that he became a lifelong friend. Years later he visited us at our island home, The Brackens, on the Muskoka Lakes in Canada. My brother and I met him at other times in London and, when I was taking my training as a midwife there, he was kindness itself to me. It may have been because of my deep affection for him that my adolescence took a profound although not a happy religious turn. I don't recall any particular attraction to religion in my early childhood. Theology, especially the grim theology of that day, repelled me. My mother gave us Christian principles without a theological bias. She had us memorize whole chapters from both the Old and New Testaments, and these have been a blessing to me all my life.

It could have been my adolescence, or the raw climate of St. Petersburg with the dark winters, but I was not well during the two years that I stayed there. I was much worse the second autumn and winter because I didn't have enough to eat. Old Dr. Duncan had a theory that when people were not strong they should eat very little. He took me off lunch, so that between a Continental breakfast, with fruit added to it, and my evening meal I had nothing whatever. In my journal are frequent references to feeling faint and "always so very tired." This Spartan treatment pulled me down so badly that my mother insisted on my having lunch after some months of semistarvation. This experience gave me such a lifelong sympathy with those dogs who are fed only once, in the evening, that I always feed mine more often. We used to joke in the family about mutual friends who, under Dr. Duncan's care, grew paler and more gaunt over the weeks. We called them Duncanites.

Aside from faintness and fatigue during my second fall and winter in Petersburg, I was lonely. I had outgrown my sister, who was still a child, and I had almost no companions of my own age. I met three charming Russian sisters (Annie, Dina and Magda) of whom the eldest was my age. We used to combine our governesses and go

10

skating together. The skating was the one thing in Russia that I loved. I had never skated before I went there, and I have never skated since I left but, as with riding and swimming, I delighted in it. There were occasionally other amenities in a life that I often wrote of as dull. It was fun to climb into the bell towers of St. Isaak's Cathedral during Easter Week and ring the smaller bells, as everyone was allowed to do during the Russians' greatest festival. I liked the low-slung sleighs, drawn by spirited horses, that were used instead of carriages and droshkies during the long winter months. Once in a while Americans would come to Petersburg with children our ages, and we would be allowed to have tea with them. The George Lauders from Pittsburgh, with daughters called Hattie and Bessie, were among the Americans who were kind to the Legation children. I recall my mortification when Lees, who was ten years old, "drank all the cream nearly, took three cups of tea with five lumps of sugar in the first one, and saw that no sugar was left except one piece which fell on the floor and which she wanted to eat also." I must say that Mr. Lauder encouraged her in this behavior but, when Mademoiselle reported it to our mother, Lees was not allowed to go again. The only things that happened to me during all my time in Petersburg which could be called gay were a concert and two bazaars.

The Fisk Jubilee Singers came to St. Petersburg to give a concert. My father, who was most punctilious in the courtesies he extended to all visiting Americans, had all of the Jubilee Singers at the Legation to tea. As my mother had not yet recovered from her confinement, my father hauled me out of the schoolroom to preside at the tea table. It was the first time I was thrown with colored people except as loved family servants. My father told me to welcome everybody very politely, and to serve them. The Fisk Jubilee Singers were themselves among the most polite people I ever met. When my father went to their concert as a patron, he took me with him. I don't remember the music but I do remember a young secretary of the Turkish Embassy who was sitting near us. He rose to stand before my father, made a low bow, and asked him in French if he would present him to Mademoiselle, his daughter. After that, he sat on the other side of me all through the concert and entertained me delightfully during intermissions. I don't know what made this young Turk behave so kindly to a little school-girl but he certainly gave me a good time.

The two bazaars brought a real escape from my governesses for a brief while. The one at the Winter Palace was a huge affair that lasted nearly a week. The Empress herself was patroness of this bazaar which was to raise funds for one of her charities, a home for convalescent governesses. All of the embassies and legations had stalls, and all sent back to their own countries for special products to sell. Ours were numerous and beautiful. My mother was fond of a number of Russians so that a good many of them helped sell at our stall, as well as the few Americans who lived then in Petersburg. She allowed me to help in the decoration of the stall and in selling. I stood just behind her when the Emperor and Empress swept through the great rooms and stopped at the stalls to say something pleasant.

The other bazaar was not so grand but I had an even more active part in it. Through Mr. Francis, my mother had become greatly interested in an institution called the Baby Home. It was maintained, at first entirely at their own expense, by two Swedish ladies, Miss Grundberg and Miss Wenberg. The Russians allowed them to take any orphan children they liked and even to bring them up as Lutherans if they wished, provided they had them baptized in the Orthodox Church. My mother interested Lady Lascelles, the wife of the British Ambassador, in the Baby Home and, together, they held a bazaar to raise funds for it. A number of Russian women joined them as patronesses, and the Grand Duchess Marie Pavlovna, wife of the Grand Duke Vladimir, sent word that she would attend the opening with her twelve-year-old daughter, the Grand Duchess Hélène. It was arranged that Lady Lascelles' daughter, who was grown, should present a bouquet to the Grand Duchess Marie, and that I should present one to the little Grand Duchess.

At the eleventh hour, these plans were suddenly thrown into a cocked hat by the unannounced arrival of the Grand Duchess Elizabeth, wife of the Grand Duke Constantine, a charming young mother of six little children. Everyone was stunned because there were only two bouquets. I was hastily summoned and told to give my bouquet to the Grand Duchess Elizabeth. I barely had time to receive my instructions when I heard my mother presenting me. Now, one of the things most carefully taught us in dancing class was to make a low *révérence*, a curtsy for royalty, but I had never been taught to make such a deep curtsy with a large bouquet in my arms. To make matters worse, the Grand Duchess (all smiles and kind words) extended her hand. I had to go down and rise and hold out my hand, clutching the bouquet the while until I could present it. The little Grand Duchess Hélène got no bouquet.

The loneliness of my life affected me chiefly in the evenings. My little sister went to bed at half past eight; at about the same time both governesses took themselves off to their rooms. It was the rarest thing that either one of them ever offered to play a game with me or to read to me. I sat in my room until late, covering pages of my journal with complaints of dullness, loneliness, and my sinful wickedness. I also read for hours all kinds of English, French and German books. They were uniformly good books but not as a rule sprightly. Among those I enjoyed the most were Miss Strickland's *Lives of the Queens of England*.

The author I find mentioned the most during this period was Milton. I read not only *Paradise Lost* but *Paradise Regained* and all of his poetry. His language sounded to me like the deep-voiced male choirs in the Russian cathedrals. I fell in love with Milton's Satan, and it nearly broke my heart when he turned into a snake. I invented "a hero" who was to come and take me away for adventures. He had many names, among them Hector, Godefroy de Bouillon, Sebastian (in *Fabiola*), Ivanhoe, Edward the First of England, Lancelot, and Alexander the Great of Greece. I wrote that he would have "the bravery of some Vikings and exiled brigands." The plan seemed to be for us to travel back into the Middle Ages together and to live where nature was wildest and no governess would ever intrude. Not that mine intruded, really. They had a limited sense of their duties, else I should not have spent most of my evenings alone.

II

In the May of 1896, we went to Moscow for the coronation of the Emperor, Nicholas II, and the Empress, Alexandra. Our Government had rented a large house for the Legation, with a great many formal rooms for entertainment and a chancellery. In addition to our family, Commander Rogers of the United States Navy and Secretary and Mrs. Pierce, with their two little boys, lived at the Legation. The two things that I best remember about the Moscow Legation are a painting of St. Cecilia and a fire. I wrote several times in my journal of going to the reception room to look at Cecilia. She wore a low-necked dress, her lips were parted slightly, her hands clasped a roll of music, and her brown eyes were "gazing at beauty I cannot see."

The fire occurred soon after eight o'clock the night of our arrival. The house had two kitchens. As the owners did not use the large one, they had stuffed straw and rags in the attic around the flue. This they neglected to mention in turning over the house. Now, Moscow had no water works in those days. All of the water used by the great city was brought in on wagons. Ours found its way somehow to a tank at the top of the house and came down by gravity. The place swarmed with servants, of whom there were more than twenty, but it was Mr. Pierce, with a little muzhik, who climbed up on a ladder to cut through a ceiling to the fire. Everybody brought him all the water they could find, including dirty dish water. After the fire was under control, the fire department arrived. Some of the firemen carried brass trumpets and nearly every other man carried also an iron torch, on a long

13

handle like a broomstick, with an open flame. In one of my mother's letters to Grandmother Lees she wrote:

> Every now and then one of the firemen blew a blast on his trumpet. When this happened the men with the torches banged their long handles on the floor in unison, for all the world like a chorus in some comic opera. The firemen that had nothing to carry stood around, looked stupid, and got shouted at.

The weeks we spent in Moscow were the happiest I had known in Russia. Warm friends of ours at St. Petersburg, an American engineer named Mr. William Smith and his lovely wife, an Englishwoman, came to Moscow to stay with his brother who was the American Consul. As the Smiths were so kind as to take me sightseeing with them around Moscow, I saw more of the old town than my father and my mother did because they were burdened with official and social duties.

Next to the Kremlin and the Troitska Monastery (founded by St. Serge in 1342), with their curious churches and treasures, the thing that made the most impression on me was an old Russian picture gallery. I don't recall a single picture among many that was not sad or horrible. I have read many Russian stories in English or French translations (by Pushkin, Turgenev, Gogol, Lermontov, Dostoevski, Tolstoy, Chekhov) and I find in them the same strains of sadness and horror. Although these things are in the novels of all races, I do think they are more common in the Russian ones. In them there is also a sense of futility, of the uselessness of trying to change one's fate.

Other Americans in Moscow, listed as "distinguished guests," were extremely kind to the Legation children. Mr. Richard Harding Davis invited us to his rooms at a hotel to see the *Entrée Solennelle* of the Emperor and Empress into Moscow after they had spent three days outside the city, at the Petrovsky Palace, in fasting and prayer. I was immensely puffed up at being asked to sit at the windows with "the grown-uppers" and eat with them, while the younger children sat at another window with the governesses.

Americans were pouring into the Legation at all hours of the day. I was especially struck by two charming girls from Minnesota, with whom I have renewed acquaintance in late years. In their fresh, young ladyhood back in the nineties, they seemed to me like people out of another world. Another "distinguished guest" in Moscow at that time was a Mrs. Nuttall whose only child, Nadine, had been left at school in Switzerland. She recommended the school to my mother. That is how I happened to go to Rosemont-Dézaley at Lausanne.

One evening my father and mother gave a large dinner which was followed by a much larger reception with music. I was allowed to attend the reception, in a party dress down to my ankles, to listen to the music. I wrote: "It was beautiful and I would so love to give a description of the dark women and men in the queer old Russian costumes of the Middle Ages, and their wild, weird songs." When the music played the Russian National Anthem, one of the most moving of them all, the singers sang the words as we all "stood in respect," I wrote. In deference to the host of the evening, my father, these gypsy-like singers decided on one American air. The song they chose was "After the Ball"! They certainly glorified it. I never knew whether or not they thought it was our National Anthem and expected us "to stand in respect."

I came in touch with the seamy side of things for the first time in Moscow, on a walk with Fraulein through mean streets and, again, on a visit to the Foundling Asylum with my mother. Since I liked babies, the sight of so many waifs nearly bowled me over. Although we saw only about three hundred ("such tiny old-looking little creatures"), the Moscow Foundling Asylum took in between twenty-five and forty a day and kept about three thousand at a time. Anyone could leave a baby at the door. Sometimes their mothers came with the babies and nursed them. All of the babies were breast-fed, two to a wet nurse. Those that were normal were sent away at the age of one month to the homes of peasants in the country, with or without their foster mothers. The peasants were paid to look after them until the age of ten, when their services would earn their keep.

This Foundling Asylum was founded by Catherine the Great and was maintained, so we were told, by a tax on playing cards and by donations. The Russians we knew were benevolent people. I remember that on my walks with Annie, Dina and Magda, they put coppers in every beggar's outstretched hand. We had been trained to save ours for charities like the Baby Home. The point of this is that, although Russian children of the upper classes gave to beggars, their people did not neglect to support the great charities as well.

It was in Moscow, also, that I first came in touch with horror and mass suffering. A popular fete for the peasants had been arranged to take place near the city on an immense plain called Khedynoïe Polé. Every provision had been made to entertain the peasants. They were not to come until the morning, but hundreds came the night before and camped out on the field. Very early the next morning thousands more (it was estimated about six hundred thousand) began arriving and pushed against the ones already there to get to the huts where the food and vodka were provided. Someone, we didn't know who, had ordered a ditch dug in front of the huts. Hundreds fell into this ditch and were trampled to death. I heard, and wrote at the time, that nearly three thousand people were killed. The hospitals were filled with the wounded. I did not know about it as I left the Legation with Mademoiselle to drive out to the "Tribune" at Khedynoïe Polé to see the merriment with some American friends. We passed wagon after wagon, driving back to Moscow, loaded with bruised and dead bodies. Their arms and legs and even their purple heads were sticking out from under the tarpaulins. My mother, who had gone early to the Emperor's pavilion, where the diplomatic corps were seated, told me afterward that when the Emperor came and stood before the crowds that remained, the tears were streaming down his face. He excused himself early from an embassy party that evening and spent the night in the hospitals. He gave a thousand rubles to every family that had lost a member.

A gentleman of my acquaintance, so I wrote at this time, asked a peasant:

"Do you love your Emperor?"

"Why, yes," answered the peasant, astonished. "He is my Little Father."

It was in Moscow that I first had to assume responsibility for a sick person. The grippe was widespread and our baby caught it. We had located a Scottish doctor who was to come again in the evening and bring a child specialist. My poor mother, burdened with engagements, could not see the physicians herself. I felt deeply honored when she chose me as her deputy, not only to take the doctors' orders but to see that they were carried out. I took Fraulein in a carriage and went out to get the prescription filled, and then I saw that the baby got it in the right proportions and at the right times.

III

Soon after we returned to Petersburg my mother, Lees, baby Clifton and I, with Mademoiselle and Ieda, left Russia for Switzerland. Although St. Petersburg remained my home until 1898, I did not go back. The impression I carried away of the Russians I knew in my girlhood was so altogether different from the Russians of whom one reads now, that I am puzzled. The upper classes had immense charm. It was not possible for us to know the muzhik and his female counterpart, the sudeamoika, although the lower servants in one's household came from that class. The upper servants were not Russians at all. These came mainly from the Baltic Provinces. My mother, accustomed to the kindly ties that bound us to our colored servants, and to those white servants at Hazelwood who had been with my Grandmother Lees for years, used to lament the fact that she could not get in touch with her muzhiks. They were hired and fired by the maître d'hôtel. We did not even know where they slept or what they ate. Although we, as foreigners, paid higher wages than the Russians did, we never knew how much of these wages went to the muzhiks themselves. The language barrier stood always between us and them.

Twice a year, at the Russian Christmas and the Russian Easter, the servants all lined up in the ballroom, with the children of the married ones, and we gave them presents and money. The lower servants and the children kissed our hands. Those were about the only times we came directly in touch with them.

We met a few tradesmen. I remember a bookbinder who charged a ruble apiece for the paper-backed books he bound for us. I was often in his shop, with a governess, taking books to be bound or fetching them to carry home. But when we took him a heap of books, to bind at his leisure over a period of months, he shook his head and said that their excellencies could not possibly expect him to bind many books at as cheap a price, each, as he bound one. From the highest to the lowest I thought of Russians as likable but impractical people.

They fought in the First World War as I would have expected them to fight, with utter gallantry and without adequate arms. Regiments lacked rifles. Supplies failed to reach the right places at the right times. What baffled me in the Second World War was the successful handling of logistics at the Battle of Stalingrad.

The Russians did not make mockery of the truth in the days when we lived with them, and they accepted all sorts of ideas foreign to their own. Science and art were free under the Czar. News was not distorted. When the authorities did not want anybody to read it, they left it out of the Russian papers and blacked it out of the foreign papers, which were sold, otherwise, just as printed. Although Russia was one of the few countries to require a passport in those days of free travel over almost all the world, no one seemed to have any trouble in getting a passport when he wanted it, or in doing business after he got it. Our friend, Mr. William Smith, although an American, was born in Russia, the second generation of his family to work there. A number of English families had done business with Russia, and had lived there, for generations. People could travel when and where they would.

I have often thought, in comparing the old regime with the one today, that when people are not ready for self-government, and want an absolute authority at the top, their chances improve enormously if that authority is a hereditary one. Few tyrants, who seize power, are anything but cruel men. A hereditary ruler, even a weak one, may be kind, as was Nicholas II. He may, on occasion, be a forward-looking

17

man of ability, as was Alexander II. Such a ruler can enormously improve the lot of his people and train them, by slow degrees, in representative government, as Alexander II tried to do. Unfortunately for politically backward races, such are the men selected by fanatics for assassination.

Chapter 3

I

THE link between my school days in Switzerland and the Frontier Nursing Service lies in mountains. For nearly two years I lived surrounded by them then; now I shall abide among them so long as life remains to me. Although the Kentucky mountains are as unlike the Alps as loveliness differs from grandeur, yet there is a kinship between mountains and mountaineers the world over. Buckle brings this out in his *History of Civilization.* There is a likeness between the mountaineers of Switzerland, the Scottish Highlands, the Ozarks and the Appalachian range, of which the Kentucky mountains are a part, that becomes apparent to anyone who stays among them. I, who have lived in them all, feel it deeply. With this comes the realization that I am at heart a mountaineer, that I belong, that I fit. At sixteen, up at Gimmelwald in the Bernese Oberland, where I went with some of my teachers and schoolmates for summer holidays, I wrote this in my journal:

Oh, these mountains, these mountains! I am troubled tonight and as I look out on their great white peaks, they say: "How small is man and his works and pains. Look on us. We have lived calmly, peacefully through all the changes of your mortal world."

It was not until a year later that I memorized in Wordsworth what he wrote in "The Wanderer" about the hills of Athol:

> But in the mountains did he feel his faith,
> All things responsive to the writing, there
> Breathed immortality, revolving life,
> And greatness still revolving; infinite:
> There littleness was not; the least of things
> Seemed infinite; and there his spirit shaped
> Her prospects, nor did he believe,—he *saw.*

To break our journey from Russia to Switzerland, we stayed over-night at Warsaw, several nights in Vienna and a night at Innsbruck. The Austrian Tyrol, which I have not seen again, enchanted me with what my little sister called its "savage scenery." Although she was probably translating *"sauvage"* into English and only meant "wild," I liked the word "savage."

After a few days at a hotel at Bex-les-Bains, we took a chalet for the summer in a hamlet, high up in the Alps, called Les Plans. We did not attempt housekeeping but took our meals at a pension. In this valley, I was turned loose with my beloved brother Carson. He went on excursions where I was not allowed to follow but we did some climbing together high enough for me to pluck my first edelweiss. I was in rapture with the wild flowers in the Alpine meadows, many of which I pressed and some I pasted in the pages of my journal. I grew brown and sturdy as a nut. In the fall, my mother placed me in school at Rosemont-Dézaley in Lausanne and left my brother at the Château de Lancy in Geneva.

I doubt if any other girl of fifteen could write and spell as badly in three languages as I did. That I spoke and read them is small beer and skittles compared to my appalling ignorance of writing and spelling. I took a breather and got to work. At first everything came hard. Although I had not been taught to study, I found that I liked it until the examinations rolled around. I don't know why we dreaded them as we did because we all passed them. They seemed a nightmare at the time. I did very well, indeed, in English and French and abominably in German. Although I had known the language from childhood, to read and speak, I found it horribly hard to learn to write it. At one time, in my teens, Schiller was my favorite poet. I read his poems and every one of his dramas, of which my favorites were *Don Carlos* and the *Yungfrau von Orleans*. I still think that he, like Walter Scott, is one of the best authors to put in the hands of an adolescent. My German has now completely gone overboard from lack of use for over fifty years. I could not read Schiller today without a dictionary, but I cannot think of the Thirty Years' War without the throb that came to me in my girlhood when I first read *Wallenstein*.

I am not by nature an adaptable person. I have learned to be one from much shuffling about in my youth, just as I learned to eat and like many kinds of food from having all sorts of things served me here and there at different stages of my growth. It took me the whole of my first term at Rosemont to fit into boarding school life. I had wanted ardently to leave Petersburg, to be thrown with a world of girls of my own age, but when I realized my dream I was at sea. Aside from the natural homesickness that comes to all of us when we are wrenched from our people, I had to face the strangeness of the companionship of my own generation. After the first term I made the adaptation and reveled in the companionship. The friends of a lifetime came out of my school days in Switzerland.

Rosemont-Dézaley was a first-class school of the old-fashioned kind, a *pensionnat de demoiselles*. We had excellent food and plenty of it. The water was not considered safe so we were only allowed to drink it mixed with red wine. We were supposed to take a bath but once a week in the one bathroom for the school. A maid spent a whole afternoon and evening running baths and washing out the tub. We American, English and Scottish girls, accustomed to washing more often, used to climb into the sinks on our respective bedroom floors, turn on the taps and take cold showers—but this was surreptitious.

The girls at Rosemont did not come from so many countries as the boys at my brother's school, Château de Lancy. In my day there were a few German girls, several Dutch sisters whose father had held an administrative post in Java, a little South American, and a number of British girls. The only two Americans besides myself, Edith Richie and Nadine Nuttall, had both been brought up in Europe; Edith in England and Nadine on the Continent. One of the English girls, Evelyn Hill, was to become closely linked with the Frontier Nursing Service. As Mrs. Arthur Bray she has visited us several times, and she calls her house in Yorkshire, "Headquarters of the Frontier Nursing Service in England." Her niece, Alison Bray, has twice come to Kentucky as a courier.

In a letter to my mother, after I had been at Rosemont for over a year, I wrote: "I am so happy here that I like everyone and believe that I am liked in return." Madame planned our lives at school in such a way that we had a great variety. We spent many afternoons and sometimes whole days in making excursions by train or boat to such parts of Switzerland as were within reach, and to the Savoy in the French Alps across Lake Geneva. After leaving train or boat we walked for hours to see legendary places like Chillon, or meadows with narcissus, or shy little lakes tucked into faraway places in the hills, or caves with hidden streams and waterfalls. In the late spring and early autumn we were taken down to the shores of Lake Geneva (or Lake Leman, as the Vaudois called it) to swim. I had learned to swim in the Gulf of Finland and have enjoyed swimming, next to riding, above all other sports.

The language of the school was French; we were only allowed to speak our native tongues on Sundays. All of the lessons were in French except that elective German and English lessons came two or three times a week. I got permission to give up the English ones when I moved into the upper school. We were taken, with our parents' written permission, a few times, to concerts (one was by Sarasate)

21

and once to an opera, *La Dame Blanche*. The first moving pictures I ever saw, and they were probably among the first in the world, were brought to Lausanne by a strolling entertainer. They were projected on a screen much as lantern slides were then but they flickered badly. Their wonder lay in that the pictures moved. One saw a man playing with a macaw, a baby feeding itself, a train coming into a station and people pouring out of it. Only once did we go to the theater, to a children's play called *Les Enfants du Capitaine Grant* by Jules Verne. We were not allowed to go to grown-up plays. This seemed odd to me because we studied grown-up literature. For example, we happened to be studying Racine's *Phèdre* at the time that Sarah Bernhardt came to Lausanne to play in it. A number of us begged Madame to be allowed to go to this play. When she refused, we cooked up a letter to Sarah Bernhardt to ask her to intercede in our behalf. I don't know how we happened to lose our nerve but we didn't send it.

In modern things our reading was rigidly restricted to books suitable *"pour les jeunes filles,"* but in the great French classics we roamed freely—Molière, Racine, Corneille. We took different parts in reading these plays. The sonorous beauty of the French language, in its classical form, moved me as deeply as had Milton's use of English, as the language of the King James translation of the Bible has always moved me.

We were extremely well taught in the things we learned and above all in writing. We had to put into our own words our opinions on what we read. I have always been grateful for this drill in which I had had no experience whatever under my governesses.

Of mathematics or science, nothing was taught at Rosemont. Oddly enough, there was a course in chemistry in the upper school, given by a professor from the University of Lausanne, a Monsieur Krafft, during which we heard a great deal of exquisitely precise French but in which we learned no chemistry whatever. There were no laboratory, no experiments, no formulas even. Near the end of the course, M. Krafft gave us one formula, H_2O, of which he rightly said, *"Ca court les rues."* That is how chemistry was taught to young ladies in the nineties.

Our education was designed to give us the history and literature of the past in order to enable us to speak and read and write with social grace. It was not known whom we might marry nor in what walks of life we might move. We had to be prepared to marry anyone and go anywhere. In my third term, I was promoted to the upper school, to my great joy. I now attended the lectures given by professors from the University of Lausanne, who were masters in their fields. Old Professor Dandiron, who wore a black cape over his shoulders instead of a coat, taught us history. Through him I learned a good deal about the history of Switzerland, which seems to me in microcosm a picture of what the world will be some day when it has outgrown what Saleeby calls, "the rude foreshadowings of the civilization that is to come." Here in this little country, with three languages besides dialects, three races of people, with two religions as antagonistic as the Catholic and the Calvinist, everybody got along together. The children of the educated classes were bilingual. One saw advertisements in the papers to the effect that a lawyer of Zurich would like to exchange a twelve-year-old son or daughter with a lawyer of Geneva, for a year or two. The Zurich boy or girl would go into the home of the Geneva child, attend his school, and speak his language until he knew it as he did his own.

That part of M. Dandiron's lectures which most profoundly affected me was his discussion of the War of the Sonderbund, Switzerland's baby civil war in 1847, which grew out of the revolt of seven Romanist cantons in defense of what they held to be their religious rights. It lasted only from November 10 to November 20. Fortunately for Switzerland, the Great Powers were otherwise occupied and the Swiss were allowed to settle their own affairs themselves. The rebellious cantons surrendered but were not subjected to indignities and the problems at issue were compromised.

I, who had been nourished from infancy on the rights of states versus a central government, followed M. Dandiron's every word, and thought, even then, how much more civilized Switzerland had been than the United States in handling such disputed issues. Not that I had been trained to think that the question of states' rights was the determining factor in our Civil War; I knew, even as a girl, that not many people are capable of reasoning on emotional issues. Great masses of free men do not fight for such an abstract idea as an interpretation of the Constitution; nor do questions of property affect the common people who make up the bulk of all armies, because most of them have no property. Probably not one man in a hundred in the Confederate Armies was a slaveowner. Such men will fight only when they think their homes endangered. Had invasion not threatened the South, there would have been a paucity of men in the Armies of the Confederacy and several states, including Virginia, would not have seceded at all. The Federalists, on the other hand, fought to keep the Union, whose preservation was worth to them even so costly a price.

We had French literature under Professor Sansine. In connection with his lectures he gave us books to read (or extracts drawn from his own *Chrystomatie*) on each of which we had to write a critique to be submitted to him. Occasionally he had one of us read her critique to the class and asked for a discussion on it. Once, when the book was Chateaubriand's *Génie du christianisme*, I was called on to read my critique. I had written that Chateaubriand was *"profondément re-ligieux."* Mr. Sansine said he was *"superficiellement religieux,"* that his religion was all form. My private opinion on this, written to my mother, was: "I knew that Chateaubriand admired best in religion its beauty and poetry but thought him sincere in his way." When I finished reading, Monsieur asked me if I had written my paper quite alone (I had) and then he opened the discussion. One of the girls said, *"C'est très bien."* "You think so, Mademoiselle?" Monsieur asked in his exquisitely ironic French, *"et en quels points?"* She did not know, so Monsieur discussed the weak points in my paper himself, and then summed up: *"Je trouve, Mademoiselle, que votre critique n'est pas très bien, mais c'est bien, et c'est beaucoup pour la première fois. Vous avez bien travaillé et je vous félicite, Mademoiselle."*

From that time on, I lived to get a commendation from M. Sansine that would not only be good but very good. This happened not long after with a critique on a book by Madame de Staël. After the discussion of my paper, Monsieur told me that, apart from two points which I should have emphasized, my critique was very good. He added that it showed not only good work but reflection. These words from one whom I rightly judged to be a master in his field lifted me into the highest heavens.

I have never had so inspiring a teacher as Monsieur Sansine in any subject anywhere at any time. Lamartine became my favorite poet for a while after we had studied his poetry with M. Sansine, but this was not because Monsieur encouraged us in unreserved enthusiasm for any author. We had to discuss their work and make our own appraisals of their weak points as well as their strong ones. Had M. Sansine spoken English and had I read *Paradise Lost* with him, I could not possibly have fallen in love with Satan. M. Sansine would have brought out the snake in him from the beginning.

Our headmistress in the upper school, a Mademoiselle Delafontaine from Geneva, was as remarkable a woman as M. Sansine and M. Dandiron were men. One of her duties was to tie up the threads of our history and literature lessons from the professors, so as to create for us one woven fabric of the whole eighteenth or nineteenth century. We learned through her to see how much influence literature had on history and the progress of human thought, and vice versa. She not only stimulated our own thought but our ability to make use of it in writing and speaking. Although I sometimes grieve that my education had in it so little that was to be of use to me in the later active years of my life, yet I would not give up the quality of learning I got at Rosemont. It opened up whole areas of my mind.

We did not live so much in the past as to overlook the exciting events of our own times. The Dreyfus case rent us from end to end.

When talk about it was discouraged, because we talked so much, someone alluded to it by pointing with three fingers at one foot. I was tremendously torn by news from home of the great Mississippi flood, which engulfed Oasis and the adjoining uninhabited plantations that belonged to my mother and my Uncle Will. In my journal I wrote of my Uncle Joe:

What will he, his wife and three little children do now? What will become of the hundreds of poor Negroes in his employ? Ah! my dear old South—one suffering succeeds another. . . . War and desolation all around and I live peacefully in a peaceful country. Can I do nothing? For the first time in my life I would like to be a boy. Though only sixteen I could fight, and I remain idle here! The beautiful Philippines are drenched with blood—Cuba is fighting for her liberty—Madagascar is in strife—Armenia persecuted—the Cretans massacred—Greece and Turkey fighting—the best and brightest part of my own lovely land flooded by the merciless Mississippi.

It reads like quire a catalogue of woes for a decade in history that we think of now as one of the most peaceful the planet has ever known.

II

Several of us girls, especially among those whose people were far away, stayed with the school over holidays. Madame then took us to some other part of Switzerland. One spring holiday we went to a little place high up in the canton of the Valais. There I saw for the first time women in work trousers like men's, but they wore picturesque red scarves around their necks. From time immemorial they seem to have dressed that way because they had to herd goats on the roughest of mountainsides. The women I saw looked pretty and feminine but were shy. They said that people took their pictures and they didn't like it. How well I came to understand this after we started the Frontier Nursing Service! We, patients and staff alike, have an intense distaste for photographers who come to take pictures of us for exploitation just because we, like the women of the Valais, are unusual and picturesque.

I did not stay in the school for the Christmas holidays. With my brother Carson as escort, I joined my people on the French Riviera for my first Christmas. At Cannes, to which my father had come from Petersburg to escort my mother back, we were a united family again. Lees and I learned to ride bicycles. We took many excursions by carriage, and in a boat called *Les Deux Frères*, which we hired with its boatmen, for trips to the islands in the Mediterranean. Carson and I went with the family to Genoa, where they took a steamer at night

25

for Odessa. My mother has often said that she has seldom been more depressed than she was in looking back from the deck of the receding steamer at her young son and daughter standing alone in the darkness on the Genoa docks. We made the journey from Genoa to Geneva in a second-class carriage on what must have been a very slow train. It was certainly a cold one. The only heat was hot water in long metal boxes stuck under our feet, and these became icy as the hours wore on. However, I loved it all, because I was with my brother, and because of the snowbound Italian mountains. I wrote that I wanted to go back to spend a winter there. I have always liked mountains best in the autumn and winter.

In the summer I went to Gimmelwald in the Bernese Oberland with Madame and a handful of girls which included Edith Richie and Nadine Nuttall. We were turned loose in the glorious air and mountain scenery. Although even at Gimmelwald we could not walk out unattended by a schoolmistress (such as along the footpath over which donkeys brought our luggage from Murren), yet we were allowed to scramble up the mountainsides around the place in pairs and with no restraints. Nadine and I were the great climbers. We used to take our four o'clock *goûter* with us on long afternoon rambles by a wild mountain stream up to where the avalanches fell in a mass of jumbled rock and ice and snow. We scaled enormous rocks overhanging this stream. Of these we became so fond that we gave them names. One was called Geierstein, in honor of *Anne of Geierstein*, a special book with us because the early part of it lies in Switzerland.

It was after a summer at Gimmelwald, when my imagination was still lit by the grandeur of mountains and a longing to climb the toughest of them, that I wrote my mother:

I dreamt such a strange dream the other night: that you were here and that we two, you, darling Mother, and I, we climbed the Matterhorn together!! There were other details, such as buying two little frocks for baby halfway up, etc. for dreams always leave the main point to wander. But that was a lovely dream: climbing up, up with you to regions of height, wonder, greatness and purity.

All through my girlhood I wanted to climb mountains and to wander through the most difficult and inaccessible parts of the world. I also wanted to have eight children! When my mother asked me once what I should do with them, I answered airily, "Oh, they can be born anywhere and I shall bring them home to you to take care of for me."

Love of home and children and love of adventure struggled for ascendancy, in the imagination of my girlhood. I don't seem at any time in my whole life to have cared much about clothes. This has been a source of woe to my friends on the Frontier Nursing Service committees in the big Eastern and Midwestern cities. Those who know me well say, "You cannot wear that dress again in this city. It baffles belief," or, "It is time you got another hat. You have worn that one four years. It never was any good and now it is shabby." I protest that none of this is my mother's fault. She encouraged us, even as little children, to shop with her and express a preference as well as develop a taste in clothes. The clothes I cared about were boots with nails in the soles for mountain climbing in Switzerland; brown corduroys for hunting turkey and deer in Mississippi; boating things for canoes in Canada; riding habits of which I wore out two of heavy black broadcloth in my Southern girlhood. I liked party dresses but I liked parties more. Clothes never seemed to add to my good times, or detract from them. I don't know why this is so but so it is. To think of life as more than the raiment has been my natural state, and requires no spiritual accommodation.

The farewell to Rosemont tore at my heartstrings. Then my brother, whose presence at Geneva and occasional visits had kept up a measure of family life for me, came to Lausanne to escort me to Dresden. My mother and Lees went to meet us at one station while we got off at the other, with the result that we reached the Hotel Bristol before their return. When we entered we were shown up to our sitting room, with family photographs scattered about, my mother's Bible and her sewing box, flowers, and French and English books. In a moment Anna, the baby's Baltic Province nurse, came in and took us to see him sleeping in his hotel crib. It was then that Carson smiled at me as he said, "We are home." He and I never had a home in all of our wandering youth, but wherever my mother was she created around her a look of home.

We spent several weeks in Dresden. My father left Russia in time to reach us before Christmas. My mother had kept some of the shopping for the Christmas tree for us to share. One of the things we bought to hang on it was a tiny cage with a parrot swinging in it; this stands on the buckeye mantelpiece of my bedroom at Wendover today. Dresden was an enchanting city at Christmas. My mind kept going back, poignantly, to memories of that joyous time when I read of the city's destruction. We visited the art galleries as well as the shops, and I pasted a picture of the Sistine Madonna in my journal. We went five times to the opera: *Lohengrin, Tannhäuser* and *The Flying Dutchman* were medieval enough even for me and I was enthralled by them.

Before I left Rosemont I had written my mother a letter that must have tried her soul: "I wish we could go over in a sailboat. It would be so exciting. Don't you like the idea? Our ancestors must have arrived thus, and shall we show ourselves less brave and fond of adventure than they? Won't you consider my suggestion? I am sure Carson has made it already." All of this fell flat, and we went home in January of 1898 on the *Fürst Bismarck* of the Hamburg-American Line.

Chapter 4

I

OUR homecoming to Grandmother Lees at Hazelwood was all that my heart had dreamed of family happiness. We were there in time for the marriage of my cousin Susanna Preston Lees to Henry Randolph Sutphen in February—a lovely, country house wedding.

There had been a family discussion about what should be done to further Carson's and my education. He was sent down to the University of Tennessee where our Uncle William Waller Carson was professor of civil engineering, but he left to volunteer in the Marine Corps for the Spanish-American War. He liked the Corps so much that when his temporary commission expired he stood for the examinations for a commission in the regulars, and the Marines became his lifelong career. I was sent to Miss Low's School at Stamford, Connecticut, for the rest of the school year.

I had the same difficulty in making an adaptation to my new school as I had had at Rosemont. American girls seemed to me like a new race of people. But by the end of the first term I had started on the delightful process of forming new friendships. I had difficulty also with the new schedule of work because I didn't fit at any point in the conventional American school system. In such things as history, and English and French literature, I was well ahead of the work given the first class. On the other hand, I knew nothing of Latin or mathematics. As to the sciences, these were not taught experimentally in laboratories even at an American school in the nineties. All we got came out of textbooks. Since I was not going to college, it was decided not to raise the question of mathematics, but I was tutored in Latin that spring to enable me to enter a regular class the next year. I wrote my mother: "Latin amuses me," but I added that

the declensions slightly disturb my mind. They are as bad as the German, only when I learned the German, I had the advantage of first speaking the language

29

before I thought of grammar. . . . It is not seemly of me to criticize the judgments of the wise and learned but I would suggest learning something of a language in the simple natural way of nature before studying its fundamental principles! Don't laugh, dearest Mother, I am in serious earnest.

It was not until years later that I ran across a book by Monsieur Sauveur, a successful teacher of French by natural methods to grown-up Americans, and found that he advocated learning Latin in the same way.

German was elective at Miss Low's School; my mother wanted me to keep it up so she arranged to have me tutored in that. I don't remember the name of the German teacher, but I shall never forget the reading I did with her, which included not only my loved Schiller but a good deal of Goethe and Lessing. Our French and English mistresses were the two I liked best and also the two under whom I had the most intellectual stimulus. I became acquainted with a variety of English essayists at Miss Low's, among whom Ruskin was my favorite, and I also began, for the first time, to read Shakespeare. With Mademoiselle I went on reading the French classics and wrote of *L'Avare*, "*C'est bien Molière! J'ai ri à tue-tête!*" I wrote my mother: "Serious study is a delightful thing."

The summer I was seventeen I spent with my Uncle Will's family in the South, and for the first time I had beaux. After I had gone back to Stamford, I wrote my mother for permission to correspond with one of these men. Her letter is so characteristic of the sheltered care taken of a young girl in the nineties that I quote from it:

I return Mr. Blank's letter. If it would give you any pleasure to correspond with him, I would hate to deprive you of it. But I can't think your interest in him is sufficient for it to require much self-denial for you to refuse. If we knew him better, or if we really knew anything about him, I would feel differently about it. We know his family is good and he has the appearance and manners of a gentleman—but we don't know anything about him. It seems to me, darling, that under these circumstances I would answer his letter kindly and pleasantly but I would not enter into a regular correspondence with him. If you don't like to refuse of yourself, you can say that your mother would prefer that for the present you do not correspond with any gentleman. I am not laying this down as the law, but simply giving my ideas and wishes. I wonder if you think your mother is unreasonable. She doesn't mean to be. I love you so that I only want to think of your interest and happiness.

To this I replied as follows:

I wrote to him as you desired, telling him that I could not correspond with him. Mother dearest, how could you think I would think anything you wanted me to do unreasonable! I would give up writing to any number of entertaining gentlemen if you wished it, for I know you have a reason for all you wish me to do and indeed, indeed I love you so it is a pleasure to deny myself anything because you think it best. I would have enjoyed corresponding with Mr. Blank but I enjoy not doing it and pleasing you a good deal more.

Such was the relationship between one girl of seventeen and her mother in the nineties.

With my first beaux, my mother began training me in how to handle my relationships with men. When I repeated to her the rather devoted expressions of one of them, she told me such things were lightly meant and must be lightly taken. It was excellent advice in preparation for a young ladyhood in the South. Southern men made love as easily as they breathed, with the utmost respect and no liberties whatever. It was like a game of ball in which one was always batting the ball. You were so used to such love-making that a man almost had to knock you down to convince you he wanted to marry you.

I learned to know, that summer, about a class of women of whom I had been totally ignorant until then. The Spanish-American War had brought into existence a number of camps in the South. A military young man with whom I was talking said what a pity it was that the women around camp were the only ones most of the soldiers saw. It amazed me that there should be any women around a camp. He said they were "a very disagreeable set." Suddenly I grasped his meaning and changed the subject but I wrote about it in my journal, and this is what I wrote at seventeen: "Poor, poor creatures—I would I could help you—I did not, I could not know that. Poor women, poor souls."

My return to Miss Low's School at Stamford was delayed for a bit in September until a chaperon could be located with whom I could take the trip North. At that time, and even a year later, I was not allowed to travel without an escort. I went back to school with delight. I had made the adaptation to the new environment, and I loved it. Miss Low was one of those lovely white-haired old ladies that New England throws out with each generation. Her niece, Miss Heywood, was growing into just such another woman, with manners as charming as they were kind.

Miss Low's did not lack outside attractions. We were taken to hear an occasional lecture in Stamford and were sometimes invited to parties given by the families of the day pupils. Occasionally we went by train to New York to the theater, of which I was extremely fond. One of the plays that year was Maude Adams in *The Little Minister* and another was Ada Rehan in *The Merchant of Venice*. It was not until later that I saw Sothern and Marlowe and, later yet (in Memphis), Joseph Jefferson—in *The Rivals* and in his immortal *Rip Van*

31

Winkle. To this day the memory of Joe Jefferson comes back to me in every thunderstorm.

Not many girls went to college in the nineties, even from so good a school as Miss Low's, but it could be done. One of the old girls, Jo Hartshorn, came from Bryn Mawr for our end-of-the-year school exercises. She told me I should go to Bryn Mawr and she would give me "an opening tea." I said I might think about it if she could get me in without mathematics! Much as I loved study, I loved adventure more, so that the temptation college held for me lay solely in providing an opening wedge for larger liberties. Although I longed for "a stable, unmovable home" in my homeless youth, I wrote in my journal: "I would be impatient were I obliged to spend any length of time in it. . . . It would be beautiful to return to after my wanderings and find those I love there." In other words, I wanted my people to stay put and leave me foot-loose! I wrote that, when absent from them, I could "think of them so happily in my prayers."

There were reasons more determining than my lack of mathematics as to why I was not sent to college. One was that my family disapproved of a college education for women. Years before, as a little girl in Washington, I listened to the family discussions when Cousin Willie Breckinridge's daughter, Sophonisba, elected to go to Wellesley. I recall my mother saying that the college would not be detrimental in itself but that Nisba would not want to live at home afterward. When Nisba finished at Wellesley and started on her distinguished career, my mother said with disapproval, "She refused to go back home to live." Now, my mother was broad-minded—she advocated woman's suffrage when it was frowned on. But she believed, like nearly everybody then, that the only place for a woman was at home—in her father's house while she was single, and her husband's if she married. All through the South there were elderly ladies of gentle breeding, whose fortunes had been wrecked by the Civil War and Reconstruction, who had to make their living. They had the highest social standing and were enormously respected, but the fact that they had to work was commented upon as a tragedy.

Another reason why I could not have gone to college is that it would have taken a lot of expensive tutoring to ram mathematics into my head. Even if my head could have supported such a strain, expensive tutoring was not possible then because we were hard up. We did have private resources, else my father could not have indulged in years of public service, but they were small and lay mostly in heavily taxed land. Before the Civil War, my Grandfather Breckinridge had bought a lot of land in Minnesota, some of it where St. Paul stands now, some between St. Paul and Minneapolis, some around Lake Superior, and a stone quarry on one of the Apostle Islands. When war came, a friend of his in Kentucky, who was not a Secessionist, took over this land. From time to time he sold parts of it and sent the money to my Grandfather Breckinridge to enable him to live during his five years of exile in Europe and Canada. After my grandfather had been pardoned and allowed to return to Kentucky, this friend gave him back the rest of his holdings. My father inherited a share and, whenever we got in a tight place, he sold off chunks of it. I don't recall that anything was done to develop it and get a regular income out of it. One effect of my people having been large landowners in Minnesota has been to give me a special affection for that state. As far removed as Minnesota is from my forbears, I never go there without a feeling of belonging a little bit. I have one other rather curious tie with the state and that is the little town named Breckinridge, which I have never seen. When we lived in Russia, Prince Khilkoff, the Minister of Ways and Communications, told my father that he had gone to America as a young man to learn railroading. He said his railroad construction crew had named their camps in Minnesota for the President and Vice-President of that time, Buchanan and Breckinridge, and that it was he who had nailed to a tree a board with BRECKINRIDGE painted on it. It was odd to learn of this in St. Petersburg.

My mother also owned land—a plantation adjoining Oasis—in which she and my Uncle Will had a joint interest. Uncle Joe's managers took care of it for them but not much of it was under cultivation. Since the one business my father knew was cotton planting and marketing, it seemed a logical thing for us to build near Oasis and live on our own plantation. That is what I ardently wanted my people to do. But my father and mother felt that agriculture, especially cotton, was in a precarious state, so we continued to sell land when we needed money. College for a girl (to say nothing of tutoring in mathematics), in preparation for a life of far-flung adventure, did not justify the sale of one Minnesota lot or one Mississippi acre; nor, had there been an abundance of loose money, would I have been allowed to do any of these things.

II

In June of 1899, when I was eighteen, I left Stamford and my school days were over. I have gone rather fully into what, for the lack of a more precise word, I venture to call my education because, despite its gaps, it did give me some things that were of use long afterward in the Frontier Nursing Service. Had I not known French well, I could not have organized the nursing in the American Committee for Devastated France, with the restoration of over ten thousand war-wrecked children. This was my first large piece of administrative work, and more than anything else it prepared me to organize the work in Kentucky. Had I not learned to ride horseback young, I would have found it hard to cope with an area where, for thousands of square miles, there was no motor road. As a person, I needed the constant shift in environment that was mine all through my girlhood, in order to learn to be adaptable. If my education had been more conventional, I might have missed the habit I early learned of digging out the things I wanted to know for myself from books and people. The ledger does show something on the balance side.

There are certain qualities of life that one learns only from one's people. These no education of any kind can give or take away. When I was young on Oasis plantation in Mississippi, my Uncle Joseph Carson, whom I adored, once said to me, "Although hospitality and loyalty are barbaric virtues, there are no others we should put before these." It was natural for my sister and me, as children in Washington, to move out of our nursery (the sunniest room in the house) for company when the spare room was already full. We did not think of hospitality as something you extended only when it was convenient. We also learned, so early that I don't remember when, that if you yourself accepted hospitality from someone else you could not speak ill of him afterward. Once you had been a man's guest your lips were sealed forever as regards anything detrimental to him. I have been aghast in late years to read the books of certain writers who profited by the hospitality they had received to exploit their hosts. That is one of the things, according to the code in which I was reared, that is just not done.

Of loyalty there is not enough to go around—but no principle was more fully inculcated in us when we were children. You stood by your friends and your people. These included those family friends who were not always diverting and those relations who were not always creditable, even to the third and fourth generations. We were trained in Christian principles but it was not considered contrary to these to have enemies, so long as you never hit below the belt. When it came to one's country, then loyalty mattered more than all beside. Treachery to a friend, to a kinsman, and above all to one's country, was the blackest crime.

Loyalty to friends, kinsmen and one's country is a notable characteristic of the Kentucky mountaineer. The code in which I was reared is taken for granted in my ancestral commonwealth. Although we fight our enemies too frequently, and we know it, we do stand by our friends. As to hospitality, I cannot even remember the names of all the people to whose houses I have ridden at nightfall; nor were my horse and I ever turned away. Ann MacKinnon ("Mac"), one of my

Assistant Directors who came to us in the early days, says that I told her then: "When strangers ride up to your door give them at least 'a cup of cold water' and a bed, even if you haven't one!"

Another thing that we learned as children was that talebearing was not acceptable and that slander and scandal were despised. I can't recall a single instance in which anyone, even an enemy, was slandered in our presence, and scandal was something of which we hardly knew the word. My people were clean-minded; they tore down the character of no one. I think this is implied in "Love your enemies." When I was a girl, my Grandmother Breckinridge gave me a copy of the *Idylls of the King*. As I read, "To speak no slander, no, nor listen to it," the words sang in my heart. The effect of slander upon me down to this day, whether private or public, is to imbue me with a strong feeling of the innocence of the person slandered and an everlasting pity for the slanderer. Some years after I had grown up, and had begun to read books on psychology and psychiatry, I learned a fact that I instinctively knew to be true, namely, that those who whisper nasty things about other people have either done those things themselves or have wanted to do them. Thus, the things they say about others are tantamount to personal confessions. One wants to beg them to be silent for their own sakes. Once when a scandal-mongering woman called on my mother, who was absent, my sister and I received her. She kept dropping horrid hints about people we knew. She was older than we were, so we couldn't silence her. After she had been gone an hour, I ran across my sister who said to me, "Doesn't she come back to you like onions on the breath?"

That part of one's education which matters most is the untaught part—what one has learned as unconsciously as one breathed and slept. For these untaught things of my early life, I am grateful to my people.

Chapter 5

I

THE life of a grown-up girl at the turn of the century was filled with romance and adventure, especially in the South. I was so struck with the words of Jan, in one of my hunting books, that I copied them in my journal: "These are the days of my youth, these are my golden days." We rode constantly when I was young, not only for fun but often because it was the easiest way to get about. In Southern towns where I visited, I was often out late to a dance at night and in the saddle early the next morning. In hunting on the plantation, our riding was sometimes daring and dangerous. In the old Indian Territory I forded rivers not unlike our streams in the Kentucky mountains. The years of my girlhood took me from Mississippi to Canada; from Hazelwood to the Five Nations, and to many places between. I had an immense drive as a girl that I was not allowed to put in any constructive channel, so I took it out in adventure whenever I could.

The things that one could and could not do were carefully defined when I was young. For example, you could ride alone with a man in the daytime but not at night. If a party of girls and men wanted a moonlight ride, there had to be a chaperon or the ride was called off. You did not travel with a man, but he could escort you to a dance. Gatherings of young people, however small and intimate, had a chaperon. There were many reticences. Men did not use the word "damn" in front of a woman nor did one mention a bull. Manners were formal; men did not call girls by their first names unless they had known them from childhood. Even then, in society, they reverted to a formal title. In the South, with men who were family connections or the sons of old friends, you sometimes called one by his first name but he always called you "Miss Mary." You knew men for years and formed friendships with them without changing from Mr. Blank and

36

Miss Blank to first names. No man would have spoken of a baby to you until after it was born and, indeed, such things were not generally discussed before young girls by older women.

The delicate line drawn between what a girl did and did not do was plain enough to us, however finely drawn it might seem to be. During one of my stays at Hazelwood with Grandmother Lees, my brother Carson was stationed at the League Island Navy Yard near Philadelphia. He invited Susie and Henry and me to go over for a dance and spend the night in town. Aside from wanting his Sutphen cousins, it would not have entered his head to have asked me to go without them. At another time, Susie and Henry chaperoned a group of us young people for the West Point–Annapolis game at Franklin Field to which my brother would not have invited me with other men and girls, unchaperoned. One of the Philadelphia girls I met at this game married in the Navy. Half a lifetime later she, the widow of Admiral Goodrich, became the first chairman of the Princeton Committee of the Frontier Nursing Service. I can echo today the words written in the journal of my youth: "I do like nearly everybody I have ever met from Philadelphia. They are as attractive as their city."

Men seemed to have a great deal more leisure in my girlhood than they have today. In the South, especially, they were in attendance at all hours. You rode horseback with them in the early morning and in the afternoon; they got up luncheons for you on Ladies Day at their clubs; if you were shopping for something like a martingale or a bit, a man was sure to escort you.

The only presents that you could accept from men were books, flowers and candy. When a Mississippi beau of mine presented me with a pearl-handled pistol, I was enchanted to be allowed to keep it. When you had been visiting a place and were leaving, some of the girls and a number of the men would see you off at your train. Sometimes the men came loaded with books, flowers and candy but sometimes these things were sent to the house before you left or handed the porter to give you on your sleeper. Men occasionally wrote valentines. Here is one that came to me in Arkansas just before I turned nineteen:

> Wide is the Czar's vast realm, but hers is wider,
> For she doth rule as queen o'er every heart.
> No nihilistic rebel has defied her,
> Nor will the sceptre from her hand depart,
> For all who see, such adoration feel
> That low in homage at her feet they kneel.
>
> She stood beside the Czar in his dominions,
> And though a greater potentate than he,

She spread upon the breeze angelic pinions,
And flew across the sunlit western sea
To found a broader empire on our shore
Where all her beauty's sovereignty adore.

I had five girlhood friends in the South who have remained as close as sisters all my life. Two were my cousins, Katherine Carson of Knoxville, Tennessee, and Anne Steele of Woodford County, Kentucky. Another was Eleanor Blaydes of Hot Springs, Arkansas, a place to which I went several times with my mother for her gout. The other two were Nelly Morton and Leila Kirtland in Memphis, Tennessee, whose mothers and mine had been friends in their girlhood. There were a good many inherited family friendships. A number of older people had me stay with them, and saw that I had a royal time, because of their affection for my father and mother. In Kentucky there were not only the friendships but the kindred. We young things called our elders "the older generation," and we had enormous respect for them and for their opinions. When my father, the last of his family, died in 1932, Anne said to me, "Do you realize that now we are 'the older generation'?"

The happiest hours of my girlhood were spent on Oasis plantation in Mississippi and I loved it more than any place in the world. Not only were my Uncle Joe and my Aunt Florence deeply dear to me, humorous, indulgent beyond measure, but I was fond of my two grown-up men cousins by Uncle Joe's first marriage to my Aunt Medora Montgomery, and I adored the five children by the second marriage, whom I called the Infantry. My journal is full of their entrancing ways on their pony, or when prancing with their nurse, Caledonia Pinky Ann, down to the canebrake. With Uncle Joe, with my older cousin, Montgomery Carson, who was a plantation physician, and with the young men of the family connection, I rode for miles through the primeval forests that stood there then.

I also hunted a lot, "still hunting" for turkey, and with hounds and horses for deer. The deer hunting was wild enough to satisfy the longing for adventure which never left me. It led through slimy water in a dense tangle of semitropical forests, hung with vines. You pushed your way through canebrakes higher than your own head on horseback; you were torn by brambles; you often had to jump over a fallen monarch of a tree without knowing what lay on the other side. In all of this riding you carried your own rifle to be ready to raise it and aim the minute you sighted a deer. I escaped injuries in what was really a terrible fall when my horse failed to make the jump over a giant fallen tree and fell back with me. I was on a sidesaddle, as always in my girlhood, and eased out of the situation on the left, unharmed, nor was the horse too badly stunned to carry on. The deer hunting was the roughest riding I ever did and I enjoyed it more than words could express.

When you went after wild turkey it was "still hunting" at dawn. The art lay in calling a gobbler to you with a turkey caller and in keeping the most absolute stillness until you had him within range. The charm lay in reaching the depths of the forest before sunrise and hearing the call bird open a crescendo of musical sound. There was always one bird to lead off, as there seems to be in forests all over the world. Grieg knew it when he composed his "Peer Gynt Suite." I have listened to the call bird in Canadian as well as Mississippi forests. I often listen for him now at Wendover, Kentucky, where my day frequently begins before he has opened with his first note. Since Grieg knew him, there must be a call bird in Scandinavia. After he has led off, the other birds wake up and the symphony begins.

The first wild turkey I shot was in the forests of Oasis, just after I was nineteen, when I called a great gobbler to within range of my shotgun. The man I was with sent him to New Orleans to be mounted. He stands on a bookcase at Wendover now. At Christmas we always hang a string of pearl beads around his neck. I shot my second wild turkey in another part of Mississippi, on a hunting preserve owned by an old friend. Although he had a lodge on his place, we left it to stay in tents on little hillocks deep in the swamps. Every day at dawn and dusk we left the tents on horseback to ride a mile or two through the water in the forest glades. After we had tethered our horses, we walked to beyond the sound of their movements, and took our stands with the guns. As it was the fall of the year, the turkeys kept together in flocks. I could not call this second great gobbler nearer than about sixty yards, when I shot him through the breast with a .32-40 Marlin Rifle. We carried rifles because we were still hunting for deer as well as for turkey. In looking back on this phase of my girlhood, I feel no compunction for shooting the turkeys, but my heart still aches over the one deer I shot. After that, I could not have shot another deer. There was a wildness in me that came in time to give me a sense of kinship with wild things in the forest. The man who escorted me on both turkey shoots wrote them up for *Forest and Stream* under his pen name of Tripod.

Tripod trapped a rattlesnake for me one spring when I was visiting the Bolton Smiths in Memphis, and came up by boat with it in a large box. I had a notion at that time that I wanted a hunting belt made of rattlesnake skin. Aside from this, we had read in *Forest and Stream* of hunters lost in a semitropical swamp who ran out of ammunition and kept themselves alive by killing and eating rattlesnakes. After that, nothing would do for either of us but to get ready for the same eventuality. The snake, six feet long with thirteen rattles and a button, was turned loose on the Bolton Smiths' front gallery and promptly headed for their yard. Tripod and I, with a charming Englishman who was visiting the Bolton Smiths, the master of the house himself, a Memphis girl and her escort, headed off the snake and let him coil while we jumped back out of reach of his strike. Then Tripod, with great ingenuity, lassoed him and controlled the noose with a forked stick. When he had him under control, we chloroformed him, holding down his mighty tail with our feet. We used a cornucopia, stuffed with cotton into which we poured the chloroform. This we slipped over the snake's head. When at last he lay quiet, Tripod put him back in the box and took him to a taxidermist to dismember through one small slit made in the throat. There were two sequels to all of this. Tripod took the choicest pieces of meat to a restaurant to be cooked, and brought them around to breakfast the next morning. He and I and the Englishman ate them. They tasted not unlike possum. After that we felt that we, like the men who wrote in *Forest and Stream*, could cope with being lost in a Mississippi forest, if only it were not the dormant season for rattlesnakes. The other sequel came in the form of a letter to Mr. Bolton Smith from the Englishman, after he had gone home. He wrote that everything he told his friends about American girls was believed except the rattlesnake story.

II

Two years after we returned from Europe, my father decided what he wanted to do. While we were living on the sale of land of which we still had a great deal (for the Mississippi plantation was not sold until several years later, and the last of the Minnesota land not until later yet), my father would say cheerfully, "There will always be something." Oddly enough, there always was. My father did not want to be a cotton planter again. He did not want to write a biography of his father, John C. Breckinridge, as many pressed him to do. He did not want to take presidencies of small Southern colleges. He liked public service, for which he was admirably fitted. With a profound knowledge of political science, in which he had wide experience, he combined an immense liking for people and the most charming manners I have ever known. He also had a trait, rare in human nature, of never bearing a grudge against anyone. Not only did he refrain from saying slanderous things about his opponents in rebuttal to those said about him, but he actually seemed to feel no resentment against them whatever.

A number of my father's friends in Arkansas urged him to run for a seat in the Senate at about this time. They felt that he could easily secure the nomination (equivalent to election in the South) from the incumbent who was getting old. This my father refused absolutely to do. Although both the Senators from Arkansas were older men than he, they were his friends. According to his code, one never sought a personal advantage at the expense of a friend. So that was off. In 1900, he accepted from President McKinley a membership on the Commission to the Five Civilized Tribes. After that, until the work of the Commission was finished, he spent the greater part of his time in the Five Nations, as they were often called then, in the old Indian Territory, now a part of the State of Oklahoma. The work was one after his own heart. He was eager always to have the Indians' affairs adjusted as they wanted them, in preparation for statehood, and to secure their advantage in such arrangements as could be made under existing law. We have letters from various "civilized" Indians testifying to the affection and regard in which they held him. One expresses the wish that the rights of all Indian children could be secured under his protection.

My mother was constantly in the Indian Territory with my father; Lees and I less frequently. Most of my girlhood was spent elsewhere. Lees went to boarding school and, later, she was sent back to Europe. Even so, I wished we could have built or bought a house somewhere in the Cherokee Nation. My father explained that it would not be suitable for him to own any land there, in view of the position he held. A railroad ran through Muskogee, which was a village of wooden houses then. We tried the small railroad hotel but were, all of us, so uncomfortable and so frequently sick that we gave that up to go to old Fort Gibson. One reached the place in those days in buckboards or on horseback near where the Grand, the Arkansas and the Verdigris Rivers came together to form the Arkansas. The horses were put on a flatboat ferry and taken across below the confluence of two of these rivers.

On Garrison Hill, which had been a frontier Army post, stood the old brownstone house, with wide galleries, formerly occupied by the commandant of the post. This was rented by a blue-eyed Cherokee family from the Cherokee Nation to which it belonged. They let us have several of their rooms and served us our meals at hours convenient to us. In the spring of 1901, when the woods around Fort Gibson were flowering, our group was augmented by Troop A of the Eighth Cavalry of the United States Army, with Captain Donaldson in command. I wrote, "They seem really of no use except to drill and blow bugles." Once when Charlie Kimzey, cowboy, deputy marshal and head of the corral, was driving the four horses that carried some of us in the big Commission "hack," the front team got frightened at the soldiers' pack mules. In plunging and rearing, one of the horses fell and another trampled on it. Charlie, a superb driver, kept the terrified horses from plunging off the hill although his wrist was sprained and his shoulder injured by the strain. Not only was Charlie said to be the best horseman in the Five Nations, but he was a crack shot as well. Lawless characters preferred to let him alone. He said once, "If I see one making for his gun, down comes his meathouse."

Old Fort Gibson had distinguished associations with the past. At the second of the three forts were the ruins of the house Jefferson Davis had occupied when he was stationed there before the Civil War. The schoolhouse where the explorer Stanley taught still stood near Chief Bushyhead's place across the river. Audubon and Washington Irving had both visited Fort Gibson in the course of their ramblings. More modern visitors were a senatorial committee to investigate the affairs of the Indians. One of these Senators was an old family friend who stayed overnight with us. I wrote in my journal: "His views are very liberal ones and seem free from prejudice. He sides with the Indians in some of their troubles but is against the Cherokees in this." On another page I wrote: "The Government seems out of patience with them and is not likely to bother with another treaty. I wish that it would let them more alone to manage their own affairs and settle disputes among themselves."

Late in the spring, my father, Colonel Thomas B. Needles (another member of the Commission), Captain Donaldson and one of the Commission clerks, made a trip to Tahlequah, the oldest town in the Indian Territory, capital of the Cherokee Nation, and twenty miles off the railroad then. It meant an overnight stay from Fort Gibson. As there was plenty of room in the big Commission hack, the men allowed my mother, Lees and me to go with them. With Charlie driving, the four spirited horses were kept in perfect control. The purpose of this trip to Tahlequah was for my father and Colonel Needles to be present at the counting of the Cherokee vote on what was, I presume, another treaty. The proceedings were in English and Cherokee both. The roll call fascinated me more than all else because of such names as Bullfrog, Deer-in-the-Water, Dry Water, Ros'enyears, Saunders of Growing Snake. After the business of the trip was over, we went fishing in the Illinois River. On our way there, we stopped at the house of a Colonel Ross of mixed Georgian and Indian descent. We got permission to take a picture of his little daughter, who was a strikingly beautiful child. So many of the Cherokees had intermarried with Anglo-Saxons that there were many English and Scottish names, as well as blue eyes and yellow hair among them.

We saw something of the full-bloods, who did not speak English,

42

especially after my father moved his headquarters to Tahlequah. By that time Lees and I had our own riding horses, hers named Charley Kimzey and mine Cherokee. We liked to ride with my father, his surveyors and interpreters, to the homes of the pure-bred Cherokees, even though we couldn't talk with them, because so many of them were fine people.

My experience as a girl among the Cherokees in the old Indian Territory left an indelible impression on my mind. I had first come in touch with Indians at the age of nine when we took our trip up to the Nipigon in the Far North. I have visited reservation Indians both in the United States and Canada. In late years we have had graduate Indian nurses stay with us in the Frontier Nursing Service to learn midwifery and rural district nursing. Curiously enough, we were involved with an Indian while we lived in Russia. An American circus left one behind at St. Petersburg when it moved on to Berlin. Our Legation had some difficulty with the Russian Foreign Office, as I remember it, in getting a passport for him because the Russians could not understand why he was not a citizen of the United States. The upshot of it all seems to have been a special document devised by the Legation to explain that he was "a ward" of the United States and under its protection.

Our mishandling of these "wards" of ours, the Indians, has, until recent times, been terrible. Not only have we broken our treaties with them, taken their lands away from them, used their own money to impose by dictatorship an alien bureaucracy upon them, but we have tried to break up their family life and their tribal cultures, to deny them the freedom of religion guaranteed under the Constitution, to destroy the genius of their race. Short of poisoning their wells, we have stopped at few outrages. Here and there men and women have risen from the ranks of the Indian Service, or in groups of conscience-stricken Americans, to fight on behalf of our voiceless and voteless native population. Three American Presidents, Theodore Roosevelt, Herbert Hoover and Franklin D. Roosevelt, to their honor, gave the post of Commissioner of Indian Affairs to able men with the welfare of the Indians foremost in their minds. In 1934, Congress passed the Indian Reorganization Act which forbade further alienation of Indian land and property; but one has only to follow the press reports to see that even now our vigilance must be unremitting to prevent the stealing of Indian lands, water, and other rights guaranteed them by treaty. Whenever an American gives smug advice to the French, the Dutch, the English on how to handle the colonial peoples in their empires, we should silence him with words from our own records. We, too, have a colonial empire, and none of those nations have treated a dependent people more shamefully than we have treated ours.

Chapter 6

I

AT the turn of the century, my mother took my little brother Clifton to the Muskoka Lakes in the Canadian Province of Ontario. Clif's earliest years had been spent in cold climates. In hot weather he drooped. The physicians who attended him several times in the South advised that until he was grown he spend all of his summers in the Far North. Through friends, my mother got in touch with Professor and Mrs. Alexander Murray, who owned two little islands in Lake Rosseau that they had bought from the Crown. These they called Yarrum, an inversion of their name. Mr. and Mrs. Murray consented to accept as boarding guests in the summer such of our family as could get up to Canada. When I first went there in 1901, I was as drawn to the beauty of the lakes and shores as my mother had been. After she received her inheritance from Grandmother Lees, she bought the two islands from the Murrays. She changed their name to The Brackens because of the bracken ferns which grew on the islands and from which our name of Breckinridge is derived. The Brackens was our very first home and we came to love it beyond words. My mother built a roomy house on the larger of the two islands, remodeled the cottage on the smaller one, and connected the islands with a causeway and a bridge. In a natural bay, enlarged by the causeway, she built a launch and boathouse. She created a garden of rare beauty on the shores of the bay. This work was not done until after my marriage but even before it had started we filled the islands with kin and kith. We rented a blue cat named Peter for whose delightful presence we paid one dollar per season to a farmer on the mainland. We were so fortunate as to have the same Canadian maids come to us year by year, long after my girlhood was over, and a French Canadian gardener who was also our winter caretaker.

We formed abiding friendships among our neighbors, Canadian and American, in all three of the Muskoka Lakes. Some of the families on our Lake Rosseau, including Carson kin, had boys of around Clif's age. These young things, the girls and men who came up to see Lees and me, my older brother and his friends on leave—all of us spilled over islands and lakes, in and out of boats, every summer. The water was thirty feet deep off our dock. The diving, swimming, canoeing, and the long camping trips into more remote parts of Canada crowd my mind with happy memories but none of them seem to have any special bearing on the Frontier Nursing Service.

It was during my first summer on the islands, in 1901, that we learned through a Toronto paper that President McKinley had been shot at the Buffalo Exhibition. When he died, I wrote in my journal as follows:

One of the kindest gentlemen, one of the most faithful Presidents our country has ever known, has shown us an example of how to live and how to die. His devotion in private life; his honor in public service; his integrity as a man; and his life as a Christian appeal to each of us singly and to all as a nation. His conduct under suffering deepened the affection the people of both parties bore him.

Much as I loved my people and much as I enjoyed the life I led, especially when it was in forests and on lakes and streams, I chafed at the complete lack of purpose in the things I was allowed to do. Several times I suggested to my mother that it would be nice to do something useful, but I never got anywhere with such an idea. I could range freely and read deeply. That was considered enough until I made up my mind whom I wanted to marry, and this I didn't do right away. Once, after a round of visits with my Kentucky kindred, I became so frustrated by idleness that I begged my mother's permission to go to the summer session of the University of Tennessee in Knoxville before heading for The Brackens. It seemed a harmless enough desire, especially since I would be stopping with my Uncle Will and Aunt Rachel, but it took pressure to bring it about. I wrote in my journal: "Every day I am more thankful that I carried my point and received permission." The professors whose lectures I attended were stimulating to the imagination much as Monsieur Sansine had been. Among the courses I followed was one on Shakespeare and one on the history of the South. I also took geology and discovered to my delight that it involved field work. I had been reading geology on my own because I wanted to know more about mountains and their rocks.

Writing is often an outlet for idle people but the only form it took with me was to cover pages of my journal with happenings, reflections, and the conversations of men and girls. At about the age of eight I had begun to write poetry. This I abandoned at eighteen, "I think partly because I cannot say what I want to say as I would like." I destroyed the book in which I had put my verses. I, who had been nurtured on the great poets of three tongues, could not tolerate my own base substitutes for their glorious reality. Although I continued my custom of telling stories to children (for years I made up one for Clif called Jack and Machinery Jim), I had no desire to write them down. The real adventures that I wanted ardently could find no outlet except in the musings of my journal. As the seasons of my aimless girlhood passed, I tried to effect a reconciliation between the life I longed to live and the life allowed me. This I could do when I stayed in Canada and in Mississippi. At The Brackens I wrote of

a great rock I especially love that reaches out toward the water way below it. When I come to this rock I dream of Switzerland until I am lost in a great contentment with rough and bold projections. . . . A holy breath rests over everything. . . . Life with nature is a prayer.

On Oasis plantation I wrote often in the same vein:

Sweet earth, good earth—I want to kiss the light and air and sounds . . . the trembling, palpitating forest with its silent footfall of the deer, and distant turkey call. . . . The great passion of my nature is for a wildness that I have had tastes of only in this country of my heart. That this feeling is shared so imperfectly by those dear to me is the cause of a loneliness that almost overwhelms me sometimes. Perhaps most people are alone in some things. I have always been alone in this. . . . The sadness in our world is infinite, for it filters through our every joy. Happiness is the deeper for being transient and not unmixed with pain. . . . In my forests sadness can shadow me but not engulf me—because I reach the heart of things and catch glimpses of the eternal light.

II

My mother and I were at Oasis plantation when we received the news of the death of my Grandmother Lees. I had just returned from hunting, with one of my cousins, and had not dismounted when I was called to answer the long-distance telephone. Uncle Joe, Aunt Florence and I broke the news to my mother. The next day we started on the long, sad journey from Mississippi to New York. We had telegraphed Hazelwood when to expect us so that the carriage was at High Bridge when our train dropped us there. I was startled to see Russell, the coachman, in black instead of the cream-colored livery Grandmother's coachman and footman had always worn. The funeral had been delayed until our arrival. It was such a gathering of the clan as we had not had at Hazelwood since Susie's wedding. I recalled that Grand-

46

mother had said the next family wedding at Hazelwood should be mine. Of her I wrote:

There is something glorious about the death of one that is old. The completeness of a long and varied life lived with dignity, the graciousness of past good deeds and wide hospitality, the end of a name borne proudly, the responsibility that came with gentle birth and was ended—these things made the death of my grandmother a stately thing. But it is strange that in missing her it is her sense of humor next to her openheartedness that I miss most.

A second death was to bring me a second shattering of life associations when my Uncle Joseph Carson died at Oasis plantation. All through my girlhood he had been my beau ideal. Of Oasis I wrote:

To be there and not to meet his loving smile; to be there and not see him among his books, or riding down among the cotton fields; to be there and know that I could not at any moment run to him—this would be such suffering. The flames of the big wood fire would cast their lights and shadows over the place where he should be sitting; I should be haunted by the nearness of the grave that does not really hold him; the woods would ring with the trampling of his horse's hoofs. . . . And yet not to be at Oasis ever again—I do not think that I could bear this.

My last visit to the plantation was made in the early spring following Uncle Joe's death. The Mississippi River was on such a rampage that four miles of train tracks between Memphis and Oasis were flooded by the seepage from under the levees. When I reached Memphis for a night or two with Leila and her grandmother, Mrs. Griffing, I resolved that no high water should keep me from the plantation. Nelly Morton's Uncle Grat came to my rescue. He knew Captain Agnew of the Mississippi steamboat, the *Kate Adams*, and arranged with him to take care of me to the landing at Friar's Point. Mrs. Griffing gave her consent. So did Aunt Florence, with whom I talked over the long-distance telephone, after Uncle Grat had said, "It would be both safe and proper." The *Kate Adams* left Memphis on a Monday evening between five and six o'clock and reached Friar's Point between one and two o'clock the next morning. She could not approach the levee for fear of her waves washing it, so she was tied to three half-submerged trees some distance out. Aunt Florence had arranged for friends at Friar's Point to come out after me in a bateau. Captain Agnew picked me up and dropped me down to them over the side of the ship. At the same time the roustabouts were landing thirty-six mules on skiffs, using the cranes with which they took on and discharged bales of cotton.

47

Many pages of my journal are given over to a description of the joys and sadness of this last visit at Oasis. Isabel was dead but I rode Cedric, another plantation horse of which I was fond. Old "Uncle Wright," who drove the surrey, and the house servants I knew so well made the place seem as though nothing were changed where all had changed. With my cousins, and the young men of the family connection, with the Stovalls—the old, glad mingling rippled over the depths of sorrow that lay beneath. It was a time of anxiety because of the high water. My journal is full of the trips we took with a Levee Board engineer up and down the river on a little steamboat; of rides along the banquette of the levee to watch the struggle of the engineers and planters, with hundreds of Negroes helping them, to control the mighty waters of the Mississippi. We knew that a break in the levees must come somewhere on one side of the river or the other. All regular plantation work was suspended while we fought breathlessly to control the "boils" which came from seepage under the levee. In the midst of all the strain there was love-making too, as always in the South, so that my account of my last stay at Oasis is a blended one.

Near the three-acre Indian mound, where the plantation house stood, there were two small mounds with a sunken space between them, enclosed by an iron fence. Here lay the family burial ground, and here I went to say good-by when I left Oasis for the last time. I was facing a decision. I did not know whether it would be honest to accept the man to whom I had become attached until I had uprooted my longing for exploration—a career wholly different from his. I wanted to talk this over with Uncle Joe, although I knew that

> . . . in dear words of human speech
> We two communicate no more.

I knelt by his grave and said to him, "You who were all truth, may your memory guard my soul from insincerity. May I see the real and live it." I rose comforted.

III

Marriage when I was young was an everlasting kind of thing and not entered into lightly. For a woman it meant that she gave up her own ambitions, which she might cherish otherwise in the hope of their ultimate fulfillment, to embrace the career of the man of her choice. Marriage called upon a woman for renunciation, entire and complete. In my journal I copied this fugitive bit of verse by an author unknown to me:

> We are queens in our girlhood and recklessly play
> With the heart strings of men as our fingers might stray
> 'Mid the chords of a harp; but are fain to lay down
> With the white bridal roses our scepter and crown.

The bantering and love-making of that period in the South sometimes led to very real friendships between men and girls. We followed a code in such things without reasoning about it. When men cared for you seriously, you did not speak of it even to the girls you knew best. You did not repeat the things men said to you. If you kept any of their love letters, these you destroyed when you had made your choice. If men who cared about you bored or bothered you, then you did not hesitate to break with them once and for all; but to those you liked, you offered a friendship that was not meaningless. In my journal I wrote of the meaning of friendship as Montaigne described it, and said, "Marriage should only come from such an understanding in its most complete and perfect form—for one's husband could not be more than a friend." Of my own brief marriage I shall not write except to say that it gave me all, and more than all, I had wanted in married friendship.

A few weeks before my marriage, I had written:

A journal that has been a part of one's life becomes precious to the possessor. . . . Our remembrance of abstractions is poor. If, near the end of life, a man were to sit down and write an autobiography, he would find no trouble in recalling the open events of his past. . . . But could he remember what he thought and felt then? What bearing his feelings had on his acts and the acts of others and the events themselves? . . . He would recall them only as memories, long succeeded by more recent ones. Whereas if he had written them at the time . . . he would find them fresh, ineffaceable, unmodified by subsequent impressions. . . . He could return to his youth and find it as it was—unaltered, unchanged by the long variations of years.

As I read over the record I kept of the inner as well as the outer life of my girlhood, it is as though I had had a little sister fifty years ago who had lived my life then. In the five years following the death of my young husband, I wrote eight times in my journal, in the form of letters addressed to him. The last entry, with which the journal ends, I wrote at The Brackens in Canada, and in verse:

> Across the blackness of a quiet night
> The flowers glimmer, paler than the dawn:
> Attentive larkspur, lilies clean and white;
> Ah, me! The dying breeze is slowly drawn
>> Across the cluster'd phlox,
>> And purple hollyhocks.

Across the darkness of my inner soul
Thy spirit, oh, my darling, yearns to shine,
Illuming its dull waste, throughout the whole
Piercing superbly with a love divine,
     Whisp'ring in trancèd breath
     Across the night of death.

Chapter 7

I

IT would not be honest to say that I had been interested in nursing, as a career, at any time in my girlhood because I wasn't. This record will have shown that, although much in my life had helped to fit me for the Frontier Nursing Service, the desire for such a service, or even the thought of it, did not cross my mind in the days when I was young. I liked children always. I liked to play with them, and to make up stories for them. I wanted a lot of my own. But my strong personal desire was for exploration, and not for nursing in behalf of children. When I was left a young widow, with some money of my own, and parents whose liberality sought to match their compassion, I could have started to train for the explorations I had so much wanted in my girlhood. But now I wanted them no more. I had renounced them once and for all when I married a man of larger intellect than mine whose career, on which he had embarked with high promise, lay in law and statecraft. The longing for exploration had died not so much with this man's death, as with my marriage to him. It never came back.

The question I had to face was what to do with the years of life that lay before me. To stay with my parents, the subject of their endless solicitude, was impossible. I wanted to give care, not to receive it. I read "Lycidas," "Adonais," and "In Memoriam." In the last of these elegies, which I think I read hundreds of times, I found a verse that, with a change of one word, seemed applicable to me:

> My old affection of the tomb,
> A part of stillness, yearns to speak:
> "Arise, and get thee forth and seek
> A *service* for the years to come . . ."

Upon reflection, I realized I was not fitted to be of service to anyone. I responded to an invitation from the Reverend and Mrs. Edgar

Tufts to visit them at Banner's Elk, in the mountains of North Carolina. He had founded a girls' school that received some of my Grandmother Lees's benefactions, and was named in part for her. I only stayed with the Tufts for a few days before going to a little hotel in the valley, but I put myself at their disposition. It was as I had thought: there was nothing that I was fitted to do. As I sat by a child with typhoid fever, as helpless as his own stricken mother to help him, it came over me that if I took training as a nurse I could be of use to such children. I went to New York to ask the advice of Dr. William Polk, who was a family friend. He suggested that I enter St. Luke's Hospital School of Nursing, right there in New York. He gave me a letter of introduction to Miss Mabel Wilson, who held the title of Directress of Nurses, as it was called then. My application was accepted, and in February, 1907, after a desultory and hesitant period of more than a year of widowhood, I entered the spring class at St. Luke's.

It comes over me with a shock sometimes to realize that my application to enroll as a student in any modern school of nursing would not be accepted today because I have not the minimum American education required, that of a high school graduate. But the thing I needed then was a grade school subject—arithmetic. Here the lack was total, as I discovered in my class as a probationer when we started what was then called *materia medica*. One of my classmates had been a teacher before she entered the nursing school. I engaged her to tutor me in fractions and decimals. Although she was a good teacher, who did her best by me, I never felt at home in those wretched symbols. Fortunately for my patients, I grasped at once the principle that the bigger-looking the fraction, the smaller the dose. It didn't follow even then that I could always trust myself in working out solutions, but I didn't have to—because I found a friend in old Mr. Byers, the chemist in charge of the drug room at St. Luke's. It was he who taught us our *materia medica*. To him I confided my ignorance of fractions and decimals. Although he was aghast that such things could be, he readily volunteered to help me with each problem as it came up. I made a point of calling the drug room by telephone whenever I was faced with a solution that baffled me. Mr. Byers invariably told me how to work it out.

I became deeply attached to St. Luke's Hospital during the three years I spent there, and I have continued my affection for the old place down to this day. I rarely go to New York without taking the time to visit St. Luke's again. Our school of nursing has kept, so it seems to me, the *esprit de corps* it had when I took my training there. The quality of the training in nursing that I received could not have been bettered, but the long hours of work in the wards and operating rooms have been shortened, to the immense advantage of the patients as well as the students.

Some years ago the School of Nursing moved into a new residence, called the Eli White Memorial, where the living quarters and the classrooms are all up-to-date. The only thing I found there that I could recognize was the old skeleton on which we had been taught anatomy. I wanted to kiss its fingers. In anatomy and physiology we had a truly great teacher in Mrs. Carrie E. Bath. She could make dry bones live. When Miss Wilson retired to get married, Mrs. Bath succeeded her as Directress of Nurses.

In those days senior nurses, who had executive ability, were given charge of all the wards except the infants' ward, and carried much of the ward teaching. Some among them were natural-born teachers, but under others we learned almost nothing. I remembered this when I was made head of Norrie One, a twenty-four-bed men's surgical ward, in my third year. I tried to help the junior nurses and the probationers to learn everything possible about our patients during the time they were assigned to me. I enjoyed the running of a large ward. During my senior year I wanted more advanced work with babies than had fallen my way. I cared a lot about the sick babies, with always the heartache that no baby had come to me, so I requested to be assigned the post of senior nurse under the graduate nurse at the head of the infants' ward. Although it meant demotion, I have always been glad that I asked for the experience because I learned a lot about sick babies that otherwise I might never have known. I was made a head nurse again, while the graduate went on her vacation, and became directly responsible for the welfare of the babies.

I formed enduring friendships at St. Luke's. I have kept in touch with several of my classmates, and, when I go to New York, I try to get together with those who live there. My closest friend, the daughter of a physician in Columbia, Tennessee, was Willie Biddle, one of the finest people, as a nurse and as a woman, that I ever knew. She came to take care of me years later when my son was born.

The hours of duty of student nurses when I trained were too long for either their welfare or that of their patients. Theoretically, we worked only ten hours a day, but it was rare for us to be able to leave our busy wards for our two hours off duty, or to get away at seven o'clock at night, so that we worked more nearly eleven than ten hours daily. On our turns of night duty, the hours were twelve, with only twenty minutes off for supper around midnight. During the twenty minutes we had to reach the supper room, on the fourth floor, and allow time to return to our posts. From some of the wards it meant a distance of half a city block, and back again, as well as time spent in waiting for an elevator. We always wanted two cups of coffee, to

53

guarantee alertness during the hours when the vitality of sick people is at its lowest, and that didn't leave much time for food. After these long hours on duty, we had to study, to attend classes and medical and surgical lectures. Aside from two half-day holidays a week, we had little time for recreation and fresh air, of which young nurses stand in need. We had only two weeks' vacation a year. Several of my class broke physically under the strain, and one died within a year of tuberculosis. I was one of four so hardy that I finished the three years without losing a day.

Although the routine hours in the wards were long and hard, we stood up under them pretty well. It was the service on the operating floor that tended to break us. Two surgical divisions operated on alternate days. We reported for duty at seven o'clock in the morning, as on the wards, to get the operating rooms set up. The operations lasted nearly all day with a brief period of half an hour allowed for the noon dinner, which included going to and returning from the dining room. When the operations were over, the surgeons, the house staff, and the graduate head nurses went off duty, but the student nurses stayed on to clean up. This usually took until nine at night, often longer, but allowed a half-hour for supper between five and six o'clock. After we went off duty and to bed, we were on call for emergencies—under the direction of the night supervisors. I remember once being called just as I had gone to bed. There were two emergencies, so that when I got back to my room I barely had time to take a bath and get back into uniform before returning to the operating rooms for the next day's work, which did not end until nearly midnight. This meant that I was on duty, without sleep or rest, for over thirty hours. Since no student relief nurses were assigned for emergency operations at night, this was not an unusual experience. One night, when I was cleaning up, dizzy with fatigue and lack of sleep, I pulled the great drums of dressings out of the sterilizers and found, to my horror, that the openings for steam to penetrate had been left closed, so that none of the dressings were sterile. I stuck the drums back in the sterilizer, to be run through a second time. After long stretches of responsible as well as hard work, without enough rest or sleep, one isn't very observing. It was not right for the safety of patients to depend on student nurses as exhausted as we often were in the operating rooms.

II

St. Luke's had only one affiliation with other hospitals in my day and that was for obstetrics. At some time, usually near the end of the second year, one was sent either to Sloane Maternity or to the New York Lying-In. Biddle and I were sent at the same time to the New York Lying-In. Student nurses were sent there for training in obstetrical nursing from many parts of the country. The New York Lying-In was way downtown then, and a far different place from the splendid institution, now a part of the medical center, which includes the Cornell University–New York Hospital School of Nursing. At St. Luke's everything was so well ordered, so decent, so kind, that Biddle and I could not accustom ourselves to the Lying-In, as it was run when we were there. The patients lacked necessary supplies and the student nurses lacked supervision. I don't recall ever seeing the superintendent of nurses on the floor to which I was assigned.

With its own delivery and operating rooms, mothers' ward and nursery, each floor was a unit in itself. The head nurse on my floor was as indifferent to the training of the students as she was to the care of the patients. Only one section of the floor had enough supplies, the delivery and operating rooms. These were under the direct eyes of the attending obstetricians, who were a fine group of men. I knew one of them slightly, the late Dr. Ralph W. Lobenstine, a former St. Luke's man. I was to see more of this distinguished man in later years but the very sight of him, let alone a few words with him, at the New York Lying-In in those days, gave me courage to carry on. Two of the nurses in supervisory posts at the Lying-In were tops. One was the night supervisor. She carried her responsibilities well, not only to the patients but in the instruction of the student nurses when they were on night duty. The other was supervisor of the Out-Patient Department. The district was interesting—and heartbreaking.

The appalling rookeries in which people lived then have probably all been torn down now, but in my day there were two-room tenements with many children and only one window opening on an air shaft. In the second room, a gas jet was the only light. For a whole tenement of families, there would be but one wretched toilet on the ground floor. It was in one tenement and one flat such as I describe that I found a woman, whose baby had been born in the night, dressed and cooking some food for her family.

Over three hundred years ago, a certain Thomas Dekker wrote:

> Then he that patiently want's burden bears,
> No burden bears, but is a king, a king!

The baby I had come to tend, a little princess of the Kingdom of Destitution, had not even a diaper to her name. The queen, her mother, had wrapped her in a dirty shawl. I had to go out to a shop to get clothes before I could wash the princess, and give nursing care to the queen. To reports on cases like that one, the supervisor of the Lying-In Out-Patient Department listened attentively. What is more, she arranged to have such cases referred at once to charitable agencies.

Although the district nursing tore at my heartstrings, I suffered even more in the nurseries. In the nursery to which I was assigned, both for day and night duty, there were never fewer than twenty babies and sometimes as many as thirty. The heat seemed to be turned on rather low at night and the east wind, from over the river, penetrated through the cracks of the windows. Only one thin cotton blanket was allowed to each bassinet. It was cold enough at night for us to take sweaters to put over our uniforms, but I never had the heart to wear mine. It was an extra covering for at least one baby. There weren't anything like enough diapers to keep the babies dry, the result, in part, of using them for a lot of other things. The mothers had them for face towels, and the ward maids used them for dust rags. I solved the diaper problem by taking cotton and gauze out of the delivery and operating rooms, the only places where there was a reserve of anything. While I had the nursery shift, both at night alone and in the daytime with two other nurses, we started a system of taking enough gauze and cotton to leave a narrow supply of diapers on hand for the alternate shift as we went off duty. Although none of the student nurses on my floor were known to me before I went there I found that, unlike the head nurse, most of them had the welfare of the patients at heart. We co-operated.

One fine thing about the nursery was that all the babies were breast-fed except two who had been there for weeks, one with head injuries and one with a malformed spine. The schedule of feeding in the daytime was every two hours and the babies were taken to their mothers in little carts. During the night there was only one longer period during which the babies were not taken to nurse. I think that this frequent contact with their mothers, whether they were too sleepy to nurse or not, kept the breast milk stimulated. The wave of bottle feeding of newborn babies came about with the lengthening of time between feedings. This is only a speculation, but I do know from experience that hospital nursery babies in the first decade of this century were not only breast-fed but nearly always had enough milk to gain back their birth weight by the end of the first week. Since mothers were not sent home as early as they are now, breast milk was well established before the fatigue of tenement life had to be taken up again.

During my term of night duty, I was sometimes in despair over the two older bottle-fed babies. More than once the head nurse went off duty leaving no formula for them, nor even any milk in the refrigerators. One of the young doctors, on staff duty, went out on the streets to buy milk for me when this happened. I did not report the lack of milk to the night supervisor. Student nurses in my day were silent creatures. We compensated for the failure of a superior as best we could. However, after a couple of months at the Lying-In, I was fit to be tied and had to talk to somebody. During a half-day off duty, I sought out my girlhood friend, Nelly Morton, now married to Irving Brock. Nelly was not at home, so I poured out a lot of things to Irving and then said I would look up a respectable woman to whom I would tell the rest. When Nelly returned, Irving said he couldn't imagine what was left to tell the respectable woman!

One of the two bottle-fed babies in my nursery, the *spina bifida*, was paralyzed in both legs. Her name was Margaret. Never have I known so young a creature with the personality of this baby. Her eyes were luminous and her whole expression more mature than that of babies twice her age. She never fretted. When she was hungry, or wanted attention, she called out once, and then waited to give me time to get to her. During the weeks I attended her, both at night and in the daytime, she became dear to me. Her mother did not want her. When I saw her she readily gave the child to me. I arranged with St. Luke's Hospital to let me pay for Margaret's care in the infants' ward until I finished my training. Although this baby was crippled for life, the feeling I had for her was not one of pity. There were babies enough on the East Side to drain one's heart of pity. Margaret and I had become friends. I wanted her companionship, and I wanted to make life easy for her as long as she lived. I could well afford a baby, even a crippled baby.

When it came to the transfer from the Lying-In to St. Luke's, I thought I had it properly lined up. A physician on the Lying-In house staff, who had the authority to do so, gave Margaret a medical discharge. The Lying-In's own office staff gave her a hospital discharge and my friend Biddle, who was on night duty, took the baby up to St. Luke's for me before going to bed for the day. I was in the Out-Patient Department then, and on the district. When I came in at noon, I was met by the biggest cyclone that ever swept over my head. I found that not only was I suspended but the house staff physician and Biddle were suspended too, only Biddle was asleep and didn't know it. We had to go singly before a Board to explain why we had stolen a Lying-In baby. When the district supervisor let me go, she said, in her Irish brogue, "You were trying to do a good deed." But it wasn't that; I loved the baby.

Awkward as things were at the moment, I was struck by the realization that there was a Board, and that for once it had taken an interest in one of the patients. Although the plot was mine, as I freely admitted, my suspension was lifted, with the others', after only a few hours.

The fact that the Lying-In's own office had cleared the papers to transfer the baby to St. Luke's made it difficult for the Board to raise a fuss. They got Margaret back. The curious thing to me in all of this storm was that I, the only person in the world who wanted Margaret, was not allowed to keep her.

Only two days after I had gone back to St. Luke's Hospital, they telephoned me from the Lying-In that Margaret was dead. They said I could have her body if I wanted it. Thus, the only thing I could do for my little friend was to save her body from a pauper's grave. I went back to the Lying-In to sign papers. I arranged with an under-taking firm to buy a grave in the Kensico Cemetery, and to meet me there with the casket on the first afternoon I could be off duty. I asked my Aunt Jane's minister to go with me and hold a brief service at the grave. He readily consented and was deeply kind. I have never been back to see Margaret's grave but I still own it. For that crippled baby with the luminous eyes and wisdom beyond her weeks, for that baby I have kept an affection that is ineffaceable. I hope, and expect, to see her with my own two children when I have crossed through to the other side of death.

III

In February of 1910, three years after I entered St. Luke's, I had completed my training, taken my state examinations, and was ready for the service which I had prepared myself to render. My mother asked me if I wouldn't first spend a year with my family. I had seen them only briefly in the summers at The Brackens when I went there for my two weeks' holiday each year.

My father had again solved his problem of what to do. After he finished the work on the Commission for the Five Civilized Tribes, he organized a trust company in Fort Smith, Arkansas. He knew nothing about trust company business but he had the rare gift of knowing men. With no difficulty he got together a good board of directors for his new company and chose, in John C. Gardner, an assistant who was one of the finest men, as well as one of the ablest trust company officers, in all America. In the course of time, my father retired as president of the company and John C. Gardner succeeded him.

Since my father's new venture meant that he would live in Fort Smith, my mother set about building a house. It was a pleasant place, roomy, and hospitable-looking with its long galleries, great open double doors and wide entrance hall. There was plenty of space for the thousands of books we had inherited or accumulated. They spilled all over the downstairs and upstairs halls; the library and my father's study were lined with them. A private sitting room my mother got ready for me was lined with my books. Even the large attic had shelves filled with books that nobody wanted to read. I remember once finding Elinor Glyn's *Three Weeks* up there, leaning against Baxter's *Saints' Everlasting Rest*.

To this place in Fort Smith I went after I had finished my training at St. Luke's. I found my mother far from well. It didn't take me long to pick her up and carry her back to St. Luke's for a medical consultation arranged by Dr. H. H. M. Lyle. When certain treatments were ordered for her, I realized with joy that my long summer at The Brackens would not be an idle one. I took over the running of the islands for my mother, with help from Lees and Eleanor Blaydes, who was a dear member of our household every summer. As we often had from ten to fifteen guests, besides our own family, the housekeeping was a big job in itself. My mother continued the oversight of her flower garden and lily ponds. In October I went back with her to Fort Smith.

My brother Carson and I used to say that the attractive home at Fort Smith, in its setting of forest trees, had come too late in our lives to take much of a hold on our affections. We had no roots there, no associations with our childhood or our youth. We did not, however, lack friends in a group of people among the most stimulating and heart-warming I have ever known. All of my father's generation have now crossed the last divide.

After my year at home, my mother was well enough to resume charge of her households both in the South and in Canada. I could, then, have gone to work in the Kentucky mountains. I had been back to Kentucky several times, but only on visits to my people. Although there really was nothing for me to do at home, once my mother no longer needed me, I kept deferring my plans. My younger brother was sent to school at Lawrenceville, my sister Lees was busy with her young ladyhood, and my father was occupied in watching John C. Gardner run his trust business, and with fishing. I was not needed, but I kept yielding to the pull of my family, although idleness has never agreed with me. A young widow may lay aside the long crepe veil which was worn in my day, and lighten her mourning as the years pass, but her widowhood is still a complete protection from the courtship of men, so long as she carries it in her heart.

Of my second marriage I shall not write except as it enters into the next chapter, where I tell the story of my children. The generation to which I belong think it in poor taste to discuss a broken marriage, and mine was broken after the children were dead. I was allowed by the court to take back my own name. This I did, with a feeling not unlike that in which one puts on again an old pair of workaday shoes.

Chapter 8

I

MY part in the story of the Frontier Nursing Service cannot be told without telling the story of Breckie. This is not hard to do because, although he died at the age of four years, he was such a happy child that the memories of his short span are all golden ones. To go back to Breckie is to step into a sort of fairyland full of sunshine and laughter, bird notes, winds, stars, the sweet earth, and the growing, climbing, calling things whose music was the gladness of his world.

I started a journal again when Breckie was born. I began it because of him. In the weeks following his death, I wrote a book about him for private publication before I destroyed the journal. The lives of few young children have been recorded in such detail as was his. In the annals of his four years, there are more outdoor than indoor things because he spent more of his time out of doors than in houses. With his nurse or with me he stayed out most of the daytime hours. At night, except in bitter weather, he slept on a balcony. I think one reason why he had a sweet and joyous heart is because he was never far from natural things even in sleep. The "winds austere and pure" swept over his little crib and he was awakened by the matins of the birds. It could have been said of him as Longfellow said of Agassiz:

> And Nature the old Nurse took
>   The child upon her knee
> Saying, "Here is a story book
>   Thy Father hath written for thee."

> And he wandered away and away
>   With Nature the dear old Nurse,
> Who sang him by night and by day
>   The rhymes of the universe.

It was during Breckie's infancy that the first of the great wars thundered in upon a horrified world. My mother and sister were touring Norway with my brother Carson. Since he was a Marine, and had to break his leave at once to report back for duty, they hurried home on the first Scandinavian ship on which they could get space. All cabins in the ship were given up to the women while the men, like my brother, went in the steerage. Carson was sent back to Europe as an Assistant Naval Attaché in Russia before our country entered the war. My younger brother, Clif, who was at Cornell, attended the Plattsburg Training Camp in the summer so that he would be commissioned as soon as the United States declared war. Lees went over to France with the Y.M.C.A. The overtones of war, long before we as a country were in it, pierce through all my record of Breckie's gay young life.

I have a twofold purpose in writing about this life. I cannot carry you, my readers, with me into the work I was to do for rural children, into the Frontier Nursing Service, unless I first share with you the child in whom all childhood is symbolized for me. My second reason is that I think the story of Breckie's life will be of use to those of you who have to do with young children. Perhaps you have read scores of books about them, as I did before Breckie was born, and have wanted, as I did, to follow in one normal child the laws that govern the stages of its growth. I found no such biography in the books I sought, nor is one needed for the physical aspects of a young child's development. These are well understood by intelligent people, whose children have the oversight of pediatricians. But of the mental and emotional life of young children, at each stage of their growth, not enough is known. A little child cannot be hurried through his second or his third year without doing him irrevocable harm. There are things he can grasp at the age of four that he cannot possibly take in at two. If at the earlier age he is pushed to responses that belong at four, then not only is his mental and emotional growth retarded, but this frustration will leave deep-rooted scars to plague him, and his associates, long after he has grown to be a man.

Of Breckie's physical development I shall write hardly anything. Dr. Holt's book on the feeding and care of infants was the classic for babies when he was born. I followed its directions in raising him. He was breast-fed until the age of nine months and completely weaned at one year. After that, his food was served him at regular hours at his own table in his own chair. Most of the things he ate had a meaning for him. The hens he personally knew laid his eggs. Kind people, also known to him, put up his jellies and made his bread from the whole grains. When he was old enough to have a small garden plot of his own, he raised some potatoes so successfully that they could be eaten. Great was his pride in them. He was a superb-looking child with deep-set violet eyes, fair skin, ruddy cheeks, and yellow hair that curled at the tips in what Mammy called "drake's tails."

Breckie's first nurse, Aunt Alice, engaged before he was born, was the mother of my mother's houseboy. She was a colored woman of the old school and one of the finest I ever knew. Since the old South was Breckie's inheritance, on both sides, I wanted him to drink at that spring. Before he was quite a year old, her health began to fail. She went back to her home, where, within a short while, she died. Before leaving me, she made arrangements for one of her friends to take over Breckie's care. This was the Mammy of my baby's second and most of his third year, and he loved her more than he loved anyone. As for me, I could take the long walks and horseback rides, without which my health suffered, perfectly content about my baby in the care of this devoted woman, who knew how to handle a young child. When he was with me, and she came to get him from me, she often said, "Dis chile's tired of white folks. Come to Mammy." In the course of time it was he, as he saw her approach, who called out, "Mammy, baby's tired of white folks." Years later when I had returned from France and my mother died, Mammy came at once to stay with me. At the sight of her large, comfortable figure and the dear dark face surmounted by its white cap, I went into her arms saying, "I'm tired of white folks."

The powers of observation of young children are far greater than most people realize. At thirteen months, Breckie noticed a picture my mother had brought me from Norway, that of the painting of the Resurrection which hung above the altar in the village church of Molde. He stood below it a moment, looked at the wings of the angel, then looked at me and crowed. Shortly before he was two years old he was walking with me one day in the rain when suddenly the sun shone out. "See the glorious sun," I said to him. There was a short silence and then Breckie replied, "G'owious sun take a baf." Not long after that, when I was putting extra covers on him while he slept on his balcony, he roused as a bird twittered. "Dat's a catbird," he said drowsily before he went to sleep again.

Breckie's first speech was in the soft dialect of the colored people. That is my native speech and I find that I always revert to it when I am alone with babies and beasts. If Breckie wanted an orange he put it this way: "Is yer got any owanges?" In his second year, he was eager to talk but his words could not keep pace with the exciting things he had to tell.

He reported a dream to me when he was two years and one month old. He woke up suddenly and called to me, "Bop, calfie sat down on de gwound."

"What did the calf do," I asked, "when it sat on the ground?"

"Calfie eat birdies."

"Oh, no," I said. "Calf eats grass and flowers."

But he persisted: "Calfie eat birdies on de gwound."

In an effort to call me mother, he came out with the word "Boppie." I was always Bop or Boppie to him after that. His father he called Daddy, a father who was tenderly kind to him and to whom he was devoted.

Children delight in rhymes at an early age. Before the end of his second year, Breckie was repeating fragments of Mother Goose rhymes, among them Mammy's version of "Tom, Tom, the Piper's Son," which concludes thus: "Pig got loose and killed ma goose, and dey put ole Tom in de callyboose." He loved Mammy's camp meeting hymns, especially the ones where he could clap his hands as he sang. He learned to dance for Mammy with much stomping of feet to the rhythm of such old airs as this one, that I knew as a baby:

> Step light, ladies, oh, Miss Lou,
> Neber mind de wedder, so de wind don't blew.

Soon after Breckie was two years old we noted that he had begun to build constructively with his blocks and not pile them up just to knock them down. One day when he set a row of blocks on end, I covered a few central ones and said, "Now, this is Stonehenge." Then I got out a volume of the eleventh edition of the *Encyclopedia Britannica* and showed him a photograph of the wonderful old pile. After that he often built "Tonenge," always asking to see the picture.

Although a happy, healthy baby smiles often, its face becomes intensely solemn when it is engaged in the serious business of play. The curiosity that consumes a baby, and its need to feel things in order to learn what they are, produce an absorption so profound in the play of the moment that it cannot break off quickly. Whenever he was interrupted Breckie said, "Baby's busy." Mammy and I respected that, and weaned him gently from the absorption of the moment to whatever else we had planned for him.

Before Breckie was born I had a fox terrier named for a character in one of the Uncle Remus tales, Linctum Lidy Lody Rinctum Riddletum Tinctum Tidy, and called Tidy for short. When the baby came, she adopted him with a devotion in which there was no shadow of jealousy. When he grew old enough to creep on the floor, she was always his playfellow and suffered him to do excruciating things to her eyes and whiskers with his barbarous little hands. Tidy died from rat poison, about which people are so careless, and which she picked up on one of her walks with Breckie. We wanted the boy to have a dog so we bought him an old-fashioned collie, black with white and tan markings, like the Shep of my own childhood. His name was Jock of Hazeldean but Breckie called him Gokkie. Whether he was poisoned or not I don't know, but he fell sick and died. Our last effort to have a dog for Breckie was when we bought a delightful bull terrier that we named Camp, after a dog of that breed beloved by Sir Walter Scott. As surely as I settled down alone to work among my flowers, I would see Mammy looming up across the lawn with Breckie and Camp fairly springing ahead of her. Then the baby ran off with my trowel and the dog with my dibble. Camp, too, got rat poison from somewhere. For weeks afterward, whenever Breckie found a bone, he would look around and call out, 'Come gie bone, Campy dear." Then he would echo Mammy's "Camp daid."

A fourth dog, another fox terrier, was given Breckie and named Patch. She did not care for children but took up with my father whom she worshiped. Just after she came, she was taken sick. I worked over her and pulled her through. After she was well, Breckie came to me, his eyes as big as saucers, and said, "Patchie sick."

"Patch is well now," I answered.

To this he replied, "Mammy sho' did tell Baby Patchie was sick."

I realized, to my horror, that I appeared to have contradicted Mammy. This had come from my use of the word "now," which no two-year-old could possibly understand. I had to explain, in baby vocabulary, that Mammy was, as always, right. I tried also to explain that Breckie's mother had been truthful too. Only those who have had such an experience with a two-year-old can form any idea of how difficult it is to get over to him such a thing as a time sequence.

The moral growth of young children will keep pace with their mental and physical growth if they are treated with courtesy and fairness. In the training of a young child, one should allow time, at each stage, for growth. He can learn a number of natural things correctly if his curiosity is met by truth. He will acquire polite manners if he is treated with invariable courtesy. Although he has no conception of right and wrong as abstractions, he is easily trained to recognize the right or the wrong of a given situation. When Breckie was two and one-half years old, he stamped his fat little foot on a baby chick and blotted out its life. I took him to a setting of eggs which was about to hatch and put an egg to his ear so that he could hear the little chick trying to break through. After I had awakened his interest in chicks, he never harmed another one. Until he knew about baby chicks his reaction was like that of most grown people in the presence of spiders.

Very early his father and I began to teach Breckie the difference between his and other people's property. We never took any of his things without asking his permission. We always thanked him. If he took our things, we would say, "Breckie, you didn't ask." Then he said, "Baby sowy. Please excuse him." But it is in training a little child in social customs that one is more nearly baffled than in all else, because they are meaningless to him and often to oneself as well. Each approach has to be at the level of a baby's growth and, once taken up, persisted in as patiently and as consistently as one trains the tendrils of a vine to take hold of a trellis. In the course of weeks, the tendrils grasp the trellis. It takes weeks too for a little child to learn a social convention and, when he has grasped it, his mother feels as did Wordsworth when he wrote:

> Full soon thy soul shall have her earthly freight,
> And custom lie upon thee with a weight,
> Heavy as frost, and deep almost as life!

II

When Breckie was two years old we began hoping for another baby to bless our lives as the first had done. One day I was telling Breckie about "Hot Cross Buns," winding up, "If you haven't any daughters then buy them for your sons."

"Bop," said he, "buy Baby a daughter."

"That would be a little girl," I replied.

After that nearly every day he begged for a little girl, and said that she could ride his hobbyhorse with him. All through the spring he talked so constantly of his sister that she became almost as real a person to him as to me who felt the stirrings of her life in mine. With the coming of the summer heat, my health was not good. I had to give up work among my flowers and I often felt discouraged and ill, but I continued to feel deeply the blessedness of my condition with one little child playing by me and another next my heart, and I thought of myself as the mother of children, not just of one child.

The last of June Mammy was called home by the illness of her daughter, which seemed to be of indefinite duration. Already I had noticed that Breckie was outgrowing Mammy. Neither she, heavy and rheumatic, nor I, in my condition, could keep up with him. Mammy's sudden call back to her own house brought to a head the ideas I had formed of a younger nurse for Breckie, and Mammy agreed that if her daughter was well enough she would come back to take care of the new baby when it was born. It so happened that Breckie was the last baby she ever nursed.

The nurse I wanted for Breckie was a French-Swiss woman named Juliette Carni, with whom he and I had long been acquainted. We often stopped at her house to talk, the mutual attraction at first being

65

that she came from a country where I had spent two years of happy girlhood at school, a country to the memory of which her heart, like that of every exiled Swiss, never ceased clinging. Juliette had recently lost her little baby and was anxious to nurse another child. I therefore engaged her for Breckie to whom she was to become a second mother. It was arranged that Juliette continue sleeping at her home, where she had a husband and a nine-year-old daughter, Liliane.

Between Mammy's going and Juliette's coming, there were two days in which I had no nurse and I overtaxed my already depleted strength. In addition to that, Breckie met with an accident which was an awful shock to me. Although the sides of his balcony crib reached up to his chest, he climbed over them and had a terrible fall. When I ran like the wind up the stairs to reach him, he had picked himself up and was sobbing piteously, his poor head hurt above the eyes. But the look he gave me had assurance in it that I would understand and comfort, as I raised him in my arms.

Juliette came the next day and Breckie took up with her at once in happy fashion. This was fortunate as I was then past helping in his care. After I had been ill five days, my girl baby was born prematurely, on the eighth of July, and in six hours died. She was an exquisite baby with a well-shaped head, broad brow, and eyes set wide apart. Lying by one of Breckie's yellow curls, I have yet a lock of her straight brown hair. I had not wanted her to be given my name, but when I knew she would not live I asked to have her named for me. I have always thought of her, and spoken of her, as Polly. Only six hours—and she had passed from one dark cradle to another with hardly a break between!

This short story of Polly will be read by women who have, like me, lost an infant at birth. For you who share with me a memory like this, I have a message. Keep your baby alive in your heart. Even if your infant did not live in this world at all, it is yours and it needs you. But in loving it, do not seek to hold it. You must learn the nature of spiritual motherhood, as indeed one should learn it in caring for children who do not die. The more we seek to hold our children to ourselves, the less are they ours. All of the love we give them has as its goal to set them free from us, to train them to be themselves.

> To hold by leaving,
> To take by letting go,
> Leaving, and again leaving,
> This is the Law.

Once, years after the death of my children, I saw George Arliss in the play called *The Green Goddess*. Those of you who have seen it will remember where the Oriental chief speaks to the Englishwoman about her children. He says, "Can even God give you back their childhood?" Yes, God can. But I think that if we set them free in our hearts, we shall find that we never lost their childhood, that we shared it with them all along.

<h2 style="text-align:center">III</h2>

It was a family decision that I should be taken to The Brackens as soon after Polly's birth as I was able to travel. With this to look forward to, I improved more rapidly as, in imagination, I listened to the "lake water lapping with low sounds by the shore." My mother traveled up to Canada from the South with Breckie and me, as did Juliette and her daughter, Liliane. It was mid-August when we reached The Brackens, which had been opened for our reception. Only two or three of our near ones came to stay with us in the roomy house that in other years had been filled with kith and kin. In a Canada at war, the Muskoka Lakes were quieter than we had ever known them to be in the fourteen years since we first began to love them.

Breckie was now in the second half of his third year. We turned Clif's old room into a night nursery for him where he slept in a crib near Juliette. But his playroom was the top floor of the large boat and launch house, full of all sorts of delectable things to delight a little boy: boats and tools and camping outfits, and in among them Clif's old red wheelbarrow, toy boats, and soldiers. Our French-Canadian gardener used to sit up there on stormy days, mending rugs with a long sailcloth needle and worsted. Instead of a thimble, he used a horny protector in the palm of his hand, which is sewing sailor fashion. This old caretaker was intensely proud of the sturdy baby and put him through a military drill every day. I don't know whether it was this drill or playing with Clif's soldiers, but it was at The Brackens that Breckie first began to speak of himself as a soldier. After that the highest praise we could give him when he picked himself up without crying, after a fall, was to call him a brave soldier. He adored our old caretaker and went out with him in rowboats and canoes even when the lake was stormy. Thus he early learned the most important thing there is to know about a boat, which is not to rock it.

Before the end of August I was well enough to take Breckie into the little bay and give him his first lessons in swimming. The rest of the time he played with Juliette and Liliane on his grandmother's islands. Young children are happiest when they are with Nature and their desire for knowledge of her is insatiable. Her plants, her trees, even her insects enchant them. In Thomas Traherne's seventeenth-century verse, we have, I think, the best descriptions of how a little child identifies himself with natural things.

67

This made me present evermore
      With whatsoe'er I saw.
An object, if it were before
My eye, was by Dame Nature's law,
      Within my soul.

Another thing that a young child learns spontaneously is to speak a second language as easily as his native tongue. For a few weeks after Juliette came to us, Breckie's French and English were all jumbled together, but within three months he spoke French as readily as English and did not mix the two languages. From Juliette he learned as many French poems and songs as he had learned English ones from Mammy and me. Three of which he was particularly fond were: "*Petite Poule, la Blanchette*," "*Le Petit Bossu*," and "*Cadet Rouselle*."

We did not leave The Brackens until late October. As the steamer pushed away from our dock, Breckie waved from its deck to the old caretaker who waved back at him, until The Brackens, with the golden and red glory of its birches, maples, oaks, and the darkness of its evergreens—with its lovely shores silhouetted against the lake's blue, and the homey smoke rising from its stone chimneys—had receded into his happy past. But there was always a happy future in this little child's fairyland.

IV

When Breckie and I returned to the small college where we lived, he found there a donkey, named Peter Pan, which his father had bought for him. His father, in whom he delighted, gave him his first riding lessons. Before he was three years old he could ride quite well, and dismount without assistance, but he had to have help in mounting. He had a good seat in the saddle. With his straight back and fine head crowned by short yellow curls, he was rather a triumphant-looking baby when he rode on Peter Pan.

Because of the war, we hadn't the heart to make a celebration at Christmas, near the end of Breckie's third year. But he had a tree and sang as Juliette had taught him, "*Voici Noël, O douce nuit.*" He seemed to me old enough this Christmas to grasp the idea that one gave presents as well as received them, so I suggested to him that he take five pennies out of his toy bank and buy a Christmas present for his father with them. We went down the mountain into the town, where I asked a clerk to put a row of things costing only five cents each in front of him. I told Breckie that his pennies would buy any one of these things, and he was to choose. He was fascinated with some

68

celluloid creatures such as float in baths. "Now, Breckie," I said, "decide which you want—the swan, or the duck, or the turtle, or the fish." One by one he picked them up gravely, saying, "De swan, and de duck, and de turtle, and de fish." Forced by his financial limitations to make a choice, he decided on the duck. He carried it home triumphantly, and kept it a secret until he gave it to his father at Christmas. Another lesson Breckie was old enough to learn was to give presents to people outside his family circle. During this Christmas season he donated some of his toys for the children invited to the college Christmas tree. The ones he voluntarily gave were the better, newer ones and not his battered old favorites.

I sometimes talked to Breckie about the plight of children less fortunate than he, especially the children in war-torn France and Belgium, who talked just as he and Juliette did together. I suggested to him that it would be fun to take some of the pennies out of his bank every month and let them buy milk for these children. Since he liked taking pennies out of his bank even more than putting them in, this represented no sacrifice whatever on his part, not like the benefactions of "Mrs. Pardigle's Young Family" in *Bleak House*, over which I laugh and cry to this day.

So many members of his family put money in Breckie's bank that he was able with his own money to buy a fifty-dollar Liberty Loan Bond at the first sale. He had no conception of the meaning of a Liberty Bond, but he knew what it was to be a patriot. I often talked to him about his country, and told him that, after God, his country had the first claim on him—a claim immeasurably greater than his father's or mine. To help him to grasp the idea of what his country was, I told him that the trees and ground and rocks all about him were a part of his native land. These he knew and loved already. Although he could not love his country as he loved his people, I am sure that he wished to serve her, and knew that he was first of all her son.

On January 12, 1917, Breckie was three years old. At some time during their fourth year, as many of my readers know, young children begin to want companionship of their own age. We had built near Breckie's sand pile, a slide, trapeze, swing, seesaw, and jumping board. Other children on the place, who belonged to members of the faculty, played there with him as well as a few who lived near the college. With them he took part in games, where he showed a fair-minded and a generous spirit.

At about this time, he began to like continued stories and I made up one for him about Fred and Lucy and a dog called Bumbleton. A hero named Roger appeared in the tale. One day when I had Fred and Lucy and Bumbleton hanging mid-air on the edge of a precipice, unable to climb up or down, an exit out of the danger immediately suggested itself to Breckie. "Here will come Woger wid a wope."

With Breckie, as with other normal little children, the patient process of training him in social responsibility moved forward to the stage where he could begin to learn the conquest of himself. Not long after he was three years old, he got into the way of leaving his balcony crib and climbing in again with all kinds of loot. Once I found him with two American flags, a raised umbrella, and a dish of prunes. He was too young to learn that such doings were unconventional, or to care, so I had a chicken wire top made to come down like a roof across the crib. After that Breckie and his Teddy Bear, who always slept with him, had the range of a generous-sized crib and nothing more. Nobody was vexed with him. Nobody tried to break the daring and initiative of a gallant spirit that because of immaturity, and only because of that, had failed to meet our ideas of behavior. It took Breckie several weeks to learn the lesson of the crib episode but, when he had learned it, he announced spontaneously that we could take the top off and that he wouldn't get out of bed. He had achieved his own conquest of himself. When he woke up he said, "Congwatulate me, Boppie, I didn't get out of bed," and to Juliette, "*Vous pouvez me féliciter.*"

It has been my wish to spare you, my readers, as much baby talk as I can, especially a baby talk that was first in a colored dialect and then in French. However, what we grown people call baby talk is the baby's only speech. With this inherent limitation a baby has trouble, too, in grasping the meaning of the words we use in speaking to him. The war talk all around Breckie, together with his role of brave soldier, led him to play at shooting Germans with a gun improvised from a stick. On one of his walks, Juliette discovered that he thought the Germans were large birds in trees. When he came back he told me, in amazement, Germans were people like us. Not long after that he said, "Dere are some good Germans." When I told him, tenderly, that he was right, he considered a moment before replying. Then he said, "I will shoot de bad ones only."

When a wooden gun and toy pistol had been given him, we said he could play with them if he used them as carefully as the real guns and pistols he would own when he was bigger. But, if he pointed the toy ones at anybody, they would be taken from him. They never had to be forfeited except once. When he asked for them back he promised me he would not point them at anybody again. He kept his word. He shot at chairs, saying that they were lions and tigers and the Kaiser. When he was going out with Juliette one day, he announced that he was going to shoot birds. "Not the dear little songbirds," I begged, and he replied, "I will shoot a chicken hawk only."

Little children identify themselves with the natural things around them so instinctively that they act the parts of animals and even of plants. One day Breckie came to me with some morning glories, saying that he was a morning glory and would have to climb up on a trellis. While they were in bloom, he constantly came back with flowers from Juliette's garden: honeysuckle, roses, sweet William, snow-on-the-mountain. Above the nosegays his grimy little face gleamed with an expression someone described as "shining." It could not have been said of him that he had moved among his race "and shown no glorious morning face." He also came back from his walks with old rusty wheels, nails, bits of iron junk, horseshoes, for himself. He called his possessions his creatures, using the word "creature" in its older meaning, which we have kept in the Book of Common Prayer—"these thy gifts and creatures of bread and wine."

Among his toys, the one that stood highest in Breckie's affection was Teddy Bear. In the latter part of his fourth year Teddy became a creature that could do all of the things that Breckie longed to do but might not yet achieve. Teddy, he said, would kill the Kaiser and end the war. Teddy could meet every emergency. When Breckie was poking a fire and had been cautioned about falling in, he said that if he did fall in Teddy would turn him into a bear and pull him out. Teddy even made him an apple pie, he told me, adding, "But I didn't eat only de apple part. Teddy ate de wooden part."

There isn't space to write of what Breckie's French and English books meant to him or how much he acted the parts of the characters in the books. A favorite English book was a copy of *The Pied Piper of Hamelin*, with Kate Greenaway's charming pictures, that had been in our nursery in Washington. When he turned its leaves, he invariably stopped at the picture above the line, "Little hands clapping and little tongues chattering," and said, pointing to the tiniest child in dark green with a hood, "Dat's de little girl I love." I was called on to read *The Pied Piper* so often that he learned a great deal of it by heart.

Among Breckie's most prized books were five volumes of *Natural History*. He often pulled one of them out, laid it on the floor and began turning the pages with comments on the creatures he found. A live creature seemed to step right out of the books, with the first frosts, in the fall of his fourth year, when a cricket took refuge with us. Breckie was as pleased as I was over his chirping and, when I showed him the funny brown fellow, he agreed that we should invite him to spend the winter with us. Unfortunately, we forgot to tell Juliette about our invitation and she blotted out his cheerful existence.

When I heard about it I grieved. Breckie told Juliette, in his baby French, that he knew she hadn't done it on purpose but, he added, "one must not kill the beasts that my mother brings into the house."

It was in the latter part of his fourth year that Breckie learned to keep his word. After that he could always be trusted to keep it. Gradually, slowly, but truly, he became more responsible, more trustworthy, more desirous of our approbation—and through all this process his integrity gleamed like a jewel untarnished. No pitiful need of self-defense had ever taught him evasions, no dread of punishment bred lies in him, for he was never punished. He made, of course, at times the most fantastic statements and went off into the wildest flights of imagination—after the manner of all imaginative little children—but of deliberate deception, the seeking to hide a wrongdoing or to deny it, there is not in all his history a single trace. Potentially fearless and honorable he came to us, and his escutcheon was still unblemished when it passed out of our keeping.

V

Early in November, near the end of Breckie's fourth year, my Aunt Jane came to spend the winter with us. She brought with her a grandson, Brooke Alexander, another only child, so that the two little boys might have the companionship of each other. Brooke was a year and one-half Breckie's senior, better poised and more responsible, an imaginative and intelligent child, but not so robust as Breckie at the time of his coming South. He was as dark as Breckie was fair, with a shock of thick brown hair to offset Breckie's yellow curls. Under Juliette's care, the children were always together. When they came in from the out of doors, a sort of rushing sound accompanied them, like wind in the pine trees, or a swollen stream in a hollow—two tongues talking at once, four little feet pattering, and that general commotion which precedes the headlong entrance of two sturdy boys. It was a good sound to me, more musical than music. After they had their first fuss, Breckie's father taught them the manly art of wrestling, but they rarely quarreled and the attachment between them was so real that if one fell down in climbing and hurt himself, the other grieved.

At Thanksgiving, I showed Breckie a colored picture of the First Thanksgiving. I told him that the people thus rescued from starvation were early Americans and because they had fought hard fights with primal conditions, which I described in simple language, he could play happily in the forest today.

"Since that time, Breckie," I said, "when Thanksgiving Day comes around, every American thanks God for something he is glad to have, just the way these men in the picture are doing—thanking Him on their knees for something to eat."

I then asked Breckie if he didn't want to thank God this Thanksgiving for something he was glad to have. Ever ready, he said at once, with his responsive smile, "I will fank Him for my shovels."

When Christmas drew near again, I sat in the evenings by my fire with my boy gathered in my arms and talked to him of the meaning of Christmas and of the Christ Child's birth. I told him the Bethlehem story more fully than I had told it before. When I came to the manger I said, "You don't know what a manger is, do you, Breckie?" His reply will serve as another illustration of how we confuse young children by using terms that are meaningless to them.

He said, "It's selfishness—dog in de manger."

On January 12, 1918, came Breckie's fourth birthday. After the little boys had their morning walk, baths and naps, they had their dinner as usual except that, for dessert, there was a birthday cake made of war flour and covered with powdered sugar. I asked Breckie if he wanted me to light it before bringing it in, or would he rather stick the candles on and light it himself. Naturally he chose to do it himself, his hands trembling with eagerness as he struck a match and lighted the candles. It took more than one match, for the lighter was not expert and had a wholesome dread of burnt fingers. Breckie blew out the candles and cut the cake, with a little help, and then handed the slices around. After that, he chose a comfortably spacious piece for himself and sat down to eat it—his expression one of unmixed satisfaction.

On the twenty-third of January Breckie died. Of his swift illness and death I cannot write except to say that he played his part of brave soldier while conscious life remained to him. Once, when I praised him, he said to me, "Boppie, I twy to do wight." During his unconscious hours I remembered that, and thought how hard it must have been at four years. But he had measured up to the magnitude of it. He had done right as he saw it. He had taken all the unaccustomed suffering terminating his happy life, without questioning why it had come, because he believed it was right for a soldier to be brave.

One morning, some days after Breckie's death, Brooke said reminiscently to his grandmother, "Once when we were coming back from the Dairy Hollow, Breckie said he was a bird and could fly." After a moment he added reflectively, "He was always falling down, but he said that he could fly."

Such was my Great-Heart. Even so did his soaring spirit overreach the limitations of its embodiment. "He was always falling down, but he said that he could fly." It is because I wanted other children to feel that they could fly—as well as fall—that we have the Frontier Nursing Service today.

VI

In the following words, I concluded the record of Breckie's life:

What of other children? What of childhood? From the desolated shores of Armenia to the Balkan mountains, from the plains of Poland to the Belgian and French coast and over at last to the streets of our great cities and the farms of our remoter hills travels that cry of childhood which throughout the ages has been the cry of martyrdom. This my reason cannot accept—this tortures the devout in my soul.

> Is there not wrong too bitter for atoning?
> What are these desperate and hideous years?
> Hast Thou not heard Thy whole creation groaning,
> Sighs of the bondsmen, and the *children's* tears?

There is a work beside which all other strikes me as puerile—the work which seeks to raise the status of childhood everywhere, so that finally from pole to pole of this planet all of the little ones come into that health and happiness which is their due. If everyone who had ever loved a child would but do his part this might come to pass. What if we do not understand? What if we cannot be held responsible for the way God has ordered His world? There lies nevertheless deep in the heart of every child lover a feeling of responsibility which will not let him put the thing aside. If God cherishes His little ones only in my breast, says the child lover, He cherishes them there, and I fight for them—fight until that ancient saying has come true, until He shall gather the Lambs . . . in His bosom, and gently lead those that are with young. And when the crooked paths are made straight and the waste places smooth it will be time enough for me to understand.

Chapter 9

I

NORTHERN France was a part of the world where I felt I could be of use to children in 1918, but I could not plan to go until June. Meanwhile, a ruling was passed by the State Department that no woman with a brother in the military services could be sent to the war areas. My mother went with me to Washington to see Miss Jane Delano, head of the American Red Cross Nursing Service then. Since she could not send me overseas until "the brothers ruling" was rescinded, she gave her permission for me to accept a three months' contract with the Children's Bureau, under the Child Welfare Department of the Council of National Defense. My work, which took me as far West as Montana, Wyoming and New Mexico, was to gather reports on the nation's children, and to make speeches in their behalf. Miss Julia Lathrop asked me to carry on in California as well but, by the time my contract was up, the ruling in regard to brothers had been repealed. I therefore went East to make my final reports, and to get my loyalty papers and passport cleared for work with the Red Cross Children's Bureau in France, to which I was assigned.

I hit Washington at the height of the 1918 influenza epidemic, when the sick numbered several hundred thousand in that congested city. The United States Public Health Service had charge of the medical and nursing services, with Miss Mary Lent as chief nurse. From her I learned there were almost no nurses so, with Miss Delano's permission, I volunteered. The District of Columbia had been divided into four medical areas, to one of which I was assigned as assistant nurse in charge. The head nurse of my area fell ill soon after I reported for duty so that I was plunged into the direction of nursing care for thousands and thousands of stricken people. I don't recall how many patients we had in my district at the peak of the epidemic, but it could not have been less than forty thousand. Nor do I remember how many nurses I had to help me, but I don't think there were more than five. We used hundreds of aides for day and night care of the patients with pneumonia in the families where everybody had come down with influenza. Many of these aides were clerks turned over to us for the emergency by the government bureaus, and only a few of them had received training in home care of the sick. They were, however, keen young people who had volunteered for the assignment and had a good will. We issued masks to them and gave them special instruction in the care of their hands. Not many caught the infection. We used the token force of nurses to make rounds of the houses, give hypodermics where ordered, and instruct the aides in regard to other treatments and drugs.

Our physicians were mostly elderly men, who had ceased to practice before the war, and Army and Navy doctors loaned us by the Armed Services. At our headquarters in a schoolhouse we had three telephones, all reporting new cases every minute, while a queue of people stretched out into the street from early morning until around midnight. Cars were put at our disposal so that we could get doctors, nurses and the aides off in the quickest possible time. The filing system was a madness of improvisation in which the vital thing, with thousands of patients, was the correct address of each. Some of the reports the aides dictated, after a day or night on duty, would have been comical had they not been so tragic. One said of a pneumonia who had died, "Patient's condition got pretty bad towards the end." Another, who had been in a government bureau handling food rations, reported on a housewife, "She has twenty pounds of sugar salted away!"

One of the most awful things about this Washington nightmare was the condition of the houses in which both our white and colored patients lived. They were riddled with bedbugs. We devised a system of disinfecting the beds, then pulling them out from the walls and putting their legs in tin cans of carbolic. But the bedbugs dropped down on the patients from the ceilings. Years later, when I traveled into Washington on the same train as my cousin, John Mason Brown, I told him about my struggle with the bedbugs. He said, "Yes, I see. You lost the cherry blossom approach."

During the influenza epidemic I hadn't a mind for anything but that. After it was over I found that it would take more than a few days to get my passport and loyalty papers. Upon the advice of Miss Ella Phillips Crandall, I decided to spend the intervening time with the Boston Instructive District Nursing Association for the special training and experience in public health and visiting nursing of which I stood greatly in need. Miss Mary Beard took me in at the house of the Association on Commonwealth Avenue, as a guest. I was put through an abbreviated but intensive course, which included an affiliation with the baby welfare work under Miss Winifred Rand. I was to be grateful a thousand times over, after I got to France, for all that I learned in Boston. My work in the slums lay mainly in the Italian and Irish sections. I thought the tenements even worse than the New York ones, but nowhere did I find so many bedbugs as in Washington.

The Armistice caused the Red Cross to cancel sailings of its personnel, and I obtained my release from Miss Delano. Through Miss Elizabeth Perkins, a family friend, and my cousin, Mrs. John C. Breckinridge, I was introduced to Miss Anne Morgan and was accepted by her as a volunteer with the American Committee for Devastated France. Miss Morgan was First Vice-President and Chairman of the Executive Committee of this organization, of which Mr. Myron T. Herrick was President. From the first I was enthusiastic about the Committee, and I came to love it more than I have ever loved any group except the Frontier Nursing Service itself.

II

The French name of our organization was Comité Américain pour les Régions Dévastées de la France, called C.A.R.D. for short. We who worked with the Committee were frequently spoken of as the Cards. Our Paris offices and our *entrepôt* were out on the Boulevard Lannes. I reported, immediately on arrival in Paris, to our Commissioner in France, Mrs. Anne Dike, and was charmed with her. I was to learn in the course of time that she was not only a delightful woman but a brilliant executive. War restrictions were still on, so that I could not go to the war zone until I had a military permit. I had also to get bread and sugar cards, and fill out a lot of forms. One day, as I left the gloomy portals of the Préfecture de Police, by a different way from that in which I had entered, I suddenly found myself face to face with Notre Dame. I caught my breath before this shimmering glory in stone, then I crossed over to the cathedral, and passed through its doors into the hushed darkness. No guides, no noisy clattering, as there would have been in other days—only a few women in black, praying, and some American soldiers as awed as I was.

Eager as I was to get to work among the children, I was enchanted to have a little time in Paris because my sister Lees was there. Since I last saw her she had married Warren Dunn, but my new brother was with the Army elsewhere. Lovely as it was to see something of my sister, I was glad when my papers were ready and I could report for duty in the devastated areas at Vic-sur-Aisne. Miss Margaret Parsons was the Director of the unit at Vic. From her, old in years but young in heart, I received the warmest understanding of what I had come to

France to do and soon embarked upon my work for children. But in some of our villages there were no children. The clearest way in which I can depict that war-devastated land of France is to quote from one of my first letters to my mother a description of one of our villages:

Tartier, before the war, was a village of 365 inhabitants. Now it has four men and three women—no children—who have returned. It stands on a hill above the valley of the Aisne overlooking a country so lovely that, almost, one could imagine it as it once was. But we drove up through that country on a road broken with shell holes, past fields still massed with barbed wire, and seamed with trenches and dugouts, and past those pathetic roadside graves of soldiers, with often a helmet on the cross, and a bayonet stuck in at the foot to mark them, "*Soldat inconnu. Août, 1914*," or some later date. Tartier is so old that the people don't know when it first began to be, but things like Goths and Gauls are buried in the valley below the village. It was made of the sandstone, of which all these villages of the Aisne of this region are built, and the quarries, used as dugouts by the Germans during their domination, are lived in now by the seven people whose ruined homes are not habitable. Walls of old, old houses still stand, and picturesque wells are labeled "*Trinkwasser*," just as the Boches left them.

One man and his father, named Dufour, sturdy hardy types, to whom we are sending seeds, showed us around. They pointed out the gardens they were spading, the quarry where they lived underground, and the old tower where the elder Dufour had, before the war, five hundred pigeons, and the ruins of the rabbit hutches where the younger had two hundred rabbits. The younger Dufour had just been demobilized and still wore his old uniform. His wife would soon join him, but they dared not bring the child yet. The hand grenades and un-exploded shells lay all about. As we talked, he picked up a hand grenade that lay at our feet and threw it down into the valley, where it burst with a wonderful display of starry lights. Then he took up another and threw it. We saw it drop on the ground below and a moment later it exploded with a reverberating roar that woke the echoes. The younger Dufour was bright and strong and hopeful. He said it was hard to begin over again but it had to be done, and so why not do it? The spirit of the man and his father was as everlasting as the hill they stood on. So was that of the other peasants of the group of seven whom we visited. Coming out of their lonely holes in the rock to greet us they were smiling, every one of them. The spirit of the peasants of France! It explains Verdun. You can't weep with them for you never find them weeping.

The first need for everybody in the devastated areas was for food, clothing, bedding, and a few household utensils, but especially food—what the French called "*ravitaillement*." In the parts of France occupied by the Germans, it was not a question of the people returning to their shattered homes because they were already there when the Germans withdrew, but all around them the ground, the bridges, the roads, were destroyed so that it was almost impossible to get supplies to them. In some villages in the *Nord*, people had to be fed by air-plane. With such widespread destruction, the problem of transport assumed gigantic proportions. Soon after I was sent to our sector, one train a day got through from Paris to Vic and Soissons. But the train could not go where the railroad tracks had not been restored, and most of our villages were not near railroads at all. We supplied them by trucks, or camions as the French call them, huge trucks driven down from Paris by Frenchmen, and small Ford camions driven by our volunteer chauffeurs. Some of our villages had no food but what we took to them, nor could any of them have procured a mattress except from our dépôt of supplies—not at any price, because there were no mattresses except those we brought in. As soon as a train could run, our Committee was given a high priority for carload lots of supplies.

Laon, the capital of the Aisne, where we first housed our unit for work in the wrecked canton of Anizy, had been occupied by the Germans until the Armistice and so had escaped destruction. This old-world walled city, rising on a hill beyond the Chemin des Dames, was the birthplace of Père Marquette. The children there, like all who had been under German occupation, those who had not died, were horribly undernourished, but their city had survived, with its cathedral of ageless beauty. Soissons, on the other hand, taken and retaken several times during the war, was terribly damaged by artillery fire, and its cathedral had gaping holes. On my first visit to Laon, I was sent to an office called the Tiers Mandataire, armed with a sheaf of demands for wheat seed from legions of small farmers in our villages. These the Tiers Mandataire took over and gave me in return authorizations called "*Bons*." Within twenty-four hours we had these "*Bons*" stamped officially by the village mayors, and had begun to deliver the wheat. Since ours was the only transport service in all that territory, except for a few military cars, it was our girl chauffeurs in their camions who made possible the spring planting.

From Soissons to Laon one crossed the Chemin des Dames. For miles, as far as the eye could see, where for years the two contending armies had fought, the earth was torn apart, broken into ghastly crevices, seamed with jagged openings, thrown over and over, and furrowed with huge craters. Nothing recognizable was left of what had once been a smiling and fertile country, not a weed, not even ruins for long distances. They had been swallowed up by earth so tortured that it billowed like an ocean in a typhoon. The road over which our camion passed had been mended and a military bridge thrown across the little Ailette River. It had lost its banks and wandered through that stricken country, where one hundred and fifty thousand Frenchmen lay buried.

79

The French Government allowed each family losing all a thousand francs to refurnish a household, with two hundred additional francs for each child. Although this was a heavy cost to be borne by a war-bankrupt government, it was little enough, at inflationary rates, for a family to make a new start. The money the Government gave was called an allocation and, when the French peasants got it, they said they had "touched their allocations." At first everything our Committee gave out was provided free, and the clothing from America, the medicines, and the garden seeds, were always given without charge. Later, when the peasants touched their allocations, we furnished things like pine tables and bureaus to the people at wholesale rates, minus transportation which we always paid. We started restocking families with rabbits and chickens even while the *ravitaillement* was at its peak, and we were busy in the distribution of beds and straw mattresses. We ourselves used the same narrow iron bedsteads and straw mattresses that we gave out to the peasants as they returned to their ravaged homes. Just after a shipment had been unloaded, we might have to use boxes to climb on our beds because as many as twelve straw mattresses had been placed on each of them. The next evening when we came in we were lucky to find even one mattress left, so diligent were the chauffeurs in their distribution.

At my Vic unit, we were living that winter in the ruins of two large country houses on a property that ran right down to the river Aisne. Here we had our dispensary, storerooms, dining room and kitchen, and here the members of the unit slept as best they could. The windows were gone and in place of them we had yellow oiled paper so that we couldn't see out and the light inside was rather dim. The water works and the electricity had been completely destroyed. German prisoners brought us our water in hogsheads, and we used oil lamps and candles. Our two houses were full of shell holes which we stuffed with refugee petticoats on the coldest days and nights. For service we depended on the daughters of the neighboring peasant families. We clubbed together to meet our own expenses on a co-operative basis and they came to fifty francs per person per week, not including laundry. The American Committee for Devastated France housed all of its units, some of them in wooden *baraques*, or huts, that we called barracks. The C.A.R.D. also met the cost of fuel. At that time this was the wood taken out of the trenches, and packing boxes cut up for kindling. We had fires in our rooms in the evenings only. Then we could heat a little water with which to wash.

The American Committee for Devastated France was a masterpiece of organization, not only in its handling of direct relief, under baffling difficulties, but in later developments that were to be integrated into the very heart of French life. Our chief, Miss Anne Morgan, had inherited her father's ability. The conception she had of what needed to be done was matched only by her amazing capacity to put it over. In Mrs. Anne Dike, she had a colleague of ability second only to hers. My admiration for the way we handled our work was profound. During those first weeks that I spent in devastated France, I did not think that trained disaster relief people could have met the conditions better than we met them, volunteers all of us, and inexperienced. We Cards were informal people, casual in our manner, calling each other by our last names or nicknames, but with a strict sense of discipline, and working almost around the clock in that land of stark tragedy. Our uniform, military jacket and skirt, was in the horizon blue of the French Army with their special permission. On the lapels of the jacket we wore metal *griffons* (gryphons), copied from the arms on the gateway of the ruined old château at Blérancourt—the place where the American Committee established its first unit. Of my colleagues among the Cards, many are now members of the Frontier Nursing Service committees. From the chauffeurs, I derived the idea of couriers for the Service.

My letters to my mother are filled that first winter and spring with accounts of people killed and injured by the explosives in the fields they were trying to get ready for the spring planting. I wrote: "A peasant sticks a spade in the ground and is likely enough to strike a hand grenade. Our casualties in the past week were three men and two women, of whom only two men survived, one with the loss of both hands."

The family life in provincial France impressed me by its solidarity and beauty. When the French peasant despaired, it was in the injuries, illnesses and deaths of his children. I nursed a five-year-old boy at Vic who died of meningitis. His father had been killed, and he was the last surviving child to his mother. I stood with her as he lay dying. She kept twisting her gnarled peasant hands, muttering under her breath, "What shall I do, what shall I do?" I kept thinking, "What can you do? What use is it to spade your garden when there is no one left to feed but yourself? What will you do?"

The French peasant's love of his own acres and his own house was second only to his love of his children. The French word for home is "*foyer*" or hearthstone—meaning the very heart of a home. We Americans have prostituted both the word "foyer" and the word "home." We use "foyer" to describe a vast public place, and "home" (funeral) to indicate a place where a corpse rests for a few hours.

As I came to know the French peasant well, his strong family life, his deep-rooted love of home, it seemed to me that Joan of Arc was not an accident but the spiritual outcome of her people and her class. The fragments that have filtered down of Joan's childhood, of the tenderness with which her parents cherished her, the play with her brothers in the forest, the lore of fairies and saints which satisfied her imagination, the simple duties outdoors, and inside around the hearth-stone—these things enable us to understand why Joan, her mission ended, begged the king's permission to go back to that family life at her village of Domrémy, which she cherished as the choicest blessing earth could hold.

It was because they loved their own country so much that the French we knew loved ours. You do not love other countries if you are incapable of first loving your own. This was brought home to me on the first American Memorial Day after the Armistice, when we took part in services at two of the cemeteries where American soldiers were buried. One of these cemeteries, at Juvigny, had only a few hundred graves. The peasants in the neighborhood had gathered artillery shells, from the battlefields, to fill with water and put on the graves. Into these they put field flowers. There were many old peasants, and some little children. One woman, who was sobbing, said, "They lie so close together, just like ours." When we thanked them all, as we were leaving, they said over and over, "It will always be so. They will always be to us like our own."

Chapter 10

I

ALTHOUGH my first work in the devastated areas in France was to help get food, clothing, supplies and seeds to the villages, and to meet the immediate emergencies, even as I did these things I started to give nursing care to the sick and especially the children. No civilian doctors had returned yet to our sector, but at first there were a few military doctors. To a French military hospital at Compiègne, we carried the people blown up by explosives—those that survived. We took some of our civilian sick to a hospital at Luzancy-sur-Marne, a distance from Vic of about ninety kilometers, maintained by the American Women's Hospital Association. Late in the spring the Association moved it to barracks set up near our unit at Blérancourt. At that time they assigned Dr. Ethel Fraser and one of their nurses, Miss Katherine Smith, to our Vic unit.

With Dr. Fraser's backing and that of Miss Margaret Parsons, I took up with Miss Morgan and Mrs. Dike the problems that lay at my heart. The loss of infants and young children had been, and still was, appalling. I got permission to begin in as many villages as I could tackle singlehanded a program for the war-devastated children, with special care to those under six and to pregnant and nursing mothers.

Of war-devastated children we had three kinds. First, those who had been under German occupation and were two or more years below their age in size and strength. Second, the children in places like Vic, taken twice by the Germans, held briefly, and retaken by the French. They had been frequently under artillery fire. I remember one family where the mother had been killed by a shell in her own garden. Lastly, there were the children who had been evacuated and were now creeping back with their families into the ruined villages. From a letter to my mother written on March 2, 1919, I describe one such family:

The thing I have done most in these last three days has been to help with a pneumonia baby over at Montgobert. Solange Duvauchelle is the name of the little one. Her mother is an intelligent peasant woman reduced almost to despair by vicissitudes of the past. When Solange was three weeks old, they were evacuated and the long forced march completely dried the mother's milk. From then on it has been slow starvation for Solange who is but the shadow of what she should be at ten months. They returned to their home after the Armistice, the parents and baby and three other children, having lost two others, to find the village in ruins but their own home partly spared so they can get shelter in it. But everything they owned was gone. When they reach this point French peasants always tell about their sheets. One told me she had had fifty-four of linen. Well, the Duvauchelle family had nothing left but the worn clothes they wore. We have given them bedding, clothes, groceries. Then the three-year-old boy, Serge, fell ill with pneumonia and was taken to Luzancy in one of our camions. Now the baby is ill. The five-year-old girl and Serge are pitifully undernourished. The older girl has fainting spells, as does the father. The mother always has toothaches. Why do I write about them? There are thousands of others like them. It is just that I have been so constantly with them. . . . If I could give right now a goat to every family that has a baby, I think we could go far toward saving many that are dying. There is much grippe and pneumonia among them and they have no powers of resistance. I wish I had a thousand goats right now. I wish I had fifty.

The goat idea struck my mother as feasible. My letters were passed around among members of my family, who all began not only to give goats themselves, but to start goat funds. Soon the money was pouring in, gifts of twenty dollars each, for the goats. Although the valleys of the Aisne had cows before the war, there had been goats in the hill country. Even in the valleys, the goats could serve to tide over the need for milk until the French peasant touched his allocation for a cow and could find one. But war-bankrupt France, with all of the villages to rebuild at government expense, could not give allocations sufficient to cover the replacement of livestock at inflated prices. I asked Miss Morgan to arrange through our Paris office for us to buy the goats. They came in carload lots from the Pyrenees, each car with its own goatherd to feed and milk them on the long trip across France.

The first carload lot of twenty-nine arrived when I was out on my rounds. By this time I had a dispensary at the Vic unit, called "*Consultation de Nourrissons*." As I opened the door I heard a "Baa, maa, baa," and there stood a white goat. She had gotten her feet in a box of nursing bottles, knocked over the weights of the scales, and chewed various odds and ends, and I hugged her I was so glad. My colleagues explained, ecstatically, that when the train had arrived, everyone on hand had turned out to lead the goats up from the track, with all of Vic in their wake. They told me there probably wouldn't be much

84

lunch because the cook, who was knowing with goats, had spent the morning milking them.

There were gray goats and white ones, and black and gray ones, and brown and white ones, and café-au-lait, and some had horns and some hadn't, and some were so gentle they followed you like dogs and some were wild. To each goat we gave the name of the donor and I wrote back to him or her the history of the children who received them. The distribution of the goats, with the problem of having to choose only twenty-nine families among so many, tore us to pieces. This was only the beginning of my goat crusade, for other carloads were to follow. Later, I asked the goat givers to provide money for beetroots with which to feed the goats their first winter. Meanwhile, the goats had to be bred again. Ambassador Morgenthau came to see us during this crisis and gave me the money for a fine buck, which we named Ambassador.

II

I used to agree wholeheartedly with the late Dr. Truby King of New Zealand that the only reason a woman could not nurse her baby was tuberculosis. I changed my mind that first year in France because I had learned of another reason—starvation. The few babies who came back with their parents to the ruined villages were only partly breast-fed, if at all. When we poured malted milk, and chocolate made with condensed milk, into the mothers then the breast milk increased so that the babies had only to be partly bottle-fed. This meant that we were feeding both babies and mothers with our supplies, and with goat milk. The children under six years of age needed lots of feeding and care just to keep them alive. Those in the areas that had been occupied by the Germans were riddled with impetigo and eczema.

In France I felt, as I was to feel later in the Kentucky mountains, that a program for children should begin before the children are born and should place special emphasis on the first six years of life. In France we did not have to worry about childbirth itself because the French midwives took care of that. Some were already in the villages, and others returned with the populations that had been evacuated. Their course of training then was of two years' duration, followed by a diploma to vouch for their qualifications. The course is three years now. My younger brother's birth in Russia, with Madame Kouchnova in attendance, had taught me early the value of a trained midwife. I greeted the French midwives with respect. They were delighted to have special feeding for their expectant mothers. They turned the babies, with their mothers, over to me when they were ten days old.

85

During that first summer we had a crop of what we called "Armistice babies."

Even before the arrival of the first goats, I had scouted around in various directions for canned milk, liquid or powdered, cocoa, chocolate and other nourishing supplies. The C.A.R.D. were most generous in letting me raid our own stores for enough of these things to get results. The Free Milk for France and the Trait d'Union Franco-Américain gave me a lot of malted milk and condensed milk. The Children's Bureau of the American Red Cross, which closed down its wonderful work not long after the Armistice, was most generous to me in the disposal of its stores. With Dr. Fraser to examine and prescribe for my babies and young children, and both Dr. Fraser and Miss Smith to give the typhoid inoculations and look after the sick adults and accident cases, I had my program just where I wanted it.

Early in May, I had a big windfall. One Monday morning I was told that two military doctors (captains) wanted to see me. They represented the American Committee for Relief in Belgium and France, called C.R.B. for short. They said that the C.R.B. was closing out its work in France and Belgium, and that they had about thirteen million francs of French money which they proposed to use, as long as it lasted, in feeding schoolchildren in the devastated areas. These children were to have a supplementary meal of a cup of chocolate, made with condensed milk, and a biscuit made of flour, sugar and lard, at the close of each school day. The children who were markedly underweight were to get a midday meal of meat, vegetables and bread. They asked me if we would like to be given supplies to start this program in all of our sector, and said that we would have to weigh, measure and examine all of the schoolchildren to determine which ones should have the hot noon meal. The C.R.B. was as good as its word. We secured just the right French people to cook the noon meals, while the teachers gave out the biscuits and chocolate at the end of each school day. Meanwhile, the American Women's Hospital Association placed women dentists at our units. They were godsends.

III

Early in June of 1919 our Vic unit moved from the battered houses near the river Aisne to other quarters gotten ready for us by the C.A.R.D. The new place lacked some of the points of the old one but had others in its favor. For one thing, it was not full of shell holes. Only one end of the house had been shattered. This the C.A.R.D. had rebuilt and reroofed. Real glass had been put back in the windows; the breaches in the walls were filled by stones instead of petticoats.

An old stable served as headquarters for the chauffeurs, under Louise Barney, and housed their camions. We had to put up four barracks in the grounds (encircled by a high wall in pretty good repair) to serve as sleeping quarters for some of the unit, and to house our supplies, our dental clinic, my dispensary, and a library. This library, set up like those at all our units by Jessie Carson, whose Card name was Kit, was as frequented as my dispensary by a literate and book-starved people.

The place to which we had moved at Vic was just across the road from the lovely park of an old château belonging to the de Reiset family. This château was of such historic interest that it had been placed under the Department of the Beaux-Arts to ensure its perpetual preservation. The oldest part of it, the tower, dated back to Charlemagne. The place was terribly damaged by artillery shells, with which the Beaux-Arts had not reckoned, but the Vicomte de Reiset came down in the spring of 1919 and made a part of it habitable so that he could live there with his wife and daughter, Anne. We often had tea with them in the only living room made habitable as a *salon.*

The Vicomte was a gallant as well as a charming old man. At the time of the last German occupation of Vic, the Germans mined the bridge over the river Aisne so that it could be exploded when they retreated, and delay the allied advance. The Vicomte, with one or two other old men, got down somehow to that troop-guarded bridge and destroyed the connections that would have set off the explosion. The enemy would have made short shrift of him, despite his gray hairs, if he had been caught. Anne de Reiset, a delightful girl, took an immense interest in my work for the little children and often went with me in the camion on my visits to them. She and her mother were greatly beloved in and around Vic. Madame de Reiset put one of the few habitable rooms in the château at our disposal for guests. Some of this family dropped in at our place several times a week, or we went to theirs, and we became much attached to them. The French nobility, like the de Reisets, and the modern industrialists in the Aisne had been sorely stricken by the war—their country places and their factories wrecked, or all but wrecked. Yet the concern of most of them was not for themselves but for the peasants who had lost everything. These upper-class families gave us wholehearted co-operation.

Our friends among our neighbors included the schoolteachers, most of them intelligent and well educated, the mayors, the men in the Préfecture, the priests, the large farmers who had been peasants but whose business acumen and thrift had lifted them into the bourgeois class. Not all of our varied friends liked one another, and sometimes they did not even know each other, but they met at our place and worked wholeheartedly with us. We were deeply touched that first

September when our Vic unit was decorated by that little town for what it had done in the months following the Armistice. We each received a gold medal with "LES HABITANTS DE VIC-SUR-AISNE RECON- NAISSANTS" and the year "1919" engraved on it.

Innumerable people other than the French themselves were scattered over that devastated land during that first postwar winter. We had Senegalese troops quartered at Vic, little colored men from Africa. We had German prisoners, who lived in barracks behind barbed wires at night but worked on the roads in the daytime. They were humanely treated. I never knew of a single instance of a German prisoner being allowed in the fields to get out the hand grenades which tore so many French citizens to pieces. With the coming of warm weather, hundreds of workmen arrived and camped in barracks to start repairing and rebuilding the shattered villages. We had a lot to do with them because they were always falling off things, or things were falling on them, with painful results.

When my mother wrote me that my descriptions reminded her of Lewis Carroll's Wonderland and Looking Glass books, I replied that we were often reminded of them because

This whole country is such stuff as dreams are made of. Consider, here in one fragment of a shattered land are a Napoleonic duchess, and a royalist family who keep a whole page in their visitors' book free because Sixtus de Bourbon wrote on it, and big modern industrial magnates, and *Républicains* and peasants, and secularized nuns and curés, and German prisoners who sleep behind barbed wire, and colored troops from Madagascar, and hand grenades in the fields which blow people up, and in Coeuvres the mayor is the Comte de Berthier and in Dommiers the village blacksmith, and workmen from all over the world are coming in to rebuild, under the Administration, among them English-speaking Negroes from Barbados, who know no word of French but came because they heard there was work to do, and brought wives and babies with them. Lastly, an American Committee of women tear around in camions, and are still the sole source of the food supply to many villages. All of this is jumbled in together like a loose pack of cards, and someday we will wake up and not be here any more.

Chapter 11

WHEN I started my special work for children in the *communes* (village groups) covered by the Vic unit, I began to gather information about what the French had done for children before the war, and what they wanted to do now. I subscribed for two Paris magazines, the *Nourrisson* and the *Presse Médicale*, which carried articles by leading pediatricians. I bought a number of books by French authorities, and I made inquiries of all the local people capable of giving me information. I found that the French, under a public department known as the Assistance Publique, had paid a physician to examine all babies brought to the *mairie*, or town hall, and to weigh the babies once in two weeks and give free advice. I also learned about the organization known as the Gouttes de Lait, started as a private philanthropy by a man named Boudin, which operated baby milk stations in the larger places only. There had been one at Soissons. Through the Gouttes de Lait, modified milk was supplied at cost to bottle-fed babies, but no instructions went with it and the mothers were never taught to handle the milk themselves. In other words, there was no follow-up work because there was no visiting nurse service. I resolved that I would organize a visiting nurse service, as good as the one in Boston, to cover the sector of devastated country assigned to the C.A.R.D. My plan for this work was to link it with all that was good that the French had done and add to it something France had never had, a visiting nurse service with a staff of trained nurses, qualified also for district and public health work. We would keep such careful records of our demonstration, and get such good results, so I reasoned and wrote at the time, that the French would want to copy it elsewhere even if they had to revolutionize their antiquated nursing system to do it.

I was profoundly impressed by the quality of my peasant children. Of course we had some low-grade children, for the feeble-minded are not confined to the United States. But in France, as well as in America, they are a small minority. I never forgot that Pasteur had been a peasant child and what his life had meant, not just for France, but for the world. I wrote my mother, "I believe that the best asset I bring to my work here is not my training and experience, although I couldn't do the work without them, but the fact that I can and do appreciate the appeal of the people themselves, that I love and admire them and realize they are worth saving. The world needs France."

As soon as my work at Vic was well under way, it was inspected by the French authorities as well as by the heads of our other units. Mrs. Dike then asked me to extend it to cover the rest of our sector. That was all very well, and what I wanted to do, but my experience with partly trained, and therefore poorly trained, nurses had been such that I knew I could not expand my program without fully trained nurses. The Florence Nightingale School, organized years before by Dr. Anna Hamilton, and attached to the Maison de Santé Protestante at Bordeaux, was the only hospital school in all France, except the one at the American Hospital at Neuilly near Paris.

In my need for trained nurses I wrote Dr. Hamilton to ask her if she could let me have some of hers. She promised me two to begin with, and more to come later. In September, 1919, the first one, Mlle Harrioo, joined me. I kept her a week at Vic and then spent several days with her at our Blérancourt unit in the canton (county) of Coucy, to get her work started there. In October, Mlle Mertillo came and I followed the same course with her. When the third Bordeaux nurse, Mlle Monod, came in November I gave her my beloved county of Vic with the little town and the many villages where my work had begun. It was an awful wrench to give it up, but a joy to have it taken over by so gifted a woman as Marcelle Monod. Meanwhile Dr. Hamilton had made us a visit of inspection which brought about an even closer collaboration. We took on the wrecked villages of the Soissons unit. At the turn of the year, with four more of the Bordeaux trained nurses, my service was established throughout the C.A.R.D. sector of devastated France.

As I got the nursing situation under way throughout our sector, the medical situation became acute. In August of 1919, Dr. Fraser and Miss Smith left Vic to return to America, to be followed by other members of the American Women's Hospital Association. There was an appalling scarcity of physicians in our sector, although the French Government offered them special compensation to locate in the devastated areas. I suggested to Miss Morgan and Mrs. Dike that the American Committee supplement the government grants, with a proviso that only physicians be chosen who knew something of pediatrics. To this they agreed, with the result that we persuaded three competent men to locate in our territory.

Meanwhile, my nursing work had become a fully generalized service. We gave bedside care to the sick of all ages and both sexes and did a vast amount of public health at the same time. The C.A.R.D. kept the barrack hospital at Blérancourt open—a godsend for our patients. We kept our emphasis on the care and rehabilitation of babies and children, the expectant and nursing mothers. My friends at home, bless them, continued to send money for more goats, and the circle of goat givers widened. It was wonderful to see the transformation of the children, bowed little figures with large pathetic eyes, after only a few weeks of four glasses of some kind of milk a day.

When I sent my mother a copy of my ten-page quarterly report for the last three months of 1919, I wrote her:

So much of my work now is taken up with writing, going over reports, talking, that sometimes I am a wee bit sad about it. Of course it is a sign of growth but I love the contact with the peasants best and now I have small time for that. Instead, I am having interviews with the Mayor of Soissons, the head of the Service de Santé of the Department (like our State Boards of Health), the people in the health part of the Ministère des Régions Libérées, in Paris. . . . I can hardly believe that only last summer I was alone in my loved villages.

From among the official people I met, I formed a lasting friendship with one man and his family. Dr. René Lemarchal was the President of the Medical Syndicate of the Department, a position the equivalent in America of president of one of our state medical societies. I had to see him frequently about the incoming doctors. He lived in one of the old Laon houses, opposite the cathedral, with a walled garden at the back, from which came the laughter of children.

In the middle of February, 1920, I took with me to Soissons my cousin, Katherine Carson (in France at that time, and spending two days with me) to see the city decorated by Poincaré with the Legion of Honor. I wrote:

The ceremony took place at the lovely old Hôtel de Ville against which Lombard had a grudge, because it was not near enough to the cathedral for you to enjoy both at once, until Lummie suggested that perhaps it was the cathedral's fault. Katherine and I were curious as to how one decorated a city, whether the ribbon was pinned on the walls of the Hôtel de Ville or the lapel of the Mayor's coat. In case you have a similar unsatisfied curiosity, I will hasten to say that the city receives the decoration on a cushion, which in this case was held out by a lovely young girl in black. Poincaré made a speech and the Mayor another, which those who were close enough to hear said were good. There were lots of military, and a band which played the Marseillaise, of course, and I wanted to wave and shout like any schoolchild. Then a man sang the Marseillaise, then the children of Soissons sang it. That moved me most of all. Poor babies What a hell of a five years! God send they may never have it to live through again.

At about this time, the Mayor of Soissons told me that the city meant to re-establish its baby milk station, the Gouttes de Lait. He wanted to know if the C.A.R.D. would provide a visiting nurse service to follow up on the babies and their mothers in their homes. It was agreed that we provide such a service for all the people then living in that shattered city, including bedside nursing of the sick, school nursing, and the control of communicable diseases. This meant a larger nursing unit at Soissons than we now had for the work among the villages in the county. It also meant the engagement of a first-class supervisor to direct the Soissons unit. I consulted Dr. Hamilton, remembering a visit to Bordeaux where I saw something of the splendid visiting nurse service that Miss Evelyn Walker had organized there, under the American Red Cross. The upshot was that Miss Walker arrived in Soissons in March of 1920 to become my Associate Director of the Child Hygiene and Visiting Nurse Service, with headquarters at Soissons.

At about the time we accepted the invitation of the Mayor of Soissons, the Rockefeller Foundation established one of their dispensaries for the treatment and care of tuberculosis at the Soissons Hospital. Nothing could have afforded more of a contrast than this modern dispensary in that hospital, which I considered a very good one for the thirteenth century. The Rockefeller put a trained French-speaking English nurse in charge of their work, with an assistant who was not a nurse but one of their newly trained *Visiteuses d'Hygiène*. When the nurse lunched with me at our Soissons unit, we worked out a plan of co-operation. Our people were riddled with tuberculosis. It meant a lot to us to have the Rockefeller establish a dispensary at Soissons, and one at Laon.

II

Before the end of March of 1920 I returned home on my first leave of absence. I did not get back to France until June. The welcome everyone extended to me, not only my colleagues in the C.A.R.D. and my Bordeaux nurses, but the French from the poorest on up to those of high degree—this welcome went right to my heart. I was allowed by my chiefs in Paris to continue to make my headquarters at Vic. Months before, when I began to create a generalized nursing service in all the centers and Mrs. Dike made me a Director, she offered me a car and chauffeur. I pooled them with the camions of the Vic unit. When Barney became chief of the whole motor service of the C.A.R.D., I continued to pool my car and chauffeur with the rest. The nursing work mattered as much to Barney as it did to me, and she never let us down. It was something for me and my nurses to feel that we must match the enthusiasm and efficiency of Barney and her chauffeurs, because they could not have been surpassed.

Although I made my headquarters at Vic, I now had to spend days at a time not only with other units in our field of work but in other parts of France. During the war the C.A.R.D. had established a children's colony far back behind the lines in a château called Boullay-Thierry. Now that the children, who had been evacuated, could be returned to their homes it was decided to close down the colony. We persuaded Mrs. Dike to keep it open a few months longer as a convalescent home for nearly one hundred of our children, who made no progress despite all the feeding and care we gave them.

Our next opportunity arose at Reims. Back in 1919 I had made the acquaintance of a Comité Britannique, attached to the French Red Cross and stationed not far from the military hospital at Compiègne. The director of this British Committee was a Miss Celia du Sautoy, an Englishwoman with a distinguished nursing career, who had been matron (superintendent) of a British nursing unit attached to the French during the war. Her associate, Lady Hermione Blackwood, was the daughter of the famous English statesman, Lord Dufferin. The friendship I formed with them leads directly to the nurse-midwife of the Frontier Nursing Service because in them I first knew women who were both nurses and midwives.

After the unit of the Comité Britannique had moved to Reims I went down there to see them. Although the glorious cathedral was not destroyed, only terribly damaged, most of the city even up to the cathedral walls was a shambles. Since the main purpose of the British Committee had been direct relief, and its funds were giving out, it had begun to close down its work. Word went out that the Reims unit would have to withdraw. But in Reims, the British Committee had French-speaking English nurses as well as relief personnel. The condition of the children, everywhere crowded into ruins and wooden huts, and the sickness among the people were such that the city of Reims held a meeting and commissioned Monsieur Guichard to offer, on behalf of Reims, free quarters, heating, lighting, water, and telephones if the British Committee would leave its nurses and continue to provide them with maintenance. To this the British Committee replied that funds were exhausted.

That was the situation when I went to Reims. I got a budget from Miss du Sautoy and ran back to Paris to see Miss Morgan and Mrs. Dike. I laid the whole thing before them, they saw it the way I did, and agreed to have the American Committee for Devastated France take over the Reims unit. I wrote my mother, "And thereby hundreds of little lives are saved. Sometimes when the longing for my own babies gets most unbearable, it does help me to remember that I can do for others what I could not do for my own." From that time on, the Reims nursing unit became an integral part of the C.A.R.D. I asked to have Miss du Sautoy made a codirector with me and left in complete control of the eight Reims nurses. These were placed in pairs in wooden barracks, given by the city, in the four sections of Courcy, St. Brice, Chalet and St. Nicaise. I asked to have Miss Walker made a third codirector. I wound up my requests with one for scholarships to send two of my English-speaking Bordeaux nurses (one of them Marcelle Monod) to the United States for study in American methods of public health nursing, and for travel and observation. All of this was granted me by Anne Morgan, the most wonderful chief that anyone ever had.

Early that autumn, Lady Hermione Blackwood went back to London to be near her family until after Christmas. She invited me to spend a week with her in November at her quaint little house in Chelsea, where she saw that I had a steaming tub of water to bathe in every night. She also introduced me to many of the leaders of the nursing world in London, midwives all of them, and magnificent women. Lady Hermione and I spent every day going through great hospitals like St. Thomas', poorhouses, district nursing centers, infant welfare centers, all of profound interest to us both. In the evenings, Lady Hermione's family were most kind to me. Her mother, Lady Dufferin, had me to dinner. To Lady Dufferin's beauty, charm of manner, keen mind, and courtesy, she added a quality I can only describe by saying she was gallant. It was a special joy to me to meet Lady Hermione's sister, Lady Victoria Braithewaite, who before the death of her first husband, Lord Plunket, had gone to New Zealand with him when he was governor-general. There she established the Plunket Nurses of whose work I had known for years. Lady Victoria took us to the place of all others that interested me most, the Mothercraft Training Center. It was Lady Victoria, as Lady Plunket, who had interested the famous Dr. Truby King in coming to London, with his two best nurses, to start this wonderful place where the Truby King methods of breast feeding babies were developed and taught.

In October of 1920 I told Miss Morgan that I had to go back to America for good in the fall of 1921. About this I wrote my mother:

She and Mrs. Dike won't hear of my planning to have this my last year in France, which is kind, but I am sure my work will be on a firm basis. I would never leave things at loose ends, but I do want to be getting home after another year. Much as I love France I can't turn into a sort of Franco-American. My home is in America and so that is where I belong in the end. It isn't only that I get home longing very often, although I do, and that my place is nearer you and father as you get older, although it is, but when in the course of events I have fulfilled my purpose in France and rounded out my work and trained people to carry it on, then carry it on without me they should, and something else is mine to do back in my own land. I don't know what yet, but I dream dreams and see visions and tens of thousands of children, mostly very little ones, are dancing always across the visions and the dreams. I know that the way leads back over the ocean to the country where my own children were born and where they are buried, the country whose development my own people have furthered for nearly two hundred years. After all, two hundred years would count for something even in Europe and it has made me very much of an American. I love France like a friend, a dear friend, who has been cruelly beset and is brightly courageous, but the time will come when her need for friends becomes less acute, and then, thank God, America is home. Her I love as I love my dead.

III

It seemed odd to me that in France where the training of midwives was excellent, and constantly improving, the training of nurses should be neglected. In the United States it is the other way around. Over here one has to push the need for midwifery. In France, the push needed was for nursing. The word *"infirmière,"* as commonly used in France, did not stand for a trained nurse. An *infirmière* might be a lady who during the war took a course on how to put on a bandage and give a *piqûre* (hypodermic injection), or she might be a poor drudge under the Assistance Publique. Sometimes she was a health visitor without a nurse's training.

The patients in the great Paris hospitals, like the Charité and the Pitié, with their thousands of beds, were cared for by male and female attendants called *garçons de service* and *filles de service*. At night the wards were shut up like pianos. The patients who could stagger out of bed had to wait on those who were desperately ill. A French physician told me that lack of care at night in the military hospitals had led to the loss of many soldiers from secondary hemorrhages. How the French, with their intelligent minds and their brilliant physicians, could tolerate the lack of nursing care in their hospitals never ceased to puzzle me. I came to the conclusion that the reason lay in the immense political power of the employees, under the Assistance Publique, who held the public hospital jobs. My first inkling of this came when I made my first visit to a Paris hospital.

The Salpêtrière accommodated four thousand patients, including insane, epileptic, feeble-minded, aged, and acute cases of all sorts. Within its walls are some of the old cottages which once formed a part of the village of Salpêtrière, now in the heart of Paris. The library of Charcot, one of the world's biggest men in research on the nervous system, is kept just as he left it, as is his laboratory with jars of brains preserved in alcohol. Some years before I made my visit, the Assistance Publique of Paris decided to found a modern school of nursing at the Salpêtrière. They built a beautiful house with single rooms, baths, a drawing room, and tennis courts. They outlined a good course of study and got, so I was told, a desirable group of applicants. They were about to open the school when the attendants of all the Paris hospitals struck. They said they would all go out at once if the school was opened. Their opposition was so vehement, and their political power so great, that the plan was abandoned. In place of it, a school of sorts was started for applicants who needed only to read and write and do a little arithmetic to be accepted. They obligated themselves to stay two years, during which they worked in the wards and received some instruction. I attended one of their classes. For this instruction they engaged themselves to work five subsequent years in the hospitals of Paris. But even if they failed in their lessons and had to leave the school, they might become attendants (*filles de service*) and carry on with the care of the sick poor. To this kind of school, which fed their own ranks, the employees of the Assistance Publique had no objection.

It was as obvious to Miss Morgan and Mrs. Dike as to me that the success of the Child Hygiene and Visiting Nurse Service that we had created in the Aisne was due to the quality of our Bordeaux nurses, whose basic training had been as good as that of the best nurses of England and America. When they spoke of it as a demonstration they realized as well as I did that it could not be widely copied in France unless modern schools of nursing could be established in the great public hospitals. Miss Morgan asked me to undertake, during my last winter and spring in France, an exhaustive study of the Paris hospitals and come up with a plan to establish a school of nursing in one of them. She, on her side, undertook to raise the money for such a school. Mrs. Dike introduced me to Madame Gervais Courtellemont, *Surintendante des Infirmières du Ministère des Régions Libérées* (Superintendent of Nurses under the Ministry of the Liberated Regions). Mme Courtellemont, a public-spirited French woman, but not a nurse, was convinced that neither the care of the sick poor nor the training of nurses to use later for district and public health work could be accomplished until we had a foothold in at least one of the Paris hospitals.

For months I spent a part of every week in Paris. I went through miles of wards, talking with attendants and the patients. Sometimes Madame Courtellemont was with me and sometimes I went alone. I wanted all the facts I could gather before I came up with a plan. Meanwhile Madame Courtellemont introduced me to the great physicians and surgeons of Paris. To sponsor our undertaking, we formed a committee of nationally known physicians. M. le Professeur Calmette, one of the directors of the Pasteur Institute, consented to take the chairmanship of our committee which we called Comité pour le Perfectionnement des Infirmières Françaises. Other distinguished medical names were those of Bezançon, Couvelaire, Delille, Guinard, Letulle, Nobécourt, Rist, Tuffier, Léon Bernard. We saw Madame Curie and asked her if she would come on our committee. She said no, because it would be her name only since she had no wards to give us, but she promised to give lectures in the school when we had it set up. I wrote my mother: "She was an interesting person to meet, just stepping out of her laboratory in a stained black and white apron, with her hair drawn back from her face and her hands trembling, as it is said the hands do of those who engage in radium research."

The surgeons and physicians on our committee suggested to us that instead of trying to get one of the vast hospitals we take over their own surgical, medical and pediatric wards scattered in several of them. They promised the fullest co-operation if we would provide decent day and night nursing under supervision. We all thought this a good idea and that the school building could be located at a central point. Monsieur le Docteur Marfan invited me to attend one of his open lectures and to visit his wards for sick babies. The hospital auditorium was crowded with physicians from all parts of Europe. Dr. Marfan had a number of sick babies brought to him, for demonstrations, while he talked. He handled them with great tenderness. When I went into his first ward where the babies were breast-fed, I thought it not too bad. Each baby had its own mother with it to take care of it. Then I passed into a ward with between thirty and forty bottle-fed sick babies. They were all being fed at once and the system was this. Two *filles de service* walked from crib to crib handing each baby a bottle or propping it against the baby's neck. Some of the babies were strong enough to hold their bottles, but it seemed to me that at least a third of them either made no effort to do it or let them fall. The nipples had large holes and the milk went down the babies' necks. Some of them swallowed the milk too fast and choked on it. So there lay the babies Monsieur le Docteur Marfan had diagnosed so well and handled so tenderly, starving to death. I knew what he meant when he told me how glad he would be to give his wards to our nursing school.

IV

When Madame Courtellemont and I had completed our study of the Paris hospitals and formed our committee, we sought an interview with a top authority, whose name I shall not give. We told him that the physicians and surgeons on our committee said we could have their medical, surgical and pediatric wards, of not less than six hundred beds, that Miss Morgan would finance a modern school of nursing, that all we asked was his permission to take over the nursing in the designated wards and be responsible for it day and night. He told us he would like to give his consent but that he did not dare. The male and female employees under the Assistance Publique, who were the attendants for the hospitals, were so numerous and so powerful politically that he could not risk their opposition. We pointed out that we would only displace a few of them, but the authority said they would know very well that when the camel's head got in the tent, the camel would follow. So that was off.

We were disheartened and discouraged because we knew a successful school could be established if only we had the hospital beds. I knew that the Bordeaux nurses, and a few French-speaking English and American nurses, experienced in hospital administration, could run it. I had also met in Paris a charming French gentlewoman, Mademoiselle de Joannis, who had taken a nurse's training and then established a small nursing school in the Rue Amyot. Unfortunately, it was not at that time a hospital school but Mlle de Joannis had succeeded in teaching her students the principles of nursing. She seemed to me just the person to direct the school we wanted.

Madame Courtellemont and I had failed in the first plan we put before Miss Morgan, for the same reason the Salpêtrière school had failed long before. We came up with the second plan. I was convinced from my conversations not only with the great physicians of Paris, but with many lay people, that a climate of public opinion could be formed powerful enough, even on the political level, to overcome the resistance of the employees of the Assistance Publique. Our medical committee agreed to co-operate with us towards that end.

The longing of the French to save the lives of their children was immense, and to me incredibly appealing. In their trained midwives the French had a competent body of skilled women for the care of the unborn and the young infant. They realized they had nobody to carry on where the midwives left off. The hastily formed groups of health visitors, with no grounding in real nursing, were the result of their efforts to reach the children in the towns and villages. The French did not see that the crux of the matter lay in their public general hospitals, even though it was in their public maternity hospitals that the student midwives received the best of training. Until the general hospitals had modern schools of nursing as good as the midwifery schools, not only would the care of the sick poor be shameful, but the nurses that might become the backbone of a public health nursing system could not be trained. In our Aisne and Reims demonstrations we had all the facts anybody needed to prove that the use of trained nurses in a visiting nurse service would save the lives of children. A gifted public speaker, who was a nurse, could bring all of this home in talks to groups of French men and women, through the press, through articles in the magazines, and in many other ways. Like all educational things, like everything that grows, this plan would take time but would come right in the end. When I put it up to Miss Morgan and Mrs. Dike, they concurred but said that I was the one to do it. This led to the only disagreements I had with them. Not only was I not willing to stay beyond the time I had set for leaving, but I knew that the job could be done far better by a Frenchwoman, and I knew exactly the Frenchwoman to do it. Marcelle Monod, so brilliant, so fine a public speaker, could take over when she came back from America and give her full time to the work even if it took years. I thought I had that lined up before I left France, but it fell through after I had gone home. The committee of distinguished physicians we had formed was allowed to lapse. Not long after, Madame Courtellemont died—my failure was entire, complete.

That winter, so much of it spent in Paris, was more exhausting than my first winter in the devastated areas. On the sixth of March I wrote my mother that I had just finished my long report for the annual meeting of the American Committee for Devastated France in New York, in April, and that I had to write another long report for the Director of the hospitals of Paris. I said, "I think I have walked through miles and miles of hospitals lately, such dreary, sad hospitals, with such unspeakable nursing. I am so tired, not in my body but in my head, which doesn't seem to be my head but somebody else's which I am carrying around on a platter—like the daughter of Herodias."

There were pleasant interludes during this Paris experience which helped to make it bearable. Nearly every evening at six o'clock, I dropped in at the apartment of Admiral and Mrs. Magruder, warm family friends. My cousins, John and Isabella Breckinridge, spent a short time in Paris. With them, and with such of my colleagues as turned up, I often went to the theater. The de Reisets were always glad to see me. Mrs. Dike had me to dinner more than once to enjoy the society of distinguished Frenchmen as well as Americans. The French are so quick at repartee that you have to be on your toes to keep up with them. I saw something of old General de Maud'huy, who had a profound admiration for General Lee. He called him the modern Bayard, and was writing a small book about him. Since he did not own General Lee's signature, I sent home for one to give him. André Tardieu I met often. He presented me with a copy of his book, *La Paix*, with a message inscribed in it. Colonel Winship of the Reparation Commission, a Kentuckian, and Surgeon-General Blue of the United

States Public Health Service had Mrs. Dike and me to lunch at an apartment where they were keeping house together. We teased General Blue about letting some lice slip by him, get to New York and kill a man with typhus. He protested that only eight lice got through, and they were on stowaways. He had a staff of men at every port just to keep out the lice and rats.

V

No dinners and luncheons with the French and with the Americans, no matter how delightful, could make up to me for the exhaustion brought about by my study of the Paris hospitals. When my Breckinridge cousins went down to Cannes they invited me to join them for a bit of a holiday. I got a *permission* (vacation) of three weeks and spent it with them at the Villa Allegria, a place they had taken on the Route de Fréjus. My young cousin, Mary Marvin, was in her early teens, as I had been when I had spent my Christmas holidays at Cannes. I wrote my mother that nothing seemed changed on the Riviera after an absence of twenty-five years:

There are the same monks (or they look the same!) on the Isle St. Honorat, the same gorgeous hotels, semitropical foliage, the same little Scottish church, and the same curious creatures in the sea. There are even Breckinridge children playing on the beach—but it is the next generation, preparing to lift our work when we drop it and carry on after us. . . . Isabella and John have taken me in as one of their own household. Already the tiredness is falling away from me like a dark veil (I never liked veils, you know) and the restoring sun is giving me back my enthusiasms.

In another letter I wrote fully of the pressure brought to bear upon me to stay in Europe, to take on the vast task of creating a climate of opinion that would enable our French Committee to effect an opening for a nursing school in the Paris hospitals. I said:

Well, darling Mother, a decision has come to me and not of myself. Call it what you will—I feel it definitely and will follow it with the assurance that I am doing what is right. Sometimes we are blest with a clear decision. A reform of nursing in the Paris hospitals and through them in all France is not my job—not even the organization for it. I am fortified by this knowledge to resist all the pressure in Paris. I am to work directly for little children now and always—because that is the work I can do best, in which my health and enthusiasm and happiness do not fail. Some very special thing is waiting for me on the other side of the ocean (although I don't know what it is). I am absolutely sure that I am not the person for this larger work in France. It is an inexpressible comfort and relief to know this—know it as I know that I know it. I shall be home for good within the year.

Chapter 12

I

MY letters from Cannes, in which I really let myself go, troubled my people more than I had realized they would. A shower of letters came back, urging me to come to The Brackens in Canada for a summer holiday. In reply, I wrote that "the director of a department of child hygiene in a great international committee can't jump in and out of Europe like a tennis ball." I reminded my loved ones at home that I had sent two of my best nurses to America on scholarships, and that they would not be back until the end of the summer. I told them that Miss Walker needed a vacation and that, in June, I was letting her go to New York to visit her mother. I could not leave until all three had returned.

Although we had a staff of twenty-nine nurses I could not spare even one that summer to act as supervisor for the Aisne area; I had to stay in France and run it myself. But my rest at Cannes, and the certainty that I need never tramp the wards of Paris hospitals again, had cured my exhaustion. I felt clearheaded once more and eager—this was just as well because a lot of threads had to be woven into a final pattern before my work in France was done.

In late May, I spent eight successive nights in: Vic, Laon, Reims, Paris, Rouen, Paris, Vic, Paris. A part of this time spent running around Robin Hood's barn was great fun. My cousins John and Isabella Breckinridge had turned up again in Paris. They asked me to drive with them on a visit to our Aisne units, spending a night at Laon, and then driving to Reims for twenty-four hours there. At that time we had a Hostess House at Laon. Here we found two of the C.A.R.D. Directors from America. It warmed my heart to hear their praise of our nursing service. "What have you done to the children?" they asked. "A year ago they were so pale and listless still, and now we never saw such hearty children. It strikes us the same in every village where we go." So the work of rebuilding France, not in monuments of stone but in the temples of the bodies of her little ones, had gotten far enough along to be visible to eyes which had seen the early ruins upon which we had to build.

The second night we spent at Reims, not in the little lodging house where I always put up but at a restored hotel, which included the rare luxury of baths. Reims was so horribly smashed that few buildings stood up. We invited Lady Hermione and Miss du Sautoy, who were living in the Hospice (an eleventh-century poorhouse), to come early to dinner and bathe first. They took us at our word and arrived armed with bath towels and soap.

My trip to Rouen was made with Madame Gervais Courtellemont, whose brother was the Préfet for the Seine Inférieure. His was a position somewhat similar to that of the Governor of Kentucky. Other large cities in his Department were Boulogne and Dieppe. I was eager to learn ever more and more about the things the French were doing to conserve their depleted population, and Mme Courtellemont was as eager to further my education. Among the places I visited with her in her brother's Department were excellent tuberculosis sanatoria (one for women, one for men), a preventorium for children, a home for abandoned children, a maternal canteen, a visiting nurse service at Rouen that had a real nurse at its head, Mlle Hervey, one of the best of the Bordeaux nurses. I also went over the old-world hospital of Rouen, where the nursing seemed not to have been bettered in four centuries. It was always in the public hospitals that one found the Achilles' heel of France. Although my twenty-four hours in Rouen were busy enough, I did take time to visit the lovely old church of St. Ouen and to dwell on memories of Joan of Arc, the sweetest and most gallant girl in all history.

In order to further Mme Courtellemont's education (we took turnabouts working on each other), I invited her to go with me to Bordeaux to attend the ceremony of the laying of the cornerstone of the American Nurses' Memorial building—given to the Florence Nightingale School of Nursing. This took place on Sunday, the fifth of June, 1920. The Maison de Santé Protestante, to which the school is attached, had given medical and nursing care to sailors for a generation, including hundreds of American sailors during the war. I suggested to Dr. Hamilton that her Board invite Admiral Magruder, the American Naval Attaché at Paris, to take part in the ceremony. This was done. When I had a quiet word with him, he said that not only would he go himself but he would send a destroyer to represent the Navy, and have five officers and fifty seamen attend with him. The ceremony of the laying of the cornerstone was deeply moving. When the names of our sister nurses, who died in the war, were placed by Miss Helen S.

Hay in the stone, and an American bugler sounded taps, not many of us—French or American—had dry eyes.

II

I spent the three months following my trip to Bordeaux almost entirely in my beloved Aisne sector, where I had to run my nursing service without the help of even one supervisor. I moved to Soissons, where there was now a daily express to Paris, so that when I had to go there it would not take as long as from Vic. Aside from that reason for the move, our nurses in the canton and town of Soissons were our largest group and I was nearer Laon, the capital of the Department of the Aisne. I maintained the closest relationships with Dr. Lemarchal, and with Dr. Cavaillon, Chief of the Service de Santé (Board of Health). I had borrowed Miss Morgan's limousine and chauffeur the preceding summer to take both these men on a complete tour of inspection of our nursing work at all the C.A.R.D. units. I respected Miss Morgan's limousine. Whenever she made rounds in it, she picked up anything and anybody needing transportation. As she herself said, her limousine had carried everything but a cow.

It was an awful wrench to leave Vic, my home for more than two years. "Dear Vic," I wrote, "the nicest little town in Europe! It has given me so much more, so terribly much more, than I ever gave in return, even when my work lay mostly here." I returned to Vic for an occasional week end before I went home in September, but I never lived there again.

When I moved to Soissons, Mrs. Dike gave me a personal bilingual secretary. Until then I had to write my long reports, and all of my correspondence in French and English, with such help as the Paris office and the secretaries at the units could give me. My French correspondence was so heavy that I really needed someone to whom I could say, "Please write such and such to so and so, and I will sign it." I had not asked for this luxury until now because I tried to run my nursing service as economically as possible. I had so much respect for the money people sent us from America that I wanted to be sure that every dollar of my part went into the nursing service itself, with the records of its work, and into the hungry mouths of our thousands of children. There has never been anything for which I have had more respect than the money given by charitable people. I know from experience that what you give, you go without.

It was my privilege that last summer to organize one more big thing for our French children. We were approached by a group of philanthropic Swiss people at Geneva who said that they would like to form a Swiss Section of the C.A.R.D. to aid the children of France. The President of the group was a distinguished woman, Mlle M. L. Moulin. The Swiss made arrangements to receive our children at Geneva, as soon as their Section was formed. I got the first twenty off in July. Each child had to have a passport, birth certificate, medical certificate, vaccination certificate, a paper giving parental consent, a Swiss *permit de séjour* and one or two other documents. The French railroads gave free passes to the children and the nurse who attended them. The Swiss met the children at the border and took over their entire care afterward. They placed them first in the Geneva hospitals for a real medical going over, treatments, and surgery if needed. After that the children went to Swiss homes all around Lake Geneva, where they were well fed and kept much in the open air. None of the services of the Swiss Section cost the American Committee for Devastated France anything, and some of the children were kept in Switzerland from six months to several years. In all, the Swiss Section cared for thirty-two hundred of our French children—a tender, charitable gesture from a small group of people to the children of a foreign country.

We had had a lot of scarlet fever and diphtheria in our villages during the winter. The diphtheria persisted into the summer. Just as I was finishing dinner one evening in late June, I got word there was a critical case of diphtheria over at Coucy. The nurse I had there, filling in for a vacation, was young and new to our work, so I went over at once—taking with me another nurse to relieve the one on duty. Twin babies of eleven months, a boy and a girl, had suddenly fallen ill but the parents did not send for the nurse until the morning. She went at once to find the boy just dead, and the girl battling for breath with the membrane covering her throat. Our young nurse and the nearest doctor—in the next county—took her to the hospital for a tracheotomy. They would not keep the baby at the hospital so the nurse brought it back to its home, with an oxygen tank and an order for stimulants. That was the situation when I got there. I took over the nursing of the baby (the oxygen, stimulation, and keeping the tube clean), while Mlle Laget gave serum to the other seven members of the family. We did all we could for our little one but towards eleven o'clock that night she gave up the unequal fight. When we had bathed and dressed her, we put her beside her brother. I wrote my mother:

There lay those babies, the day before in perfect health, struck as by lightning, and a broken mother who could not understand. . . . Always when I lose a baby, always while the fight for it is on, I seem conscious of another child in the room. The pale flicker of the lamp flame the other night seemed to shine like a halo above his yellow hair. When the baby died, I said, "Here, Breckie, take this little child. We have done all we could, now she goes to you." Nor do I doubt the welcome on the other side, for Breckie and I have a sort of partnership about babies.

The Municipal Council of the village of Coucy-la-Ville sent a most moving address of thanks to the C.A.R.D., in which they outlined all that we had done to re-establish agriculture, including the tractors we had given; our work in forming groups of boy scouts; our rehabilitation with food, clothing, beds—all the multifarious activities in which we had engaged. The last paragraph of this address of thanks I translate as follows:

Finally, and this is the most fruitful work and the most worthy of praise, the C.A.R.D. has, through its nurses, its devoted, courageous and indefatigable nurses, fought disease and death which otherwise, under our conditions here, would have caused a large part of our population to disappear.

The summer of 1921 will be remembered in Europe as one of the hottest on record. This added heavily to the burden of our nursing work. There were lots of flies and the country had practically no sanitary arrangements of even the most rudimentary sort, as they were the last to be reconstructed. We bought mosquito netting to protect our babies, and encouraged people to put their food in *garde-mangers* (screened containers). I drew up a special report:

On the Mortality Rate of the Babies and Young Children
under the Care of the Nurses of the American Committee,
in Reims and in 103 Villages of the Aisne and the Town of Soissons,
for the Months of July and August, 1921
(during the heat wave)

Of babies under two years we had lost twelve per thousand babies. Of children between the ages of two and six we had lost three per thousand. It was hard.

Early in August we had a shocking blow in the form of an epidemic of dysentery in the *commune* of Blérancourt, including three adjacent villages, caused by the bacillus of Shiga. I find from my four-page official report that there was a difference of opinion as to the cause of the epidemic. The physician at Blérancourt, Dr. Fournier, thought that its origin came from an old graveyard where the Germans had buried victims of a similar epidemic in 1918. The bodies had recently been disinterred. On the other hand, the Departmental Director of Hygiene, our constant friend Dr. Cavaillon, who personally studied the ground, thought that while it was not possible to locate the origin of the first cases, the fact that one of the first had been the baker would explain the subsequent spread of the disease. The water was not contaminated. Our two chief difficulties in handling the epidemic lay in the disposal of excreta and in getting enough serum. The first problem we met by having a hole, a meter in depth, dug behind each house where there was a case of dysentery, lined with lime, and covered with a specially constructed cover made in our own workshop. We did this for the first twenty families affected, and then Dr. Cavaillon sent two men to take the job over and co-operate with us.

To get the serum was a graver problem because it lay beyond our power to remedy. Dr. Cavaillon said that the surest way to break up the epidemic was to give preventive doses of the serum to all exposed people. Not only could we not get enough serum for that, but often we could not get enough to give the maximum curative dose to the sick. None died who had the maximum dose within the first twenty-four hours. Those who did not get it were gravely ill for weeks, with subsequent prostration. We had 128 cases with 9 deaths, of which 7 were children. The reason for the scarcity of serum, as reported to us by the Pasteur Institute, in Paris, to whom we sent people direct time and again, was the unusual demand for it that hot summer all over France. Only a proportion of orders could be filled.

The work of our Bordeaux nurses at Blérancourt received the highest praise from Dr. Cavaillon. Mlle Dumon was the senior nurse; Mlle Eldin was her assistant. The third nurse I sent them for several days was Mlle Coste, one of our best, who knew the Blérancourt district. The nurses gave the patients sterile, normal saline solutions by hypodermoclysis. They worked far into the long summer evenings, until the light had gone, and into the night when need be, with a selflessness beyond all praise. One amusing touch should be reported before I close the account of this period of terrible strain. The village authorities wanted to be of some help, so they fumigated the library!

III

I took only one trip during the summer. Early in July, before we got involved with epidemics, I went as a delegate to the English-Speaking Conference on Infant Welfare in London. Since my absence from France had to be of the briefest, I went by plane from Paris to London on a French air line called the Messageries, and returned from London to Paris on an English plane of the Instone Air Line. Kit, who had taken her vacations with Racky or Lummie in places like Venice, decided that she would fly with me to make a lark of it. She wanted to check up on the London libraries in preparation for her popular library in Paris. Commercial air lines were in their infancy then. The pilots had been war aces and were superb but the planes, with their inside wickerwork, looked like governess carts. The French one had room for only four passengers. The other two were a famous jockey and an English tailor, who carried a robe for an Eastern potentate to wear the next day at Buckingham Palace. The flight reminded me of the trip Alice made in a train, after she had gone through the Looking Glass, when she found herself sitting near a gentleman in white paper and a horse.

I thought the Conference worth the time and the money I had spent in going there. The London *Observer* of Sunday, July 10, 1921, called it "A Great Congress." They concluded a long article by their Medical Correspondent with words that seem as applicable today as they were then:

> We are mammals, and therefore the mother is the natural saviour of the baby. There is not—never was, nor ever will be—anything that can replace the mother in the home. . . . Our mottoes for the future should be Back to the Home and Back to the Breast. It is an ancient and perdurable ordinance of Nature that for these there shall be no substitute.

IV

I had intended to return to America early in September on a Canadian boat, to meet my mother at The Brackens and to go South with her. Although this plan was close to her heart and mine, I gave it up when Miss Morgan asked me to go back with her on the *Paris*, sailing September 24, in order to discuss the hospital-training school plans. As things turned out, I needed the extra weeks in France. When Miss Walker and Mlles Monod and Peiron returned to the Aisne, and I turned the direction of that nursing field over to Miss Walker, I had one last fling with Mme Courtellemont.

We had been working up a Comité d'Action Franco-Américain, to supplement the work of our distinguished medical committee. To serve on the new committee, we invited representatives from the nursing services of the International Red Cross and the Rockefeller Foundation, as well as from our own C.A.R.D. Miss Morgan and Mrs. Dike consented to hold high office, which was altogether right, as the C.A.R.D. was to put up the money. Mme Gervais Courtellemont took the hardest post, that of volunteer secretary. As a committee for the purpose we had in mind, it had points. To keep out of the political factions into which France was as split then as she is now, we chose people whose appointments were of a more or less permanent character. The top people rose and fell with dizzy rapidity. A committee on which they served would have had to be reconstituted every few months. Among ourselves we called our group "A Committee on

Nursing Propaganda in France." I wrote my mother that the committee would arrange to give a series of conferences this coming winter (with Monod speaking), write articles, talk to people individually and persuade distinguished French men and women, planning trips to the United States, to arrange to visit some of our leading hospitals. "Out of this committee will grow the grain I have sown but cannot harvest. As a matter of fact, there have been many of us in the sowing, and others ahead of us whose footsteps we follow only." Such were my hopes then.

On my last fling with Mme Courtellemont, I made a visit to Camier, near Etaples, on the Picardy coast. The English built a hospital of wooden barracks there during the war. These the French took over and turned into a camp large enough to accommodate between five and six thousand children. The camp had two seasons of two months each; the first for girls from seven to twelve, the second for boys. Our visit fell in the boy season. Thousands of these children, all undersized and debilitated, had come from the great cities of the north—Lille, Roubaix, Arras. In squads of forty-five, they played on the sands under the direction of their school teachers. A corps of doctors and *infirmières* looked after their health. The food was excellent. With Mme Courtellemont I stayed overnight at the camp. My French hosts were exquisite in their courtesy as well as in their hospitality. The American flag flew over the Administration Barrack in my honor.

To my mother I wrote:

Rarely have I been more moved in a land where so much is moving than on the second afternoon at Camier, when we passed around the dunes and came onto miles of shining sand and glimmering water—a seashore like Tagore's, "of endless worlds where the children meet with shouts and dances." Scattered all over the beach they were, digging, gathering shells, listening to fairy tales, chasing one another, playing in the pools left by the outgoing tide. It was a shore for children —no fashionable promenade, no ugly buildings—nothing but a glory of sun and sea and sand, and one German wreck that had washed ashore in 1914 and still bleaches there.

My last days in France had to be spent in Paris "on final work with Mme Courtellemont for our nursing propaganda committee and inducting my Monod into its bypaths," so I wrote in my last letter before sailing. On my good-by visit to Reims, I stayed in the poorhouse with my English friends. We talked far into the night. My last rounds of the nursing centers in the Aisne, my last visits to old friends near them, were to say adieu. My work in them and for them had ended. I made farewell ceremonial visits to the officials at Laon, among them my friends, Dr. Lemarchal and Dr. Cavaillon. "As we sped back over the familiar road from Laon to Soissons, across the Chemin des

Dames toward the setting sun, the early autumn lay in the bits of yellow here and there in the living trees. But soon we were in the dead ones, which know no season, and mournfully stretch their sapless arms out to those of us who never will forget."

The Vic unit of the C.A.R.D. had a good-by party for me with toasts and songs. The songs harked back to the early days when I gave personal care to babies and children, before I got drawn into the net of administrative work in which I lost touch with the peasants. My good-by party at Soissons was a dinner given me by our nurses. They invited a number of my C.A.R.D. colleagues to attend, and Miss Morgan and Mrs. Dike honored us by coming down from Paris. Marcelle Monod had been chosen to make the farewell speech. She handed me the last part of it, written out like a citation, and signed by all the nurses. Because I treasure this more than any citation, I translate a few lines:

You cherished all our French children. You dreamed of the day when all of them, in country and in city, in mountains and on seashore, would be placed under the guidance of nurses . . . and we, your little army of nurses, we shall remember you as we carry out our daily tasks, forcing ourselves to follow in your footsteps, having learned from you that the most precious qualities are those of the heart.

The reason why I have covered my years in France so fully—the devastation where we of the C.A.R.D. went to work; the people of all classes with whom we mingled; the beginning of my nursing service for children and its growth; our search for a solution to the nursing problem of France—is not for old affection's sake, although that would be reason enough to me. But in this part of my book I try to tell of the things which prepared me for the work that lay ahead in the Frontier Nursing Service. Nothing better prepared me for this than my years in France. I learned then that it is wise to begin small, take root, and then grow. I also formed a habit, indispensable in new undertakings, of learning all I could about native customs so that new things could be grafted on the old. Finally, I gained a respect for facts—old and new—with the knowledge that change is not brought about by theories.

V

Early in October, I was with my mother, my gallant mother. With a heart at one with theirs, she had seen her four children volunteer for war. The youngest was still with the Army of Occupation in Germany when I went home. No matter to what parts of the world her children scattered they knew that she went with them, that distance was no barrier to love and faith like hers. To me, whose life had twice been shattered, she transmuted the sustaining power of her courage and her tenderness. After my long absence from home we had much to tell each other. We had long, quiet hours for a deep exchange of thought before she left me, in less than a month after I had gone back to her from France. On November 2 she passed "to where beyond these voices there is peace."

Chapter 13

I

IN France midwives were not nurses. In America nurses were not midwives. In England trained women were both nurses and midwives. After I had met British nurse-midwives, first in France and then on my visits to London, it grew upon me that nurse-midwifery was the logical response to the needs of the young child in rural America. Although my life was dedicated to the service of children, there was no partiality in my regard for them. Whether in city or country, they mattered more to me than all the world beside. But in America much had been done for city children, whereas remotely rural children had been neglected. My work would be for them.

Work for children should begin before they are born, should carry them through their greatest hazard which is childbirth, and should be most intensive during their first six years of life. These are the formative years—whether for their bodies, their minds or their loving hearts. Our health records in America have no name for children between the ages of one and six years. At one year and one minute old they cease to be babies—save the mark! They become schoolchildren at the age of six. During the intervening years they have no title of their own but are called pre-school, as one might say sub-deb. In England they call little children toddlers on their health records. The French called them *"jeunes enfants"* (young children). Their word for schoolchildren is *"écoliers,"* a nomenclature of a different root. With the development of nursery schools in many of our cities, some like the Merrill Palmer in Detroit of outstanding quality, I have thought that we might substitute the title "nursery" children for "pre-school" children. But whatever we call them, their short span of years after babyhood are the formative ones. Only through the use of imagination can grown people understand young children. We remember what it was like to be six years old, but we don't recall our point of view at eighteen months. From this it follows that our memories are of no use to us in understanding nursery children. It might help to awaken our imaginations in their behalf if we classified them under a name of their own.

Thus reasoning, I came in time to see that I could be of use to children if I worked for them in a remotely rural area and, most intensively, from the period preceding their birth to the school age. But I realized that I would be faced with a staff problem even more difficult than the one I had had in France. Over there we left child-birth and early infancy in the hands of the splendidly trained French midwives. My difficulty then had lain in getting nurses qualified to take on the job where the midwives left off. For work in rural America, on the other hand, I could get nurses but the lack of qualified midwives would be total. This led my thoughts to England and the nurse-midwife. But first I needed to learn more about America.

It seemed to me, as I reflected further, that I would do well to spend an entire school year in Teachers College, Columbia University, to get abreast of developments in public health nursing and allied subjects. After that I should spend a summer riding through the Kentucky ,nountains to learn, at firsthand, of conditions there and to become acquainted with leading citizens. Only after these two things had been done would I go over to England to take my training as a midwife and to study the work of nurse-midwives in the rural parts of the British Isles. It will be seen from all of this that my plans were practical. I had the same conception of the way to go about my work for the children in the Kentucky mountains as I had had for the children in the devastated countryside of the Aisne. In both cases I thought it better to do something before talking about it. It was not until our demonstration in France had been successful and had produced results, supported by statistical findings, that we were ready to awaken public opinion to the need for enough trained nurses to get these results elsewhere. The same reasoning applied to America. First, we must give a demonstration in a remotely rural area of the value of nurse-midwives and only then, backed by statistical findings, would we be ready to awaken public interest in the development of the nurse as a midwife. In my childhood at Hazelwood I had read an old book called *From Do Nothing Hall to Happy Day House,* which told of a magic key called "Do it yourself."

II

Although the winter and summer following my mother's death were poignant ones for me, they have little bearing on the Frontier Nursing Service. Since none of us would ever live again in either of my mother's large houses, they had to be closed and left ready for sale. My father went with my sister to Fort Caswell on the East Coast where her husband was stationed. He stayed with her most of the time until he and I had a home together in the Kentucky mountains. With my older brother at the Naval War College in Newport, the younger one in Germany, and my sister expecting her second baby, it naturally fell to my lot to close the two places. I was so very tired that I had to rest awhile in each of them first. My Aunt Jane spent the winter with me in Fort Smith; Eleanor Blaydes came for several weeks. Old friends there were deeply kind. My older brother had a week to give me during which he went through tons of papers—fishing catalogues, plantation payrolls, receipts for ice cream we ate as children, interspersed with letters of historic value—and made bonfires of most of them. Those of our loved family possessions that we wanted to keep— from the Sully portrait of my great-great-grandfather, John Breckinridge, to the little chairs that were my father's as a boy in Kentucky, and my mother's as a girl on Airlie plantation—all such things were put in the hands of packers and shipped off to fireproof storage. After I had gone, the house was sold.

My brother Carson and I were in Canada together the early part of the summer. It was hard to be at The Brackens without our mother. During the twenty years since we bought the islands—the first home we as a family had ever owned—my mother had nearly always gone there as early as May and stayed until late October. Her children, in their roving lives, knew they had a home to go to, if only in thought— and a mother in it. On the larger of the two islands stood my mother's roomy house. From one of its long verandas her garden stretched down to a little bay where it ended in water lilies. All was just as she had left it the preceding summer and, as Carson said, "abjectly lovely."

Carson decided to buy The Little Brackens, connected by a causeway with the large island, from my mother's estate to keep as a place where he could spend a month's leave occasionally. Although he kept it until his death twenty years later, lending it to friends to enjoy, I think he was able to get back but four times. My father, Lees and Clif never returned. The problem of breaking up the big island was made less difficult by my brother's decision to keep the small one.

Breckie's godmother, Mrs. Jesse Turner, was one of the friends I had invited to spend my last summer at The Brackens with me. When the summer had ended, and I went on to New York, she came with me to enjoy a few weeks of music. We put up at a small hotel within walking distance of Teachers College. Miss Adelaide Nutting, the great leader of the nursing department at Teachers College, was still in her prime when I went there. She often invited me to talk with her in her apartment, so it was my privilege to know her well and to have the seal of her approval on the plans I formed for work in the Kentucky mountains.

Due to my lack of education, I could not matriculate at the college. Since no one could have had a more humble opinion about my education than I had myself, this was quite all right with me since I could get the work I wanted as a nonmatriculated student. In fact, under that classification, I could get more of the work I wanted since I did not have to follow a rigid schedule. With the kind help of my advisor, I chose the courses that would be of most use to me in my future work. Several were in the social sciences, nursing education and public health. One of the latter was given by Dr. C.-E. A. Winslow of Yale. I took a course on the principles of statistics, which interested me intensely. I took biology for fun.

The first of the two semesters I took general psychology, of which I knew nothing except from William James's book that I had read because I liked it. The second semester I took child psychology. During the whole year I followed a course in psychiatry, or mental hygiene as it was called, under Dr. Charles Lambert of Bloomingdale. A profoundly interesting professor to me was Dr. Whitley in psychology and child psychology. I thought hers one of the ablest minds with which I had ever come in contact. Through her I came in touch with Dr. Ella Woodyard, not only my warm friend since then, but a friend of the Frontier Nursing Service even before its work began. She was doing research with Dr. Thorndike in the Institute of Educational Research, but she had been a teacher of mathematics. The manner of our acquaintance came about through my weakness in the matter of decimals and fractions. I told Professor Whitley that unless I were tutored in those two dismal subjects, I could not calculate the medians in her psychology class assignments. When Dr. Woodyard took me on, she was most reassuring. She convinced me she could fill the parking space in my head where decimals and fractions ought to have been. She did. I passed all of my examinations successfully, including the ones with medians. After that, for the second time, I forgot all about decimals and fractions.

During the Christmas holidays I made a visit to my sister at Fortress Monroe, Virginia, where I delighted in her children. Her boy, "Dusty," was halfway through his fourth year. I found him sorely puzzled over the munificent intervention in his life of what he thought of as three old men. Uncle Sam owned the house where he allowed Daddy to live; Santa Claus had given a hobbyhorse to Dusty, but God sent the baby. When anything new turned up, he would ask if it was from Uncle Sam, Santa Claus or God. His puzzlement over God's share in his benefactions was further complicated by our Southern pronunciation of "guard." When he pointed one out to me he said,

"Dat is de one dat cawies guns, not de one dat sends babies." Oh, the bewildering world through which the young child has to grope his way!

A great happiness came into my life on December 27, 1922, when my older brother was married to Dorothy Throckmorton Thomson at the Church of the Holy Spirit in the Shenandoah Valley—a small stone church built on land given from her ancestral home of Hawthorn. Until my brother's marriage there had been considerable family discussion about getting a place in the country, not too far from the seacoast and the railroads, to serve as a center where we might foregather once in a while. We were an attached family. But this plan was so impractical and costly that we had given it up even before my brother married. After the marriage, we knew he and Dorothy would be the family focal point whenever they were stationed within range of any of us—as, indeed, they always were.

In the spring of 1922, after closing my mother's place in Fort Smith and before going to Canada to close The Brackens, I had made one of many visits to my kindred in Kentucky. At that time I also made my first approaches towards the work I had in mind to do. In 1923, with a whole summer free to spend as I liked, I spent it in the Kentucky mountains. Since my plans would take me in the autumn to England for a long stay, my father and I wanted to be together as much as possible that summer. He came to Kentucky on a visit to Cousin Molly, Cousin Letitia and Cousin Cabell Bullock in Lexington, and then moved to the Boone Tavern in Berea where I could get to him for an occasional week end. It was on these visits to him that I first met Dr. William J. Hutchins, later to become one of the Frontier Nursing Service trustees. I never shall forget his deep interest in the plans I had afoot, or how charming he was to my father and me.

III

In 1793, when my great-great-grandfather, John Breckinridge, brought his family from Virginia to Kentucky, he must have crossed the Appalachian mountain range farther north than the route through Cumberland Gap, because he and his party traveled in boats from Red Stone in southwestern Pennsylvania to Limestone, now Maysville, Kentucky. They were eight days on the water. A letter from him to his father-in-law, Colonel Joseph Cabell in Buckingham, Virginia, said that his party saw no Indians and little sign of any. He added, "Polly has written—I am sure my little children were never all so fat and healthy." In this letter, now owned by the Filson Club in Louisville, he relates that his party reached Fayette on the third day after their boats landed at Limestone.

Of John's wife, Mary Cabell, one of whose wedding slippers is still in the family, I thought often as I rode through the Kentucky mountains that summer. More than a century before, an earlier Mary Breckinridge had ridden trails not unlike those I was following then. Of one thing I felt certain—she was better mounted than I was or she never could have reached her destination.

That summer I rode thirteen different horses and three mules. Among them was every variety of sore, ringbone, kidney disorder, and other equine complaint. Only two were even fairly good saddlers. The bridles were often pieced with rope and the girths tied on with wire or string. The blanket was often a meal sack. The shoes were in such poor condition, with blacksmiths and forges few and far between, that I made it my custom to carry in my saddlebags a couple of shoes of the size worn by my horse of the day, and turned to fit him. I traveled approximately six hundred and fifty miles on these animals, reckoned on a basis of three miles an hour, which is conservative as on some roads and some mounts I made four. I would have bought a horse for the summer's travels but for my frequent visits to my father. Several times I left the mountains at the spur of railroads that led eventually to Louisville or Lexington, to make my way to Berea. After a day or two with my father, I would go back into the mountains via another spur that would land me perhaps three days' horseback travel from the place of my departure. Under such conditions, it just wasn't possible to depend on any one horse.

It is not within the scope of this book to give a report on the mountain midwives I visited, the families they served, the condition of the babies and young children. From the daily notes I kept, I wrote up my investigation as soon as it was completed, with tabulations on the 53 old midwives that I had interviewed. The total age of the 53 was 3,193 years, and their average age 60.3 years. Nineteen years later in the *Quarterly Bulletin* of the Frontier Nursing Service for Spring, 1942, I published the investigation and its tabulations in full—seven thousand words. Here it suffices to say that the care given women in childbirth and their babies, thousands of them in thousands of square miles, was as medieval as the nursing care of the sick in the public hospitals of France.

Contrary to popular impression, many of the midwives were intelligent women whose homes were tidy and gay with flowers. At least sixteen of those I visited, even six in windowless log cabins, were women of more than average ability. Ten of the fifty-three were filthy, as were their homes. The rest fitted in between. Some of the better-class midwives were to become my friends, but even before I knew them well I respected them, despite their superstitious practices. Most of them had taken up midwifery, after their own families were raised, in order to help neighbor women who had no one else to stand by. In just the same way must our own great-great-grandmothers have gone out to help their rural neighbors, making use of the practices of their day.

Even the most intelligent midwives had no advance knowledge of possible complications in their maternity cases because, unlike the midwives in France, they had had no training whatever. A few of them had attended conferences held by nurses under the State Bureau of Child Hygiene. But the nurses themselves were not midwives and, therefore, unable to teach them how to look for abnormalities, even if such things could be taught in conferences. In hundreds of square miles there was no licensed physician but, as always happens under such conditions, there were men claiming to be doctors and practicing medicine. I met two who could not read or write. They were the least harmful because they made use of old-fashioned "yarbs" as remedies instead of store drugs.

One story will serve to illustrate the maternal tragedies that came about because of these conditions. Among the finest of the old midwives with whom I talked was one called Aunt Tildy. She was a touchingly honest and unassuming person and deeply grieved by the recent loss of a young mother. The baby was "crossed" she said. She could not reach either head or feet and, after trying all day and night on a Friday, she sent Saturday morning for two "doctors." From then until Sunday morning she and they all tried unsuccessfully to deliver the patient. At last, after over fifty hours of labor, they sent "a fur piece" for a real doctor. But before he reached the house, the young mother had died. Had it not been for the pseudo doctors—nearer at hand—Aunt Tildy would probably have sent Saturday for the real one and there might have been one less maternal martyrdom. She described to me the despair of the young woman at leaving her family, how she called for her sister and told her to "take keer" of her little children, and how the terrible "miseries kep' up" until they had "kilt her."

Since there are few colored people in the Kentucky mountains, it didn't surprise me to find only one colored midwife among the fifty-three that I visited. A native of Virginia, she had come to Owsley County as a child with a family to whom she belonged and was, when I saw her, seventy-three years old. To one like me, whose ties with old colored people were those of lifelong affection, this midwife was something special. As soon as I told her my name, she burst out with a jingle I had never heard before:

John C.
Breckinridge, he
Beat de Bell of Tennessee

117

When we sat down to talk, she told me her story. An only slave of a poor hard-working man and his wife, she had been raised with their daughter of about her own age, and loved them all dearly. One day in the sixties, while she was in her teens, she and the daughter of the house had worked in the fields together as usual. When they came in, her master said to her, "You are free." When she asked him what he meant, he said, "Hit means you don't belong no more." She pointed to the daughter of the house and asked, "Don't she belong?" Her master replied, "She does, but you don't belong no more." "Then," she told me, "I bust out cryin'." Except for this early shock, her life on the whole had been a happy one. She married a colored mountaineer and raised all of their seven children. After his death, she had tended her white neighbors, as midwife, for thirty years.

From the point of view of my investigation, the greatest difficulty I had with the old midwives was in finding them. Only nine or ten lived on the principal waterways. They lived mostly on the smaller and rougher creeks, on the forks of those creeks, up the branches above the forks, and at the gaps where the branches headed up. To see one midwife would sometimes require five or six hours' riding. This meant that sometimes I had to sleep wherever I happened to be when night overtook me. I shall never lose my gratitude for the hospitality extended to me in the lonely little homes of these remote places. Rarely ever was I allowed to pay anything for myself, although fifty cents would usually be accepted for the feed and care of my horse. I nearly always got a bed to myself. Although a bath was harder to manage, it was not the problem for me that it would have been to people who grew up with plumbing and had never left it. At the end of each day's ride, I begged the loan of the one hand basin and kettle while the housewife was getting supper. After shooing out the children, I took possession of the room where I was going to sleep. With a basin of hot water, my washrag, soap and towel, I disposed of the dust of the day's travel. Then I put on the fresh set of crinkly underwear carried in my saddlebags, refilled the basin with hot water from the kettle, and washed the set of underwear I had been wearing. Then I hung my wet clothes on the limb of a tree to dry out during the night. After that, I washed the hand basin, refilled the kettle from the well, and returned them both to my hostess. Except on rainy nights, my underwear as well as I myself was beautifully clean.

When I could plan ahead on my travels, I put up overnight with the larger landowners in six- and eight-room houses where I was entertained with fried chicken and other delicacies. I stayed also at the Hindman and Pine Mountain Settlement Schools in Knott and Harlan counties. Miss May Stone and Miss Lucy Furman were the only two of the early group of workers, which had included one or two of my cousins, still at Hindman. On one of my stopovers at Pine Mountain, I was warmly greeted by Mrs. Ethel deLong Zande; the next time I turned up, my old friend, Miss Katherine Pettit of Lexington, was there as well. Especially memorable to me was the hospitality often given me by Miss Mary Rose McCord at the Wooton Community Center in Leslie County, and that of Miss Lila and Miss Mabel Buyers at the Presbyterian Girls' Dormitory in Hyden. With Miss Lila and Miss Mabel I remained in close contact until their retirement years later.

At Hyden I made my first acquaintance with Judge L. D. Lewis and his wife, as well as several other citizens who were to become lifelong friends but whose part in this story comes later. With Judge Lewis I was immediately and completely at home. His roomy mind was stored with Kentucky history. He had known several members of my family and knew more about those long dead than I did myself. His greeting to me was that of an old friend who welcomes an exile that has at last come home. Through his courtesy, I received introductions to other leading mountaineers and stayed at the homes of several of them. When I spent a night with Albert Hoskins and his wife on Stinnett Creek, I little thought that he was to become the chairman of the Beech Fork Committee of the Frontier Nursing Service. Unforgettable is the night I spent with the Henry Chappells at Chappell on Greasy Creek. Aunt Jane Chappell, as in our deep affection we came to call her, was the soul of hospitality. With a small hand lamp she preceded me into my room at bedtime to see that everything was comfortable.

One night I stayed with the Huffs on Wilder Branch. The old couple had had three sons, all of them in the First World War and one of them killed. We sat in an old log room where a log fire burned on the stone hearth and talked about the graves of the American soldiers in the Aisne, on which I had placed flowers, and the surviving soldiers here at home in the Kentucky mountains. One of them, Elmer Huff, a son of the house, became not only chairman of the Confluence Committee of the Frontier Nursing Service, but one of its most valued trustees. He lived to see his sons and kinsmen in another war where the lives of some of them were lost in Europe and in the Pacific.

On most of my journeyings I rode alone, but occasionally someone from one of the settlement schools went out of her way to keep me company for a day or more. One day as I was leaving the Pine Mountain School to ride down Cutshin Creek, Mrs. Zande asked if I would mind stopping off on Maggard's Branch to see one of their former students, now a young married woman in broken health. They wanted me to send back, with a horse they had loaned me, a full report on her condition. This I did. Later I learned that her father had shown ingenuity in getting her taken by mule sled to Pine Mountain.

From there the School sent her to Dr. Irvin Abell in Louisville. He afterward told me that she had the worst case of uterine cancer he had ever seen in a young woman, that she was inoperable, and that she had died. This was the first time I came in touch with the brilliant surgeon, the kindly man who was to serve, until his own death in 1949, on our National Medical Council. More than once that summer I acted as go-between with a patient and her remote physician. Among the homes at which I stopped was that of Mr. and Mrs. Carlo Hoskins, who became our warm friends forever. When Mrs. Hoskins learned I was riding out by way of Hazard, some forty-odd miles away, she asked me to take a report about her to Dr. R. L. Collins of Hazard. That was how I first met the man whose life was to be more interwoven with the early years of the Frontier Nursing Service than that of almost any other.

IV

During the last two weeks of my travels, I had the joy of the companionship of Dr. Ella Woodyard. She had begun to ride in Kansas at as early an age as I had begun in Mississippi, so that days of horseback travel held as much interest for her as they did for me. I had invited her down not only for the pleasure it would afford us both but because I wanted mental tests made of some of our children by a brilliant psychologist who was an expert in this technique. I wanted to be able to answer questions I knew people would ask me about the mental level of our Kentucky mountaineers. While I talked with the midwives, Dr. Woodyard took individual mental tests of 66 children, using the Stanford Revision of the Binet-Simon test. All of these children were from six to ten years old. They were picked up at random as they played in front of their homes by the creeks and branches. Of the 66 children tested, one had an intelligence quotient of 135, and one was a high-grade imbecile, with an intelligence quotient of 82. Such a child might not have been found in a school group but as Dr. Woodyard was taking the children as she met them he was included in her estimates. Without him, the median intelligence quotient of the 65 children would have been 102. With him, it was 99.5.

Dr. Woodyard is now the Research Director of the Frontier Nursing Service. Recent careful testing by her of 810 of our young children, ranging in age from 35 to 40 months, gives a median I.Q. of 108.3, a mean or average of 108.0. As most people know nowadays, intelligence quotients are compared with a norm of 100. It is no surprise to me, who know them so well, to find that our young mountain children show a higher average of intelligence than the national norm.

V

It was on one of my rides alone that I first saw Wendover. Of course it wasn't Wendover then, but I knew it would be. It was purely by accident that I happened to be riding along the Middle Fork of the Kentucky River. I was on my way to Stinnett and Beech Fork where the direct road lay up Muncy Creek and across a gap down to Stinnett Creek. A dear girl, Pauline Brashear, whom I had met at the Buyers' dormitory in Hyden, begged me to turn off at Muncy Creek and follow a detour of some miles along the river that would take me past the home of her people. She went on ahead of me to tell them I would be there for the noon dinner. So, for the first of many thousands of times, I rode down Muncy Creek, forded the Middle Fork and rode slowly along its banks. I thought I had never seen anything lovelier than the lay of the land with its southern exposure facing the great North Mountain. When I raised my eyes to towering forest trees, and then let them fall on a cleared place where one might have a garden, when I passed some jutting rocks, I fell in love. To myself and to my horse I said, "Someday I'm going to build me a log house right there." Two years later I did.

Chapter 14

A SKETCH of the evolution of the nurse-midwife just naturally
has to come in this part of my story to explain why I became
one. Although not much is known about the women who acted as
nurses and midwives before Florence Nightingale, they are symbolized
forever in Dickens' immortal character of Sairey Gamp. When Florence Nightingale used the money the grateful British people gave her
in 1860, following the Crimean War, to found a training school for
nurses at St. Thomas' Hospital in London, she created modern nursing.
Before that time the sick poor in the hospitals of England and America were cared for by ignorant and degraded women. So much was
this the case that it was believed no respectable woman would take up
the career of a nurse. The first Nightingale nurses brought to America
to start the system in public hospitals of New York and Philadelphia
were rotten-egged.

Not many people know that Florence Nightingale was interested in
midwifery as well as in nursing. Among my most cherished books is
one written by her and dedicated "without permission" to the shade
of Socrates' Mother! It bears the quaint title:

Introductory Notes
on
Lying-In Institutions
Together with
A Proposal for
Organizing an Institution for Training Midwives
and Midwifery Nurses
by
Florence Nightingale

This book was given me by Miss Adelaide Nutting, who sent me a
note to say it was given her by Florence Nightingale's cousin, Henry

Bonham Carter. On the flyleaf of the book Miss Nutting wrote: "To Mary Breckinridge—With affectionate regard."

It was one of "Miss Nightingale's Young Ladies" (as nurses were called then), Miss Rosalind Paget, later Dame Rosalind, who took up and followed through Miss Nightingale's schemes for the modern education of midwives. Like Miss Nightingale, she was a handsome girl of ample private means when she decided on nursing as a career and received in 1879 a certificate from the London Hospital. She was not long in learning that a Nightingale nurse needed to be a midwife as well. In co-operation with other gentlewomen of like interests, Miss Paget founded the Midwives Institute in 1881—the year in which I was born. In 1882 she took a course at the British Lying-In Hospital in order to get such training in midwifery as was possible then. Although ladies of birth and fashion did not often become nurses it was permissible to do so following Miss Nightingale's example, but that ladies could become midwives was not acceptable in English-speaking countries. One of Miss Paget's friends said to her, "My dear, I wish there were another word for you, it would be so awkward if we used it just when the footman came in to put on coals."

The condition of the sick poor and of maternity cases in their homes as well as in hospitals aroused the compassion of the British people. When a large sum of money was given Queen Victoria by her loyal subjects to commemorate her Jubilee in 1887, the Queen acted in the spirit of this compassion when she dedicated the gift to the creation of the Queen Victoria's Jubilee Institute for Nurses. After Miss Paget had been selected as the first Queen's Nurse, she started her district work in the most degraded parts of London of which "Tom-all-Alones" in *Bleak House* was typical.

In this book I can't pause to give the history of the Midwives Institute, of which I have been a member since 1924, of its long struggle to secure legal recognition of midwives, to provide adequate training for them, and postgraduate training in midwifery for nurses. Suffice it to say that in 1902 the bill promoted by the incorporated Midwives Institute passed through Parliament and received Royal Assent. Under this Midwives Act, the Central Midwives Board became the authority for all midwives in England and Wales, whether they were nurses or not. The Scottish Act came later. Later yet, the Midwives Institute was granted a Royal Charter and is now called the Royal College of Midwives.

II

When I wrote my English friends that I was going over to the Old Country to take training as a midwife, they were eager with kind

123

offers of help. I could have chosen any one of several first-class mid-wifery schools with the backing of graduates of those schools. However, my choice was determined in another way. During my winter at Teachers College I met Miss Carolyn Van Blarcom through my friend Ella Phillips Crandall. Miss Van Blarcom, widely known for her excellent book on obstetrics for nurses, had made an investigation of midwifery in England for the Russell Sage Foundation years before. I gratefully accepted from her an introduction to Miss Paget, whom I had not met on my visits to London, and I followed Miss Paget's advice in the selection of my school. The one she chose for me was the British Hospital for Mothers and Babies, in the Woolwich dock-yard section of southeast London, midway between the Arsenal and the Thames. The institution, with its modern blocks of brick buildings, was a lineal descendant of the old British Lying-In where Miss Paget secured such training as a midwife as was possible in 1882. In the fall of 1923, after my rides through the Kentucky mountains were ended, I went over to England and entered the British as a pupil-midwife—the name used for a student of midwifery.

I put up at a London downtown hotel until I could get my uniforms. I had been sorely puzzled over the directions sent me about these—that the bonnets should not be trimmed with lace was one requirement. I finally got outfitted in both outdoor and indoor uniforms—none with lace—and, in the dreary moistness of a dripping evening, I drove to the place which was to be my home for several months.

A number of American nurses have taken their training as midwives in Great Britain since I made the plunge in 1923, but at the time I thought it something of an adventure. For one thing, I had stepped back into the kind of work I did as a student nurse, with extras added. The British or Woolwich, as we often called it, was a model institution in the care it gave the patients and the training it gave the pupil-midwives—but it was the dampest place in which one could live, short of a frog pond. The shoes seemed to mildew on my feet, water to ooze out of the walls, and the sheets felt like cerements from the tomb of the Capulets. The only places that ever dried out were the delivery rooms and operating theater, where central heating was in constant use. The climate of London is surely not more raw than that of northern France, and heaven knows our early housing there was so shattered as to let in wind and rain, but in France we were constantly out of doors in thick uniforms, whereas in Woolwich I felt as though I lived in a dripping cave—and in cotton. I suffered.

Since Americans are not as a rule familiar with British midwifery schools, a few words of explanation seem in order. In 1923 the mid-wifery course for untrained women at Woolwich was of twelve months' duration, longer than the legal requirement in England. For trained nurses the course was of four months' duration, the legal requirement for all of the English midwifery schools then. The course for trained nurses was increased to six months, after 1926, under a directive of the Central Midwives Board. There have been further changes instituted by the Board in late years, but into these I need not go. During our four months' course in 1923, we trained nurses served in rotation in the mothers' wards, the nurseries, the labor wards, the prenatal clinics and on the district. We were called in rotation for our own deliveries and, whenever possible, to observe all deliveries. Under the rules laid down by the Central Midwives Board each of us had to deliver personally, under supervision, a minimum of twenty normal cases of childbirth. We were allowed to attend the abnormal cases delivered by the hospital physician, who, in my day, was a man, Dr. Wise. A surgeon was called in for Caesareans. In my day she was a woman, Miss Bolton. (The British do not use the title "doctor" before the name of a surgeon.) The superintendent of nurses in any British hospital is always called Matron and is addressed by her title and not by her name. The head nurses and supervisors are always called Sisters and are addressed by that title. Our medical lectures were given by one of the attending physicians. Our classes in midwifery were conducted by the Sisters, and one of them by Matron herself.

When one of the attending physicians made rounds of the hospital, as was done every day, a bell was rung. Then all the pupil-midwives who could leave their work followed behind the physician, listening to his comments on the patients. It was a useful part of our instruction. A bell was rung whenever a woman was about to be delivered in one of the labor rooms. Again, all of the pupil-midwives who could leave their work filed into the labor room to watch the delivery, conducted by one of them with a Sister in charge. When we were assigned a maternity case of our own for delivery, then we followed straight through until the mother was back in her own bed. This meant that we were often on duty for long hours at a stretch, but this was essential in order to give the mother consecutive care by one person. She was never left alone. If the case terminated after midnight, we were allowed to sleep until noon the next day. However, we had no holidays, not even half-day holidays, so there was no way of recuperating after a particularly hard strain.

Although the babies had nurseries, on the different floors, they also had metal beds attached to their mothers' beds. They were nearly all breast-fed and were allowed to remain with their mothers as long as the mothers wanted them, except during visiting hours in the afternoon. They were all dressed in pink, white and blue woolly sweaters and pants and looked like teddy bears. From my point of view they were kept much too cold. I have known the temperature in the nurseries to stand below sixty degrees when we bathed them. It consoled me to remember that they were British babies and an early Spartan system might be necessary to get them inured to their climate. We had stone hot water bottles for them as well as for the mothers, and that helped. Our normal maternity cases were delivered without anesthesia and remained in the hospital for fourteen days.

A midwife's course of training cost forty pounds. There were no incidental expenses except textbooks. A number of British nurses who were training with me were on scholarships given by the agencies which were going to make use of them after they had passed their Central Midwives Board examinations. These examinations, conducted at the same time at various regional points over England, loomed up before us as the climax of all of our hard training. In order to qualify for them and, indeed, for credit as a graduate nurse to take the shorter course of training, I had to submit a detailed statement from St. Luke's Hospital School of Nursing in New York about the length of the course, the number of the patient beds, and the kind of training I had received there. When this was accepted by H. G. Westley, Esq., the Secretary of the Central Midwives Board, I ran into another snag.

Mr. Westley asked me for a birth certificate or infant baptismal certificate. When I explained why I had neither, the Central Midwives Board consented to accept the declaration of birth my parents signed years before for my passport, and ruled that I could qualify for the examinations on the same basis as the British nurses. Meanwhile, I was struggling to prepare for them. Aside from delivery room and bedside teaching (which is as essential in midwifery as in other branches of nursing) and the notes I took down from my lectures, I got the most help out of a textbook for midwives by Dr. John S. Fairbairn, a great obstetrician and a member of the Central Midwives Board. I came to know him and his wife very well indeed and dined more than once at their house on Harley Street—but not while I was in training.

My greatest handicap as a pupil-midwife was the fact that I was always chilled to the bone. I think it takes generations of unbroken continuity to withstand a raw, damp cold when it is in a house. My ancestors, both Scottish and English, left the Old Country so long ago, and lived in southern climates for so many generations, that I just didn't have it in me to react like a chip off the old block. I thought of a way to stay alive through the winter if the three women who ran the hospital would consent. The Matron, Mrs. Lelia Parnell, was an elderly woman and a daughter of an ex-Confederate who had gone to England after the fall of the Confederacy and stayed there. She had an exact sense of what was suitable for everyone in every situation. For example, when one of the hospital maids wanted a copy of Robert Browning's poems for Christmas, Matron said firmly, "She has asked for Robert but I shall give her Elizabeth." To Matron there would be nothing unsuitable in allowing an American from the South, parked on the dockyards of the river Thames, to thaw out occasionally. The Honorary Secretary, as she was called, Sister Gregory, a daughter of the late dean of St. Paul's Cathedral, was a fine woman who raised most of the money for the hospital, but in a glacial atmosphere not unlike that of a cathedral she felt at home. The third of the triumvirate who ran the British was Sister Maud Cashmore, brilliant administrator, and a person of such unlimited compassion that she could not see a fellow creature succumb to cold without a reaction of distress.

In all of our bedrooms at Woolwich there were gas heaters but no one was allowed a key to turn on the gas. "One misty, moisty morning when cloudy was the weather"—all the mornings were like that—I went to my three chiefs in their own sitting room, at the ten o'clock tea hour, to ask if I could use the gas fire in my room when I studied in the evening and pay the cost. They concurred at once, even Sister Gregory, who looked upon me as an effete scion of a mighty race. I never knew how much gas I burned in my twopenny heater, and they wouldn't bill me, so I gave them fifty pounds when I left and hoped that I had not used more gas than that. I do know that I burned a hole in one of my legs without even noticing it, and had to be under medical care for several days. They never got over that at Woolwich! Despite the chill of the place I liked it because there was no lack of warmth in friendly hearts I found there. Sister Maud Cashmore and Sister Lillian Neild had sunshine enough between them to disperse a lot of fog.

The only two things about Woolwich that I did not like were the damp cold, about which I have said enough, and the lack of any time for rest and relaxation. Sister Gregory said that the only two things needed in a dedicated life were religion and work. The work was well done and the religion, Anglican of the High Church wing, was sincere and centered in the hospital chapel. But there was a good deal of respiratory illness among us all, including those who set the pace, which might have been avoided by weekly periods of refreshment. After I came down with something resembling the grippe, the Matron, Sister Gregory and Sister Cashmore were kindness itself to me. What is more, they told me I could take a week off and make it up later. I went to Garland's Hotel in downtown London, where Henry James used to put up, had a fire of coals in my room morning and evening, and slept from ten to twelve hours every night. I took in several plays of which the one that most profoundly impressed me was *Outward Bound*. I saw a lot of Miss Paget and other English friends, and the Americans I knew who were then in town. I was a member of the

English-Speaking Union even before we had a Kentucky branch. Their clubrooms in London made a delightful center for meeting people. I went more than once to two places of which I am extremely fond, the Church of St. Martin's in the Fields and the National Portrait Gallery.

When I returned to Woolwich I started the district part of my midwifery training under Sister Card, as fine a supervisor as she was a woman. From then on everything was easier for me because I was out of doors and in the homes of the people. The perpetual drizzle and fog didn't really matter when one was walking briskly under a heavy topcoat and a bonnet without lace. In every house where the mother lay with her newborn baby there was a fire in her room. As you went in the door, the mother would call out from her bed, "Have a good warm, nurse, do." I respected the dockyard workers, their dependability, their steady heads, and their loyal hearts, as much as I liked them. I never saw poverty more decent than it was in Woolwich, a family life sweeter or more wholesome. After months of depressing institutional life it was reassuring to feel its stability and warmth— "from our immemorial joys of hearth and home and love" to be "one with its silent stream." Then, too, there were the dogs—members of nearly every household—and so respectable.

The first delivery that I attended alone was that of a young woman living in an overcrowded lodging house with a husband who had been out of work for months, and two small children. Her sister—a stout, plain widow of a sergeant—who stayed with us, put one hand on my patient's shoulder and said, "It's me, right by you, old pal." The baby with an old, sad face was born prematurely. Since I was a pupil-midwife, Sister Card followed me up almost at once and got a doctor for the baby before it died. She also put me in touch with a mission station of the English Church just back of the lodging house, down by the Thames, so that I could arrange through the mission workers to meet the expenses of the baby's burial. It is a cardinal rule of nursing that nurses must never be almoners—or their influence is injured—but one can get around this when one must.

Things were amusing as well as sad among the East End Cockneys. One of my patients, who loved to eat, spoke of herself as "'oggish and gorgeous." There was another who was equally fond of eating and had the means to gratify her taste. I found that she could be diverted through the long hours of the first stage of labor by talking about the things she had eaten, the things I had eaten, and the things that in sublimated moments we both might eat. In this fascinating conversation we were joined by the charwoman who was helping me and who talked like a stage character. Out on the district I formed a high opinion of the dependability of British charwomen, British dock workers and British dogs. The names of some of the district people were as delicious as those in Dickens. The one I liked best, emblazoned over the owner's little shop, was that of Treacus Tidy.

III

The Central Midwives Board had a ruling in my time that you did not sit for your examinations until a month after you had completed your training. This allowed for a record of your training, including the reports on the twenty or more cases you had personally delivered, to reach the Board before it held the examinations. A week after the written examinations you came up for the oral ones, called the Viva. With Matron's permission I took a three weeks' holiday before putting in the week I had lost at Woolwich. Sister Lillian Neild invited me to go with her on a visit to her uncle and aunt at Oxford—the uncle a don and a mathematical genius.

My stay of almost a week in Oxford, where nearly everyone had lost sons in 1914, like my visits with Nadine at Cambridge, like my work with the Woolwich dockyard people, brought me an understanding of what the first great war had meant to England, not unlike the understanding I had of what it had meant to France. A generation of young men who could have carried the nation successfully through the years between the two wars, and might have prevented the second one, that generation was dead. In England, with no conscription during the first war years, it was the pick of the land that went no matter from what class it came.

From Oxford I went to Cornwall for two weeks of sea air and, by God's grace, some sunshine. There I found a world of moors stretching endlessly, a bloom of yellow gorse reaching down to sea beaches. The place was St. Ives, immortalized by the man with seven wives and many cats. I stayed at the Tregenna Castle, a country house turned into a country hotel, where I could have big coal fires. All morning I spent on the moors and all afternoon down by the sea watching the fishermen's children at play. Often there was a friendly dog as well. Unfortunately, I caught the "flu," which was wandering all over the Cornish coast but, even so, I gained new strength, as I always do, from hours lived in touch with the earth and in country air.

I went back to London for the week I had to make up at Woolwich —all of it spent on the district—and my examinations under the Central Midwives Board. These I passed successfully and became an American certificated English midwife! The program I had outlined in preparation for my work in the Kentucky mountains included a study of the Highlands and Islands Medical and Nursing Service in Scotland

129

and further study and observation in England. I deferred these plans until later in the year and went back to America for two reasons, of which the first was that I felt too tired to do justice to any more work right then. The second reason was even more compelling. My sister-in-law, Dorothy Breckinridge, was expecting her first baby in May. She and my brother both wanted me with them for an event almost as desired by me as by them. The bond between my brother Carson and me was so close that neither of us ever refused a request from the other. So I arranged to leave England April 19 on the *Minnewaska* of the Atlantic Transport Company, sailing from, of all places, Wool-wich.

Chapter 15

I

SOMETIMES an experience is so deeply creative that you respond to it with everything that you have, not only in retrospect but at the time. When I went to Scotland in mid-August of 1924 to make a study of the Highlands and Islands Medical and Nursing Service, I knew that weeks of enchantment lay ahead of me, but I could not know until it happened what it would be like to enter a strange country and feel at once that I had come home. Scotland, its soil, its people, and its traditions became mine—not by inheritance as before, but actually through the response my spirit made at every hour to their appeal. I had come back to my "ain countree." Clad in tweeds, I moved through it in a state of alert exaltation and in one continuous drizzling mist. When the sun came out for several hours on a glorious day in September, I heard one Scotsman say to another, "Trrropical weather we're having, trrropical."

In the spring before I left England I had been in correspondence with Sir Leslie MacKenzie, a great public officer of the Civil Service whose investigations in 1912, under the Dewar Committee, led to the creation of the Highlands and Islands Medical and Nursing Service. I had read enough about his work to know that I should study it at firsthand. It is important to tell about it here because the system used by the Frontier Nursing Service is an adaptation of the methods used in the Highlands and Islands work, and Sir Leslie and Lady MacKenzie came all the way to Kentucky to dedicate our Hyden Hospital. In the rough country of northern Scotland and in the islands off its western shore, Sir Leslie had found a combination of social, economic and geographic difficulties characteristic of remotely rural areas, and necessitating exceptional treatment in order to secure medical and nursing care for the mothers and children, of whom Sir Leslie wrote that they were "the most delicate and fluid part of the population." "Expectant mothers," he said, "are at the mercy of distance and the winds and the waves." When he wrote of regions rugged, roadless and mountainous, his description fitted vast areas of our Appalachian mountain range as completely as it did the Scottish Highlands. In one of his reports where he outlined what should be done to meet the medical and nursing needs of inaccessible citizens, he said, "If I know anything of our people, the response of the nation will be positive and handsome." It was indeed.

The way in which the Highlands and Islands Medical and Nursing Service was financed and operated was characteristic of the British philanthropic genius of that day—private enterprise aided by government grants to bridge the gap between what could be handled by local efforts and the magnitude of the job to be done. The direction of the Service lay in the hands of a voluntary committee affiliated with the Scottish Board of Health. This committee annually received a crown grant of some eighty thousand pounds. Decentralization was assured through local administration, by voluntary committees, in the various shires of northern Scotland and the islands, and direct administration was left in the hands of these committees. They raised what money they could in donations and through the small fees charged the patients. The crown grant allocated to them whatever else was needed to give medical and nursing care. In remote areas like those of the Outer Hebrides, this amounted to as much as eighty per cent of the costs. In the more habitable sections, like those of northern Perthshire, where there were a few wealthy and generous local landowners, only a small part of the costs came from the crown grant.

The operation of the Highlands and Islands Medical and Nursing Service provided for nursing districts staffed by qualified nurses who were midwives as well. In an area with several nursing centers, a medical center was located and staffed with a physician who had had some training in obstetrics and pediatrics. Rural hospitals were set up to serve even larger areas, and transport for patients was arranged out of the Highlands and Islands funds. The nurses were paid salaries and provided with living quarters and uniforms. The fees charged the patients for their services were arranged by their local voluntary committees and were, therefore, suited to the varied economies of each region. In some nursing districts in the Outer Hebrides as small a sum as two shillings (about fifty cents) a year would insure nursing care to a family. In others the charge was eight or ten shillings annually. An added charge was made for the nurse's care as a midwife in a confinement case, when the patient could pay it.

The methods used for the payment of physicians were of two kinds. In the more habitable areas physicians were paid on a mileage basis. For example, a shepherd living in Perthshire in a remote glen, ten or twelve miles from a doctor, paid exactly the same price for a medical visit as if he lived next door. The extra mileage charge was met by the Highlands and Islands fund. The shepherd was not penalized for his inaccessibility, and the doctor was compensated for his time. In the more remote parts of the Hebrides, the physician was given a flat salary and a house. The small sums that the patients could pay went toward that salary, but the greater part of it was met out of the crown grant. This second method is the one we have used in the Frontier Nursing Service—except for the crown grant!

I got some of the information outlined above from reports, but most of it came right out of a small black notebook I carried around with me on my Scottish investigations, where I jotted down more than eleven thousand words—gleaned from conversations with the chairmen and secretaries of many Highland nursing committees, with physicians and nurses, and with Sir Leslie MacKenzie himself and the chiefs of his divisions. They were profoundly interested in my tour, which they outlined for me in Edinburgh as we pored over a map of Scotland. They gave me a letter that bore on the envelope a legend to the effect that it was "On His Majesty's Service." I found this letter an open sesame wherever I went.

Before leaving Edinburgh I made a visit to the headquarters of the Scottish branch of the Queen's Jubilee Institute for Nurses, in Castle Terrace, of which the superintendent at that time was Miss Whyte and her assistant was Miss Weale. Since the greater part of the nurses under the Highlands and Islands medical and nursing scheme were Queen's Nurses, fully qualified, with graduate training in public health, district nursing, and midwifery, I wanted to know all about them before I started on my investigations. The heads of the Queen's gave me the names and addresses of some of their best nurse-midwives in the remotest and most difficult parts of the Outer Hebrides.

The family letters that I had sent my mother from France now went to my father. They constituted a sort of journal filled not only with my experiences but with the impressions which I drew from them. I wrote pages on the charm of Edinburgh, the loveliest city I have ever seen. Interspersed with my rhapsodies of its incomparable castle are accounts of visits with the local district nurses on their rounds in the Canongate where the exquisite houses, once built for noblemen, were now considered insanitary for Edinburgh's poorest citizens. I will say this for the Canongate: the houses there are the only beautiful slums I ever saw.

The Scottish Board of Health and the Queen's Jubilee Nurses both agreed that their outstanding piece of work which covered a county, or shire, as the Scots call it, was in Perthshire. They advised me to go there first and see things as they someday hoped to have them in all the shires, where the good pieces of work were only here and there in local bits. Sir Leslie told me that the superb piece of organization in Perthshire had been made possible largely through the efforts of the Duchess of Atholl. She was by birth a Ramsey, daughter of a Cambridge professor whose mental gifts she had inherited. It was she who induced the small local committees in Perthshire to affiliate with a central committee while maintaining their own local responsibilities. To Perthshire, accordingly, I went first.

II

In Perth I called at once on Miss Williamson, the Superintendent of Nurses for Perthshire. She invited me to dine that evening at her headquarters, 7 Barossa Place, just off the Inches bit of ground where occurred the famous fight Scott tells about in *The Fair Maid of Perth*. I found Miss Williamson a delightful woman, a sister of the minister at old St. Giles in Edinburgh. With her, or with her assistant Miss Cameron, I covered many of the more than two thousand square miles of Perthshire. Only the northern part of the county received help under the Highlands and Islands grant. The southern part was a lovely rolling country with no geographic difficulties. But the nursing of the whole shire was under Miss Williamson's administration, acting in co-operation with the educational authorities and the Perthshire Board of Health. There were fifty-three nurses, all of them midwives, and their work was on a generalized basis. They took the maternity cases alone or under a doctor. They nursed the sick. They did the school inspections and followed up the children who needed attention. They regularly visited the babies and the toddlers up to school age. They did the follow-up on all cases of tuberculosis. The work in Perthshire was admirable. When I reflected that only two years before my visit the county had over thirty committees with divergent aims, methods and standards, each organized locally and employing its own nurse, and that now all was harmonized into this one big work, with the local committees still functioning and still backing their individual nurses—meeting, receiving their reports—and yet all co-operating in the larger program, I understood why the Scottish Board of Health and the Queen's Nurses in Edinburgh had directed me to Perthshire to see their system at its best.

In going about Perthshire I was particularly interested in two things. First, in the quality of the local committees, their chairmen and secretaries, and the degree of support each committee gave to its own nurse. Where the committees were "of the clan"—landowners living on their own land, and townspeople of inherited responsibilities—their support was magnificent. But where the landowners were absentees, living on other estates in the South and coming up for about ten weeks for the shooting, or letting their places to those beings known as "shooting tenants," the support was small and ineffective.

The second thing that interested me greatly was how the nurses lived. Each of the fifty-three local committees worked this out for its own nurse. Two nurses at Crieff, a prosperous little place, were lodged in one cottage with a nice white-capped maid. They had a complete dispensary. Several nurses were in lodgings where their meals were served them, by their landladies, in their own sitting rooms before a coal fire. Their nursing and medical supplies were kept in large cupboards. In many of the villages there were no water works but in one, where water was laid on, the local committee had put a large bathtub in the nurse's pantry, where it did look odd. It stood right next the sink. I wondered if the nurse washed herself and the dishes at the same time.

Many of the nurses were provided with bicycles. But often they had to leave their wheels and go over the moors afoot. With several of the nurses I made calls on the shepherds out on the moors. I remember one shepherd's family where the man had over a thousand sheep to tend alone except for such help as his young sons gave him in the lambing season. But he had two collie dogs—real Scotch collies, with their broad intelligent heads, stub noses and coats of black and white and tan. He told me that the dogs took care of the sheep. All through the mainland of Scotland I kept meeting droves of sheep that were handled almost entirely by the dogs, who deployed them to the sides of the road, out of the way of motor vehicles, and then back in the road again. We in America have turned that sagacious beast, the collie, into a long-nosed, low-headed dog with the plumage of a Buff Orpington rooster, and in so doing have lost his brains and his incomparable heart.

In Perthshire, as in other parts of Scotland, I often found myself passing regions familiar to me all my life in stories and songs. I went about with the nurses in a country where Lady Nairne lived in her youth, in the Auld House of Gask, and wrote "The Land o' the Leal," and such melting Jacobite songs as:

> Sweet's the laverock's note and lang,
> Lilting wildly up the glen;
> But aye to me he sings ae sang—
> Will ye no come back again?
> Better lo'ed ye canna be,
> Will ye no come back again?

From Perthshire I went over to Argyllshire, where I stopped first at Oban, on the mainland, because the county health people had headquarters there. I presented my letter and was received with immense civility. With their help, a map, the mail coaches, the mail boats, and a few motor tours for tourists, for whom the season was only just closing, I got to see many of the district nurses in Argyll. I found that almost everybody was named Campbell—many of the nurses, three out of the four honorary district secretaries of the nursing service, and practically all of the patients! The most moving place of all to me in Argyllshire was the island of Iona, where every stone, and every bit of sand and moor, held a prayer.

Up until now I had pushed steadily west from Perthshire clear to the Inner Hebrides, but my plan was to give most of my weeks to the Outer Hebrides. Now the time had come to move north into the shire of Inverness, where I could get a steamer for Stornaway. I lingered on the mainland of the shire only long enough to visit three district nurse-midwives and their local committees before heading for the Kyle of Lochalsh. This was my jumping-off-place from where I could cross the Minch to the island of Lewis. Since the Minch is an arm of the open Atlantic, and rough, it amazed me to find that my steamer, a roly-poly little boat called the *Sheila*, was smaller than the boats on the Muskoka Lakes in Canada on which I had traveled so often to The Brackens. As I stumbled over coils of rope and milk cans on the *Sheila's* tiny deck, I reflected that on just such boats, except that they used sails instead of steam, must my ancestors have crossed the Atlantic in the long ago, and I saluted them. When we docked in the night at Stornaway I realized with a quickened pulse that I had reached the Outer Hebrides.

III

Since few Americans, or Englishmen for that matter, visit the Outer Hebrides, it takes a map of these islands, to the west of Scotland, to make my wanderings through them clear. The largest island and the farthest north is Lewis. Just south of it comes Harris. Lewis is in the shire of Ross and Cromarty but South Harris, and the islands still farther south, are in the shire of Inverness. They sprawl on down through the Atlantic Ocean from North Uist to Barra, with many smaller islands between them and around them. Some of the Hebridean islands are Roman Catholic and some are Presbyterian, depending on whether the chiefs of the clans changed to the new religion or kept the old one in Reformation days. The people depend almost entirely on the fisheries for a living but they also hold bits of land called crofts, on which they can grow something to eat with their herring. They are all Gaelic-speaking. Few of the children learn English until they reach school age—and almost none of the old people I met could speak it. In the Hebrides the Highlands and Islands Medical and Nursing Service had special administrative problems. Every doctor and nurse had to be Gaelic-speaking. Those in the Catholic islands had to be Catholics, and those in the Presbyterian islands had to be Presbyterians. I found it like that wherever I went. The Presbyterian minister, whether Established or Free, served on the nursing committees of the Presbyterian islands. The Roman Catholic priest served on the nursing committees of the Catholic islands. In one small island, Benbecula, lying between North Uist (Presbyterian) and South Uist (Roman Catholic), the population was of both religious faiths. Here I found a Presbyterian minister and a Catholic priest both serving on the nursing committee.

Lewis is like no other part of the planet. One old Scotsman put this well when he said to me, "To the man of Lewis the island is his home and his warrrkshop is the warrrld." Celts and Norse and Scots and Picts and Druids, early Catholic-Christians—the ruins of whose sweet chapels are called temples—and later Presbyterian-Christians, succeed one another in a history of legends, warfare, Viking raids, fisheries. Poor Prince Charlie landed on Lewis after Culloden in the "45." His friends concealed him in a shepherd's hut, called a sheiling, on the shores of a loch which still bears his name.

Except at Stornaway, most of the Lewes, as the people of Lewis are called, lived in "black houses." These were made of stones piled up roughly to form walls, with roofs made of the roots and stalks of barley, thatched on and tied down with ropes of the same. In many of the black houses there was no window nor chimney and the smoke seeped through the roof from a fire laid on stones in the center of the room. At one end of this room the family slept and at the other end the cow and hens. In one such house, which I visited with the Garrabost nurse, we were having a confidential conversation with the patient when an old hen came and stood by, her face turned to one side, quite obviously listening. Meanwhile, a cow ruminated like a gum-chewing girl in the "byre" or far end of the room. But I will say this for the black houses—they were the only warm ones I found in Great Britain. I was entranced to see fires that gave out heat and were large enough to warm the toes of all. The smoke really mounted up and got out quite well through the thatched roof, induced thereto by the open door. Through the roof and the door, which had to stay open to let in light, there was good ventilation. The owners of many of the black houses had put in chimneys, and separate enclosures for the cow and hens. They had also cut windows in the thatch—such a pretty covering, green with grass and gay with a yellow flower. The peat smoke is so nourishing that the Hebrideans changed the roof every year, putting on a new thatch and using the old for manure. When I was in Lewis, the Government had already started to get modern cottages of stucco or stone built. If that scheme went through, then the Hebrideans are now as cold and damp as everybody else in the British Isles. I loved the black houses and I could have lived happily in one of them with a cow and hens in a byre—but I am like that.

The "warrrkshop" of the Lewisman is truly the "warrrld." In one black house I found such a nice old man and his daughter, she speaking English. He had sons in New Zealand, South Africa, Australia, and daughters in Canada and the States. The men followed the sea as sailors or fishermen, often returning in the spring to put in the pitiful bits of crops they wrested from an unfriendly soil in an inclement climate. Much of the land is only fit for sheep grazing, much is scenery, acres of it are the peat which gives the people their fuel. I saw the women carrying heavy loads of it in large wicker hampers on their backs. There was almost no timber on the island—rolling, dark moors and over six hundred lochs. Almost everyone lived in fishing villages, and there had been much suffering during the two years before my visit, owing to a failure in the herring fisheries.

Two of the six days I spent on the island of Lewis I gave to Ness—a village of several scattered hamlets where about four thousand people lived, nearly all in the black houses. To reach the Butt of Lewis and Ness, I took the twenty-seven-mile drive across the moors in a baker's cart. The two fine nurse-midwives at Ness had arranged for me to stay at an inn called Thule House, which made me think of William Black's old novel called *A Princess of Thule*. Much in the Hebrides reminded me of that story, as, for example, the fact that the servant classes were of the clan and, therefore, distant cousins of the heads of households. The princess, in Black's book, was served by a cousin.

On my trip back to Stornaway, I rode in a public conveyance with wooden side seats. It was full of Lewis people, including a girl called Marget just leaving to join her brothers in Winnipeg, with her bit of luggage and such a good face. People followed her out of the black houses and down the road, weeping and talking in Gaelic. Then the schoolmaster came and said in English: "You'll no be homesick, Marget. It's the lads that are homesick and no the lassies." But Marget's heart was "sair" and her poor eyes red with long weeping. She made me think of the song of the Hebrideans in Canada:

> From the lone sheiling of the misty island
> Mountains divide us, and the waste of seas—
> Yet still the blood is strong, the heart is Highland,
> And we in dreams behold the Hebrides.

IV

When I had absorbed all the district nursing and midwifery, medical interviews and local committee conversations that I could glean from Lewis, where I met with unending kindness from everyone, I engaged a motor to drive me the thirty-six miles to Tarbert at the tip of North Harris—a place of about two hundred people. Here I expected to find, and did find in Miss MacLean, an exceptionally fine nurse living in a cottage hospital with a small operating room and accommodations for four or five patients. Miss MacLean did a generalized nursing service, including midwifery, for eighteen scattered villages. She was lucky in that the physician for that area, Dr. Ross, lived at Tarbert so that she could get in touch with him quickly. Both doctor and nurse thought their chief difficulty lay in getting about. The winds were so terrible that bicycles were almost useless and they had to walk miles over the moors to reach their patients.

A day at Tarbert was enough for me so I booked passage on a fifty-year-old boat of 180 tons register, called the *Plover*, due to sail that evening around six o'clock. She did sail, but never got beyond the point of land at the end of the bay where she ran into the terrible autumn gales of the North Atlantic. Her skipper moved back into the bay where we rode at anchor all night. Except for the stewardess I was the only woman aboard. Curiously enough, I was also the only person with playing cards—something that could have happened nowhere but in Scotland. To a disconsolate group of men in a stuffy little lounge I gave one pack of cards and kept the other for my own solitaire. The faces of all brightened and soon the whole lot of them, two educational authorities, a young English angler, and several nondescripts—with matches for counters—were having a good time.

Out of this night on the *Plover* I formed two lifelong friendships. The educational authorities were Mr. James Grigor, inspector of science and art for the Scottish schools, and Mr. Murdo Morrison, superintendent of schools for the shire of Inverness. I had met them through the Millers at Stornaway—charming men, both of them, and rare companions of the road. After we had all three spent the rest of that day and the next night at Tarbert, and the *Plover* was still storm-bound, Mr. Grigor and Mr. Morrison told me that it was absolutely necessary for them to push on with their tour of inspection and meet their appointments on the island of North Uist. They said they had engaged a small boat as a ferry to put them over the Sound of Harris, and would I go with them? I joyously accepted their invitation. They had gotten hold of a motorcar, of which there were few in the Hebrides, and in it we drove the sixteen miles to the south end of Harris through a deer forest. Like all the deer forests that I saw in

Scotland, it had no trees. It was just a stretch of wild moorland on which the deer were kept out in the open. We came out on a shore of bold and desolate beauty, with the Sound of Harris between us and North Uist. There our ferry awaited us—an old herring-fishing boat, about twenty-five feet long, with the sail pulled down and a motor put in, and manned by three hardy men. They needed to be hardy because it was a rough crossing and we got more than one wave over us, entire. At North Uist we landed on some rocks because there was no wharf at that point. Here a car, for which Mr. Grigor and Mr. Morrison had wired ahead, met us and took us to Lochmaddy—a place highly reputed for its fishing and with a fairly good hotel. As the anglers came in from their sport, they received me kindly. Two of them had wives, nice Englishwomen who were friendly. When they saw my wet tweeds and heard I had ferried across, they put me next the fire.

That night the *Plover* came wandering in and announced that she would go to Castle Bay at Barra (where she should have gone when she stayed all night at Harris) although she was scheduled for Dunvegen in Skye. So the people for Dunvegen stayed off and I got on, being the only one for Barra. My appointments with people were such that I was due to go first to Barra and then work back up the islands to North Uist. The *Plover* puffed into Castle Bay between four and five in the morning. A little maid met my boat and lugged my suitcase up to the inn, declining assistance. There were not one but two hot water bottles in my bed—the sort of personal kindness to which one grows accustomed in the Highlands.

Of all the islands I have ever known anywhere, from the Mediterranean to Canada, Barra is the most beautiful. The sands are golden and long, craggy rocks reach out far into the sea, cutting the yellowness of the sands into bays. Back inland the country is mountainous with deep purple moors, matched by the purple and green of the ocean breaking against the rocks and along the sands. The whole island had only about twenty-two hundred people, who lived along the coast where they fished, caught lobsters, and tilled their bits of crofts. The road, the only one, runs around the thirteen miles of coast. There had never been a motorcar on it. The only doctor on Barra, under the Highlands and Islands scheme, rode a horse.

Barra is one of the Roman Catholic islands. The people, like all the Hebrideans, speak Gaelic and had many legends of the sea. One was of sea horses, which are inimical to man, and sea bulls which are friendly. I was told that if I found a tired man who asked me to hold his aching head and stroke his hair I should notice carefully if it were seaweed. If it were, he would be a sea horse in disguise and would utterly destroy me unless a sea bull rushed to my rescue.

Most of the black houses had been replaced with modern cottages which were much colder! That afternoon Nurse MacMillan, the Queen's Nurse at Castle Bay, took me for a walk of several miles along the west coast, seeing patients en route, and stopping with Father MacIntyre and the schoolmaster for tea. He lived near the church and school in a group of crofts called Craigston. It was a happy afternoon. From Mr. Grigor and Mr. Morrison I had already learned something about the way the Scots handled their school system. The school at Craigston was typical of other remote ones that I visited. The schoolhouse was well built, of stone, with the schoolmaster's house attached to it. Twenty-seven children attended this school and Mr. Riley, a university graduate, had an assistant who was a normal school graduate. The greater part of the money to maintain a remotely rural school at that level came from the central Scottish funds, so that these poor fisher children had as good a primary education as the children of Edinburgh. Those who showed an aptitude for secondary education were given bursaries to enable them to go to the nearest place where a high school was maintained. There they were boarded with families, under the supervision of the school. At Stornaway there was a hostel for such children—in other words a public boarding school for children from remote regions. So much did this democratic system pay off, so Mr. Morrison told me, that from ten to twelve per cent more men, in proportion to population, went through the universities from the Highlands and Islands than from all the rest of Scotland. The rural children, all given a first-class primary education in well-built and well-lighted country schoolhouses, really made their own decisions as to whether they were to go on to high school or not. If they reached a certain level in the highest primary grade, money and distance were no bar to the continuance of their education.

The next day was Sunday and I went with Miss MacMillan to her church in Castle Bay where my friend, Father MacIntyre, was preaching. But as the service was mass, in Latin, and the sermon was preached in Gaelic, I didn't understand either. I loved the reverence of the fisherfolk who crowded the building. I found this reverence also in the Presbyterian churches whose services I attended—Established, Free, and Wee Free.

In the afternoon Father MacIntyre lent me his trap and driver. With Nurse MacMillan I drove around the island to North Bay to spend the night with Nurse Gatt. There being no inn of any sort and she having, so I was told, only a single bed, I had telegraphed from the post office to know if I could be put up for the night and received a reply that I could be. It was getting dark when we reached Miss Gatt's cottage, and I bade good-by to my Castle Bay friends. After tea, I went with Miss Gatt to see a baby she had brought into the world at five o'clock that morning, and its mother. They lived four miles away, but we cut off a mile by crossing the sands in the bay at low tide. When we had made the mother and baby Margaret comfortable, and built up their peat fire, we started back across the bay which was a mile wide at that point. We had gotten about halfway across when we found we could no longer get around the pools of water which were spreading into one long shimmering silver floor. Said Nurse Gatt suddenly, "I have miscalculated, it is the tide returning." We mended our pace and got out with the water only midway between our ankles and knees. Oddly enough, it was not cold.

When we returned to the group of houses known as North Bay we found that the priest, Father MacDonald, had not liked that I, a stranger woman, should be given the vacant bed kept in the community for commercial travelers. It was in the post office, quite by itself, and had no covers. So Father MacDonald had arranged with his housekeeper to take me into the guest room he kept for bishops. Although it was nearly ten o'clock at night, they had a fire ready for Nurse Gatt and me and had cooked a fish for our supper. They dried out our wet things, and were so kind with their simple resources that I shall never forget them. Then the housekeeper, who had lent me her clothes, filled a hot water bottle for me and put me to bed in the ecclesiastical guest chamber.

The next morning I arranged with a being called "Coddy"—from his fancied resemblance to a codfish and the Highland habit of nicknames —to rent a fishing boat, with three fishers, to take me to the island of Eriskay. Here Prince Charlie first landed in Scotland, and hardly anybody has landed since. It lies across the Sound of Barra not very far from the tip of South Uist. It had no doctor but a splendid Queen's Nurse-midwife, Miss Martin, in whose work I was keenly interested. Her nearest physician, on South Uist, could reach her on call when the seas were not too high.

As I was leaving North Bay, Miss Gatt and Father MacDonald asked me if I would take two sickly children with me and leave them at a cottage hospital on South Uist. Kitty and John they were, small and motherless. Coddy's boat landed us all safely at Eriskay where we were warmly greeted not only by Nurse Martin but by Father Mac-Isaac, the secretary of the Eriskay District Nursing Association, eighty per cent of whose funds were met out of the Highlands and Islands grant. I left the children with Father MacIsaac while I went with the nurse to see some of her patients. The poorest-clad children that I saw anywhere on my travels in the Hebrides were those of Eriskay. Later, when I was back at Edinburgh, I went into a shop, and then went broke—buying warm woollies for them. All of the nurses who had been kind to me needed things for their work and it was a joy to send them, but Eriskay was the only district where I found the children markedly underclothed.

That afternoon I chartered another ferry, a sailboat with two men, to get over to South Uist with Kitty and John. We caught a mail car which took us to a hamlet called Deliburgh. Here I left those precious children with Sister Mary at a cottage hospital, built and maintained by Lord Bute—who didn't live there or even own land. Here I found the Highlands and Islands doctor, who handled all the medical work for that area and for Eriskay, and another one of those fine Queen's Nurse-midwives. The secretary of her committee, Mr. Lomax, a university graduate and head of the local school, walked with me the two or three miles to Loch Boisdale to a small inn entirely occupied, except for me, by Englishmen fishing. I decided to ease up on my wanderings and stay there two nights so as to climb Ben Kenneth, a jagged rock of a mountain rising sheer out of the sea, and approachable only over the moors on its inland side. It happened to be a clear day else I should not have ventured, as people do lose their way in the mists, sink into quagmires and die of it.

The last house I passed, as I left Loch Boisdale, was one of the blackest of the black ones. An old woman stood in front of it who called out to me, but I could not understand her so I smiled and went on. I got to the top of Ben Kenneth, with my luck still holding for the mists had not come up. I saw a wonder world of sea and sky, the surf breaking on distant islands and the land below me so littered with water—sea lochs and inland lochs—that there seemed to be more water than land. As I started my return trip, the mists began to rise and I could not see clearly what was boggy and what was safe going on land lovely to look at, with its red mosses and heather, and sinky to walk on. But I made it down to the black house, between four and five, and very wet and boggy I must have looked. At the black house stood the same old woman waiting for me and obviously anxious. She took me by the hand and pulled me into her house, which had an uneven dirt floor, peat smoke everywhere and such poverty—one broken chair only, a bench, and a box bed built in the wall—no table, no cow. The old woman put a kettle on the peat fire, shooed the hens off the china, selected a cup they had not offended, dug a scone out of an old black chest, spread it with cheese, pulled the kitty out of the milk jug, poured me tea with milk in it, and served me with the simple grace and unapologetic hospitality of a great lady. I was a tired stranger and she a Highlander. It was enough.

All the time she was getting the tea ready, the old woman kept talking in Gaelic, interspersed with occasional English words where everything was "she." There was no other pronoun, not even for Ben Kenneth. I gathered that she had been anxious about me and would have sent to the inn for men to go out after me if dark had closed in before my return. Then she began running off the names of English counties—Suffolk, Norfolk, Essex. I caught her meaning and said, "American." I doubt if she had ever met an American woman before. She ran right to me and grasped my hand and shook it and beamed. The thought of her and of her poverty haunted me long after I had gone back to the inn, where I wrote down her name. She was so great a lady that I did not dare to send her anything that would look like repayment of her hospitality. When I had gone back to cities, I chose two large colored pictures of animals and children, nicely framed, and sent them to her. I thought she wouldn't mind a gift like that, and that they would look gay in that black house.

The next morning I engaged a car and drove twenty miles to the northern end of South Uist, where I was just in time to get across the ford with a horse and trap before the tide rushed in over it. This put me on the island of Benbecula. It lies between the islands of North and South Uist and the three of them are often called the Long Island because they just miss being one piece of land. In fact, when the tides are out, they *are* one piece of land. The south ford I had just driven over is short but the north ford, between Benbecula and North Uist, is about four miles long and skirted with quicksand. Many and grisly were the tales I heard of people lost in that ford. The tides rush through both fords with fearful velocity. A little miscalculation as to time, or a false step into the quicksand, and it is all up with the traveler. Even when the tides are out, and the three islands are the Long Island, it is not easy to cross the fords on foot because little streams of the Atlantic Ocean still run through them here and there.

I spent several hours with the Benbecula nurse. When I got to the north ford the tide had come in nearly full. It would be hours before it got low enough to cross with a trap and then too dark, so I got hold of a wee sailboat manned by two good Scotsmen and we started across. Now here is the oddity about that unfinished bit of land. When it is fordable it is full of dangerous currents so that parts of it are always wet. When the tide is up and it has to be ferried, the boat gets caught on sandbanks here and there and has to be pushed along with an oar, so that really it is never land nor water. With its quicksand (which is a mixture of both), it is one of the most unhealthy localities to which I have ever been. The nurses in those parts visited some of their patients on bits of islets, fordable at low tide only. They tried to make their crossings then, in order to save boat hire, and often ran danger from the incoming tides and from the quicksand. Their work was heroic.

On North Uist I caught a mail cart that dropped me off with the Fergusons of Clachan who handled the mails and ran the only store.

They kept me to tea, warmed me, and located the district nurse-midwife for me to meet. North Uist had four of these wonderful women and a doctor—all under the Highlands and Islands grant, and with keen local committees. As I wondered how I could get to Lochmaddy for the night, Mr. Morrison and Mr. Grigor turned up. Our paths crossed more than once in the Outer Hebrides. They had a hired car and took me in it to Lochmaddy. They told me I had brightened the routine of their inspection and that they could not hope for another American woman to pass that way again. Years afterward, when my back was broken in the Kentucky mountains, Mr. Grigor wrote me, "When I learned of it I feared that you would become an almost helpless invalid for the rest of your life. It would have been very sad to think of one of the three who braved the passage of the Sound of Harris, one autumn day in 1924, having to spend long years of inactivity." My parting from my two Scottish friends was in a free rendering of the words of Malcolm Graeme, "Earth holds no glen, so lonely but we meet again." But we were not to meet, except through the exchange of letters and in our unforgettable memories. Mr. Grigor has now crossed over deeper waters than those in the Sound of Harris. With Mr. Morrison I am still in this-world communication.

V

The time had come when I must leave the Hebrides. I have tried to tell what they meant to me. To the Frontier Nursing Service, in after years, all that I gathered from those islands was to mean more than I can put into words. As Sir Leslie MacKenzie said of his own wanderings through them, "No words of mine can match the subtleties of the reality . . . words are only symbols of an incommunicable experience."

I had two courtesy calls to make before I went away from the Highlands. For weeks I had traveled through the western fringes of the shires of Ross and Cromarty, and of Inverness. I could not leave these shires without calling on their health officers and tendering my thanks to them. When the *Plover* meandered in to Lochmaddy, I went aboard her for the last time. The next afternoon I left her at the Kyle of Lochalsh. Here I caught a train on the Highland railway that took me through a yellow sunset into the lofty scenery of Ross and Cromarty. Although my destination was Dingwall, the capital of the shire, I got off the train at Garve. The next morning I caught a mail coach for the thirty-odd miles to Ullapool where I spent a day and night in study of the nursing thereabouts. This, the northernmost part of Scotland I reached in my travels, lay in moors of indescribable beauty.

The bracken on them, from which comes my name, had yellowed, giving them a tawny look. The effect of their rolling masses, with the wind sweeping over them, was not unlike that of billows of a monstrous ocean. Before the dawn of history, man lived on these Scottish moors. I wrote my father that no one had described them better than Stevenson in his:

> Grey recumbent tombs of the dead in desert places,
> Standing stones on the vacant wine-red moor,
> Hills of sheep, and the homes of the silent vanished races,
> And winds, austere and pure.

At Dingwall, Dr. MacLean and his wife overwhelmed me with courtesies, driving me everywhere, feeding me lavishly, and introducing me to their dogs and their friends. From Dingwall, I went on to Inverness to see Dr. MacDonald. He too was all that is kind. "Then," so I wrote my father, in my last letter from Scotland,

> I caught an evening train to Edinburgh—and as it swept on down through the Highlands into lowlier land, and the dying and misty sun touched the hills into blacker shadows, the closing lines of *The Lady of the Lake* came back to me:
>> Harp of the North, farewell! The hills grow dark,
>> On purple peaks a deeper shade descending. . . .
> Never will I cease to love the Highlands, reverently love them and their people. As De Quincey says, they pass out of my life and "into my dreams for ever."

Chapter 16

I

FROM Edinburgh I went straight to London. It seemed to me that if I were going to organize and direct nurse-midwives I should know more about midwifery than it was possible to get in the four months' course I had taken—good as that was. The York Road General Lying-In Hospital, in the Lambeth section of Southeast London, across the Thames from Westminster and the Houses of Parliament, had an affiliate called the Post Certificate School, on Southampton Street in the Camberwell district—also in the East End. I had arranged in advance to go there as a postgraduate student of midwifery. Since I was now a certificated English midwife (Number 62718) I could take cases alone on the district.

The Post Certificate, or Southampton Street as we called it for short, occupied two neighborhood houses thrown into one, poor quarters—plain and cramped. The neighborhood was congested and the streets were so dirty that I wondered the unemployed were not set to cleaning them, for pay, instead of sitting in despair on a dole. My room looked out on a back yard planted with dahlias, Michaelmas daisies, and asters. Sister Turner, the Director of the school, and Sister Doubleday, the Sister Tutor, were as High Anglicans as my friends at Woolwich, and two of the best as well as most devout of women. Although they worked long, hard hours, they liked their staff to get off duty now and then and have a bit of gaiety. To me they were deeply kind.

Sister Turner determined to keep me as well as the Scottish Highlands had made me—so she persuaded me to spend week ends with such of my friends as did not live in slums. Sometimes I stayed in London at Garland's Hotel in Suffolk Street, behind the Haymarket. I became so much attached to this old inn, with its elderly employees, that I truly grieved when I heard it was bombed to bits in the war. My bookseller, Hugh Rees, was within easy walking distance and I went there often to get books for myself and my friends. To this day I keep an account with Hugh Rees, and correspond with Mr. Weekley who can always find English books I want, even those that are out of print. Whenever I was at Garland's on a Sunday, I went in the evening to have supper with Miss Paget. I was made welcome in her circle of friends. In her drawing room, among her Reynolds pictures and Chippendale chairs, she was a lovely embodiment of young old age.

As a graduate student of midwifery I had a wide range of opportunities—more than I can describe within the limits of this book. I attended lectures at the Royal College of Surgeons (two of them by Sir Arthur Keith), and at the Midwives Institute of which I was a member. I took a short instruction course for teachers of midwifery held at the Royal Society of Arts, in the Adelphi, and conducted by various distinguished nurse-midwives and physicians. Among the latter was my friend, Dr. J. S. Fairbairn, about whom I wrote home: "He has the simplicity of all big men in general with the special simplicity of the Scotch added—so you see he really is simple!" The greater part of every morning I spent in the antenatal clinics of the General Lying-In Hospital on York Road. Occasionally I took cases on the district and one whole week, at my own request, I did nothing else. From Monday to Sunday I had six babies, an average of one for each day.

I had spent two weeks in London when I was thirteen years old and had seen many of its historic glories then. While I lived in France I had made my two visits to London, when I met people in all walks of life and saw many fine charitable institutions. But it was not until I worked in London that I began to feel myself a part of her teeming millions. I wrote how I felt about this, at the time, and this is what I said:

In one of the "leaders" of *The London Times* the other day I read these lines: "The secret of London's charm is not revealed to a careless glance. . . . It can only be given, perhaps, in its completeness, to those who will share the burden of her life." So much have I felt this during the past year, that I have added London to the places where some part of my spirit, in the fullness of many memories, will always abide. The town was known and loved by me, through Dickens, as a child. Now since I have lived in mean and twisted streets such as he describes, among the millions of plain people whose throbbing hearts *are* London, and stood by them in the supreme hours of their lives, and yearned over the quiet heroism of their suffering, and watched the beauty of their family ties, which are among the strongest I ever knew, and welcomed their new babies, and threaded my way back in the misty starless night carrying a heavy bag along the same mean and twisted streets, now I have a oneness with London in a sense not unlike Dickens' own. I won't say that in order to know London you have to be a midwife. But I will say that midwives know it right well.

My patients were puzzled by my accent. Sometimes they asked me

148

if I came from "the North Country." As a rule I smiled and shook my head and left them puzzling. Since I was the first American to become a London midwife, they rarely if ever guessed the truth. They called me Nurse Breckinridge—as is the custom in the British Isles, where the title is used for nurses. Dear Cockneys! As I read of the obliteration of so many of you from bombs in the Second World War, a hundred recollections of Woolwich and of Camberwell poured back into my mind to wring my heart.

II

Among the distinguished nurses whom I had met several years before, when I visited Lady Hermione Blackwood in London, was Miss Peterkin, the Superintendent of the Queen Victoria's Jubilee Institute for Nurses in England and Wales. This burdensome title was later changed to the Queen's Institute of District Nursing, of which Her Majesty Queen Mary is the patron. First set up by Queen Victoria, to give nursing care to the sick poor in their homes, the organization was quick to include midwifery in the preparation of the Queen's Nurse. With the advent of preventive medicine, the Institute added the training of "health visitors," as the British call public health nurses. I visited the principal training center at Plaistow, where graduate nurses were taught district nursing, health visiting and midwifery.

In 1924 the Queen's, so Miss Peterkin told me, was fully organized in all but three English and Welsh counties, in affiliation with local voluntary associations and over-all county voluntary committees. That year their nurse-midwives attended 80,147 confinements—roughly two-thirds of them as midwives and one-third as maternity nurses working under a physician. The figures for 1924 were not available in 1924. I got them later from a paper by Dr. Fairbairn, printed in the *British Medical Journal*, which he sent me. The maternal death rate of the Queen's Institute, computed per thousand deliveries, habitually ran below two per cent. This was considerably lower than the national death rate for England and Wales and much, much lower than ours in America at that time. We have had a number of Queen's Nurses on the staff of the Frontier Nursing Service during the last quarter-century. We consider their preparation in district nursing, midwifery and public health the best of any who come to us.

Miss Peterkin told me that the nursing and midwifery in the county of Hertfordshire were exceptionally well organized and well run. So, upon leaving Camberwell, I went to Hertfordshire to make a study to parallel the one I had made of Perthshire. Miss Harrington received me warmly and gave me most of her time during the week I stayed in her county. She was the superintendent of nurses, and also the official inspector of midwives, for a county population of over three hundred thousand people. Some two-thirds of these people lived in twenty-two small towns or "urban districts." Over one hundred thousand of them were rural—but not remotely rural as in Perthshire. Working under Miss Harrington were 140 nurse-midwives. They nursed the sick in their homes; made what the British call "health visits" (with special supervision of children up to the age of five); attended school clinics, baby and toddler clinics, tuberculosis clinics, and did the follow-up visiting for them all; and, finally, they attended, as midwives, nearly three thousand mothers a year. Physicians with special training in obstetrics held modern antenatal clinics to examine the midwives' patients. Physicians with special training in pediatrics held clinics for babies and children under the school age. Medical examinations were held in the schools, at which the nurses assisted. As a system of generalized nursing, including midwifery, it was complete.

The way in which this service was organized and financed was so characteristic of the British philanthropic genius of that day that it needs emphasis. The voluntary committee for the county, of which the Marchioness of Salisbury was the active chairman, employed Miss Harrington as their superintendent of nurses, but a grant was made from the county for her work as inspector of midwives. The educational authorities paid grants for the services of the nurses with the schoolchildren; local authorities all chipped in through their local associations to help out on such things as the nursing of the sick poor, and the follow-up work on babies and toddlers. The county committee and the local associations collected money from those able to give anything, from a few shillings up to many pounds. The patients paid small fees suited to their means. There was even an insurance scheme that covered some of the costs. It will be noted that, although the work was assisted by public grants in aid, its administration was left in the hands of private voluntary groups. Such was the English concept then. It was sensible and effective.

In 1949 the Queen's Institute sent me the copy of an address given at their annual meeting by Mr. Ronald W. Raven, O.B.E., F.R.C.S. The whole paper is an impassioned plea that the Queen's Institute not be swallowed up by the modern National Health Organization; that it be allowed to continue "unhampered and unfettered" along the road of progress it had followed for sixty-two years. He spoke sadly of areas where the local district nursing associations have ceased to exist as such. "Have the sick poor disappeared?" he asked. "There are many more who are poor and the chances are they will be as sick as ever." It is because I am a nurse, and because this book will be read by many nurses, that I give some of the closing words of Mr. Raven's address:

We are living in an age which is painful and toilsome, full of dangers and packed with great labours. It is finite-minded and secular. Eventually, a civilization is doomed which is governed by a secular philosophy. We, therefore, look for the greater age which is spacious, secure, and where the fruit of immortality is found. But how vast is the agony of earth; and where is the pity for the sickness of this world? I feel that much of it is embodied in the Queen's Nurse, seen in every city, town and village of our land, and in lands beyond the seas, following in the footsteps of the Master "who went about doing good," and applying her art in the homes of the people, helping them to a nobler, better way of living. She has a majestic mission—one of the highest vocations of all.

III

I did not sail for home (January 14, 1925, on the *Rotterdam* of the Holland-American Line) until six weeks after my visit in Hertford-shire. There were still several things that I wanted to do. Mrs. A. M. Dike begged me not to leave Europe without a return visit to France. She offered me her car and chauffeur, old Camille, who knew all of the places I would want to visit again. She said she would use Miss Morgan's car which was "eating its head off in the stable." So I went to France on a trip in which pleasure and heartaches were mingled. Several of my old French friends were dead, among them Mme Gervais Courtellemont and my little godson, Jean. Those who were living overwhelmed me with flowers and kindness—among them the de Reisets, Jeanne de Joannis and Marcelle Monod. Our work at Reims had closed down long before, but much of the Aisne work had continued under the name of the Association d'Hygiène Sociale de L'Aisne (Fondation du C.A.R.D., 1923). Marcelle Monod was no longer connected with it but I met again a few of the Bordeaux nurses of our early days.

From France I returned to Garland's Hotel. In and around London there were several hospital training schools for midwives, baby welfare stations, and other institutions and nursing units that I wanted to see before my long preparation for the Frontier Nursing Service had ended. I forbear to give the names of any of them, but from all I gleaned useful facts about labor bags and their contents, records, breast feeding, supervision, treatments, and lots besides. These all went into my notebook for future reference. While I was busy with all of this my friend, Mary Beard, who had been so kind to me when I had gone to her Boston Instructive District Nursing Association, came over to London to make an investigation of midwifery for the Rockefeller Foundation. We made many trips to institutions together, and it was a joy to me to introduce her to my professional friends.

Those who feed on Jane Austen will remember that Mrs. Allen and Catherine Morland, in *Northanger Abbey*, yearned for "acquaintance" when they first went to Bath. In London I had an extensive "acquaintance" as well as friends, who were not all in the nursing world. For some years I had been interested in psychical research, in which I had read deeply. For example, I have in my library at Wendover all of the books by Sir Oliver Lodge on that much-slighted branch of knowledge. Through his courtesy, I was given a ticket to attend a lecture (in French) by Professor Richet, famous French physiologist, given under the auspices of the English Society for Psychical Research, with Sir Oliver in the chair. Professor Richet described demonstrations he and Sir Oliver had conducted together. He commented on the fact that they both testified to their reality and that they were not "*des imbéciles,*" those two! He then went on to say that although Sir Oliver thought that the power which produced these demonstrations came from a life beyond death he, Richet, had not yet reached that conclusion. He added that if such a conclusion is reachable, "*Ce sera une vérité splendide.*"

Through my membership in the London Spiritualist Alliance (an old and studious group) I had made friendships with other people who were, like me, interested in psychical research. I spent week ends with some of these and with school chums of my Rosemont days. My "acquaintance" in London included my friends of the days in France, Lady Hermione Blackwood and Miss du Sautoy, and several people I had met on my visit to Lady Hermione. Among the latter was Mrs. Bedford Fenwick, founder of the International Council of Nurses, with whom I dined in an enchanting old house in Westminster. Her interest in the Frontier Nursing Service remained keen throughout her life. When Florence Nightingale's house at 10 South Street was torn down, she sent us one of the bricks. In 1949–50, when we built the Margaret Voorhies Haggin Quarters for Nurses at our Hyden Hospital, this brick was placed in the stone chimney of the sitting room, above the buckeye mantel.

Several times I went out to Woolwich to see all that I could of my friends, Maud Cashmore and Lillian Neild. The wards at the British, where I had begun my work as a pupil-midwife, and formed my first attachments for the dockyard people, were bombed into rubble during the Second World War. Maud Cashmore wrote me afterward that the patients had all been moved into the cellars (St. Michael's in the Basement, they called them) and no one was hurt, but "it was horrid," she said, to see the open night where the roofs had been.

The great English exhibition was on at Wembley. To this I took Sister Laura Turner. I engaged a Cook's guide so that we could do it in style and in one afternoon. I am still of the same mind about exhibitions as I was when I wrote home:

We were rushed through the sights—the last way under heaven to see mellow sights but the best for exhibitions. The kaleidoscopic view so obtained of the extent and variedness of the British Empire was unforgettable. But I didn't enjoy it, not really. I don't care for rows of ears of corn and miles of machinery and heaps of photographs and skeletons done in ivory out of tusks and artificial lakes and mixed architectures and coasters and East Africans in shells and the insides of Canadian Pullmans and crowded tearooms and uncut diamonds and the Prince of Wales in butter. That is my third large exhibition and my last. The first I went to as a child in Geneva, the second as a girl in St. Louis. This London one finishes me off. I am never going to have to do that again.

As Christmas drew near, the theaters were enchanting with their pantomimes, their revival of Barrie's plays, and the *Midsummer Night's Dream*, at Drury Lane, with Mendelssohn's music. Although it was my second Christmas season in London, it was the first in which I had had time for such things. Miss Paget took me to Drury Lane, and to what I loved most of all—the medieval "Bethlehem" play given in the Church House of Westminster Abbey. During the play the choristers danced down the aisles, as was the old custom, singing "The Holly and the Ivy." To the Abbey I went often to stand by the tomb of the Unknown Soldier, and the tomb, in the Cloisters, of little Jane Lister, who died some two hundred years ago. Under her name is engraved, "DEARE CHILD."

IV

My oldest friend, among them all in England, was the daughter of the American engineer and his wife that we had known and loved in Russia. She had married an Englishman and lived in Derbyshire at a place called The Yelt. The ties between us were such warm ones that she and her husband asked me to be the godmother of their first son. While I was staying at The Yelt with Frances and Tom, reveling in country life again, a plan went through that was to take me to York, and the beginning of an adventure from which there is no turning back, in this world or the next. Since it is hard to recapture the freshness of a first encounter, I shall tell you, my readers, about this in the words I wrote my father then:

I went on to York to see Sister Cashmore's sister Adeline, who is an anchoress and lives in the Church of All Saints on North Street. I love Maud Cashmore so much and admire so deeply her splendid administration of the maternity at Woolwich, her unselfish and intelligent devotion, that I wanted to meet this loved sister of hers—but I would have been no more surprised to learn she was a zebra as an anchoress. She has taken no vows, but seven years ago she came to the conclusion that she could best help the world by prayer instead of through social work, which was what she was doing, and came to live in the cell of this old church, last inhabited by another anchoress five hundred years ago, and she divides her time between prayer (not for herself but for others) and acting as sacristan of the church—which gives her many hours of practical work to do. The church is in the heart of a slum. She also sees special people, but only by appointment through the local clergyman as otherwise she would be much interrupted, and often by curiosity seekers only. My object in going to see her was because she was the sister of my friend, in whose active goodness I have unbounded trust. My appointment was made through a quaint old clergyman, by letter, and it ran like a timetable:

1:00 P.M. Sext

1:05   Me

1:10   A.C. (for Adeline Cashmore)

I didn't know what the "Sext" stood for. Frances and I puzzled over it at length and concluded it meant the sexton, but it turned out to be a devotional service. That sort of thing shows the immense latitude allowed in the English Church. Frances, a lifelong member of that church, had never heard of a Sext, because she was Low and it is High—and St. Martin's in the Fields which I love to attend in London would be called Broad, given over to good works, seeking to express religion much in terms of life, and even in some of its services departing from the prescribed rituals altogether for silent community prayer.

I was at All Saints by one and was greatly struck by its old-world charm. It is indeed quite a famous small church with some of the best stained glass in England. The clergyman has gotten up a beautiful book about it, for he knows its history and its art intimately. I sat down on a bench. There came into the church the loveliest woman I think I ever met, smiling and happy, with hands outstretched to greet me and a sort of white light coming from her that could be felt and almost seen. I was most deeply moved by her. After Sext (!) and after I had had five minutes with the old clergyman, who received me kindly because of my friendship with Maud Cashmore, but with a series of questions not unlike those put to me at the Bow Street police station when I went to register as an alien, and had taken in the friendly atmosphere of the place, with the two comfortable-looking elderly aunts of aforesaid clergyman bustling about with parcels, Adeline took me to the "anchorhold," which was the cell of the former anchoress of five hundred years ago, and is still just a stone cell, reached by a worn flight of stone stairs.

The thing which quickly impressed me was that there was no pose of ancient-ness. The furnishings consisted of an iron bed without pillows, a cheap modern rug on the stone floor, a cheap modern nickel clock, a deal table, and electric light and heat introduced because it was easy and cheap, and could be used for what cooking she does. But of course a little electric contraption doesn't really warm that damp cell. Modern windows had been cut in and they were all open. I shivered, but she quickly closed all but one and lit the contraption, turned it on rather, and gave me the only chair and sat opposite on her bed, and we talked

154

for two hours. I told her about her sister and about Sister Neild, our mutual friend, and she was so natural and merry and kind that I cannot describe her. Think of the sanest, the sweetest, the brightest person you know and you will approach a conception of Adeline. In such a general letter I cannot go into the other things we talked of, but the gist of them was that God is love and that no one who loves is far from Him, and that He doesn't despise broken and contrite hearts.

Of course I don't explain Adeline. I can't try. She is a fragrance, a light, an unexplainable suggestion of the real things of which we are shadows, most of us. She is a mystic and thinks that prayer is the channel by means of which the human is brought in touch with the divine, and that one can help that meeting by holding the thought of others before God in prayer. It is not asking for things, not formula, not telling God what to do. It is obeying a spiritual law as real as the law of gravitation, the law by means of which people come in touch with God and learn to do His will, and one can do it for others, just as one can nurse others or clothe them. It is like washing windows for the light of God's love to shine through. But I am explaining it badly. . . .

I had one more meeting with Adeline before I left England. I was a coward about Christmas, and especially the Christmas of 1924 when I had no hard and useful work to do. Among the letters that my father kept is one written to him and to my Aunt Frances and my Aunt Jane in Kentucky, in which I said that I did not know how I was going to get through the Christmas of 1924 until Adeline told me I might spend it at York. For the first time in seven years I was in peace.

I went to the midnight service at All Saints. On Christmas Day I had two hours with Adeline, only two, but tons of aching pain went out of me in her presence. Then I walked for hours along the river Ouse, and made the circle of the town on the top of the old wall, and hung about the Minster, and felt it was true that:

> Dull must he be of soul who could pass by
> A sight so touching in its majesty.

After that I went to my room at the hotel and had a fire, and still it was peace.

The day after Christmas I saw Adeline again before I caught an afternoon train back to London. Then the little old-world church and cell, and the lovely person who transfigured one's life in them, and the children from the mean streets who ran in and out and played about Adeline while she did her work as sacristan—these all passed into that realm of spiritual things where reality begins. Adeline said to me, "There is no time—spiritually I think there is no past or present—that is just one of our purely natural seemings, and memory, which brings past things into living reality for us, is the shadow of a spiritual fact."

V

It is a rare thing in this world to know a saint, and the impact upon one's life of such a person is stupendous. During the thirty years which lay between my first meeting with Adeline in York and her death in India during the war, I don't think I saw her more than thirty hours in all. But her letters guided me, and I knew that she took me with her through that real world where she habitually lived, of which our world with its memories is but a shadow.

In my halting way—with failures to come innumerable—I began at York an adventure in the life of the spirit. It is as though one went through the Looking Glass, not to travel in a land of phantasy but to reach the only country where things are real. All values are turned inside-out on this journey. I can best describe it as a slow movement from our grown-up childishness, with its instabilities, to childlikeness.

No road is harder to follow than the inside-out one—where shams and evasions must be fought each mile of the way—but it is the road to which Christ pointed when He said we must become as young children in order to enter the kingdom of God. Breckie was a Great-Heart; Adeline a Valiant-for-Truth. In their company traveled one called Mr. Ready-to-Halt. But even to this one, a post came from the celestial city, who said, "I am come from Him whom thou hast loved and followed, though upon crutches; and my message is to tell thee that He expects thee at His table to sup with Him in His kingdom."

The story of the Frontier Nursing Service could not have been told but for Adeline. Until her death in South India, she held us in her prayer—as I am sure she does now. The blunders we have made were ours. The good things we have done came to pass because Adeline carried us, and our endeavors, with her to the Source of all good. Her windows were kept so clean that Life and Love and Light streamed through them—to reach the maimed and the halt and the blind.

What did she get out of it all for herself? In her many letters of counsel and encouragement, of humor and charm, she wrote almost nothing about herself, but I remember a service at All Saints in York where a hymn was sung which gives our answer:

> The King of love my Shepherd is,
>   Whose goodness faileth never;
> I nothing lack if I am His
>   And He is mine forever.

156

Chapter 17

I

EARLY in 1925 I came back to Kentucky. The years spent in getting ready to work for children had ended. It was time to begin. If I had known all that lay ahead of me in the next quarter-century, I wonder if I would have had the courage to launch the small movement destined to grow into the Frontier Nursing Service. One day, when I was overwhelmed by the responsibility we had assumed, I sought out Scott Breckinridge to ask him how we could have taken on so much and if we could not carry less. He replied that we would have to carry more, not less. He said, "And had we failed to do it we would have been untrue to everything that has come down to us from the past." *Noblesse oblige?* For him, yes, but not for me. Scott and I had been raised by the same family code—one which did not admit the shirking of responsibility. But, insofar as I am concerned, the steps I had taken since Breckie's death had not so much been chosen by me as thrust upon me, by something inside of me that came from beyond me. Although I seemed to make my own plans, I doubt if I did. But I was free to bungle them.

Elsewhere in this book I have given the reasons why my work for children placed its emphasis on the little ones and, among these, the country dwellers. If my readers have accepted these reasons, then there are two questions which may occur to them—in fact, have occurred to many people—and these are: "Why did you begin in Kentucky?" "Why did you not extend the work to other areas, such as Puerto Rico and Alaska?" I shall answer the second question first. Administrative costs of a demonstration are much higher if the demonstration is located in several areas, and in scattering you do not reach more people.

There are several answers to the first question. Not only was there no reason why the Kentucky mountains should not be chosen, but we had the best of all reasons for choosing them, namely, their inaccessibility. I felt that if the work I had in mind could be done there, it could be duplicated anywhere else in the United States with less effort. From the beginning I had the wish to do the work so well, and to keep such accurate records of it, that others would study it, be trained in its techniques, and then, in other remotely rural parts of our own and other countries, repeat the system we used. It would be possible for us to reach only a few thousand children directly, but hundreds of thousands of children could be reached by others because of us. Our inaccessibility was a priceless asset. None who wanted to copy our work could plead that it would be more difficult for them than it had been for us.

A second advantage to me in setting up the demonstration in Kentucky was that I would be working in a part of the world where my family name was known and I would be accepted without explanation, because I belonged. As an example of this, I recall speaking at a rally of mountaineers at a place some twenty-odd horseback miles from a railroad. The rally had been called by local leading citizens who had asked us to place one of our nursing centers in their section. They indicated what they were prepared to do in the way of gifts of lumber, use of mule teams, a site for the nursing center, several days of free labor from men before they took pay at the prevailing rate of fifteen cents an hour. Then the chairman of the rally introduced me, so that I could explain what we had in mind. He said that he didn't know me but that my people had held "high office" in Kentucky, and none of them had betrayed a public trust. Therefore, he was willing to guarantee that the local citizens could trust me too.

A third reason for the choice of Kentucky, a vital one, was Dr. Arthur T. McCormack, Health Commissioner for the Commonwealth, an imaginative man of rare ability. Many were the conferences I had with him that spring of 1925. He not only approved of what I wanted to do but he, almost alone, understood it. It was his suggestion that we establish our first nursing center on the Middle Fork of the Kentucky River, in Leslie County, in the heart of a thousand-square-mile area covering parts of several counties, where some fifteen thousand people lived without benefit of one resident state-licensed physician. He gave me a certificate licensing me to practice midwifery in Kentucky.

A final reason for locating the demonstration in Kentucky lay in the fact that I had hundreds of kindred and family friends in that state, who were willing to back me up. A few of the physicians who were my cousins—among them Scott Breckinridge, Josephine Hunt, John Scott, Julian Estill, Waller Bullock—knew what I was setting out to do. Waller said to me, "There isn't one of us, Mary, that won't stand by you." All of that helped—God! (and I say it reverently) how it helped!

Among Kentuckians there is a strong sense of family solidarity not unlike that in the old Scottish clan. We stand by our own people unto the fourth and fifth generations. In my family there is as much English as Scottish blood, but the clanship probably comes through the Scottish strains. As I went about my work of forming a committee to back me up, I stayed with members of the clan. Before the spring was over I had completed the organization of a group of nearly seventy people. We called ourselves just what we were—a Kentucky Committee for Mothers and Babies.

Our members came from highlands and lowlands, from town and country. Five of them did not live in Kentucky at all. They included prominent ministers of various denominations, well-known politicians of both parties, physicians of many specialties, and men high in the educational, business, legal and newspaper worlds. Represented also were those who had been active in establishing the mountain settlement schools. Early mountain workers on a heroic scale were Miss Linda Neville and Dr. J. A. Stucky. They had started the cleanup of trachoma, and were more instrumental than all others in getting the U.S. Public Health Service to take it on.

Of the members of that first committee I wrote Breckie's godmother: "They are our nucleus—first fruits of public sentiment—and they have been garnered 'one by each'—not in a bunch. It couldn't have been done without the Spirit."

II

On May 28, 1925 the Kentucky Committee for Mothers and Babies held its first meeting in the Assembly Room at the Capitol Hotel in Frankfort, Kentucky, to form an organization and to elect its executive officers. The secretary then, Mrs. W. H. Coffman of Scott County, has been our Recording Secretary for twenty-six unbroken years. In her minutes of this initial meeting, two things stand out as significant. One is the fact that the goal at which we were aiming was clearly seen by everyone that took part in the formation of what was to become the Frontier Nursing Service. Judge Edward C. O'Rear of Frankfort, who opened the meeting, said that he was impressed by the program, by "its sublime audacity," and felt sure of its success. He said he knew of the conditions and possibilities of the mountains from having been a part of them; that wherever you find a highland people they are the seed corn of the world. The other thing that impresses me now is the flexibility of the early plans we made. Research is a continuing thing. As one acts, one gets an insight of what is best for the next action. It is better to begin small, as we did, without theoretical ideas of methods of administration, expansion, and finance.

We provided for essential things—an annual audit; accurate records of the work we were to do; arrangements for medical consultations and hospital care for our patients (too far away, but the best we could do then); the status, legal and professional, of the nurse-midwives of whom we expected to make use; the choice of a place where "the value of this service shall be demonstrated first," with reciprocal membership provided between a local committee and the central committee; honorary membership on the Kentucky Committee of the State Health Officer *ex officio;* an executive group, with officers, which would have all the powers and responsibilities of the Kentucky Committee when it was not in session, and which should "pass on names for membership and present them to the Kentucky Committee meetings for ratification, receive and disburse funds, determine budgets, receive and distribute reports, organize auxiliary committees in other states as requested, determine questions of finance, supplies, records, policies, in co-operation with the directing nurse-midwife, and, wherever policies are local, with the Branch Committee." These essentials were embodied in a series of Resolutions, which Mrs. S. C. Henning of Louisville presented to the meeting for adoption.

It was not until the following November that Judge O'Rear drew up articles of incorporation for us, and we adopted them, with flexible by-laws. It was not until 1928 that we amended these articles when we changed our name to the Frontier Nursing Service. By that time we had many more committees than the initial Kentucky one, with its first local reciprocal branch committee, and our work had taken on the national significance inherent in it from the beginning. At our initial meeting we elected our executive group and officers. We chose Dr. Alexander J. A. Alexander of "Woodburn" in Woodford County as our first Chairman and Mr. C. N. Manning, President of the Security Trust Company of Lexington, as our first Treasurer.

The members at this meeting asked me to send out printed reports of the progress of the work throughout the year. That is the genesis of the *Quarterly Bulletin* of the Frontier Nursing Service. Volume I, Number 1, June, 1925, has: "Application for entry as second-class matter is pending." This continues to be printed in every issue until Volume III, Number 1, May, 1927, which shows that our application had been accepted and we were entered as second-class matter at the post office in Lexington, Kentucky, where our *Bulletin* has always been printed. Volume III is the first volume to be a true quarterly and have four issues in the year. The first two volumes had only three—something that puzzles librarians when they ask for a complete file.

Seasons instead of months are first used in Volume VI, Number 1. The *Bulletin* was not copyrighted until Volume VIII, Number 1.

At the Frankfort meeting I asked for a motion that was the result of my conversations with Dr. McCormack. He had told me that no matter how much we were able to lower the death rate of women in childbirth and of babies in the first month, and the first year, of life; no matter whether we had fewer stillbirths or not—we would have no way of knowing we had done so unless we first made a survey of all the births and deaths in Leslie County (where we intended to begin) to find out how many had not been reported since registration became legal in 1911. Dr. McCormack introduced me to Mr. J. F. Blackerby, Chief of the Bureau of Vital Statistics of the State Department of Health. He said he would give us forms to fill in for the families in Leslie County if we would arrange to visit each family and get hold of all unreported births and deaths of the past fourteen years. This was indeed a monumental task, but it had to be done. Although Kentucky had come into the United States registration area in 1911, the registration of births and deaths was incomplete in the mountain sections, particularly where there were no physicians. After a conference with Dr. McCormack, Mr. Blackerby, and the latter's brother, Dr. Phillip E. Blackerby (a dear man, who meant much to us in the years to come), I accepted their argument, and cast about for the person to put in charge of this survey. In Sir Leslie MacKenzie's report on the *Physical Welfare of Scottish Mothers and Children*, I had read this:

Miss Bertram Ireland acted as Secretary to the Inquiry. She visited, by herself or with some other investigator, many of the localities and institutions described. To her skill, tact and patience in collecting and recording facts, the Report owes much of its most valuable material.

Correspondence with Sir Leslie gave me two pieces of information—that Miss Ireland could ride horseback; that she was doing a special piece of work in the United States. Correspondence with her led to a leave of absence for the summer months to allow her to make our survey. This led to the motion that we engage Miss Ireland for our survey of births and deaths.

We now had all we needed to get going—except money. In calling my group together, I did not ask any of them for money because I was sure that most of them, and others as well, would volunteer to give it once we had made a beginning and shown what it was all about. To Mr. Manning, when I asked him to become Treasurer, and to others of the Executive Committee when it was formed, I promised to underwrite the work for the first three years and meet whatever deficits we incurred. This was not known by anybody else for twenty-five years. I didn't want to do this, because it would have to be done out of my capital and I liked having an independent income. But no other way to get started opened up, so it was plain I had it to do. It was just one of those things.

Shortly before our first meeting in Frankfort, my Aunt Mary Maltby ("Aunt Jane") told me that she would give $100 as an indication of what people of moderate means should subscribe to get the work started. About the same time I had a letter from Mrs. Dike in France stating that she wanted a finger in my pie and enclosing a check for $50. To these two gifts I added $1,000 to carry the summer's work—but I put it in the name of my Grandmother Lees from whom my money had come, and in memory of my mother. Thus the first money to come to the Frontier Nursing Service, and all there was until the fall, when others subscribed spontaneously, stood for old ties of Kentucky, of France, and of the Hazelwood of my childhood. It was good to have it start like that.

III

The heroine of the summer was "Ireland of Scotland," as we called Miss Bertram Ireland. In a June letter to Cousin Cabell Bullock I wrote: "She has begun her work on 'Hell-fer-Sartin' Creek and Devil's Jump Branch—really! She is blistered, sore, stiff, and undaunted." With a detailed map issued by the Geological Survey Department and a darling horse, Rickie, she started out to cover all the houses in a county of 376 square miles, with a river, many creeks, their forks and branches, and innumerable high mountain gaps and steep trails. We had bought a couple of horses at Berea. As the easiest way of getting them into the mountains, we rode them in ourselves. The distance was not so long as the one followed by the motor road today, which is ninety miles, because there was no motor road and we took several short cuts.

After Ireland of Scotland had done three weeks of traveling, it was obvious to us both that she couldn't possibly complete the survey that summer without help. Among the leading citizens I had come to know well was Miss Zilpha Roberts, a teacher, born in Leslie County, with an intimate knowledge of some of its most inaccessible sections. She gladly gave us two months of her time. A quick and accurate worker, she covered a lot of ground but even she said that "the next census should be taken by airplane and parachute!" As she dismounted one day at a rough gap she stepped on a long snake, which liked the contact as little as she and moved away fast. To her horror, she stepped on him again and then a third time so that, in her own words, she "danced a jubilee on that old snake all the way down the mountain."

But even two efficient workers were not enough to complete a survey carried forward on horseback. When Miss Freda Caffin and Miss Edna Rockstroh, the first nurse-midwives we engaged, arrived towards the end of July we had to ask them both to help with the survey before starting their nursing work at Hyden. They consented at once, and managed to give advice, bandage sores, and bathe wounds while traveling as rapidly as their horses could take them from one house to another, gathering statistics.

The difficulties of this study did not lie only in the hard travel and the discomforts of sleeping in overcrowded houses wherever night fell. It was not easy to gather data covering a period of fourteen years in a country where calendars and diaries and marriage lines and birth certificates and even clocks were so uncommon as to be of little help in marking the passage of time. As to burial permits, there were none. Where the births and marriages and deaths had been put down in the family Bible, the interviews could go along quickly enough—but where a loose sheet of paper or an old notebook or even a store catalogue had to be hunted up from a certain old box kept in the depths of a trunk, then the interviews took longer. When memories had to be relied upon, and consultations with the whole assembled family were necessary, our workers tried to forget their fear of not getting over the next mountain in daylight. They heard tales of dark nights when wildcats cast themselves on the heads of tired travelers. They met snakes slithering along the bridle paths. Although it was a dry summer there were enough storms to bring small tides in the creeks and river which made travel difficult, and sometimes dangerous or impossible, for a day or two. The one compensation for our workers, and it never failed them, was the consideration and courtesy of all of the people whose homes they visited. Miss Ireland said she could not recall one instance of anything but patience and helpfulness. She said the people were truly a "clever" people, using the word in its old meaning of generous, hospitable.

By September the survey was finished, with not one family in Leslie County unvisited. Our forms went to Mr. Blackerby at the State Board of Health in Louisville. When he and his assistants had finished their tabulations we learned that we had secured ten per cent more births than had been reported during the fourteen years and seventeen per cent more deaths. We now had the facts we needed as a basis of comparison with our own records in the days to come.

It was not only in the tabulations of the results of our survey that we were indebted to Mr. Blackerby. He, like his brother and Dr. McCormack, feared I was unmindful of the difficulties that lay ahead of me. Although they brought many of these to my attention, they backed me up and cheered me on. Of the two who are no longer with us, Mr. Blackerby has written me: "To the day of their deaths, nothing thrilled Dr. McCormack and Dr. Blackerby quite as much as recounting to friends and audiences the success of your venture."

IV

While our workers were busy with their survey, I ran across them from time to time as I rode over Leslie County engaged in my immediate task of enlisting the co-operation of leading citizens to form our first branch committee. It was a pleasant task because I had friends in many parts of the county dating from the summer two years before when I had covered so much of the same territory. Then, too, I had met the J. D. Begleys of Hyden at a conference in Alpine, Tennessee. Judge L. D. Lewis, Judge Theophilus Lewis, and their wives, took me under their wings. The names of other friends will crop up later in the story.

My chief woe during the summer was the lack of a decent horse. With the help of my cousin William Preston, I had bought a magnificent horse, Teddy Bear, who was to become one of my closest friends in the years ahead. I didn't have time to ride him into the mountains from Lexington myself, so I engaged a man to do it for me. He put him overnight in a barn that had a nail sticking out of the studding. On this Teddy Bear caught his leg just above the foot. With his foot hanging, and not liking it, he pulled out a piece of the barn and tore himself badly. Teddy Bear's rider had the sense to take him to Dr. Cleaves, the Clay County Livestock Inspector and a fine veterinarian, who gave him serum and other treatment, but there was a bad abscess. It was not until the autumn that Teddy Bear could be ridden. A second horse we had ordered for the Service turned up with a sore eye. I wrote Cousin Cabell that it would have been convenient to have eye and nail on the same horse, leaving one for riding purposes. I had to hire a right old mule. A mule with a good running walk is the best of all saddle animals, but my mule wasn't that sort at all.

As I rode from place to place I gave such nursing care as I could to the sick people I met, especially the babies. So many of those in their second summer had such terrible dysenteries that I carried two tiny catheters with me in my saddlebags in order to give them colon irrigations. Sometimes I was able to hand a pink baby back to a mother who had given me a blue one. When I had done all I could for the child, I talked with its mother, and with other mothers who gathered around me, not only about how to take care of the sick babies, but how to feed all the second summer babies in such a way as to keep them well. It was because my nursing skill helped the sick babies that

164

the mothers welcomed my suggestions. Most of them had potatoes. I explained why these should be baked and not fried, and eggs boiled and not fried. I told them tomato juice was good but not to give cucumbers—which I found more than once to be part of the diet of a baby in its second summer. As to bread, I told them to take the crusts of the corn bread and bake them in the oven for the babies. In one of my many letters to Cousin Cabell Bullock, who did endless errands for me in Lexington, I find one of August 2 from Hyden which says:

I have returned from the eastern end of the county. Yesterday I passed by a schoolhouse where they were voting, and the women had come with their children. When they heard I was there (I haven't any idea how they knew it, or that I was a nurse—I had stopped off only to see a leading citizen for my committee) they came crowding around me with their sickly babies—so many it fairly broke my heart—and begging for a nurse for their part of the county, and offering to house her (heaven help them, their overcrowded cabins hardly hold themselves), and I stayed over an hour holding a little clinic, washing out one very sick baby that had dysentery, etc. The crowd of mothers with their little ones looked like a Biblical picture.

I had to ride to the railroad several times during the summer, and in September, to meet with members of my committee and to get supplies. Before we started our regular nursing work, we knew that we would need tons of typhoid serum because typhoid fever was endemic in Leslie County. We would need diphtheria serum too, smallpox vaccine, treatment for hookworm and other worms, and basic supplies in advance of setting up our first clinic. I also wanted to put orders with the printers for our first nursing records. On one of my trips out, I made a visit to Dr. Lillian H. South (Director of Laboratory Service of the State Board of Health) who arranged to send us quantities of typhoid serum and to get for us the toxin-antitoxin which was used at that time for diphtheria immunization. I never shall forget her kindness to me then, and to all of us in the years that followed. Pages of my early letters back to the nurses at Hyden are filled with her advice. I made a connection with an old drug company, Peter-Neat-Richardson, and told them to honor all orders that came down from Hyden. I find that as early as September I had croup kettles sent up from another house, hypodermic needles, baby scales, fish kettles for boiling supplies, lanterns for the barns, fire screens—all kinds of things to be hauled across from Krypton (on a spur of the Louisville and Nashville Railroad) while the river was low enough for fording. Even before our survey and the organization of our first local committee had been completed, we ran into patients that just naturally had to get out of the mountains for medical and hospital care. These we invariably routed through my cousin, Dr. Josephine D. Hunt, who, like Scott

Breckinridge, is one of the people without whom our work could not have gotten under way.

In midsummer, while I was like the man in the *Nonsense Novels*, riding madly in all directions, I had a letter from my younger brother Clif that started me off for the railroad, and Lexington, as soon as I read it. He, now Captain Breckinridge, had come back to the United States from Germany not long before, was about to leave the Army, and could meet me at Lexington on short notice. It was in my heart to give him a homecoming that would put him in touch with his people and make up, insofar as I could, for the loss of his mother and his homes during the years he had been in Europe. We stayed with the Carter cousins at Shirley in Woodford County. Desha Breckinridge engaged one of the country clubs near Lexington for me, so that I could give Clif a family party to which I invited all of the kinsmen within driving distance—around a hundred people. This party has a place in the story of the Frontier Nursing Service because it was there I met my first secretary, Martha Prewitt of Dunreath in Fayette County. I might add that in the same girl Clif met his future wife. Although Martha had been invited as one of the young dancing crowd, she and Clif were cousins of sorts, through the Rodes branch of the family. In fact, her given name was Martha Rodes and his Clifton Rodes.

The climax of my summer's work came on August 22 when we inaugurated our first branch committee. We had an attendance of thirty-five members at the county seat of Hyden, in the courthouse, turned over to us during a term of court through the courtesy of the district judge. Many members had ridden their mules and horses for hours to be present, one woman spending the day in the saddle, coming and going, with her baby over one arm. The courthouse was jammed to capacity with interested onlookers. Three of our state executive officers, Mrs. Henning, Mrs. Carter and Judge O'Rear, came up to the mountains to open the meeting, and welcome the local committee into the state group. We presented our program in detail. It was accepted in thrilling speeches by Judge L. D. Lewis, by Mr. J. H. Hart, the County Superintendent of Schools, and by Judge John Muncey, the editor of our weekly, *The Thousandsticks*. Mr. Walter Hoskins of Hyden presented a set of Resolutions which were adopted unanimously. "From now on," so I wrote at the time, "in our plans as in our aims, we move together."

V

Elsewhere in this book I have written of my liking to begin small, take root, and only then start to grow. A tiny plant above ground was the Frontier Nursing Service when its roots began pushing deep into the culture of its native soil. Over the years the plant has grown, throwing out branches, as it has sought to become a banian of the forest, "yielding shade and fruit to wide neighborhoods of men."

Hyden Hospital and Health Center with its large acreage, many buildings, Medical Director's quarters, Graduate School, laboratory, X-rays, came to pass bit by bit over the years, but we made a start with what we could get and could afford, namely, the only vacant house in Hyden. This was a two-story dwelling in bad repair, long since torn down, but there was room for a dispensary and there was a barn for the horses. We had no plumbing but the outside conveniences were decent, and we had a clean well.

The medical, nursing and teaching staff of today, and the nurse-midwives at our outpost centers, were then a part of the undisclosed future. But the two nurses with whom we made a beginning were fully qualified in public health and midwifery, and carried the welfare of the mothers and their babies—of all the children—in their hearts. Today there is a suite of rooms at Hyden Hospital and Health Center for the huge out-patient clinics. But the one-room dispensary with which we started was clean and had the indispensable equipment for taking blood pressures, giving typhoid vaccine, and all the rest.

Our trained statisticians were to come later, through a grant from the Carnegie Corporation, but from the start we had records and report sheets and kept them carefully. A bookkeeper was yet to be, but we held on to our vouchers, and our auditors said we gave full accountability for every dollar spent. In the years ahead we were to have offices at Wendover, an executive secretary, a staff to carry the volume of our growing work and correspondence. Hyden was to have a hospital secretary, and a secretary for the Medical Director. But when we started, I had no secretary at all—because we couldn't afford one. I had a 1912 vintage typewriter, and I was so strong that I could spend half the night writing orders and letters after a day in the saddle. Our blue-gray riding uniform has been ours for so long that I find it hard to remember we had no uniforms at first—just riding togs. We still own and use many horses. In addition, we have now a station wagon ambulance, a truck, twelve jeeps. But there wasn't a motor road within sixty miles when our work began, so that horses and mule teams provided all the transport we had. It's been rather like Edward Lear's jingle of "The Jumblies":

> They went to sea in a sieve, they did,
> In a sieve they went to sea,
> In spite of all their friends could say,
> On a winter's morn, on a stormy day,
> In a sieve they went to sea.

And when the sieve turned round and round,
And everyone cried, "You'll all be drowned,"
They called aloud, "Our sieve ain't big,
But we don't care a button; we don't care a fig:
   In a sieve we'll go to sea!"

And in twenty years they all came back,
In twenty years or more.
And everyone said, "How tall they've grown
For they've been to the Lakes and the torrible zone,
And the hills of the Chankly Bore."
And they drank their health, and gave them a feast
Of dumplings made with beautiful yeast.
And everyone said, "If we only live,
We, too, will go to sea in a sieve
To the hills of the Chankly Bore."

Chapter 18

I

Kentucky was first explored by the Anglo-Saxon race, about the middle of the eighteenth century. It then formed a vast hunting-ground upon which the savage tribes of the south and of the north killed the elk and buffalo, and occasionally encountered each other in bloody conflict. No permanent settlements existed within its borders. Its dark forests and cane thickets separated the Cherokees, Creeks, and Catawbas of the south, from the hostile tribes of Shawanees, Delawares, and Wyandots of the north. Each, and all of these tribes, encountered the Anglo-American pioneer, and fiercely disputed the settlement of the country.

—*Outline History*, 1846, quoted in
COLLINS' *History of Kentucky*, 1874

THE Kentucky mountaineer has been written up and talked about as though he were a special kind of *Homo sapiens*. I have knocked around the world a lot in my time and have never found any people in it but men, women, and children—with no two of them alike. This delectable variety is as true of Kentucky mountaineers as of everybody else. But the picture that people from beyond the mountains hold of them is uniform. They see a lean man with a gun tending his moonshine still, while his wife and fifteen children clutter his one-room log cabin by night and plow his hillside by day. If he speaks at all before shooting, it will be in words too archaic for comprehension.

The Kentucky mountaineers do undoubtedly hold certain characteristics in common. They are all of British descent, with here and there a sprinkling of Huguenot and Pennsylvania Dutch. They, unlike the people of the seaboard colonies, have only recently emerged from pioneer days—but this is startlingly true of all old stock Kentuckians. "Miss Doll" and "Miss Jo" Carter, who lived in the oldest brick house in Woodford County, in the Blue Grass, were alive only a few years ago—and their mother had been carried away by Indians! She was about five years old at the time and the settlers did not get her and her little sister back until she was nearly twelve. The only English she remembered, and had taught to her little sister, although neither understood it, was the Lord's Prayer. This they repeated every night during their long captivity. I used to look at her portrait, that of a highly civilized woman, and think how strange it was that I should know the daughters of a woman who had been carried off by Indians.

The recent pioneer inheritance that the mountaineer shares with other Kentuckians of the old stock is more acutely his in modern times because the modern world is just beginning to come up with him. His ancestors—trail blazers, Indian fighters, individualists all—chose to take possession of the Kentucky mountains where they would be beholden to none. When the lower lands had been subdued to what is called civilization, the highlands remained out of touch because of their extreme inaccessibility. This resulted in two things. First, the customs and the language of an earlier Anglo-Saxon age continued to flower. All sorts of lovely words of Chaucerian and Shakespearean descent remained in use, while legends and ballads that go back to the Old Country were passed on from mother to child. Within the memory of living men, the Julian Christmas on the sixth of January—Old Christmas—was observed instead of the Gregorian Christmas of today. At midnight, the beasts in the barns talked together in human speech, and the alders budded along the creeks. Words now thought to be obsolete are still in use in this last pocket of Anglo-Saxon culture. For example, our older people speak of "yarbs"—which is correct. We have turned the "y" into an "h" and the "a" into an "e," so that we have a word the English call "herb" and we call "erb." Both of us have corrupted the true word, which is "yarb."

The second result of the Kentucky mountaineer's isolation from modern times has been the retention of a pioneer code of honor long after it had been abandoned by the outside world. Our mountaineer is chivalrous to women. Our nurses go out on calls with any man, anywhere, at any hour of any night, if he comes for them. Our young couriers can ride alone over the most remote trails with a safety that would not be theirs in some parts of our great cities. They can count on service when they need it and they have no fear of molestation.

Another example of the pioneer code is that stealing is held to be a greater crime than shooting an enemy. After a man had been sentenced to the penitentiary for a killing, we heard one mountaineer say to another, "Two years is too much for a killing. For stealing, now, it would be all right, but two years is too much for a killing." This is not to say that we don't have our scalawags in the mountains, and people who steal among them, but they lose social caste, whereas no one loses social caste for having shot his enemy.

170

This business of shooting it out with an enemy doesn't derive from pioneer days only but also from the old custom of the duel. Duels were fought in the United States long after the famous Hamilton-Burr engagement. My Grandfather Breckinridge's dueling pistols are still in the possession of our family. Although I never heard he had occasion to use them, this amusing bit of her family history from Mrs. William R. Blair, Jr. of Sewickley, Pennsylvania, suggests how liable men were to duels in my grandfather's day:

Apropos of nothing, did you ever know that my grandfather heard that one of the Breckinridges had said something outrageous about him? He galloped away from the Mexican War—they met in California, all was explained, all was love and kindliness—grandfather packed up his dueling pistols and galloped back to the war. It is all written in French to my grandmother.

To me there is a real distinction between a killing and a murder. With the coming of the motor roads my heart sinks at the thought that cold-blooded murder—hitherto unknown to us—has come with them. The old shootings were always personal except, occasionally, when they were accidental. Kentuckians have a reputation for shooting too easily and too much—but this is true of all of us and not just of our mountaineers. Around the turn of the century, when the famous Colson-Scott shooting occurred at the old Capitol Hotel in Frankfort, a traveling man was descending the winding stairs leading down to the lobby. In his terror he fell over the banisters onto the lobby floor where he lay with a broken leg shouting, according to the story as my father told it to me, "My mamma told me not to come to Kentucky! My mamma told me not to come to Kentucky!"

The Kentuckian, in fine, particularly in the mountain pockets where he has been isolated, is stamped down to this day with certain pioneer characteristics which mark him as the product of an earlier and more rugged age. These have made him even more of an individualist than the average American. But in the shaping of the Kentuckian who is also a mountaineer, other forces came into play. For more than a hundred and fifty years he has lived in mountain country and has gained thereby certain traits one finds in mountaineers the world over, and only in them. Where the land is rough and steep, nature is not easily conquered even after wild beasts and wilder men have been subdued. There is about the mountaineer a dogged determination to survive that keeps his body lean and his mind alert. His dwelling place in awesome regions tends to give him dignity of manner. This is accentuated by his sparse use of words. One night many years ago I stopped off with a widow on Jack's Creek. When we went to bed I told her I wanted to get off in the morning at the break of day. There was so little light before sunrise that I could barely distinguish her kind face under its black sunbonnet when she bent over me and said, "Woman, get up." What a chatter there would have been in the lowlands! "I hate to rouse you so early, but you did ask to have me do it. The coffee is on the stove. The boy is saddling your horse." Well, the coffee was on the stove and the boy was saddling my horse. No rite of hospitality had been neglected. My hostess said all that was needful. She knew that I was a woman who wanted to get up.

II

Now that we have named certain characteristics the Kentucky mountaineers hold in common, we shall go back to that divergence of all individuals from each other which is as true of Kentucky mountaineers as of the rest of the human race. Since the tone of every community is set by its best men, I shall describe some of those at Hyden who influenced our work profoundly in its early days. In any part of the world these men would have stood out for what they were —leading citizens. All have crossed the Great River in recent years, and cannot be embarrassed by any praise I give them now.

Mr. Sherman Eversole, the banker, was so conservative and capable a financial man that his little bank at Hyden, and he the only man in it, rode through the period of bank failures unscathed. He was a man of probity, of business and personal integrity. As Secretary of the Treasury of the United States, he could have served America well.

Mr. M. C. Begley ("Mr. Mitch") had not only a fine legal mind but he was, barring none, the man with the most mature emotional balance of any I have ever known. He took no cases of criminal law but derived a good income in retainer fees from companies outside the mountains who held undeveloped coal and timber rights in our section. He had no enemies in a land of strong personal antagonisms. The fairness of his judgment, the courtesy of his speech, had to be known to be credited—as did his compassionate heart. Once when we asked Mr. Mitch if anything ever broke his composure, he said, "When I hear something unkind—and therefore untrue—said about the Frontier Nursing Service, I get red all over."

Judge L. D. Lewis ("Judge Lew") had a massive intellect. His legal acumen and his justice, on the bench, were such that the appellate courts rarely reversed his decisions. It has been said that this is "the best criterion we know for gauging the record of a circuit judge." His knowledge of Kentucky history, including the most minute details of genealogy, was unsurpassed outside the ranks of professional historians. But whatever he happened to be reading popped up in his conversation at the most unexpected times. Once, when the river was rising,

Teddy Bear and I rode swiftly out of Hyden, in a hurry to get over the Muncy ford before it became too swift and too deep to cross. When we met Judge Lew, riding back towards town, he caught hold of my reins and said without preliminary greeting, "Now that fellow Napoleon, at Marengo . . ." and then he launched into a description of the battle. I fairly gasped, "But, Judge Lew, does it matter at the moment?" When he let me go, Teddy Bear and I pushed on towards the ford, I brooding over Napoleon. I didn't remember enough about him to discuss him intelligently with Judge Lew so, when I visited my brother Carson at a post of the United States Marines, I asked him for a biography of the Corsican. From his bookshelves he pulled out *The Riddle of Napoleon* by Raoul Brice, Surgeon Lieutenant-General of the French Army, and I devoured it. When I next met Judge Lew I was prepared to discuss Marengo but he, as I recall it, was thinking then in terms of Frederick the Great! Judge Lew's interest in those of our nurses who were British was enhanced by his own pride of British descent. To some of the neighbors he said, "Our nurses are the descendants of your ancestors."

These three old friends of mine would have gone to the top in any part of the world where they had chosen to make their careers. They had left the Kentucky mountains to complete their education, and came back to them because they loved them, because they belonged. To their names I want to add that of a fourth old friend who only two years ago joined them on the other side of death—a death foiled of its mark during the First World War, when he faced it head on. While Sergeant Will Sandlin served in France with the Thirty-third Division he attacked a machine gun nest at Bois-des-Forges with only a pistol and grenades. He accounted for twenty-two of the enemy in his first attack and, with a bayonet from one of those who had fallen, he killed two others who had escaped his grenades. He had a grenade wound in his head and a shell fragment wound in his leg at the time.

Sergeant Sandlin received the Congressional Medal of Honor, and decorations from many lands, but he refused to capitalize on his fame. He came back to his own land on Owl's Nest Creek not far from Hyden, where he lived with his wife, Belvia, and their children, and ignored the offers of wealth that could have been his had he gone out to the platform and the radio. He and Belvia threw themselves into the activities of the Frontier Nursing Service from its beginning. As members of our Hyden Committee, they attended most of the meetings, and shared in all of the work. Sergeant Sandlin was in ill health, off and on, until his death at the age of fifty-nine, as the result of poison gas he had taken into his lungs in the Argonne Forest. It was our privilege to attend him during his illness, and to reckon his friendship among the closest we have known. Through him, as well as through the other three leaders of whom I have written, I gained an understanding of the pioneers who had explored the wilderness of America and founded the habitations that were destined to grow into a great nation.

III

During the summer and autumn of 1925, I started the building of Wendover. Early in the summer I bought the site with which I had fallen in love two years before, and engaged local workmen to build a log barn. They then began work on the log cabin. Men felled the logs on the mountainsides, and snaked them down by means of mules hitched to them with chains. Our local workmen could handle the barn and the cabin but, as the weeks passed, I realized I couldn't expect them to construct a large two-story log house, with an attic, and with plumbing, unless they had expert direction. I rode over to Hazard in October to see Mr. and Mrs. Roy Helm and Mr. and Mrs. L. H. Stiles (among our early friends there) to ask for help. They gave me the name of a local contractor who could build the Big House.

Until the time came to bring in plumbers, and a carpenter or two to finish the inside, the local workmen were the only men the contractor had, and a fine crew of men they were. Stone masonry is traditional in certain mountain families. The tools and the craft pass from father to son. Such masons built the great stone chimneys in the Big House and in the cabin at Wendover. The logs for the second story of the Big House, and for the attic, were raised by means of a contraption called a "crab," with a pulley system used on the branches of the giant beeches. Although mine was not the only two-story log house (my neighbor, Elihu Mosley, lived in a lovely old one on Muncy Creek), it was the only one with a third story in the form of an attic.

I opened an account at Hyden Citizens Bank to cover my weekly payrolls and other obligations incurred in building Wendover. Mr. Eversole had huge checkbooks printed, with my name on the longest checks I have ever seen. This turned out to be just as well because rarely were the checks returned until the backs of them had been covered with signatures. There was so little "cash money" in our section then that my checks were used like legal tender. A man would endorse his weekly pay check to a neighbor for the purchase of a hog, the neighbor would endorse it to someone else for fence posts, the third person would use it to pay a bill at the country store. After that it wandered back to the bank and into my hands weeks after the date on which I had signed it.

My father did not wait until Wendover was built to join me in the Kentucky mountains. On one of my trips out to Lexington I met him, and rode in from the railroad with him and his fox terrier, Patch. This was the same Pitchy-Patchy given Breckie long before, who had settled her undying affections upon my father from the first. My father was seventy-nine years old when he took this first ride from the railroad into the Kentucky mountains—where he had not been since his boyhood. In Lexington, Cousin Letitia Bullock said to me, "You are taking an old man and an old dog." But my father did not seem old at seventy-nine, nor for several years after that. He regularly rode horseback from the railroad to Wendover in the spring or early summer, and back to the railroad again before bitter weather set in.

All that fall my father and I made our headquarters in the Hyden house the Kentucky Committee had rented, on the site where Miss Huston's house, "Cherry Corner," stands now. He insisted on taking care of the nurses' horses, grooming and feeding and watering them. He bought a small set of tools and put himself at the disposal of the nurses for minor repairs about the place. In another way, my father was of more use than he realized. He became a member of our Hyden Committee and attended the meetings we held monthly while our work was getting under way. His knowledge of parliamentary law got everything off on the right footing, and his geniality gave the meetings ease and friendliness. I was struck by the costume he always wore at these meetings—heaven knows why. Although he kept to the khaki riding trousers and leggings which were a part of his regular daytime dress, with them he wore a frock coat made for him by Pool, in London, years before. The upper accessories were those that went with a frock coat. He looked like a statesman from the neck to the hips, and a horseman from there on down.

Another pleasant older person, Mrs. Caroline Caffin, joined her daughter in Hyden as soon as we had a house. She was not nearly so old as my father but combined with him to give our little establishment a family feeling. Mrs. Caffin undertook, as her share of the work, the hardest post of all—that of volunteer housekeeper. With one of our neighbors in by the day to cook our meals, and the help of a man to clean out the barns and do other work too heavy for my father, we got along comfortably enough, and pooled the living costs among us. Unfortunately, the horses had no proper horse lot so they came up on the porch to eat the tomatoes and lettuce set out on the railing. When they walked across the porch, the whole house shook. It was so designed that you had to go out to come in, at every room, and was so sketchily constructed that the air blew in from a thousand cracks. In one of my many letters to my cousin, Dr. Josephine Hunt, I find this plea: "Josie, darling, please telephone Blank Hardware and ask them if they have drunk the Pyrene extinguishers and fillers. This old house is not safe with its loose chimneys. Ask them to speed the order up."

Many of my letters written to outside firms carry the same note of chaff in urging them to make shipment. Sometimes, however, when things had been hauled across from the railroad, and turned out to be the wrong sizes for whatever they were to fit, my letters took a piteous tone, such as: "If you all had a heart, you would check your order before shipping it." Then I would explain all over again about the long haul in, the long haul out (when things had to be returned), and the long, long delay.

As I compare the costs of things in the 1920's with the costs of things in 1951, I am struck by the difference. For example, I find that by the end of our first year of work we had ordered the following articles for horses—7 saddles; 7 bridles; 4 halters; 3 curry combs; 4 brushes; 8 blankets—at a total cost of $123.66. In 1951, these things would cost $611.45. Our first saddlebags, from surplus Army stock, were much too small for our supplies. On the ride Ireland of Scotland and I took from Berea to Hyden, we met a man at Tyner in Jackson County who made saddlebags by hand, out of the softest and finest quality leather, for $13 a pair. This man made all the large, roomy bags that the Frontier Nursing Service nurses, couriers and guests know so well, with metal buttons inside to which we fasten our washable linings. Even in our early days, each nurse had two of these bags, one with a white lining for midwifery only, and one with a blue-checked lining for general nursing. The midwifery bag, packed, weighs thirty pounds. The utmost care has to be taken to have the weight evenly distributed or there might be trouble with the horse's back. A bad back on a horse in the Frontier Nursing Service has always been the same kind of disgrace as a bad back on a patient in a hospital bed.

Early in our work we found we needed layettes for our babies. A baby in a black and white calico slip and nothing else, and another in red serge with its neck raw, sent me scouting for baby clothes. Few things in those early months gave us such happiness as a gift of forty layettes, generously donated by Dr. G. De Jong of the Dutch Reformed Cottage Hospital at Gray Hawk in Jackson County. Ireland of Scotland and I stayed with her overnight on our ride in from Berea to Hyden. Before the end of our first fiscal year, I had groups of women sewing for our babies in several parts of the United States—and groups of women are sewing yet.

IV

In October, Dr. Cleaves wrote me that although Teddy Bear's ankle was still swollen, he could be used and would be the better for regular

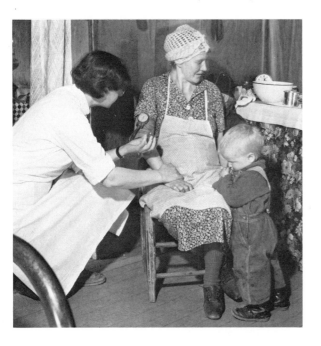

In the early years of FNS, much of the nursing care was provided in the home. *Above:* A nurse makes a prenatal visit
in a mountain cabin. *Below:* A posed picture to illustrate
an old saying. When mountain children asked where babies
came from, they were told, "The nurses bring them in their
saddlebags." Photos, 1937, by Marvin Breckinridge.

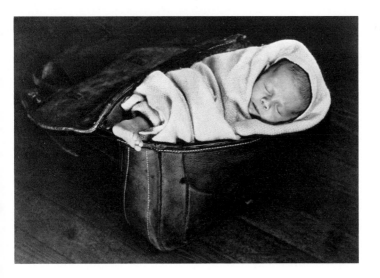

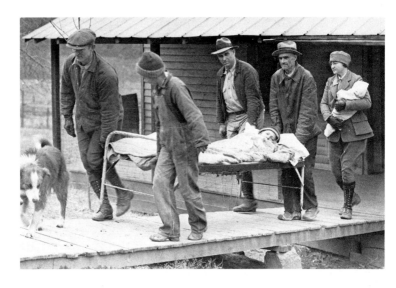

A young mother and her newborn baby are transported from her home and across the Middle Fork of the Kentucky River to Hyden Hospital for treatment. Photos, 1937, by Marvin Breckinridge.

Part of the children's ward of the old Hyden Hospital in 1937.
The hospital, built in 1928, had facilities for twenty patients.
Photo by Marvin Breckinridge.

Above: The "Big House" at Wendover, built in 1925-1926 as Mary Breckinridge's home and as headquarters for the FNS. It is now on the National Register of Historic Places. Photo by Debbie Callahan, courtesy of the *Leslie County News.*

Left: An FNS nurse opens up for the day at Hell-for-Sartin Clinic in 1953. Photo by Thomas V. Miller, courtesy of *The Courier-Journal.*

The new Mary Breckinridge Hospital in Hyden, opened in 1975. It admits nearly 2,300 patients a year. On the hill above is the old hospital, now used for administrative offices. Photo by Gabrielle Beasley.

The new home of Oneida Nursing Center, opened in 1976. The FNS operates five district nursing centers to serve a four-county area. Photo by Gabrielle Beasley.

Above: A Home Health Agency nurse visits with a homebound patient. The agency, a branch of the FNS, makes more than 7,000 such visits each year. *Below:* A nurse-midwife and an obstetrician conduct a joint prenatal examination at Mary Breckinridge Hospital. Photos by Gabrielle Beasley.

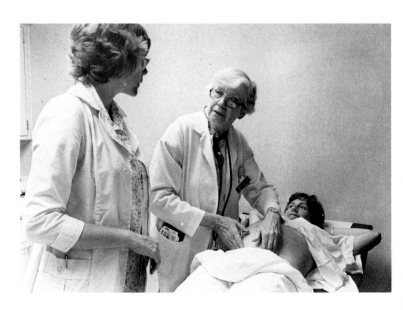

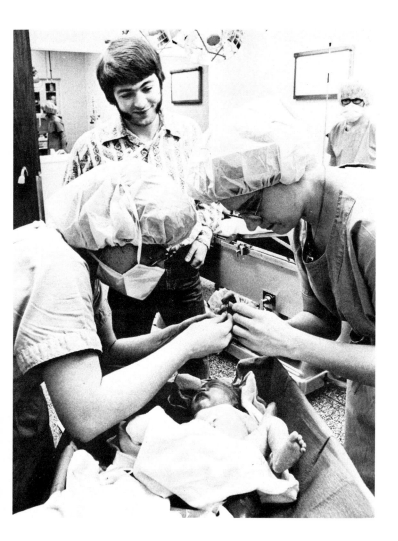

A proud new father and his daughter, age five minutes, at Mary Breck-inridge Hospital. More than 350 babies were born at the hospital in 1980. Home deliveries are now rare. Photo by Gabrielle Beasley.

A family nurse-practitioner checks on a broken finger during a follow-up visit to Beach Fork School. Photo by Gabrielle Beasley.

use. He suggested that I spend a night with him and his wife, and ride Teddy Bear back to Hyden. This I arranged to do, on my return from one of my visits to Lexington. I don't recall the name of the little way station, on a spur of the Louisville and Nashville Railroad, where I left the train, but Dr. Cleaves had a man with a buggy to meet me there to drive me to his place. As we went through a dark and lonely bit of forest, the man said to me, "They do say these woods is hanted. Strange and terrible things happens in them at the edge of dark." He little knew that I would have been enormously interested in the happening of anything of a psychic nature, and would gladly have held his hand with one of mine while I took notes with the other. At the Cleaves place, Teddy Bear came tearing out of the barn to meet me— not the glorious-looking creature William Preston and I had chosen weeks before, but spirited and intelligent still. The next day I mounted him and rode off. Dr. Cleaves advised me to give three days to a ride that Teddy Bear could easily have done in two before his injury and illness. I spent one night at Oneida and the next night at Big Creek. Despite all the care I had taken of Teddy Bear and his ankle, the rubbing down, the careful bedding, he was a mighty tired horse when he rode with me down Rockhouse Creek to Hyden.

It was good to have my own horse at last and I needed him because I lived in the saddle in those days. The nursing work, as well as the midwifery, piled up on us with almost unbelievable swiftness. I often had to take my turn on the district and in the clinic. Mrs. Martha Lewis, who lived on Flackie, claimed she was my first patient, and she was certainly one of the first. She had severed an artery in her hand. Her husband had the sense to put on a rough tourniquet, which had been on over an hour by the time they came in, riding the same mule. When I took it off, the blood spouted almost to the ceiling. I felt that younger eyes than mine were needed to clamp off that artery so I sent to the Presbyterian Dormitory for Leona Pace who rushed over to help me. We took the tourniquet off again and, while I swabbed, she caught the artery in a clamp. Then we tied it off. Martha Lewis stayed all night with me and was none the worse for her accident.

Leona, a Leslie County girl, had taken a nurse's training in Pennsylvania and was a tiptop young surgical nurse. She married Gillous Morgan soon after I first knew her. In later years she was chief surgical nurse at Hyden Hospital, riding horseback to and from her house for her hours on duty. Although she finally had to give up nursing for her home responsibilities, she has remained one of us down to this day.

Teddy Bear and I got lost one afternoon when I was making some district calls. Winter had set in early with heavy snows. Somewhere on Thousandsticks Mountain we lost the trail, which was a faint one even without untrodden snow. As night came on, I decided the only way for us to get home was to start off in what we knew was the direction of Rockhouse Creek, and just naturally go there regardless of obstructions. We came onto a mountain so steep and so heavily timbered that it was impossible to ride down it. So, Teddy Bear and I just sat down on our haunches and slid. We went over a frozen waterfall and came down off a cliff onto an open space. To our joy, we found we were on Rockhouse Creek. It was nothing, then, to follow the creek down to Hyden. When I wrote about this experience to Adeline at York, she wrote back for me not to forget that my guardian angel was always with me. Our guardian angels need skis to keep up with us at times, now as then.

V

We began to make ready for Christmas. I sent a little circular, asking for toys and money, to everybody I knew. My friends and kinsmen supplemented my lists with lists of their own. It was our first appeal. We have sent one in advance of Christmas every year since then. At Hyden, where the Buyers and other leading citizens never let Christmas go by without a celebration for the children, we pitched in with them to ensure that every child was remembered by the toy it most wanted, that the poorest families got the warm clothing sent us, that all had candy. Up at Wendover, my father and I made plans to combine a splendiferous party with the dedication of Wendover itself.

As far back as October, Breckie's nurse, Juliette Carni, her husband Henri, and her young daughter by an earlier marriage, Liliane, had all come to me at Hyden where I boarded them until the cabin at Wendover was roofed. Juliette and I loved each other so much that we wanted to spend the rest of our lives in close companionship. She agreed to become my cook-housekeeper, use Liliane for household duties and let Henri be the barn man. They brought with them a magnificent dog, part Saint Bernard, part collie, named Fino—pronounced "Feeno"—who was about ten times the size of Pitchy-Patchy. These were the first of a long line of Wendover dogs. When the Carnis could move into the cabin, I boarded the contractor with them so that he no longer had to ride between Wendover and Hyden.

Before Christmas the contractor had the roof of asphalt slate shingles on Wendover Big House but there were no stairways to the second story or the attic and there was no chinking between the logs. However, in planning our party, my father and I felt that all we really needed were great fires in the chimneys downstairs and a kitchen stove attached to the kitchen chimney. Our guests would be cold as all outdoors, but under cover. We needed the kitchen stove because Juliette started cooking on a vast scale long before Christmas Day. My father insisted that in such cold weather everyone who came must have a substantial meal. He bought tons of hams. The odor of their baking came out to greet me every time Teddy Bear and I rode up to Wendover. When Juliette had the hams laid by, she started in on puddings and cakes. It was to be a feast. For a drink we had a new wash boiler full of hot cocoa made with condensed milk, well sweetened. That part of the refreshments and the candy, which we put into little paper bags, were given by friends on the outside who responded to my circular with enthusiasm. My cousin Clay Hunt, of Bryan-Hunt Company, sent us a big shipment of hard candies. In later years, up until his death, Clay established the custom of getting gifts of candy from other wholesale houses in various parts of the United States to add to his own.

The ladies on our Hyden Committee helped with the ham baking and made quantities of bread. They filled all the candy bags for Hyden and Wendover. The men on the Committee who had mule teams hauled all the toys, also given by friends on the outside, up to Wendover free. Our women members had sewing bees at which they freshened up those of the pretty baby things sent us that were not quite new, and dressed the dolls that came naked. As we had not yet started a nursing district at Wendover, we didn't know the children and could not set aside, in advance of Christmas, suitable toys for these boys and girls. We didn't even know how many babies there were.

The only thing to do was to have all the toys stacked around under the great tree and arrange a committee of leading local citizens, whom I had met, to pass the children in one by one and let each child choose the toy he wanted most. This was terribly hard on the boys as they stood with dazzled eyes in front of balls, harmonicas, little red trucks. As for the girls, there was not one but wanted a doll and there weren't enough dolls to go around. Although we ran short of dolls, we did not run short of toys or of food. The weather was bitterly cold and the river barely fordable so only some five hundred people came to our first Wendover party. To it I had invited everybody in the county—some ten thousand people. I had notices about the housewarming put up at all the crossroad stores and post offices and said that everyone would be welcome. This struck Cousin Cabell Bullock so forcibly that he wrote me as follows:

I hope your Christmas housewarming will be a success. What stands out in noble proportions is the number of the invited guests—10,000 of them. It puts me in mind of Ed Turner's story of your grandfather's special admirer, in telling of the reports from the Battle of Shiloh: "After they fit and fit again, up come John C. Breckinridge and asks the privilege of the field for an hour. They told him to wade in, and, gentlemen, they do say he slew a hundred thousand men."

So many people came up the river from Hyden to Wendover to

help with the housewarming that we had mule-drawn wagons as well as mules and horses to accommodate the crowd. But all transport for this great occasion was given, by those who had it, as a courtesy. My father came in Jonah Begley's wagon with several other people, among them Miss Lila and Miss Mabel Buyers. They all sat in split-bottomed chairs on the wagon bed. Jonah hoisted a tarpaulin above them, in case of snow. As the wagon jolted over the ford in the river, it hit a rock—and over went all the chairs! As Teddy Bear and I rode alongside, we heard Miss Lila call out, "Are you all right, Major?" and my father's reply, "No, Madam, not quite all right." They were, all of them, sprawled over the wagon bed with the chairs and tarpaulin strewn over the top of them, and nobody could be sorted out until they reached yon side of the river. But no mischances occurred that were serious enough to mar the beauty of our day.

My father and I wanted a religious observance at Christmas as well as the social one. A group of Hyden school boys and girls who came to the housewarming sang "Come All Ye Faithful," "O Little Town of Bethlehem" and "Silent Night." The Reverend Isaac Wells offered a prayer. Judge Lew Lewis and my father made brief addresses of welcome to our guests before my father dedicated Wendover. I told the people it was built in memory of my children, to be used in work for their children. A bronze plaque on the chimney in the living room of the Big House commemorates the day in these words:

TO THE GLORY OF GOD
AND IN MEMORY OF
BRECKIE AND POLLY
DEDICATED CHRISTMAS 1925

Such was our first Christmas at Wendover. In the following years we added other festivities to the Christmas season, such as a square dance for the young people—"Winding the Ball of Yarn," "Boxing the Gnat," "Wild Goose Chase," "Cage the Bird"—and a Santa Claus with the Christmas tree. The deeper meaning of Christmas is expressed through a Nativity play. This is done by the younger children, in pantomime, while the older ones form a chorus to sing the carols. In Mary and Joseph, the Wise Men, the shepherds, the angels, there are parts for many young actors.

We make much of Christmas at our outpost centers, too. But for the first Christmas at each of them, as at Wendover, there were not enough dolls for all of the girl children who wanted them. They gazed with adoring eyes at the real dollies, even while they hugged their make-believe ones. The doll of one such little girl was a piece of old blanket, tied around the middle with a string, with a stone fastened at one end for a face. But she loved it, with that creative instinct older than recorded time, which springs up anew in every girl baby. Why must she needs mother something, with the first outreaching of her tiny hands? Why plead so early for a life whose sword shall one day pierce her own?

When Christmas comes we understand a little less dimly. The Light of the World could only come to His own through a woman's body. Only a woman held the mysteries of His advent, and pondered them in her heart.

Chapter 19

I

WHEN our work in the Kentucky mountains had gotten off to a start, my friends and relations began sending in checks just as I knew they would, bless them. Mrs. Henning opened her Louisville house in Cherokee Park for an autumn meeting. Afterward, many of the Kentuckians sent in their subscriptions, as did a scattering of friends from beyond Kentucky. Two of these, from the old C.A.R.D. days, my chief, Miss Anne Morgan, and Miss Elizabeth Perkins, wrote me to come to New York right after New Year's Day, and have meetings at their houses. This I did. It was the first of the tours to which I have given from six to twelve weeks nearly every year since then. Although I have lived and worked in the mountains for more than a quarter-century, I have gone out periodically to report to our supporters in other parts of the United States—wherever some of them wanted me enough to arrange for meetings.

In New York we had wonderful meetings that January, not only at Anne Morgan's large house and at Perky's smaller one but at the Colony Club, through the courtesy of Isabella Breckinridge. We also held a meeting at Riverdale, sponsored by Mrs. Cleveland H. Dodge, Mrs. Archibald Douglas, Mrs. Francis Boardman and others. Riverdale formed a committee to back our work and started the first sewing circle to make layettes for our babies. This committee, small in number but great in loyalty, has maintained its own nurse in the Frontier Nursing Service from that day to this, sometimes meeting her support and that of her horse as well, sometimes falling below the full support—but never failing to put out its own appeals and glean all it could from its own neighborhood.

While I was in New York, Mrs. Robert Lovett, wife of the distinguished surgeon, and another member of our old C.A.R.D., invited me to Boston for a meeting in her house. She got the meeting together, collected subscriptions afterward, took the first chairmanship of our

Boston Committee, and enlisted the interest of Mrs. Draper Ayer, a cousin of mine through the Prestons, who gave us the money for our first outpost nursing center, the Jessie Preston Draper Memorial. Boston, New York and Riverdale provided our first three committees outside Kentucky. At the instance of my cousin Anne (Mrs. Waring Wilson), we had our first meetings in Philadelphia, but they were on the Main Line at Bryn Mawr and Rosemont. Our first large meeting in Philadelphia itself was held another year at the home of Mrs. John Markoe, who was a member of our Philadelphia Committee until her death.

In addition to my main engagements, I spoke to various clubs, churches, nurses, and other groups of people as I have done ever since. Among these, I recall particularly that I made my first talk to the Kentucky Women's Club of New York early in 1926. At none of these engagements did I ask anybody for money. I didn't even hint. This seemed to me then, as it does yet, the right approach. I was so sure my plan for remotely rural babies, children, and their mothers was practical that I backed it with all I had. The people to whom I spoke caught my enthusiasm by a sort of contagion. I felt that those who did would want to support our work, and should be left free to do it in their own way and at their own time. If they didn't want to give to us, then why should they? It is the duty of all to support their local charities which, in these days, usually means the Community Chest. But people should have the privilege of choosing which national charities they wish to support, and they should be under no compulsion in making their choice. I feel this so strongly, and I dislike so intensely asking people for money while they sit helpless before me, that I have never willingly departed from the system I laid down for myself in the beginning. I did depart from it for a few years, and during that time people were asked at some of our general meetings to leave checks as they went out. This was done at the request of friends of the Frontier Nursing Service whose opinions I valued. I don't think we took in more money than we would have gotten by a follow-up appeal which the same people could have read when the glamour of the meeting was over.

One good thing came out of this asking for money at meetings—it cured me of any vanity I had as a speaker. I don't always speak well, but usually I do. It is only too easy to take credit to one's self for a natural gift, and feel a sense of pride in it—and that is shameful as well as silly. The distaste I felt when I had to end a talk with an appeal for money knocked all of that kind of nonsense out of my head so completely that it freed me from this vanity. I have become so detached from myself as a speaker that when people come to me and tell me I spoke well, and I know that is true, I have to check myself not to answer, "Yes, I did." On the other hand, when I have not spoken well and someone compliments me, I find it hard not to reply, "You are mistaken. I was not at my best today." Within three minutes after I start speaking, I am either *en rapport* with my audience or I know that I shan't be. The matter seems to be one over which I have no control. Sometimes, even when I am seedy, I can swing right into my talk. At other times, even though I feel quite fit, I don't seem able to make the grade. When I catch hold of my audience, I am able to draw an immense amount of power from them and throw it back at them—but now and then, for no reason that I can see, I fail in this. I don't know how much this is true of other spontaneous speakers, but such is my own experience.

II

At the end of December, just before I went to New York, we had an Executive Committee meeting in Lexington. Of the greatest significance to me, personally, is a sentence culled from the minutes of December 30, 1925: "On motion of Dr. Hunt, it was voted that Mrs. Breckinridge be empowered to employ a secretary, in the event that funds are secured that will justify the expense." Money was now pouring in not only from Kentucky but from New York and its environs, Philadelphia and its environs, Riverdale, and even from a scatteration of places where I had not spoken. Supplies came as well as money, including the layettes we so terribly needed for our babies. It began to look as though we could afford for me to have a secretary.

While I stayed with John and Isabella Breckinridge in New York, they had employed a secretary to take care of my engagements and my correspondence. The freedom it gave me passes human belief. I could go to sleep at night when my day's work was done. Back in Lexington I ran into Martha Prewitt, who had once taken secretarial training. I asked her if she would like to go back with me to Wendover. Her reply was as characteristic then as it would be now: "Why I'd just love it. When do we start?"

We could not start for a few days because I had a spot of work to do in Louisville. I had tried to get a fire insurance policy on Wendover through the Hazard Insurance Agency. Mr. E. H. McGuire said the agency would be delighted to give this insurance, and also to insure houses belonging to the Kentucky Committee when we built them, but that the big insurance companies refused insurance on remotely rural property. I arranged with Mr. McGuire for us to have a meeting in Louisville with the state agents of five great insurance companies from New York, Hartford, and Philadelphia. Mr. McGuire started the discussion by saying he considered our business, in spite of its remoteness, a good risk because of the character of the people backing it. He said that people like that were always a good risk—nothing better. When Mr. McGuire finished speaking the five agents opened up as with one voice. From their point of view, they said, there were insuperable drawbacks to remotely rural risks. First, they didn't know a man willing to make the long horseback trip from Hazard to Wendover to inspect the property. Second, if we put in claims for small losses from small fires, they couldn't send an inspector to check on such claims. Third, there was no way they could see where we could get any fire protection whatever, and certainly no way they could check on it if we said we had it. I never met five more skeptical men than those five agents.

When it came my turn to speak, I had to do in about half an hour as big a job of salesmanship as I have ever tried to put over. I told the agents that if any of them ever built anything two days' mule-team travel from a railroad they would understand how ardently I wanted to protect my Wendover property from fire, so I would never have it to build again. Nobody in his senses would go through the anguish of construction under circumstances like ours if a little forethought could prevent a fire. Second, I told them that since we were as eager as they not only to prevent fires but to put out small fires before they became big ones, they need only tell me what to do and we would do it. I already knew that rural buildings should not be too close together and had carefully spaced Wendover Big House, cabin and barn accordingly. We already had fire extinguishers. I promised to get as many more as they advised and throw in a few extra for my own peace of mind. On Wendover Big House I had put fire-resisting shingles to minimize the danger of sparks from the chimneys and I promised to do this on every two-story house built in the future. I told them that on the mountain behind Wendover I had a great stone cistern, from which came the water for our plumbing, with sufficient pressure to reach the roofs of the buildings, and that I would buy a regular fireman's hose to carry the water in volume. I said we would install the same system at Hyden Hospital when it was built. As to the nuisance of small claims for small fires, I promised them that I would never make such claims. We have had several such fires since then about which we kept mum.

In winding up my argument, I referred to what Mr. McGuire had said about the character of the people who sponsored the work I was doing. I told the five agents they would have to take my promises on faith but, if they did that, the years ahead would bring them a nice lot of new business. They were delightful men, those agents. We put it over with them, Mr. McGuire and I, but they insisted on dividing every policy, even one for a barn, among all five so that each company carried only a fifth of the risk.

Some several years after this meeting, Mr. McGuire told me that the state agents of the great insurance companies said they considered the Frontier Nursing Service the best risk they had in all eastern Kentucky, and yet not one building of the many the Frontier Nursing Service owned by that time had received a single visit of inspection. When the highway from Hazard to Hyden had gotten as far as the Middle Fork of the Kentucky River but not so far as Hyden itself, around 1931, the first fire insurance inspector turned up. A stout, middle-aged, red-faced man, he had to leave his car half a mile from the hospital and climb straight up the mountainside. Miss MacKinnon (Mac) was so stunned by the look of him as he plodded up towards the hospital veranda that she called for water and aromatic spirits of ammonia. He reached the steps, sat down, loosened his collar, began to gasp, and turned purple. When he was revived, he looked up and without any other greeting asked, "Is God in?" He figured he had indeed "climbed the steep ascent of heaven through peril, toil, and pain."

III

Wendover Big House was habitable that spring of 1926 although the inside work had not been finished. Juliette, installed in the cabin, wrote me often during my absence. Her letters were filled with homey things about the chickens she had started to raise, the breaking of the ground for the garden, the brood sow she bought and called Edna—the first of a long line of Wendover Ednas. She began her letters, "*Ma bien chère Boppie*" and ended with expressions like "*Bien des baisers de Juliette*." The name Breckie had given me did not die so long as she and Mammy lived.

From our family furniture, stored at a fireproof house in Louisville, I sent to Wendover only such things as were suitable—some of the old walnut, bedding, many books, and enough of my mother's linen sheets and pillowcases to use for members of the staff who might have fevers in hot weather. I took none of the silver, family portraits, old mahogany, fine china, or oriental rugs—except one for the living room. I had to buy suitable china, the draperies for the windows and a lot of other practical things. All of that took time—a commodity of which I had very little then as now.

Martha and I camped out in the Big House while the workmen were still there. One morning at sunup an old man placed a ladder up to Martha's bedroom window, started climbing in, saw she was still in bed, withdrew. He came to me and said, "Your clerk sleeps late."

186

Thousands of people have traveled to Wendover since it was first built and know the character of house it is. What they can never know is how crowded it was until we built Hyden Hospital. For nearly three years Wendover was used as a cottage hospital, and often overflowed with sick people. One patient, a child with pneumonia, stayed there for weeks as did several marasmic babies. When home conditions were unsuitable for a confinement, we took such cases in at Wendover. I remember one poor young thing who called to know if she could have her baby there. When I asked if her husband didn't have a house she said, "They don't accuse me of being married."

The dogtrot that runs down through the middle of Wendover Big House was a true dogtrot when the house was first built—open all the way through. The expression "dogtrot" puzzled the people in eastern Kentucky. It is a relic of my Mississippi days. Carson said, on a winter visit, that a dog would certainly have to trot in the place to keep warm. In time I had glass put up at the two ends of the dogtrot but it retains its character of inside walls like outside walls—rough logs— dividing the house in its lower story into two houses. In the early days I kept a long sofa there which could be used to put up anybody overnight. We had a bed in the dispensary, and a cot that could be turned into a bed in Martha's office, which became the post office. I had Breckie's crib for a sick child and we could always improvise cradles for the babies.

Far as we were from the railroad, a certain number of guests came in to see us. All were my personal guests in our early years, whether they were sick people, local or outside friends. In the first six months after Wendover opened I entertained 35 guests who stayed a total of 295 days. This did not include the people coming and going up and down the river who stopped off for a meal with me. Some of these were strangers, like a boy of about eighteen who rode in on some errand, stayed to lunch, and said on leaving, "Thank you for the nourishment."

Sometimes people dismounted at Wendover just for the luxury of a tub bath. Leslie County had only five bathtubs at that time and of these I owned two. To own two-fifths of the bathtubs in a region of ten thousand people sounds like a lot of plumbing—but it only meant that I had one bathroom upstairs and one bathroom downstairs at Wendover Big House. The downstairs tub received so many visitors that I threatened to give it a guest book, bound in blue and white linoleum. Ireland of Scotland gave Wendover its first real guest book. The remarks people wrote after their names in those days were a scream. When Dr. Hunt made her first visit in to us, got off her horse after a ride of nearly thirty miles and staggered over to the guest book, she wrote, "Fatima's brothers came from here"—an allusion to the length of time it had taken the brothers of Bluebeard's wife to come to her rescue. But Wendover's long breezy dogtrot, its bathtubs, and the shade of its giant beeches were a refreshing spot to anyone who had spent a summer's day in the saddle. Whenever I rode up to it myself, I thought of Cowper's lines:

> Oh for a lodge in some vast wilderness,
> Some boundless contiguity of shade . . .

It seems to me, in looking back over my first few years in the mountains, that I was always riding up to Wendover or riding away from it. That first summer in my home, I wrote to Mrs. Dike in France, "I am beginning to commute between Lexington, Louisville and the mountains. During the last two months I have gone in and out on an average of every ten days and as that means nearly a day in the saddle and a night on the sleeper each time, you can see that it is tall commuting."

IV

The first Wendover nurse-midwife, Ellen Halsall, had come in the spring. She was one of many people—nurses, guests, patients—that I brought in from the railroad with me, the natural result of my commuting. She had never been on a horse in her life. To get her mounted behind the Hazard railroad station near a shunting train was no small feat. But some men and I did it and I led her up Town Mountain Creek, as we called the way out of Hazard in those days, she sitting petrified on old Rick. Until we got over that first mountain and down on Brown's Fork of Big Creek, I held Rick's reins. Then I told Ellen she need only sit in the saddle and let the reins hang loosely in her hands because Rick would follow like a dog behind Teddy Bear. I had only ridden a few steps, at a slow walk, when I heard a muffled shriek behind me. Teddy Bear and I hastened to the rescue of Rickie, who was standing on his hind legs (his forepaws wagging like a dog's) and looking at me with imploring eyes. I quickly released the tightened reins and told Ellen not to pull on them but to leave them loose. This time we rode a few yards before Rickie was again drawn back up on his hind legs, forepaws wagging, with that piteous look in his eyes. Meanwhile, poor Ellen sat petrified in the saddle. She would have been quite all right if only her hands had been petrified, as well as her seat and her legs, because all she needed to do was to stop pulling on the reins. After one or two more tries, I gave it up and led her the twenty-five to thirty miles from Hazard to Wendover.

No wonder this experience gave me an idea! From that time on I required every new nurse who came into the Frontier Nursing Service to take five lessons in riding so she would know how to sit quietly on a horse and hold the reins. Some weeks later Ellen told me she died a thousand deaths not only on the way in to Wendover but for days afterward every time her horse skirted the edge of a precipice or forded a river. She was asked to write an account of her experiences for the English nursing publication known as *Nursing Notes and Midwives Chronicle*—the oldest nursing magazine in the world. When she brought me her article to look over before mailing, I read this: "In America the cities are very far apart and in between them everybody rides horses and mules."

The next two nurse-midwives to arrive, Gladys Peacock and Mary B. Willeford, came on August 1 of that summer. Their riding was no anxiety because Peacock, who was to become a good rider, could stick on a horse and Willeford, a Texan, was an expert rider. When I first knew Peacock, an Englishwoman, she was one of the chauffeurs in the old C.A.R.D. days. Both girls had trained as nurses in America at the Walter Reed Hospital and as midwives at the York Road General Lying-In Hospital in London. Up until now we had not had to give any scholarships to our nurses for overseas training in midwifery, as they had all taken the course on their own.

During our first year we engaged several nurses who were not midwives to help out on the general nursing, and the hundreds of inoculations that Dr. McCormack had asked us to give. We had in mind, even then, that if these nurses liked our work, and proved suited to it, we would send them overseas for their midwifery training so that they could return to us as full-fledged nurse-midwives. This policy met with the approval of Dr. McCormack, who gave licenses to practice midwifery in Kentucky to those American nurses who had taken this postgraduate training in the Old Country, and to the British nurses who already had the training when we engaged them. Through this means we were able to work out a system of replacement for those of the early nurses, like Miss Caffin and Miss Rockstroh, who moved on to other fields of work. They went to California in 1927, after two years in Kentucky. We had a French nurse with us in the summer of 1926, Annette Dohring, who had been one of my staff years before in the Aisne and was brought to this country on a scholarship by Miss Morgan.

We needed all the nurses we could lay our hands on. Typhoid and diphtheria were endemic in our early days in the mountains. As to the typhoid we not only had the sick ones to nurse, with the same care in the disposal of excreta that I had used in the dysentery epidemic at Blérancourt, but wherever typhoid was reported we felt it our duty to send nurses to inoculate the whole creek. One of the first things

Peacock and Willeford had to do when they came to us was to go for four successive weeks nearly a day's horseback journey to a creek where there was typhoid, for the inoculations. One always had to make four such trips because many people turned up for their first shots on the nurses' second visit. Typhoid broke out even in the county jail at Hyden. We took care of the patient, scrubbed the place with Lysol and inoculated the other prisoners.

As to diphtheria, the first we would hear of it might be something like this: "Baby had a risin' in the throat and choked to death." In the territory we covered with our district nursing, which soon included Beech Fork and the Middle Fork upriver, where the Jessie Preston Draper Memorial Nursing Center was started in 1926, we gave every child over six months toxin-antitoxin shots as rapidly as possible. It was not long before it became routine for every one of our babies to get these shots at that age. My experience with diphtheria in France and in the Kentucky mountains has made me dread this disease in children more than any other.

V

Although I have not begun to tell of all the guests, patients and outside people alike who stayed at Wendover that spring and summer, I think I have written enough for it to be plain why I had to get out of the house myself, and live in a tent. There is a limit to the capacity of even the most elastic house. Wendover reached that limit when my Aunt Jane consented to come up and stay four months with my father and me. With more joy than I can express I prepared my own room for her reception, had a couple of platforms built on the side of the mountain for tents and moved into one of them. During six weeks of Aunt Jane's visit, her grandson, Brooke Alexander, was with her too— the Brooke who had been Breckie's playmate. He was now fourteen years old, knew how to ride, and was of immense use to me in taking horses to and from the railroad, as well as riding on errands up and down the river. Our tents were only a stone's throw apart and I put mosquito bars over the cot beds to keep the spiders off our faces. The habit these insects had of descending from ridgepole to face, while we slept, might have been of absorbing interest to naturalists but not to Brooke and me.

It was my Aunt Jane who gave Wendover its name. Even before I started to build, I asked her to choose a name for my place that would be Anglo-Saxon and restful. After her trip in she probably felt like other arrivals who said the place ought to have been named "Scramble-over." Although I had prepared Jonah Begley's wagon for her the way we did for the stretcher cases we transported to the railroad—with bedsprings, two mattresses and many pillows—the jolting was so terrible, and the wagon tipped so much, that Aunt Jane said she felt like Esther in the presence of Ahasuerus. Teddy Bear and I rode alongside from Krypton to Wendover. It took all day, with the river to be forded eight times. It was near the edge of dark when the wagon passed through Wendover's big pull gate. As Aunt Jane was lifted down, she forgot her soreness and stiffness to smile at me and say, "My Matron's home, I have come to my Matron's home." Matron was a name she had for me from the time of my first marriage. The bond between her and me had been closer than is usual between those of different generations. In a letter of that period she wrote me, "Nobody, now living, understands you as I do and I trust your love and understanding of me."

My Aunt Jane's presence that first summer at Wendover gave the place the final blessing it needed. Often as I returned from one of my long, hot rides from the railroad or from upriver, I would find Aunt Jane and my father strolling together along the trail by the Middle Fork, followed by the old fox terrier, Patch. Then I would dismount so that Teddy Bear and I could walk beside them. They were both full of plans for the improvement of the property at their own expense. Aunt Jane built an addition to the barn, which is still standing, and my father began to build the stone walls and culverts which have made a terraced garden possible at Wendover and have prevented its steep slopes from washing down the hill. The brother-sister tie was close between those two, the more especially as my mother had been Aunt Jane's friend since they were girls at Hazelwood. That trail along the Middle Fork reminds me more of them than of all the many who have walked and ridden it in all the years since then.

Chapter 20

I

OUR work had no sooner started at Hyden than I began to plan for the Hyden Hospital and Health Center. I aimed for this to be not only a center to house the district nurse-midwives, but a hospital of about twelve beds. With that assured we could have a Medical Director to assume responsibility for the hospital patients, one who would be available for district calls as well. Sometimes these were desperate. Our effort to provide medical care on a mileage basis, as was done in the more accessible parts of the Scottish Highlands, proved to be as unsatisfactory a system for our remotely rural area as for the Outer Hebrides, as will be shown by the following case histories.

In July of 1927 we had two women with *placenta previa*—a grave obstetrical complication. For the first of these two cases, during a period of three days and nights, we sent to four counties before we could get a doctor. One who lived just beyond the territory we covered was away for the summer. The next nearest, at Beverly in Bell County, was off getting married. The third, in Harlan County, could not or would not come. All of the trips involved long hours of horse-back travel because there were no telephone connections with any of these places. Meanwhile, we put special day and night nurses with the patient, who lived in a one-room log cabin on a remote creek in the upper end of Leslie County. Finally we sent to Hazard in Perry County and Dr. J. P. Boggs answered our call. He rode his horse Snip to Wendover, arriving in the early hours of the night. There we gave him a fresh horse, sandwiches, and a guide. Then he rode on through the night to the Jessie Preston Draper Nursing Center, from where he was taken to the patient on Upper Bad Creek—thirty-three miles of riding in all. With two of our nurse-midwives to help him, and by the aid of flashlights, he did a version. The baby was dead but the mother's life was saved.

In the second case of *placenta previa* the baby was so premature that the nurse-midwife was able to do a version herself and so save the mother's life. We had sent for Dr. Boggs as soon as the case was reported but it was many hours before Snip could bring him to the creek beyond Hyden where the patient lived. On July 23, Dr. Boggs wrote me:

I sure was glad to hear about both patients getting so much better. Also was glad to find Mrs. Blank better when I got there. If Miss Caffin had not had the nerve to plunge and take hold she would have been a dead patient by the time I got there. So we certainly have to commend her for bravery.

These two cases determined me not only to have the small hospital we needed but a Medical Director of our own on whose services we could rely, and for whose vacations we could plan in advance. There would always be emergencies, I knew, when the nurse-midwife would have to act even before our own doctor could reach her, but it was terribly unjust to her, as well as to her patients, to leave her totally without dependable medical aid.

A twelve-bed hospital, with living quarters for its nurses and the district nurse-midwives at Hyden, meant more expensive construction than Wendover and the outpost centers. But we needed it so badly that I had to give the time it took to round up the money. I made a start right at Hyden the first summer after our work began. Our Hyden District Nursing Committee appointed a subcommittee consisting of Miss Oma Lewis, Mr. Joseph E. Hart, and Mr. George N. Morgan (Long George) of Short Creek, to conduct a drive for funds for Hyden Hospital. We set a quota of one thousand dollars but the drive exceeded it. Not all of the gifts were in money, but gifts of stone (from Judge L. D. Lewis), timber, rough lumber, locust fence posts, the use of teams, and free labor were of just as much value as money.

With no funds on hand except what our own citizens had raised, we started to get out rock. We paid the stone masons forty cents an hour but each one gave his own labor for one day as his contribution toward the hospital. By the autumn, they had quarried twenty-five hundred blocks of stone. With these "we went to sea in a sieve, we did," for we hadn't a place to which we could move our rocks, and yet we kept on quarrying more of them. Then our Chairman, my friend Alex Alexander, gave us the money for the hospital site and we started hauling the stone down to this site, one or two blocks at a time, on wooden sleds drawn by mules. We still had no money to do anything with it after we got it there, but we "called aloud":

        . . . "Our sieve ain't big;
    But we don't care a button; we don't care a fig:
    In a sieve we'll go to sea!"

II

During the coming year I had not only to raise the budget for our district work but somehow, somewhere, I had to find the money with which to build Hyden Hospital. This business of sailing in a sieve demands endurance as well as courage. For me it meant travel in and out of centuries. It took as long to go from Hyden to Lexington then as it takes to go (by air) from Kentucky to England now—a day in the saddle, a night on the train. Then, in a week or two, a night on the train and a day in the saddle. Each time I made the trip I moved from the nineteenth into the twentieth century, and back from the twentieth into the nineteenth. Well, I was born and raised in the nineteenth century and I have always felt more at home there than in the twentieth, but I had to learn to shift centuries with a frequency that made me dizzy sometimes, and tired often. I wrote Breckie's godmother, Mrs. Jesse Turner: "I never am caught up and never will be because the work gets bigger than I get faster. . . . I have had to talk so much that I fear I am digging my grave not with my teeth, but with my tongue."

I have no record of how many times I changed centuries during the summer and fall of 1926 but I know that in August I was up at York in Maine for about a week. My friend, Miss Elizabeth Perkins of C.A.R.D. days, had organized something she called the Film Mutual Benefit Bureau, in New York, to sponsor, on a nonprofit basis, the taking, the distribution and the showing of motion pictures of a high quality. As soon as Wendover was open to guests, she offered to come down with a young assistant to take pictures of our nurses at work, mountain scenery, and things like old water mills. I put this up to our local committee who invited her to shoot the pictures, and gave her a lot of help. She presented us with a set of four reels which she called *The Trail of the Pioneer*. While I stayed with her at York, I gave four neighborhood talks with them, only one of which has significance in the story of the Frontier Nursing Service. Miss Naomi Donnelley of Chicago was staying with her mother at the Marshall House in York Harbor. After my talk there, they came up to me and introduced themselves. Later, they sent us a subscription and invited me to have my first Chicago Committee meeting at their house. Naomi became one of the early trustees of the Frontier Nursing Service, as well as one of the most faithful.

By September I had commuted back to Wendover but I had to go out again in October for meetings in Cincinnati. My Executive Committee decided that I would get many more invitations to speak if we had someone to go to cities ahead of me and organize groups of people willing to sponsor my meetings. Jessie Carson (Kit), old C.A.R.D. friend, had come back to America from France full of zest for new adventure, so we engaged her to be my advance agent, or contact secretary as we called it. I invited her to Wendover so that she could see our work at firsthand and know what she was talking about. Even that first fall she did a magnificent job. In Cincinnati she had three talks lined up for me when I joined her there. Among the people we knew in Cincinnati, although he lived on the Kentucky side of the river, was Mr. E. O. Robinson of the Mowbray & Robinson Lumber Company. Judge O'Rear had brought him to visit me in the summer. Mr. Robinson was as impressed by the quality of our citizens as by our work, with the result that he sent us the first of the thousand-dollar checks he gave annually throughout his lifetime. The best thing Kit did in Cincinnati, in my opinion, was to persuade Mrs. Davis C. Anderson to be our first chairman. She was one of the most charming gentlewomen ever to be associated with our work.

When I shifted back to the Kentucky mountains, Kit moved on to Detroit and Cleveland. The engagements she made for me in these two cities, with several I took in Louisville, used up all my time from late November to mid-December. Kit lined up eight speaking engagements for me in Detroit, with such varied groups as the Board of the Visiting Nurses Association, the National Society of the Colonial Dames of America in Michigan, the Girls Protective League, the Merrill-Palmer School, the Nurses Association of Detroit, and people in three private houses—one of which was the home of Mrs. Henry B. Joy at Grosse Pointe. This was my first acquaintance with one who became not only my friend but a trustee of the Frontier Nursing Service, one whose intelligence, devotion and generosity are rarely matched in the annals of trustees. At a luncheon in Detroit I sat next to Mrs. Henry Ford. She immediately offered us the gift of an outpost nursing center—the Clara Ford on Red Bird River. She, too, was later to become a trustee, one who followed our work with unbroken affection until her death. Not long after this Detroit visit we formed a committee there, of which Mr. Gustavus D. Pope took the chairmanship.

From Detroit my tour took me to Cleveland where I spoke to the nursing associations and in the home of Mrs. Chester C. Bolton, who was already my friend. She offered us the money for another outpost nursing center—the Possum Bend at Confluence on the Middle Fork. From that day to this her joy in our work, and her generosity, have not flagged even through all the heavy demands of her distinguished public career. Before long we had a permanent committee in Cleveland, of which Mrs. Leonard C. Hanna was the chairman. An exquisite woman she was, one in whom a deep sense of social responsibility blended with a childlike gaiety of heart that kept her forever young in this world, and fitted her for that far world where she is now.

III

On November 22, 1926, my father celebrated his eightieth birthday at Wendover. My engagements beyond the mountains kept me from home but Juliette carried out the plans we had made to give him a stag dinner to which I had invited, unknown to him, the men who were his special cronies from the Hyden and Wendover neighborhoods. They brought him small presents—handkerchiefs, packages of cigarettes—as tokens of their affection. Juliette herself carried in the birthday cake with its eighty red candles. He wrote me it had been "an undreamed of birthday." A few days afterward, during an open spell of weather, he took the long horseback ride to the railroad, and came down out of the mountains for the winter before I went back in.

That year the December rains fell upon us in torrents. Three tides in ten days left us with inundated roads, heaps of mire and quicksand, great washouts and gullies. When Christmas Day dawned, half our supplies for the holidays were still at the railroad. We had had no second-class mail for ten days, and had no prospect of any for two or three weeks to come. Our nursing units at Hyden, Wendover, and the Jessie Preston Draper upriver were marooned from one another by a waste of angry waters tearing madly down the craggy slopes into the creeks and branches and bearing with them to the river logs and boulders and the earth itself in landslides. It was a bit disheartening. But our nurses made plans to have their Christmas parties on or near Old Christmas Day, on January 6. Meanwhile, they crossed precarious swinging bridges and climbed mountains on all fours "to catch" five babies who made their advent during the storms and floods.

At Wendover Ellen Halsall was called out in the early morning for a case on Coon Creek six miles away. The man who fetched her said the back water from the river covered the road for the last mile and his horse had sometimes to swim. Ellen rode off with him into the gray dawn. Eight hours later her horse, Nellie Gray, came back dripping wet, saddlebags dangling, and riderless. I often felt that if my hair turned white every time these things happened I should soon have been crowned with snow. But this time the strain was not long. Before a rescue party could start after her, Ellen came down the trail. She had been dragged off her horse but was uninjured. She took the experience composedly, this nurse who had told me in her early days of riding that she had "died a thousand deaths."

On the thirtieth of December, I had to leave Wendover to meet outside engagements and I had five patients to take with me. One was Juliette. She was expecting a baby in January and she had not had a living one in nineteen years. When Dr. Hunt came to Wendover in October, she had examined Juliette and said we must get her down to Lexington. The other four patients were children of whom one, a boy of eleven named Joe Morgan, was a bad heart case. Since overland travel was impossible for us, I decided to turn the floods to our advantage and go out in a boat. My neighbor across the river, Taylor Morgan, had some planks; I had pitch. With these he built me a flat-bottomed boat which we named "The Ambulance." On the thirtieth we floated down the river from Wendover with Juliette and Joe, picking up the three other children whose homes lay farther down. In the bow of the boat stood Taylor Morgan, guiding our destinies with the branch of a pawpaw tree. Next, on a plank, sat two sisters, Mallie, aged three, and Hannah, aged six. I sat on the second plank with Joe, who was warmly wrapped in blankets and woolens. On the third plank sat Juliette with a crippled, cross-eyed child of six, named Jean. Lastly, in the stern, on the luggage, which included supplies for any emergency, sat Martha Prewitt, alternately baling out our leaky vessel with a tobacco can and steering with a shingle.

Thus we made the sixteen miles with the current downstream. Twice we landed our precious freight, to portage the worst rapids, while we took the boat through them—at the mouth of Hurt's Creek, and in that foamy bit of water known as Judy's Whirlpool near the mouth of Betty's Branch. Across from Confluence, where we built Mrs. Bolton's nursing center a year later, there is a creek called Trace. We abandoned our boat at Trace and got hold of a mule team. Only four miles and one mountain lay between us and the railroad but it took us three hours to cover those four miles by wagon in the dark. There was no road—just rocky, flooded creeks up to the gap of the mountain and down the other side.

We had left Wendover at eight o'clock in the morning. At eight that night we stood by the tracks at the way station of Krypton when the train came thundering through. I felt Joe's and Hannah's hands tremble in mine. They had never seen a train before. "Won't hit git us?" gasped Joe. Later, in his Pullman berth, sinking back on white pillows, he added, "I thought hit was goin' to be like a waggin." Then he turned his big, sad, brown eyes up to mine and said, "I stood this better'n I thought I could." As the train thundered on down out of the mountains we counted our little boatload over—every one of them safe—with grateful hearts.

197

Joe Morgan had been living upriver near the Jessie Preston Draper Center where our nurses Gladys Peacock and Mary B. Willeford had discovered him. His father was serving a term in a Federal penitentiary, for making moonshine, and his mother had died in childbirth some years before. The neighbors had divided the children among them. Clarence Jones took Joe and was kind to him. When our nurses were called in to see Joe, they found his feet badly swollen, his face bluish and dark circles under the eyes. In the course of weeks we succeeded in getting a doctor to see him who diagnosed his case as endocarditis. The Children's Hospital in Louisville said they would receive him. I had solved the problem of how to get him out of the mountains. Before the third tide, while horses could travel, I asked my neighbor, Elihu Mosley, to go up the river after Joe and bring him down to me. I sent a heavy coat with Elihu for Joe to wear, a coat given us by another Joe from "the settlements"—the word our mountaineers used then to describe the far-off country of the lowlands.

Late one gloomy afternoon, Elihu came riding through the Wendover pull gate with Joe astride the horse behind him. As soon as he saw me Joe said, "That was a warm wrop what you sent for me to wear." Thus Joe's first word of greeting was one of courteous appreciation. I wondered where he had learned it. The second day after Joe had come to Wendover he asked me if I could write. When I said that I could, he asked, "Will you back a letter for me to Clarence? He was kind to me." Again I marveled. For the first time in my life I realized that the bread-and-butter letter was not just a thing of social etiquette. It is the outcome of a grateful heart. But Joe had more surprises in store for me. He pulled out of his pocket five cents that Clarence had given him—all the money he had—and presented it to me. Said Joe, "If you bust this nickel, you can pay for a stamp for that thar letter." This waif, who had depended upon the charity of a neighbor, had not been beggared. He wanted to meet his obligations.

During the few days that Joe spent at Wendover, he stayed close to the stone chimney, with its big wood fire, in the living room. His circulation was so poor that he felt the cold bitterly. Once when I stopped to speak to him, he raised his big, sad eyes to me and said, "Do you reckon when I git back from the settlemints I could go to a home with room near a big fire? There's allus so many children at Clarence's there hain't much room near the fire." Well, I had a big fire at Wendover and the only children it warmed were those who came and went, like Joe. I promised him that when he got back from the settlements, his place would be at my hearth. But Joe was not to "git back from the settlemints." When he died, Julia Henning (a granddaughter of the famous Confederate cavalry leader, General John Hunt Morgan) had his wasted body buried in her family lot. She said, "This child was a Morgan, and I shall claim kinship with him."

Of all the children I have known in the mountains, Joe has left the most unfading imprint on my memory. This homeless boy of eleven, whose mother had died in childbirth, whose father had been a moonshiner and was serving his term in a Federal jail, this boy who thanked you for sending a warm wrap to cover him, who thought of a thank-you letter to his host and paid for the stamp himself out of the only nickel he had in the world, who bore uncomplainingly the pangs of his mortal illness and twelve hours of exhausting travel, this waif, with a knightly code of courtesy and honor—whenever I think of him I recall the divine promise: "And they shall be mine, saith the Lord of hosts, in that day when I make up my jewels."

Chapter 21

I

THERE is nothing like underwriting a budget yourself to learn the value of a dollar and squeeze one hundred pennies out of it. But, although I had to find our money and to budget it, both, I had nothing to do with its accountability. When Mr. Charles N. Manning, President of the Security Trust Company of Lexington, Kentucky, agreed to become our Treasurer, he said he would help me to set up a budget in which he hoped there wouldn't be too many deficits for me to have to meet. He summed up the problem for me by quoting Mr. Micawber, in the debtors' prison, where he told David Copperfield "that if a man had twenty pounds a year for his income, and spent nineteen pounds nineteen shillings and sixpence, he would be happy, but that if he spent twenty pounds one, he would be miserable." After which, so the tale goes, Mr. Micawber borrowed a shilling of David to spend on porter . . . and cheered up!

Mr. Manning always had time to give me when I went to his office. Nothing brought to him was too small to receive his attention. As the months passed and my association with him became more intimate, as the acquaintance ripened into one of the warmest friendships ever granted me, I began to grasp some inkling of the burden he carried for us all. Not many large matters turned up in our early days but, later, when we began to get endowments and to receive legacies, Mr. Manning discussed the investment of our funds at the Executive Committee meetings and gave thoughtful advice. We never lost a dollar from his investments of our endowment funds during the twenty-two years he served us as Treasurer—from 1925 until his death in 1947. The same sound principles have been carried on by Mr. Edward S. Dabney, who succeeded him both as President of the Security Trust Company and as Treasurer of the Frontier Nursing Service.

Mr. Manning arranged for a certified public accountant, Mr. W. A. Hifner, Jr., to be our first auditor, and the firm of Hifner, Fortune and Potter handles our annual audits down to this day. These were printed in full in our *Bulletins* all through our early years, as were the names of all donors, with the amounts given, except where anonymity was requested. When thousands of people began giving to us annually, the printing of all their names became too expensive. Mr. Hifner then put into operation his system of numbered receipts. These are kept in triplicate; the original goes to the donor, one copy stays in the Treasurer's office, and one copy is sent up to us at Wendover. Just as we owe the careful handling of our funds to Mr. Manning and Mr. Dabney, we owe the careful accounting of them to Mr. Hifner.

I did not meet Mr. Hifner until it became time for me to take him our vouchers of expenditures, our pages of inventories, to add to Mr. Manning's bank statements of receipts at the close of our first fiscal year. To me he was an auditor, therefore a person moving in realms of tabulated figures where no common garden woman could follow him. The first impression I had of him was an awesome one, tempered only by his courtesy and kindness. Ten years later he gave his first impression of me in a letter of transmittal to Mr. Manning of his annual audit report. I quote several paragraphs:

In transmitting to you, Mr. Treasurer, the annual audit report of the Frontier Nursing Service for the fiscal year just ended, I wish I had the ability to convey to you the succession of exquisitely beautiful pictures these annual reports have visualized to me.

I shall never forget the first audit we made for the Service. The Director walked into our office, a total stranger; dumped on the floor an old rusty pair of saddlebags, and calmly announced that she wanted her accounts straightened out. You will please note that I say "accounts" and not "books," as the Service survived the first several years of its existence without the aid or impediment—according to one's point of view—of books of any kind.

I do not know how familiar you may be with saddlebags, but that was my first introduction to the species, and I am still amazed at the enormous mass of papers that first pair of saddlebags disgorged. They reminded me of nothing else quite so much as an old ragbag my grandmother kept hanging on the inside of her closet door as a receptacle for the most varied assortment of cloth, of every hue and texture, it has ever been my lot to inventory in any department store.

And, just as the contents of that humble old ragbag, under the deft fingers of my grandmother with the aid of her looms and frames, were gradually transmuted into some of the most beautiful quilts, rugs and carpets it is possible to describe, so, also, did the simple contents of that first visitation of saddlebags, and its annual successors, when assorted and assembled, depict the realization of hope and the futility of despair; the glory of tasks well done and the satisfaction of service rendered.

I shall not attempt to describe to you all the beautiful scenes these annual reports have brought to my mind, as they are too many and too varied. Their predominating motif, constantly recurring, seems to be the spirit of an intrepid adventurer and pioneer, wearing a girdle of courage, a mantle of faith and hope, a banner of mercy, and a shield of duty; a spirit imbued with an overwhelming and intense love for little children.

In the collaboration of these reports I have been accorded the privilege of witnessing history in its making: where the warp and woof of a better civilization, in an area larger than many principalities, has been fabricated through the piecing together and skillful application of an infinitude of small contributions from the four corners of the globe, to the end that generations yet unborn will be endowed with better minds and hearts by reason of a natural heritage of better bodies.

II

There was so little "cash money" in the mountains for years after we started our work that our five-dollar midwifery fee (which included complete care in childbirth, prenatal care, and nursing visits for ten days after the baby was born) was rarely paid in money. In lieu of this fee we accepted quilted "kivers" from the women, homemade split-bottomed chairs from their husbands, food from those who had a small surplus, and the husband's labor in mending fences and whitewashing barns. The one dollar a year that we asked each cabin to pay for general nursing care was more often paid in cash if it could be paid at all. Most of the region we covered was desperately poor. In 1932, the Frontier Nursing Service published a book called *Income and Health in Remote Rural Areas* by Mary B. Willeford. This was the thesis she had written for her Doctor of Philosophy degree. In the Bad Creek and Marrowbone magisterial districts of Leslie County, where her study was laid, she found in the year July 1, 1930, to July 1, 1931, that the modal per capita income (the more typical average) for the four hundred families in those districts was $85.70 a year. The bunching of the frequencies in the lower income groups was very apparent, only five families having per capita incomes of over $340 a year. These figures included not only money received but home products consumed as well. The per capita income figures were secured by dividing each total family income by the number of persons dependent on the income. The modal total money income, or that which occurs most often, was $183.53, which was $36.70 in cash for a year for each person in the average size family of five. The modal money income was exceeded by only two per cent of the four hundred families.

Since our people could not afford to haul supplies to the railroad to sell, even if on mountain land they could raise more than they needed for the support of their families, their mules, and their cows, the question often asked us was how did our people get "cash money" with which to pay taxes and to buy shoes, along with the other indispensable supplies they could not raise. They got it in two ways. First, a great many men, when their crops were harvested and molasses had been made from their sorghum cane, rode over to the railroad to get jobs for the winter months on what they called "public works." The coal mines that had been commercially opened along the railroads took on extra men during the winter months. These spurs of railroads, which ran into the mountains, had been built to transport the coal. They too could often use extra hands for a few weeks at a time. So common was this custom of going over to "public works" to earn "cash money" that syphilis was called in those days "the disease that comes from the railroad." There was almost no venereal disease in our section in our early days. We think that the pioneers who explored and settled the mountains must have been free of it.

The second way people had of making money was in felling the big timber, making rafts of the logs, and floating them down the river on the "tides"—the Middle English word still in use hereabouts to describe a risen river. There are big tides, little tides and even flood tides. Giant logs of white oak and black walnut, linden, and poplar were cut through the winter months, snaked down the sides of the mountains, built into rafts and moored for the first spring tide. The timber depreciated in value if there was a delay of even a few weeks in floating it out. Not only did the timber bring money to its owners, but many men were paid to get it out and to build and man the rafts. This work was hard and dangerous. On the Middle Fork it took from thirty to forty hours for the rafts to reach Beattyville, where they were turned over to their purchasers. Three men went down on each raft to steer, and to fend the rafts off the rocks with huge poles. Sometimes, for all their skill and hardihood, the rafts would be tossed by the river's swift current onto rocks and broken to pieces. Although men were sometimes drowned, the employment was eagerly sought after. I have seen more than fifty rafts pass Wendover on one spring tide.

III

I now come to a part of my narrative that is so sad for me I would pass it over if I could. My Juliette, Breckie's Juliette, had a girl baby in Lexington nearly a month after our boat trip on the swollen river, and died eight days afterwards. All that skill and kindness could do for her was done by my people and my friends but I was not with her. I had gone on to New York for a number of early January engagements to be followed by an operation at St. Luke's Hospital. Hard riding had not been good for me, nor had it been wise to defer the operation for so many months. But I long ago learned that consideration for one's body cannot come first in the planning of one's time.

Dr. H. H. M. Lyle, great surgeon and family friend, had expected me to make a slow recovery because I was tired, but the telegram telling of Juliette's death nearly finished me. There are times when all of us feel as I felt when I wrote Josie Hunt then, "Isn't life hard? One's heart is broken too often and too much." When Dr. Lyle gave me morphine, I passed into restless dreams where I seemed to be making that boat trip over and over again, with Juliette and Joe and the other children. I came to, muttering, "There is too much water," and then rows of gentlemen in white collars stood up and sang, like an antiphonal chorus, "Too much water." It was difficult for me to control this latest grief because it hit me when I was down and out.

In early April, with Dr. Lyle's permission, I made the trip back into the mountains. The boat on which we had come down the river in January was still at the mouth of Trace Branch. I rode over the mountain from Krypton on a quiet mule, accompanied by a new nurse, Doris Park. My neighbors, Taylor Morgan and Jink Ratliff, met me at Trace where they took charge of the boat. Going upstream was harder than going downstream had been. The men could use paddles for propelling the boat over the deep parts of the river, and poles where the water was not so deep, but when it came to the rapids, Parky and I got out and walked while the men, up to their waists in water and chained to the boat, pulled it up the swift currents. After two or three days at Hyden, I rode on to Wendover—a homecoming incredibly sad for me because I missed Juliette at every turn.

From a distance I had made new domestic arrangements for Wendover. Henri and Liliane had gone back to St. Louis. I saw the baby, my namesake, while I was in Lexington before it was taken by Juliette's married sister to be cared for by her. The people who now came to stay with me were Jahugh and Belle Morgan from Camp Creek, with their two youngest children and their niece, Lulu Morgan. They were with us for so many years that hundreds of the people who read this book will hold affectionate memories of them. Mrs. Belle Morgan, a famous gardener in our part of the world, took over the planning and direction of the Wendover garden on which so much of our subsistence depended. With her help, I gave more time that spring and summer to my flowers than I had been able to do before. The lovely word for a flower bed in the mountains is "blossom patch." My father, who kept two men employed for months each year on his stone walls and drains, had my blossom patches terraced so that the soil would not wash down to the river. He laid out the vegetable garden in a series of levels, supported by walls, not unlike the mountain slopes he had seen in the Austrian Tyrol and in Switzerland. He used to point at his stone walls and say to Jahugh, "Jay, these will be here long after you and I have gone."

The question of subsistence in the mountains during the winter months was difficult for everybody because for weeks at a time the mule teams could not make the trip to and from the railroad. I got hold of my uncle John Steele's Woodford County recipe for smoking hams and had Edna's progeny cured and hung for winter use. I built an apple house where apples and potatoes could be stored. In the early autumn I had enough supplies hauled in to last for months—things like matches, candles, kerosene and, for food, barrels of mackerel, flour, sugar. Like all of our neighbors, we canned many of the vegetables we raised. Only those who live in a remotely rural country know what it is like to plan ahead for the winter months. Among our neighbors the best housewives were the good providers who canned their vegetables, put up their fruit, and salted their meat. As for the others, some had such poor land that they never raised enough to eat, while some were grasshoppers among the ants. All of us had to see that they didn't starve.

IV

Throughout the summer following my operation, I lay low. A telephone of sorts had at last come to Wendover, which was a help. I had Brooke Alexander back with me again and another young kinsman, Joseph Carter, Jr., aged fifteen. With these eager boys as messengers, I kept in pretty close touch with our work. Dr. Lyle took all restrictions off me in the fall of that year and I was able to get back to my old system of commuting in and out of centuries. Kit Carson did brilliant work in rounding up sponsors for meetings for me in new cities, and committees we had formed the year before seemed really glad to have me back. While I followed on Kit's trail in the Middle West, she made another trip into the mountains in early December to get the feel of the country in rough weather. Ahead of her arrival I wrote my crowd:

She has no riding clothes with her at all, only shoes and galoshes. She would look a little odd wearing only them. A pair of my riding trousers have been meeting trains all fall. Ask one pair kindly to go to the railroad and get Miss Carson. Somebody's shirt must go but it should be the shirt of a tall person like Parky. Send my cousin Anne Wilson's fur coat which we have wisely kept for such emergencies.

Such good advance work had been done for me, and so diligent was I in following it up, that at the end of that fall and winter we had new committees working for us in Baltimore, Chicago, Pittsburgh, Minneapolis, and St. Paul. Dr. William H. Welch took the first chairmanship of our Baltimore Committee which was honored by several world-famous medical names. Mrs. Frederic W. Upham was the first Chicago chairman of a committee that has grown in strength and resourcefulness over the years. Although my tours took me to Philadelphia in the East and St. Louis in the West, it was not until a year later that we had permanent committees in those places. I also covered Washington, D.C., and Rochester, New York, where homes were opened to receive me, but permanent committees in both those cities were not formed until two or three years after that. It is easier to get a group of effective people to sponsor a meeting for a charity than it is to weld such a group into a permanent committee. In fact, rarely can this be done until someone all like, and know to be a good worker, consents to take the chairmanship. People have a dread of flops. They demand leadership and, if they are capable people, they rate it.

Such leadership was ours in full measure in Pittsburgh. Mrs. Charles S. Shoemaker, an old C.A.R.D. person, was so impressed by what she knew about our work that she agreed to be the Pittsburgh chairman even before we had our first meeting there—which was the best first meeting I ever had in any city. Everybody liked her and she liked everybody. One of the people she drew into her first committee was the same Mrs. William R. Blair, Jr. whose grandfather nearly fought a duel with a Breckinridge. Among the others were Mr. and Mrs. George H. Clapp, two of the little handful of trustees who kept us going during the depression years.

V

In going from Hyden and Wendover to Lexington, in the early years of the Frontier Nursing Service, we made use of three stations on the Hazard spur of the Louisville and Nashville Railroad. One was Hazard itself. Another was Typo, way station on the North Fork of the Kentucky River, to which the horses could go and return the same day—about thirty-two miles round trip—in fine weather. But Typo had two disadvantages. The station stood on the far side of the river and could only be reached in a leaky flat-bottomed boat; there was no place to leave the horses if, as might happen, one went lame and could not make the return trip.

Krypton was another way station but on the same side of the North Fork as the trail which led to it. In dry weather, we used it more often than Hazard but the seven fords of the Middle Fork, between Krypton and Hyden, made it an impassable route for horses and mule teams when the river was in tide. One morning I got off the train at Krypton and engaged a man and his mules to take me up to Hyden. He said we would probably have to swim the deep ford at Confluence, and his mule did. My mule reared up, its hind legs clinging to the river bottom while it paddled with its forefeet—half walking, half swimming. I kept on his back by throwing my arms around his neck and gripping the saddle with my knees. It was fastened on with a piece of wire instead of a girth, and tended to slide away from me. Under conditions like that Hazard, with several mountains to climb but only one river ford to cross, was the better route.

The U.S. Mail was brought to Hyden, in a mule-drawn cart, by the Hazard route. When the roads were impassable for the cart, then the first-class mail came in on muleback. One winter's day I had to ride to Hazard at the tag end of a blizzard. Teddy Bear, shod with ice nails, was "rarin' to go." Before we had traveled far, the sun came out and shone gloriously—but without warmth. We had the trail to ourselves for the first five or six miles and, then, we heard the jingling and jangling of harness and met the U.S. Mail—first-class only—coming in by mule pack. The mail carrier rode the lead mule, followed by three other mules laden with sacks. After that encounter, we rode on for miles without meeting another soul. Smoke poured from the cabin chimneys and I thanked God, as I have so often thanked Him, that ours is a country of coal and timber where even the poorest families can afford fires.

When we started down Big Creek, we ran into so much ice, and some of it so thin, that Teddy Bear broke through it often and his injured ankle, which always remained a bit swollen, began to bleed. It was then that we met two men I knew traveling towards Wendover. This gave me a chance to get Teddy Bear back to his own barn for the night. So, I exchanged horses with one of the men and pushed on towards Hazard.

By now it was getting late, and our progress was slowed by the ice in Big Creek, through which we crashed at every step. I remembered a short cut I had taken in fair weather. It went over a mountain to the head of Brown's Fork of Big Creek—with only one more mountain between us and Hazard. I led the horse up to its summit by a snow-covered trail. The sun set, as we reached the top, in a panorama of color. It was wonderful to look at but I felt lonesome in that icy world. Night descended fast. Since it was not possible to ride down the mountain, the horse and I slid down on our haunches. I reflected wryly, that if one of us broke a leg we could lie there until a thaw before anyone came our way.

It was pitch-black when we reached Town Mountain. In the darkness ahead, I saw the flares of lights that miners wear on the front of their caps. It cheered me no end to find human beings near at hand. As we pushed on towards them, suddenly they all ran away! In a moment I knew why. After a thundering blast, rocks and earth fell all about us. There was nothing to do but keep going, and so we did. The horse was stabled and I made my train—but only just.

The trains from Hazard to Lexington figure often in my story of our early years. Until a motor road was built down to the Blue Grass, there were two passenger trains that carried Pullmans, with colored porters who were kindly men. When my father took his spring and fall trips in and out, he always gave his porter a five-dollar bill saying, as he did so, "Now you be good to those nurses and children when they come down on your train." I am sure these men would have been good even without the admonition and the tip. They not only cleaned the mud off the children, but played with them. To my father they were devoted. For all of us, wearied by such riding as I have described, they had broad smiles of welcome.

Chapter 22

I

IT was a year after we began to quarry rock and haul it to the site on mule-drawn wooden sleds before the money was given us for the two wings of Hyden Hospital. The money came as an indirect result of one of my many talks, this time to the Women's Club in Louisville. Mrs. S. Thruston Ballard sat in the audience. She came up after the meeting to tell me she would be glad to give the support of one of our nurses for a year. Her interest in the work once awakened, she followed all the details of it with such concern that within a year she consented to become a member of our Executive Committee. She recognized our need for a hospital without my having to put it into words. So often during the years of our association I was to find that her mind grasped a problem before it was stated. This was true of all kinds of problems and not just of financial ones. Mrs. Ballard said she would give one wing of the hospital in memory of her daughter, Mrs. David Morton. She then arranged an interview for me with Mr. Bethel Veech, President of the United States Trust Company in Louisville and administrator of a charitable fund left by another Louisville woman, Mrs. Mary Parker Gill. Mr. Veech said he would give the accrued income from this fund for the second wing, to be erected in memory of Mrs. Gill. Both Mr. Veech and his legal advisor, Mr. Percy Booth, who concurred in this gift, were to become members of the Executive Committee of the Frontier Nursing Service.

I have been asked more than once why we built where we did—on a narrow bench of Thousandsticks Mountain above the county seat of Hyden. This always reminds me of one of my father's stories of the Confederacy. A martinet, in the form of a senior officer, made a visit of inspection to one of his juniors and hauled him over the coals because he had not fired a salute. In explanation the junior said, "Sir, there were three reasons why I did not fire a salute, and the first is that I had no ammunition." Many are the reasons I could give why it was better to build our hospital high above Hyden. The little town lies in a narrow valley where Rockhouse Creek flows into the Middle Fork of the Kentucky River, and where the mists rise early. On the mountain there is less damp and the air is clearer. Although the problems of getting a clean water supply and proper sewage disposal are more complex on a mountain than in a valley, they can be handled with less danger than is possible near other people's wells and insanitary privies. It was quieter on the mountain than in the valley. In those days our young men, for lack of anything better to do on a Saturday night, used to ride their horses madly through town, shooting in the air—a noisy custom. However, all these were subordinate reasons for our taking the bench on the mountain as a hospital site. In a narrow valley, like the one at Hyden, where the surrounding mountains are high and steep, all available land that was even semilevel had been occupied long before. The first reason, then, why we built where we did was because we had no choice.

Money for the hospital assured, the next problem was to build it. Even down to this day we are our own contractors. I had gone through the throes of building Wendover so I knew a little something, but only a little, of the headaches and heartaches that lay ahead of me. Our chairman, Alex Alexander, and I went to see Frankel and Curtis, a firm of architects in Lexington, Kentucky. They readily agreed to design the hospital for us and furnish the blueprints without charge. In addition to this they agreed to give us the names of reliable firms in Louisville, Lexington, and Cincinnati for heating, plumbing, and electricity, to receive their bids and estimates, and to pass on them for us. The one thing, said Mr. Curtis, that the firm could not do was go up to the mountains to inspect the site, in advance of drawing up the plans, or to inspect the building afterward.

II

Boards of Trustees who build hospitals in cities haven't the foggiest idea of what it means to build a remotely rural hospital. After their building is wired for electricity, they have only to turn on the switches to get it. Their plumbing once installed, they need give no thought as to where the water is to come from, and how they are to dispose of the sewage. They know they can get all the pasteurized milk they need for their patients once the hospital is occupied, so they don't have to think about that in advance. The Board of Trustees of a remotely rural hospital, on the other hand, has to build a barn and buy cows before there will be any milk. City hospital people don't worry much about manure. Remotely rural hospital people must build a screened manure bent and see that the cows' manure is removed from the stalls to the bent every day of the week except Sunday. All of this must be planned for in advance, and you get no help on it from any hospital publication that I have ever seen.

When you build a hospital off the beaten track, you have to pay heavily for modern installations. This is something else that city people don't understand unless they are members of a Board of Trustees like ours. They only think how lucky you are not to have to pay city prices for labor. True we could hire first-class stone masons at the prevailing rate of forty cents an hour, common labor at twenty cents an hour and plain carpenters at prices ranging between these two. But nobody in our part of the world could plaster walls, install a heating plant, wire a building for electricity, or put in plumbing. All such things had to be arranged for by contract with various outside firms who charged us extra because they had to send their men to the mountains. We bought our cement in carload lots at a reduced rate and received from the Louisville and Nashville Railroad a rebate of fifty per cent on all freight. But hauling to the hospital site had to be done by mule teams that took two days to go to the railroad and return and the cost, moderate enough in all conscience, was one dollar per hundred pounds.

The first thing we did, even before actual construction began, was to appoint a building committee at Hyden composed of Mr. Sherman Eversole, Mr. "Mitch" Begley, Mr. Walter Hoskins. They persuaded Corbett Brown, a first-class contractor in Hazard, to oversee our work and charge only for the time he spent on the job. It is awkward when your builder lives a day's horseback ride from the site of the building and can only spare occasional days to come over to see how the men are progressing. Members of the building committee were indefatigable in going to the site themselves to help the foremen with the knotty problems that came up between Mr. Brown's visits. They lined up fifteen mule teams, under Jonah Begley's direction, to meet each of the three carload lots of cement and plaster, in turn, as they reached our shipping point at Krypton. In those days the Louisville and Nashville Railroad allowed people at Hyden four days' leeway to empty a freight car before they put on demurrage charges. Sometimes all fifteen teams had to make two trips, each involving two days, to unload one car of cement. Jonah had our authorization to open, unload, and relock freight cars on his first trip, so the supplies would be safe until he and the other teamsters got back two days later. He saw to it that every teamster we employed had a tarpaulin. So well was the cement and plaster protected by these wagon covers that we didn't lose a sack of either from rain, nor would Jonah take the teams through the river fords if the water was high enough to wet the wagon beds.

But the local problems we faced, the building committee and I, lay within our capacities. We who lived in the mountains were geared to a nineteenth-century mode of travel. It was otherwise with the electricians, plumbers, plasterers, and steam fitters who came to us on contract from the outside. These men, from the settlements, were what the mountaineers in those days called "brought-on" or "fotched-on" people, "furriners." Most of them had never ridden a horse in their lives, and none of them liked mule-team travel. They hit Hyden one by one, sore at us and sore all over. I used to think the only thing that kept them until they finished the work they had come to do was their dread of the return trip.

One of them, a Mr. Chope, who came from a Louisville firm to install the hospital heating plant, had left Hazard on the little mail cart. He described his experiences to me thus: "We jolted along for several miles and then the wagon give out. The postboy and I got on the mules, with the first-class mail, and then the mules give out. We started to walk, and then I give out." Chope was so good-natured about his grievances that we took a liking to him at once. The thing that pleased him most was fudge, so we made it for him twice a week. The mountaineers who worked with him liked him too.

The size and weight of the heating and plumbing supplies that the "fotched-on" men brought with them were almost matched by the size and weight of their tools. And they all had to be hauled twenty-odd mountain miles by mule team in old-time wagon beds. The massive outside doors for the hospital weighed enough in all conscience, as did the seasoned, planed lumber. We had no lumber in the mountains that was not rough and green. But doors and lumber, although awkward in shape, weighed as nothing compared to the hotel-model kitchen range, the deep-well engine, the yards of flue tile to line the stone chimney. And then the tools! The ones the plumber brought with him weighed nearly four hundred pounds. Chope's tools were no light matter to haul either—and as for boilers! To meet the needs of the deep-well engine, we ordered a Standard Oil tank to be buried in the ground with a pump attached. This tank held five barrels of gasoline. But three barrels filled a wagon and gasoline was something we never hauled in combination with anything else.

The hardest part of all this lay in the planning. The "brought-on" plumber and steam fitter came in twice because the roughing-in had to be done before the walls were plastered. The second time they came (with their tools!) was to install such things as bathtubs and radiators. Before they left I had a deep-well engine expert brought in for a testing party, when the pressure was first put on Chope's boiler.

III

The toughest problems we had to meet in building Hyden Hospital and Health Center had nothing to do with the construction of the building. The local men who worked on it had a pride of craftsmanship which was beautiful to see. Our chief stone mason, Mr. Hence Stidham, a staunch member of our Hyden Committee up to the day of his death, led me to an opening for a door and said, pointing up to the arch, "I did that personally." No arch was ever better proportioned, in my opinion. The pains those stone masons took to build chimneys that wouldn't smoke, the eagerness with which they hoisted the great rocks for the hearthstones, was only equaled by the pride of the carpenters in their studding and their hand-hewn buckeye mantels. Nor did we have too difficult a time with our "brought-on" technicians once we had assuaged them after their trips in. They were competent men who knew their work and liked it so well that they put up with their hardships good-naturedly. No, the toughest problems we faced in the building of our hospital did not lie in its construction.

Only four of our problems really mattered. These were Water, Sewage, Slides, Electricity—and were they tough! In building Hyden Hospital twenty-three years ago we contended with Water, Sewage, Slides, Electricity. We have contended with them ever since then. We contend with them now. For so many of the more than twenty years since she came to us, I have been able to shove these horrors onto the competent shoulders of our Executive Secretary, Agnes Lewis, that one might think I could forget the anguish of the days when I myself had to handle them. But I cannot forget any of it in this world, and I doubt if I want to forget in the next. I think I shall helpfully haunt all builders of remotely rural hospitals on this planet, with my comprehension and my sympathy.

WATER

We got the best advice we could for the location of our first Hyden Hospital well and employed a firm of well drillers recommended as reliable. Their machine drill had to be hauled across from Hazard by four mules. After it had plunged its mammoth tongue 112 feet into the ground, the driller reported an abundance of water. A year later, when the hospital was opened and dedicated, in 1928, we found the water supply was as nothing compared to our need.

We called in consultation Mr. S. S. Snowden, a hydraulic engineer in Lexington, who found that the driller had so tapered our well at the bottom as to make it impossible for any drill to carry on any farther down. Mr. Snowden, who was a kindly man, went about exclaiming, "Poor Miss Mary, they built her a taperin' well! Such a good charity, such nice ladies, poor Miss Mary!" That was the end of Well Number One.

Well Number Two was drilled on the same level as Well Number One, again on the best advice we could get. To the right of and below the hospital site, a steep ravine runs down to Rockhouse Creek. It was assumed that we could get water somewhere in the earth at the level of this ravine. We did indeed get water, but it was salt water! After consulting with one of the professors in the School of Engineering at the University of Kentucky, Mr. Snowden came back to study our new problem. The only thing he and the engineer could suggest was that the well be shot with Nitro-Jell, after the salt area had been walled off, and saltless water obtained by creating fissures in the solid rock above the salt area. If this failed, the well would have to be abandoned. It was abandoned.

Well Number Three was sunk in the summer of 1929 on a few feet of land we bought for that purpose next the Hyden High School grounds. When it was finished we seemed at last to have enough water, although we had to pipe it a great distance through the property of three people, all of whom were so kind as to give us what Mr. Begley and Mr. Hoskins called "easements." Then the Presbyterian Church and its dormitories, perennially short of water, sank a well on their property in the same neighborhood. Our water left us at once, all of it, and ran over to them. They felt terribly about this, but since neither they nor we knew any way of getting it back, and going halves on it, we abandoned Well Number Three. Meanwhile, almost all the water used at our twelve-bed hospital had to be hauled in barrels on mule-drawn sleds. We got enough for drinking, brushing teeth, and bathing babies by installing a tank to catch the rain water from the roof. Upon the advice, freely tendered, of a mining engineer from Hazard we dug a sump hole in a cave below a coal vein on the mountain above the hospital. A small spring in the coal vein ran into our sump hole. This gave us a spot of water.

Late in 1929 we drilled Well Number Four on land given us by Mr. "Mitch" Begley. This was so near the ravine that we soon struck water. Then a dreadful thing happened. We found we had tapped the same water supply that Walter Hoskins used on his place, lying just a little below the site Mr. "Mitch" had given us. As our well gained water, his lost it. Mr. Hoskins, one of our staunchest friends, made no complaint but we sent the well driller over to his well to dig it to the same depth as ours. Then we shared the water. This was enough for a private family but not enough for a hospital. However, we made do with it for several years.

Our hospital plant was enlarged late in 1930 after Mrs. Warren

214

Thorpe and Mrs. John E. Rousmaniere of our New York Committee came down to see us. They gave us the money for an annex to be erected high up behind the hospital and connected with it by a bridge. Here, a suite of two rooms and a bath was set aside for cases of communicable disease. We used the rest of the annex as bedrooms for the nurses until they got their own building years later. This enlargement put such a strain on our water supply that we could only run the gasoline engine an hour at a time. Then we had to wait hours for the well to fill up before we could run it again. This had to be good enough until we could do better, but Mrs. Thruston Ballard promised the hospital a new well when we could locate a sure site for drilling it.

In 1934 a member of our Executive Committee, Miss Mattie Norton of Louisville, gave us the site where Joy House now stands and all the land below it down to the road. This land slopes from both sides to the middle. A mining engineer from Hazard assured us that we should find water in abundance between these slopes but he could not suggest where it would be advisable to drill. All he really knew, he said, was that the lay of the land indicated that water would lie under it, but at what subterranean depth or in what quantity he could not say. By this time I had learned there was only one thing to do and I did it. This was to ask a dowser to be so obliging as to come over to Hyden and tell us where to sink Well Number Five. Mr. Oakley Spurlock on Red Bird River is a person with the rare gift of water divining. He is most obliging in offering his services without charge to such of his friends as want wells.

One of our own nurses, Mary Cummings, had discovered that she too was a water witch when she helped Mr. Spurlock locate the site for the well at the Clara Ford Center on Red Bird River. Thus it came about that Oakley Spurlock and Mary Cummings chose the place where we drilled Well Number Five. It was fascinating to watch them move slowly down the gully between the two slopes with peach tree switches in their hands. The switches bent over at the right and at the left of the gully, indicating water moving towards the center. At one spot, at one spot only, the switches pulled down so hard that they twisted Mr. Spurlock's and Mary's hands completely around. This must have been where the two streams joined together into one large one. We drilled right there. At 210 feet we got what old Uncle George Duvall, our driller, called one of the biggest flows of water he had ever reached in twenty-five years of drilling—inexhaustible. Had we sunk our well only ten feet up the gully above the place located by the two dowsers, we would have found water but nothing like enough.

In Uncle George Duvall, a driller from Lexington, we were so lucky as to get not only an experienced man but an honest one, who took pride in his work. Every day during his weeks of drilling, we got his reports on the strata through which the great tongue of the drill moved down into the earth. He reported when he first found water and, after bailing, said it was not enough. When he tapped a subterranean river, with water to supply the biggest hospital plant we could ever build, his gladness matched ours.

This should have brought the section on wells to an end except that troubles with wells never end. Two years after it was dug, Well Number Five had a sand slide some hundred feet or more down in the earth. Uncle George Duvall, whose arm had been torn out of the socket by the chains of his well drill, was then living on an old-age pension down in Lexington where we kept in touch with him. But he could not help us again. This meant that Agnes Lewis had to locate another drill and bailer. It took about a month to get the sand out and install a brass strainer. We have had two sand slides since then, and more than one breakdown of pump and engine. But, for several years, we have had the help of our trustee, Mr. Chris Queen, an engineer, to pull us through these later catastrophes.

It now only remains to be told how we supplied the hospital with water when we got it out of the wells. After the sinking of Well Number One, we bought a cedar tank holding thirteen thousand gallons of water which we had set on a stone and concrete foundation about three hundred feet on the mountain above the hospital. There the water, when at last we got it, came down by gravity not only to the hospital but to the fire hose hydrant and to all the other buildings that were erected later on our Hyden acres. But the tank did not hold enough water to tide us over the more or less frequent breakdowns of the engine and pump, or the dislocations by slides of the buried water mains. Later, we built a second tank of approximately fifteen thousand gallons, this time of stone and cement. Both are kept full so that we have a sufficient reserve of water to last the hospital plant about a week, with care taken in its use, whenever there is a breakdown.

SEWAGE

Mrs. Ballard gave the hospital its first sewage system. I saw Mr. F. C. Dugan, Chief of the Division of Sanitation of the State Board of Health in Louisville, and laid our situation before him. He gave me a blueprint for a septic tank and told me the number of feet of drainage tile we should lay with it. Now a septic tank is a comparatively simple thing to build and there is no trouble even on mountain land in finding a level enough place on which to put it. It is otherwise with drainage fields. The trenches dug for them in the mountainside, and the water flowing through them, loosen the terrain and start slides in a region where slides start anyway with the least provocation. The original septic tank for the hospital is still in use but the drainage field had to be moved to another level below Aunt Hattie's Barn. This first septic tank and drainage field were only the beginning. When Mrs. Henry B. Joy of Detroit gave us Joy House, the home for our Medical Director, we had to put in another septic tank and drainage field. When Mardi Cottage, quarters for our Frontier Graduate School of Midwifery, was built with money given by New England friends, that called for a third septic tank and drainage field. When at last another of our dreams came true and the Margaret Voorhies Haggin Quarters for Nurses was given us, we built a fourth septic tank and drainage field. The only place left for this, within our boundary of 35.46 acres, was the hospital horse lot.

After we had coped for years with drainage fields, the slides they caused, and the way in which the effluent broke out of bounds and had to be piped and carried by culverts into a ravine, we decided to find out if it would be possible for us to arrange for a central sewage system. We again sought advice from the Sanitary Engineering Division of the State Board of Health. After an inspection trip they told us to call in a private firm of sanitary engineers. This firm advised that we assemble all of our sewage in one gigantic line and take it down to the playground of the Hyden High School, on a bottom by Rockhouse Creek. Here, they said we should build our drainage field. They figured the total cost, in 1945, at over fifteen thousand dollars. The High School authorities were quite willing to give us an easement, provided we built the drainage field when school was not in session and restored the playground afterwards. It might or might not have been possible to persuade someone to meet the cost. However, here again was a situation that reminded me of the martinet in my father's story. Under half of the playground there is a layer of solid rock.

SLIDES

From sewage one naturally drifts to slides, although not all of them, by any means, are caused by drainage fields. Faith isn't the only thing that moves mountains. Sub-zero temperatures crack them, as do torrential rains. Wherever they crack, they slide. The biggest and most awful slide we had at Hyden Hospital seemed to come from the sheer weight of the building and its foundations on the mountain bench. The long slope that lies below the hospital down to the winding road had been denuded of its forest covering, and planted in corn. Like millions of other acres in the Appalachian range, it was too steep for the planting of any kind of crop, least of all corn. When this slope began to slide, it slid from the hospital steps on down. The building itself did not move because it was too firmly pillared on solid rock, but it began to look as though we would need a derrick to draw the patients up to it and let them down. The donors of the hospital came to the rescue. Mrs. Ballard paid for a great retaining wall to be built about twenty feet from the hospital steps. Mr. Veech gave, from the Mary Parker Gill Fund, the money for a second wall to be placed above the winding roadway far below. These walls were built by "brought-on" contractors who employed our own stone masons to help them. To the State Highway Department we were indebted for engineering supervision, given without charge, by their Mr. W. S. Carrington.

As soon as the walls were finished we planted a forest on the long slope between them. From the heads of families around Hyden we accepted trees in payment of their annual nursing fees. Scores of men rode in with either hard- or softwood young trees lying across the pommels of their saddles. These they planted where we wanted them, and each got his receipt for his dollar annual fee. Some of these trees are now more than forty feet tall. For quick results we planted wild honeysuckle and, much later, had to pull most of it up because it choked the life out of the trees.

Our retaining walls, which are greater in depth below the ground than in height above it, put an end to our worst slide. But in between them the land kept slipping so much, despite our forest, that it broke the top off the lower wall. The slips were caused chiefly by wet weather springs. Finally, in the fall of 1941, the American Rolling Mill Company (Armco) at Middletown, Ohio, one of whose officers was the late Mr. W. Walker Lewis, the brother of our Agnes Lewis, became interested in our problem. This isn't the first nor the last time that a big business has shown a big comprehension of our problems and given us big generosity in meeting them. Armco sent two of their engineers to Hyden to make a survey of the hospital mountain and to draw up plans to control the slips. Armco followed this up with a gift of the 220 feet of perforated galvanized metal pipe called for in their drawings. By this means we got the worst of the underground water under control.

ELECTRICITY

It isn't possible to run a modern hospital without electricity. There were no power lines in all our territory of hundreds of square miles when we built, or for years afterwards. We tried to persuade the power company in Hazard to run a line to Hyden, with its three hundred inhabitants, and bring light to us all. But they were not willing to do this until after a modern highway had been cut through.

Mr. Veech gave us two Kohler of Kohler engines which we installed in a wee stone house hard by the hospital. This gave us not only light but enough power for our sterilizers and our first two refrigerators, which were also gifts. But the power was not enough for an X-ray machine and, whenever we ran the autoclave for our dry dressings, it took all the power we had with none left for refrigeration or light. In a region of lamps and lanterns, our hospital with all its lights on of a dark night looked like a great airship riding above the mists of the town.

The hospital had been built six years before the Kentucky–West Virginia Power Company sent lines in to Hyden. We connected with them about a year later, after much dickering on my part to bring their rates down to charity size. We connected with heartfelt relief because, although our engines were good ones, we had no electrician to take care of them. A man had to come up from Lexington every time one got out of order. Until he came, the hospital was without light, ice, or sterilization. When at last we got the blessing of public power, and only those who have run rural hospitals without it know what a blessing it is, we were able to install a good many things we needed. Mrs. Ballard, who had become our chairman after Dr. Alexander's death, gave us an electric engine and pump for her well. This did away with the use of gasoline. Mrs. Morris B. Belknap, our fourth chairman, who learned of our work and began to support it while the hospital was a-building, gave us our X-ray machine. We also had two more refrigerators given us. All of these needed and welcome gifts added to the load on our circuits. They sizzled. To stop that, we installed more circuits. At the same time we substituted rigid conduit for the BX cable with which the hospital had been wired.

Such, in brief, has been the struggle of one remotely rural hospital to have and to hold its share of light and power.

III

Hyden Hospital and Health Center was ready for dedication in June of 1928, but that is a chapter in itself. The two buildings, connected with each other, housed the district as well as the hospital nurses and had only twelve patient beds. Great verandas ran the full length of the Gill Wing on both floors. Years later, through the generosity of Mrs. Joy and of Mrs. Belknap, these were enclosed and heated. This enlargement gave us eighteen beds and eight bassinets upstairs, and much larger clinic space downstairs. It was not until 1949, when the Margaret Voorhies Haggin Quarters for Nurses was built that we got all of the nurses out of the hospital and its annex.

Now Hyden Hospital has twenty-five beds and twelve bassinets, with two extra beds available for isolation. Even so, it is not spacious enough to meet the demands upon it. Another wing will come someday, although now it shines only in our far-off dreams. As Thackeray says at the end of *Vanity Fair:* "Ah! *Vanitas Vanitatum!* . . . Which of us has his desire? or, having it, is satisfied?"

Chapter 23

I

FROM the Scottish Highlands to those of Kentucky was "a fur piece" in the eighteenth century but there were not lacking men to undertake the dangerous journey. The little sailboats of a few hundred tons' burden broke the ocean's track for the sea palaces which have succeeded them. Bold was the spirit of the men who went down to the sea in ships in these earlier times, and bolder yet the spirit of those who left the settled coastlands of Virginia to plunge into a mountain wilderness. Among the most daring of the early adventurers was a Scottish Highlander called Roderick MacIntosh. Men of the MacIntosh breed, whether in Kentucky or Scotland, go back in their ancestry to an origin older than human recorded time, their destiny shaped always by the determining forces of mountains. The mountaineer, individualistic and deep-rooted, has a kinship of thought and emotion with every other man and woman bred like himself.

We wanted a Scottish Highlander to dedicate Hyden Hospital and Health Center and set our aim at the greatest Highlander of his generation, Sir Leslie MacKenzie. We wanted Lady MacKenzie to come with him to represent in her person the pioneer wives who crossed the ocean with their men, and rode with them through trackless forests and innumerable dangers to found Kentucky. It seemed to us that Sir Leslie MacKenzie, whose work had done more than that of any other living man to make "regions, rugged, roadless, and mountainous" safe for women and children, should dedicate our hospital on the bench of Thousandsticks Mountain, at the foot of which lies the grave of Roderick MacIntosh.

To bring Sir Leslie and Lady MacKenzie from Edinburgh to Hyden did not involve sailboats and trackless forests but it took a spot of organizing, of which the simplest part was the decision of our Executive Committee to invite them, and their immediate acceptance of the invitation.

The two things that needed careful planning in advance were hospitality and transport. Nearly fifty people were coming in to us from beyond the mountains to be entertained overnight. For luncheon on the day of the dedication we expected about a thousand local citizens as well. Hospitality was the easier problem of the two because everyone at Hyden came in on it. We could put up a number of people in the rooms and wards of Hyden Hospital, because no nurses or patients were to move into it until after the dedication, and the leading citizens of Hyden offered their spare rooms for the other guests. As to the food and its preparation, that too was under control. Nearly everybody at Hyden gave food and half the women had volunteered to cook and serve it, with some of my Blue Grass cousins to help them.

The transport of fifty people by horseback and mule team twenty-two miles from the railroad at Hazard presented a more complicated problem than feeding them, and putting them to bed, after they got to Hyden. A convoy of around thirty horses and mules had to be taken over to the railroad the day before, and stabled overnight. Since Mrs. Ballard and Sir Leslie and Lady MacKenzie did not ride horseback, we bought a buckboard for their trip in. Jonah Begley undertook to drive it, with his fine team of mules. Three wagons, their beds covered with hay, were lined up for such other people as did not ride. A fourth wagon was assigned to the luggage, and a fifth to the Perry County miners' band, under the direction of Mr. Christian Mahr.

John Breckinridge's daughter, Marvin, who was our first girl courier and had come to us just after her graduation from Vassar, was given the post of transport officer. She was to have Brooke Alexander as an assistant, with several men to help in taking thirty or more horses and some of the wagons to the railroad the day before. When everything had been lined up, I left the mountains to meet the MacKenzies and take part in the honors and festivities that had been arranged for them in the Blue Grass and in Louisville. A day or two before we were to bring the MacKenzies to Hyden, a tragedy in Marvin's family called her home. At the same time I learned that Brooke had come down with German measles. The only person left to handle transport was Martha Prewitt. She had married my brother Clifton the preceding March, but came back to Kentucky for the dedication. To her I assigned the task of bringing the guests in, while I hurried back to the mountains in advance of their coming.

II

In setting Tuesday, June 26, for our Dedication Day, we had been afraid that it might be too hot, especially for Sir Leslie and Lady

MacKenzie, but none of us dreamed it would be too cold and too wet. The heavens opened, the rain fell in blinding torrents, and the creeks and rivers rose rapidly. Our guests, escorted in special Pullman cars by Mr. E. S. Jouett, Vice-President of the Louisville and Nashville Railroad, reached Hazard in the early morning. There they were met by a deputation of leading citizens, under the chairmanship of Mr. Judy, who took them to a hotel for a big breakfast. After this sumptuous entertainment, they went off, under Martha's guidance, into the storm.

At Hyden, some of us got on our horses early and rode two-thirds of the way along the road to Hazard to meet our incoming guests— their number augmented by a Hazard contingent. The riders were strewn all along the trail well in advance of the buckboard and wagons. More than twenty were men, among them two reporters and a rotogravure photographer from the Louisville *Courier-Journal*, and Paul Porter from the Lexington *Herald*. A scattering of women rode with the men, among them Mrs. Ballard's granddaughter, Jane Morton, who was escorted by her father, Dr. David Morton. All were in high spirits; all were soaking wet. The one I had most wanted to meet on that trail, our chairman, Alex Alexander, was already stricken by the mortal illness which took him from us within the year.

Leaving the riders for Martha to guide, we pushed on past them to meet the buckboard and wagons. Everybody had been wet through to the skin, had dried out at a road construction camp, and had been wet all over again. Although the dear things in the hay did not look as cheerful as the horsemen, their sportsmanship left nothing to be desired. The first wagon I met was covered completely with a tarpaulin. I said to the driver, "Is this the luggage?" He said no, that it was the band. With that, the tarpaulin seemed to lift itself up before my astonished eyes, exposing a bunch of men, wind instruments, and a drum, trying to protect themselves from the rain whilst rocking and swaying over the stones. In the buckboard, Sir Leslie sat next to Jonah Begley, Lady MacKenzie and Mrs. Ballard on the back seat. To the end of his life, Sir Leslie cherished one incident of his travel on the Hazard-Hyden road. When the buckboard balanced on the edge of a precipice, Jonah called out to a man standing near, "Charlie Gayhart, if you just keep holt of the right corner, she won't capsize." The picture that I remember the most vividly is of Lady MacKenzie standing on the trail, while Jonah urged his mules through an impasse, exclaiming in triumphant tones, "I am in the MacIntosh country." She was up to her knees in the mud of the MacIntosh country.

When at last we neared the Middle Fork of the Kentucky River, with the deepest ford that lay between us and Hyden, runners met us who said to hurry, as the river was rising rapidly. It wet the beds of the buckboard and the wagons and, needless to say, drenched the hay and the seats of those who sat thereon. But everybody got through. As we pushed up the winding road that in those days led from the river to Hyden town, a bunch of boys began shooting off their pistols, whether in welcome or sheer exuberance of spirit we did not know. But we told them to cut it out. The last of our guests were safely delivered at the hospital, where a welcoming party greeted them with bright fires and plenty of hot food.

Everybody had met the strain of that twenty-two-mile ride with imperturbable good humor. Their sporting qualities never failed, not even when they had to climb out of buckboard and wagons to creep along ledges above precipices, or when the rain and the rushing water in the river ford wet them through and through. Nor did they complain that night when their luggage failed to reach them. The last of the wagons, the one which carried the luggage, could not be driven over the ford without wetting everything. While their clothes dried, we dressed our guests in such odds and ends of things as people had sent down to us. We had to put some of the men in skirts. Dr. Mc-Cormick wore a sheet, which gave him the effect of a noble Roman in a toga. Since their slippers had not come, they all had to go barefoot until their shoes dried out—all that is but Mrs. Ballard and the Mac-Kenzies who had overnight bags in the buckboard. It was a gay party.

When the Dedication Day dawned fair over a watery landscape, our guests were still in a state of imperturbable good humor, even to the reporters whose struggles to get their reports out over the telephone system can better be imagined than described. Soon after breakfast people began to arrive for the ceremonies but there were only around five hundred of them. By that time the river was past fording. Our Possum Bend nurses contrived an ingenious way of getting to Hyden. They had men take them across the river by boat, but first they turned their horses into the stream and slapped them gently to make them swim across. Among the nurses who had come to us not long before was one Scottish Highlander, Ann P. MacKinnon (Mac), from the island of Skye. She, who was with us then, when Scotland and Kentucky met at Hyden, is with us now.

III

The dedication ceremonies took place on the hospital veranda above which we had placed the Stars and Stripes and the Union Jack. The Leslie County Judge, William Dixon, presided with dignity and charm. Dr. William J. Hutchins of Berea gave the invocation. Then Judge L. D. Lewis made a stirring address of welcome. All through the morning the Perry County band played with such spirit and feeling as only miners who have been half drowned can play. After Sir Leslie had finished his address and words of dedication, and the band struck into "Hieland Laddie" and "Annie Laurie," nobody's eyes were dry. Before the ceremonies they played "My Old Kentucky Home," and they closed them with "Auld Lang Syne." Mr. Jouett, whose services in giving passes for the sick on the Louisville and Nashville Railroad were deeply appreciated in our section, was called on for a few remarks as were Dr. Arthur McCormack and Lady MacKenzie. To her Mr. Manning presented a bedspread made by our Kentucky mountain weavers and colored in the native indigo dye—"blue pot."

Sir Leslie's address was published in full in the *Lancet* of London, July 21, 1928, but he departed from the written words many times because the occasion moved him deeply. He began by saying that roads like ours, if in Great Britain, would be venerated as scenery but not used for travel. He described the Highlands and Islands Medical and Nursing Service, telling us that the ten million acres of land covered by this service had a scattered population of less than that of the city of Edinburgh. "The more one studies things as they are today," he said, "the more one is impressed with the infinite complexities of the growth of peoples." He spoke of the aim of the Highlands and Islands Medical and Nursing Service to bring the care of physicians and nurse-midwives to those isolated citizens for whom they were otherwise unobtainable, and to meet the bulk of the costs. "We aimed at eliminating from the charges the fact of distance." He brought out the complexities of administration for such diverse areas as northern Perthshire and the Outer Hebrides. He said, "No doubt, it is these varieties of difficult administration that have fascinated Mrs. Breckinridge in looking for a parallel with the difficulties of the Kentucky mountains, and there are many parallel conditions in the two countries. But most striking, perhaps, is the parallel in character and outlook, the disposition due to the necessity of facing the forces of nature alone, the relative sterility of the hills and glens, as well as the ferocities of the wind and water."

Near the conclusion of his address Sir Leslie said:

I have been speaking of Scotland, but I have been thinking of Kentucky. With you, as with us, there is the ever-recurring tragedy of hardship and death. . . . All our institutions for the welfare of mothers and their children have their tap-root in the one great fact that, when the child dies, the race dies, and when the race dies, the great fight between life and nature is over.

This hospital is the radiating center of the nursing service in these mountains. The maxim of the trained nurse is: "You need me? I am ready." The hospital is a temple of service where the lamp never goes out. . . . That is what inspires the skilled and brave nurses to face the day's duty without misgiving; to feel that the least of duties is a great and holy thing and to live for all their working days in the atmosphere of creative friendship. Here, in their hours with one another and their tales of adventure, they will keep warm the fires of woman's social genius.

Sir Leslie quoted the words of the memorial tablets, set in the stone of the two buildings, before making his

Act of Dedication

In all reverence, I dedicate this hospital to the service of this mountain people. The act of dedication will have consequences beyond all imagination. It will evoke responses along the many hundred miles of these mountain frontiers and among the millions of their people. The beacon lighted here today will find an answering flame wherever human hearts are touched with the same divine pity. Far in the future, men and women, generation after generation, will arise to bless the name of the Frontier Nursing Service.

IV

After the luncheon on Dedication Day, many of the "brought-on" guests headed back for the railroad and in so doing missed the glory of the evening. We had bought quantities of Roman candles and sky-rockets. After night fell, the sky above mountains and valley was illuminated for nearly an hour by the first display of fireworks our children had ever seen. This part of the ceremonies had been planned for them. Judge Lew's only son, Jesse, took charge of it with the help of eager volunteers from among the older boys. The children, even the "least ones," were enraptured. Miss Ruth Huston's moving pictures show children with their fathers and mothers climbing the long slide up to the hospital bench on Thousandsticks Mountain. Mr. Ballard Thruston, who took photographs of everything and everybody, caught the faces of some of the children—but not as they looked when they saw the skyrockets.

My father and I had invited Sir Leslie and Lady MacKenzie to rest for a few days at Wendover before setting out again on their travels, which were to take them to Canada before they sailed. This was the only time I regretted the overlapping of patients and other guests at Wendover. We could not move the patients to Hyden Hospital immediately after the dedication because we had discovered the shortage of water in Well Number One, and the inside painting had not been finished. During the MacKenzies' visit, I had a crippled child (awaiting transportation to the railroad) on a sleeping porch just off my only double guest room, where I had to put the MacKenzies. In the clinic was a mother with a newborn baby. Our patients included Enos and

Eva, motherless infant twins, of whom more later. One of our nurses was sleeping on a cot in the post office, to be within call of the young mother, and within earshot of the cries of the twins. With the three babies and the two other patients in the house, it wasn't as quiet as my father and I would have liked it. But the MacKenzies, who were genuine through and through, accepted with pleasure the interlude we had arranged for them in their hard schedule.

When it came time for them to leave, Jonah Begley drove them to the railroad in the buckboard, while Teddy Bear and I escorted them two-thirds of the way. After they reached the cut for the new highway, they were over the worst of the trails. When the MacKenzies climbed out of the buckboard for the last time, so that Jonah could lighten his load for a particularly bad bit, she looked up at me and said with a smile, "I am still in the MacIntosh country." She was again up to her knees in MacIntosh mud, this time on the borders of MacIntosh Creek.

In one of Lady MacKenzie's letters, written soon after her return to Edinburgh, she wrote that she had had slides made from Mr. Thruston's photographs, and was about to give twenty lectures with them—from Nairn in the north of Scotland to Dumfries in the south. "Scotland will know something of Kentucky before I am done with them," she wrote. In the same letter she said: "Now the year has gone and it feels as if Kentucky filled it all. Very few days pass that your wonderful country does not get talked about. Often have we longed for the artist that could fix forever that sudden swift sweep of a woman on horseback round that side road on the hill. But we have many pictures and many memories, and Kentucky now is part of ourselves and of our life." In another letter she wrote, "Truly, we are homesick for Kentucky."

We in Kentucky were often homesick for those dauntless ones, who came to our mountains, in the latter years of their lives, to bind in a common tie their Highlands and ours. The way we felt about them is expressed in the words of my favorite Jacobite song:

> Better lo'ed ye canna be,
> Will ye no' come back again?

But they could not come back. For them it was to be as it had been for me, after my travel through the Outer Hebrides, an experience not to be relived, except in memories and dreams.

Chapter 24

I

THE six outpost nursing centers of the Frontier Nursing Service were built during the years 1927–30. After nurse-midwives were stationed at all of them, we covered an area of approximately seven hundred square miles in which we carried bedside nursing, midwifery, and public health for nearly ten thousand people. Our aim was to cover, in the same intensive way, approximately twelve hundred square miles. This would have brought us to within from six to ten miles of the three spurs of the Louisville and Nashville Railroad, which approached our territory from the south, west, and northeast. Had we been able to do this, we would have left no territory uncovered, and no people uncared for, within the range of our demonstration. But, after 1930, we could expand no further. In fact, during the early thirties, we had to struggle like the Red Queen, just to keep a toehold in the area for which we had assumed responsibility. We call the country that lies adjacent to ours, between us and the railroads, our "fringe territory." Hyden Hospital, the only hospital for this territory, is open to the people who live there, especially those maternity cases who have no one at hand to take care of them, and the children, for whom our beds have always been free.

The principle of organization in a remotely rural field of work is one of *decentralization*. In such a country *time* and not mileage is the factor involved in daily travel and in all emergencies. It is not a question of the patient's distance from his nurse but of how long it takes her to reach him. This is as true of travel by dogsled in the Labrador snows, or travel by boat in the Outer Hebrides, as it is of horseback travel in the Kentucky mountains. It is the crux of the problem to be handled, not only for medical and nursing care, but for every local situation. Schools cannot be consolidated where there are no motor roads. They must be decentralized, else the children could not reach them. Voting precincts must be decentralized, or many

228

citizens could not vote. Even the bulls, with which cows should be bred annually, to keep up the milk supply, must be decentralized. The more rugged the country, the greater the need for more bulls.

When a nursing center in our horseback country was opened, in the heart of a five-mile radius, its nurse-midwives covered about seventy-eight square miles of ground with a population of approximately a thousand people. In a service that combines midwifery, bedside nursing, and public health, two nurse-midwives at such a center will be kept very busy indeed. But their farthest patients are only five or six miles away in any direction and, on a good mount in good weather, can be reached in about an hour even when travel is through rocky creek beds and across the gaps of mountains. It will take longer to reach them on a January night in a blizzard. When one adds to the nurse's time spent in getting to an emergency case (whether a gun-shot man or a woman in childbirth), the time a messenger has taken to reach her, there may be a good two or more hours between her and the patient who needs her.

In a service designed, like ours, for a remotely rural area, the hospital and medical director are like the palm of a hand from which fingers radiate in several directions. It is possible, under this system, for a hardy physician to be responsible for the medical needs of some nine thousand people annually, many of whom he does not meet, whereas he could serve little more than a five-mile radius without his nurse-midwives. A fine physician in Owsley County, with whom I talked when I made my investigation in the Kentucky mountains in 1923, said to me, "It is impossible for me to reach every hoot-owl hollow in my section in time to be of any use to a woman in childbirth. Midwives are essential here. I wish they might be nurses as well."

II

In building our outpost centers we located them from nine to twelve miles apart so that where one district nurse-midwife's territory ended another district nurse-midwife took over. We paid no attention to county lines, which have a way of running right through the middle of a community, sometimes even through the middle of a house. They are even less relevant to natural geographical features, which determine the early settlements of people, than state lines, and heaven knows these are irrelevant enough.

In developing the area covered by the Frontier Nursing Service we followed the waterways, the natural arteries of travel and trade in our part of the world. This meant that we built along the two rivers in our section—the Middle Fork of the Kentucky and Red Bird River—and on their tributary creeks. The creeks head up in mountain ranges. As a rule, few people live between the head of a creek, on one side of a mountain gap, and the head of the next creek on the other side. Since we could not place outpost nursing centers everywhere that they were needed, we tried to place them in such a way that the districts they covered stopped at the gaps of mountains. We covered about sixty miles along the Middle Fork of the Kentucky River, and its tributary streams, from Beech Fork Nursing Center in Leslie County to Bowlingtown Nursing Center in Perry County. On Red Bird River in Clay County, where we have three outpost nursing centers, we followed the same principle. When the last two outpost centers were built in 1930, and for years afterward, it took seven days in the saddle to make rounds of all eight of our stations, starting either from Wendover or Hyden Hospital and staying overnight at each center. At the upper and lower ends of our territory we crossed the gaps of the mountain ranges that lay between the two rivers and, in that manner, eased over from one river and its tributary streams to the other.

In putting up all of its buildings everywhere, the Frontier Nursing Service has been careful about two things. First, that the excavation for the building must reach solid rock so that the foundations will not sink. Second, that every building, down to the barns and chicken houses, must be located well above the highest floodwater mark. The initial temptation to build on bottom land is great. Wells are easily sunk, there is plenty of room for a septic tank and drainage field, there will be no slides. But anyone who knows this country will resist the temptation. Sooner or later the bottom lands would be flooded, resulting in an appalling mixture of well water and sewage, and a foul debris left in the houses themselves, even if parts of them were not undermined and washed away. I knew, from talking with old-timers, that floods had come and would come again. I foresaw the day when the forests on the gaps would be subject to destructive lumbering and there would be little cover left to hold back the melting snows and the pounding rains of late winter and early spring. Because of the destruction of this forest cover, the floods that come now are more frequent and higher than those the earlier generations of our people knew. It is bad enough for the Frontier Nursing Service to have feet of sand deposited upon the best parts of its pastures, and fences washed away, in every flood, but its buildings are safe.

JESSIE PRESTON DRAPER MEMORIAL NURSING CENTER
"Beech Fork"

Our first outpost nursing center was also the first place to be built after Wendover. Gladys Peacock and Mary B. Willeford had been with us about two months, in 1926, when I told them to go up to Beech Fork to open up the district there and build the nursing center. They said that they knew nothing whatever about building. I replied that neither had I known anything about it when I built Wendover. If I could learn by doing, so could they. The site chosen was thirty-two miles from the shipping point which was Pineville in Bell County. It took the mule teams four and sometimes five days to go to the railroad and return with supplies. Peacock and Texas rode off with the light hearts of those whose ignorance is total. Since there was no trained builder anywhere near that section, and no possibility of getting one to go in, I had ordered, with the permission of the donor, Mrs. Draper Ayer of Boston, a ready-built house to be shipped to Pineville and hauled across to Beech Fork. Its plumbing was to come with it. The circular about it implied that a child could put it up, with a little help from daddy and mummy. I sent a man to the site to drill a well. This was so abominably done that I fired the man in the Middle Fork with the river rising so quickly that, tall as Teddy Bear was, it had reached his belly. There wasn't time for argument. I sent the driller out on one side of the river while I rode out on the other. A second well man drilled a decent permanent well, later.

Peacock and Texas stayed with our old friends, Mr. and Mrs. Carlo Hoskins at Hoskinston, near the mouth of Salt Well Creek, two and a half miles below the site of the nursing center. Their first job was to build the barn, and get the foundations for the house laid in advance of its arrival. They did not want to show their ignorance of the task to which they were assigned, but it took a lot of bluffing on their part not to lose face. The first morning after their arrival, they got to the site at seven o'clock and found twenty-five men all grouped around the beech trees, all wanting to work, and all waiting for directions from them. After they had told some of the men to cut down the trees where the house and the barn were to go, others to dig the foundations, and those who could quarry to get out stone, Peacock was approached by Mr. Carlo Hoskins who, because of his experience and intelligence, had been chosen to be foreman. He said to her, "What about sills?"

"What about what, Mr. Hoskins?"

"Sills."

She said afterward that she felt swamped. What were sills? Surely he could not be talking about window sills yet, before the foundations were even dug. She looked wise and thoughtful.

"Well, Mr. Hoskins," she said, "I'll ask Miss Willeford. Mrs. Breckinridge may have said something to her about them."

So Peacock went down the hill to the barn site where she found Texas. She called her to one side and said, "What about sills?"

"What about what?"

"Sills."

"What the dickens are sills?"

Peacock replied, "Well, look here, old sport, Mr. Hoskins has asked about sills. What are we going to do about it? We can't let him think that we don't know what they are. We've just got to bluff."

They scrambled up to where the foreman was standing. "Mr. Hoskins, Mrs. Breckinridge did not say anything to Miss Willeford about sills." Here Texas chipped in casually, "Er—what would you suggest, Mr. Hoskins? You know these parts so much better than we do."

"Well, I reckon you can get all you want off Luther Moseley's land. He said you could have all the timber you needed."

So it was timber!

"How soon do you think you'll be ready for them?"

"I reckon we'd better be getting them out right now."

They delegated four men to go with Mr. Hoskins, who climbed the hill at the back of the house site for about half a mile. Peacock and Texas slowly followed at some distance away, out of sight. They meant to find out what a sill looked like. Soon two enormous trees came rolling down the hillside, splashed into the water, and floated down the river until they landed on a shallow spot. Four mules, dragging large chains and hooks, were attached to the trees and snaked them up to the site. The sharp blows of four axes rang out. Little by little, slowly and evenly, the men hewed until the two large trees were made into four even blocks thirty feet long and eight inches deep. So these were sills. The whole of their house was to rest on these blocks. No wonder that Mr. Hoskins thought them important!

Peacock's racy story of the Beech Fork Center, which we printed in one of our *Quarterly Bulletins*, is the only complete description we have of building one of our outpost centers, and it is not typical because it was the first and last time we tried to use a ready-made house. When Peacock and Texas had hauled the contents of two freight cars (full of house) in twenty-four mule-team wagons, a distance of thirty-two miles, and then gone through the anguish of putting it all together, where every piece of board had to be mitered to fit the next one—when they had done all of this, they convinced me that a builder at almost any price would be no more expensive. These two nurses were to open up four more nursing center areas, and build the four houses for them, but from then on a builder was put in charge.

During the weeks it took Peacock and Texas to get their house hauled in and fitted together, they struggled with stone masons. These competent men will use rock near at hand for foundations, but in all of our buildings everywhere it has seemed to us that the only rock they consider suitable for chimneys had to be hauled by mule sled from one to three miles. The huge oak barn also had to be erected and the shingles to roof it hand-hewn out of solid oak. A white oak tree, suitable for shingles, is called a "board tree." More than one man gave a "board tree" as his donation toward the building of the barns at all of our centers. With every barn, a manure bent must be put up on a solid foundation, with a round of wire screening inserted under the roof, to let in the air, so as not to have spontaneous combustion from overheated manure. Peacock and Texas had the usual struggle, "tore their hair," as they expressed it, over the septic tank and drainage field.

Plumbing seemed to us the one essential modern thing to install in building our outpost nursing centers, with connections from the well or spring to the house, and connections from the house to the septic tank. We did not want our busy nurses to pack water, or otherwise do the work that iron pipes can do better. To install the plumbing that came with the ready-made house, I sent Perl Lewis with a few plumbing tools. He had helped the "brought-on" plumber install the Wendover water works, and learned something about such things then. When everything seemed to be ready, Peacock and Texas turned on the taps. Nothing happened. Then they climbed under the house, disconnected the pipes and discovered the trouble. The next time they turned on the taps, the water poured through and didn't stop running. At the same time the most terrifying noises came from the engine and the pump until, mercifully, the engine stopped stone dead. Water works are among the modern things that are not easy to install and operate in regions where they are unknown.

At the same time that Peacock and Texas were building the Beech Fork Nursing Center they were busy on their districts. This dual responsibility of building and nursing had to go forward with each outpost center we organized. From the moment the nurses arrived in a new area, there were constant calls for them day and night. They were also given the responsibility of organizing leading citizens into a local committee, but this had to be done slowly as they came to know the people. Mr. Walter Hoskins of Hyden, son of Mr. and Mrs. Carlo Hoskins, was our mainstay in setting up our Beech Fork Nursing Committee, where for years, until his death, we had, in Mr. Sherman Cook, one of our finest local chairmen. No labor on behalf of the nursing service ever seemed too hard for him to undertake. When Beech Fork was finished, Peacock and Texas gave a housewarming to which everyone came from miles around. Each workman looked upon it as his own nursing center. He had given some days of free labor toward the building of it. It was his house. Since the original ready-built house proved to be nothing like large enough for the crowds of people who made use of it, Mrs. Draper Ayer gave an addition to it several years later. This consists of a huge waiting room for the patients with two bedrooms above it. When it was built, of local lumber, the neighborhood took as much pride in it as they had in the original building. The men who worked on it took up a collection, in cash money, and gave it to us to buy a clock to hang in the waiting room as a testimonial to the joy they had taken in their work.

FRANCES BOLTON NURSING CENTER
"Possum Bend"

Our second outpost nursing center was built in 1927 with money given us by Mrs. Chester C. Bolton of Cleveland, Ohio. We bought blueprints for a two-story house and were so lucky as to get hold of an experienced builder, Mr. Nick Lewis, back home at Hyden for a visit that summer, to take charge of the construction. Since blueprints were an everyday matter to him, he was able to give me exact specifications of what he would need to put the house up. The citizens in the area around Confluence Post Office were so eager for one of our nursing centers that they invited me to attend a rally, and tell them what they needed to do to co-operate with us. Mr. Boyd Campbell, our first chairman, donated three acres of land for the house, the barn, and the pasture. Other men lined up with their pledges, to the value of $500.

I sent Ellen Halsall down to open up the district and handle construction problems with Mr. Nick. She established herself in a one-room log cabin close by the river, with a young girl called Dolly to be her housekeeper-maid, and with Pepper, a magnificent bull terrier who was a gift to us from Dr. Hunt. All three lived in the one room, fitted up also as a dispensary, where they kept a cot for my visits. The dispensary was screened off from the rest of the room by curtains, made from yards of yellow cotton that had been used in the decorations for the Queen of Rumania's visit to Louisville. Enough of the stuff was left over to make covers for the cots. The effect was gay. A sort of shelf was stuck on to the back of the cabin, which served as a kitchen. But the cabin was in a bottom too near the river. In mid-November, before Possum Bend was quite ready to inhabit, the rains came down so terribly and the river rose so rapidly that Ellen and Dolly decided to move their belongings up to the new center while travel was possible. They made three trips on horseback, the last one with their horses swimming. "But," as Ellen wrote me triumphantly, "we made it."

The Possum Bend Nursing Center at Confluence is twelve miles down the river below Hyden. Like Beech Fork, it is a white house with green blinds. Although it stands high above the river, which is broad and deep at that point, it is only a few yards from the bank, as the crow flies. From the upper windows, the view across the river to the great mountain, rising sheer out of it, is a majestic one. When the river is in flood, the rush of the sweeping waters adds to the majesty. The river makes several sharp turns below our nursing center, the first around Mosley Bend, the second around Possum Bend. When I used to ride through that territory in the early days, on my way to Hyden from Krypton, I thought that not many people could be living where the mountains were so steep. But from the time we opened our center, we have served the nursing needs of over a thousand people, living chiefly in the great bottom lands on the bends, and on the creeks and branches. The most famous of the creeks, written up long ago by John Fox, Jr., is Hell-for-Certain. We often had reason to dread the quicksands at its mouth, which came after every tide.

CLARA FORD NURSING CENTER
"Red Bird"

This, the first of our outpost centers to be built on Red Bird River in Clay County, was the second one for which Peacock and Texas were responsible. They moved over there from Beech Fork in July of 1928, with a wagonload of stuff, and took possession of a two-room cabin, which they whitewashed and screened. Their housekeeper-maid was a widow with a baby. One room served as a kitchen, with a curtained-off place for her bedroom. The other room had dispensary supplies and three cots, the third one for me whenever I went over there.

When Mrs. Henry Ford gave this nursing center, she included with her gift enough money for an electric light plant. The place was so well wired that when the Rural Electrification Administration ran a line up Red Bird River, many years later, and we connected with them, we had only to turn the current from D.C. to A.C. The Ford Motor Company owns thousands of acres of land in that section, where they have a camp of engineers and surveyors, with well-constructed permanent buildings located about a mile up the river from the land they donated to us.

The chief engineer in 1928 was Mr. S. E. Puckette, a South Carolinian, who showed us a thousand kindnesses in the building of our center and its great oak barn. Nothing could have been more picturesque than the site Mr. Puckette chose for us, overlooking Red Bird River, unless it was the house itself, the only house we have, except at Wendover, that is built entirely of logs. Mr. Puckette's offer to give us all the logs we wanted from the company forests made this practicable. He put me in touch with Mr. Oscar Bowling of Big Creek, an extremely able, hard-working man, of few words and transparent honesty. The Clara Ford Center was the first building we put up under his direction. He has built all of our places since then, several of them from 1939 to 1945, when he worked for us on a salary as maintenance man. He left us to become a contractor in the mining towns, but gave up this lucrative work twice to come back to us when we needed to reroof Hyden Hospital and Wendover Big House. He came back a third time to build the Margaret Voorhies Haggin Quarters for Nurses in 1949.

It was just as well for Peacock and Texas that they had so much help from engineers, surveyors and Oscar Bowling, because the neighborhood was so quickly responsive to their presence that they were almost overwhelmed by the volume of nursing work. During the first six weeks they delivered two women in childbirth, and registered nine more expectant mothers. They gave nearly fourteen hundred inoculations against typhoid and diphtheria, and were booked for weeks ahead. They enrolled almost all the babies and toddlers for regular care, and were called in for so much sickness that they had to send several times to Manchester (eighteen horseback miles away) for the two physicians that lived in Clay's county seat. While all this was going on, they organized an excellent committee with Mr. Cicero Feltner as its first chairman.

The kindnesses of the Ford Motor Company engineers did not end with the Red Bird Nursing Center. They handle our engineering problems, from the foundations for houses to retaining walls. When Mr. Puckette retired and went back to South Carolina, he was succeeded by his assistant, Mr. Chris Queen, who with Mrs. Queen lives at the Ford Motor Company camp down to this day. For years he has been one of our trustees, and we have no other who is more at our beck and call.

In 1929, Mr. Puckette and Mr. Queen made a detailed map of the Frontier Nursing Service area, and contiguous territory, which included the sites of the two nursing centers we built a year later. We had large copies of it made to hang at all of our places, and small copies, mounted on linen, that folded up and could be carried in a pocket of the saddlebags. With that map, it was possible to ride the most remote trails and not get lost.

CAROLINE BUTLER ATWOOD MEMORIAL NURSING CENTER
"Flat Creek"

The money for this nursing center was given us by Mrs. John W. Price, Jr. of Louisville and her sister, Miss Jane Atwood, in memory of their mother. The location we chose in 1929 for our fourth outpost station lies at the mouth of Flat Creek where it flows into Red Bird River. Here three acres of land were given by Mr. Shelby Bowling, with the privilege, in perpetuity, of piping water from a spring above it and walling up the spring to protect it from contamination.

When the citizens of this section first asked us for a center, I rode over there with Mr. Walter Hoskins and Dr. P. E. Blackerby (on a visit to us from the State Board of Health) for a rally, called by Mr. Bascombe Bowling who became the first chairman of the Flat Creek Nursing Committee, and is our chairman now. This gathering was enthusiastic, with many pledges of support aside from the gift of the land and rights to the spring. Dr. Blackerby made a splendid address, lucid and complimentary. The next step was for the Ford Motor Company engineers to survey the site for us. Then Walter Hoskins drew up the deed. The third step was to send Peacock and Texas up there with the supplies we now called our "mobile unit." In between building centers, these supplies were stored in the loft of one of our barns. As surely as early summer came around, they were packed again in a wagon and driven off to the site of the newest center to be.

Peacock and Texas installed themselves as usual in a cabin, given us rent-free by a local citizen. This three-room house, located on Hog Wallow Branch, was so unusually spacious that they called it Buckingham Palace. It had a barn of sorts and a little pasture, but the well was infected so that the water they used all summer had to be boiled. They were hardly installed when I turned up on rounds, knowing there would be a cot for me. The young widow and her baby were the only persons at home when I arrived, so I turned Teddy Bear into the pasture and curled up on my cot with a book.

Soon the nurses returned from a clinic where they had been giving T.A.T. and typhoid inoculations. They had had an experience! The parents had given their consent to have the children inoculated, but we always have to have the children's consent too, and in this instance a young teacher stood up before the group and said, "Children, I am sure it is going to hurt very much. You don't want to have it, do you?" And all the children chorused, "No." So then Peacock and Texas turned to the teacher and said, "It's our personalities against yours!" and talked over half an hour in tones of such glowing fervor that when they called for a volunteer to be the first, Maurice, aged nine, a child of good stock, piped up and said, "I will be the second." At that a tall, lean father, named David Ledford, who was standing near the door, rolled up his sleeve and said gravely, "Take me first." Maurice, gallantly true to his word, stepped up and was second, and then they gave over one hundred inoculations to children and adults.

At Flat Creek, our two mobile nurse-midwives were kept very busy from the beginning. Within their first ten days, five maternity cases registered with them, some of them for almost immediate delivery. Then they had the horrible shock of having three children come down with scarlet fever right next door to one of their maternity cases. The nurse who had been on the scarlet fever cases had to leave all the midwifery cases to the other nurse. One of the children was desperately ill, and a Manchester doctor, nearer Flat Creek than our own Medical Director at Hyden, could only make one visit on the whole situation. But he was a tower of strength then, and the patients all made a good recovery.

Flat Creek Nursing Center was built of local materials except for the plumbing and a hot air furnace, which we found it advisable to install at all of our outpost centers. Our nurses got hold of a windfall for this center in the form of local hardwood, that had been hand-planed and dried, and could be used for the inside floors. Before the end of autumn, these two indefatigable pioneers had completed the job assigned them of building the house, with its great chimney, and the barn, walling off and connecting the spring, laying the septic tank and drainage tiles, fencing all the property, planting the first grass seed in the pasture, while at the same time they organized the local nursing committee and carried enough work in bedside nursing, public health, and midwifery to have kept any other two people fully occupied.

BELLE BARRETT HUGHITT MEMORIAL NURSING CENTER

"Brutus"

MARGARET DURBIN HARPER MEMORIAL NURSING CENTER

"Bowlingtown"

In the summer of 1929 we were approached by the citizens who lived along Bullskin Creek with an offer of free land and many other gifts if we would build our fifth outpost nursing center in their territory. Soon after this, the citizens around Bowlingtown, on the Middle Fork, approached us with the same offer. Before the summer of 1930, when we could build again, we received gifts for these two centers. Mrs. Charles Frost, Mrs. Alfred Granger, and Mr. Marvin Hughitt, two sisters and a brother in Chicago, gave us the money for a center to be built in memory of their mother who had been Kentucky-born. At about the same time, Mrs. Hiram Sibley of Rochester, New York, gave the money for our sixth outpost nursing center in memory of her Kentucky-born mother. In this manner it came about that two girl babies, of early Kentucky days, were a blessing to scores of babies born more than a hundred years after.

Brutus and Bowlingtown, the last two outpost nursing centers we were able to build, are the two that lie at the lowest end of our territory. Bullskin Creek, in Clay County, flows into Red Bird River some eight miles below the Belle Barrett Hughitt Nursing Center. Bowlingtown, in Perry County, lies on the Middle Fork River about twelve miles below the Frances Bolton Center at Confluence, by way of the great bends of the river. It is, however, only about nine miles from the center by way of a short cut over one of the steepest mountains in all our territory. In going from Bowlingtown to Brutus, one fords the Middle Fork at Bargers, rides up Leatherwood Creek, crosses over a narrow gap of the mountain range, and then rides down Panco Creek to Bullskin Creek. The distance is about eleven miles. From Brutus to the Clara Ford Center on Red Bird River, it is about the same distance, over a terribly steep mountain called the Flatwoods, because the top of the mountain flattens out enough for a few families to live there. It will be seen that in building our fifth and sixth nursing centers, we followed our custom of making districts contiguous to one another. Both of the new centers were to be built in the summer of 1930 and, since they were only about eleven horseback miles apart, we gave Peacock and Texas the task of building them simultaneously. This was not so hard as it sounds. By now these two pioneers had coped with three other centers. They had Oscar Bowling for the builder of one of the new ones and his brother, Floyd, for the other. Floyd Bowling is the same fine type of man as Oscar, and an experienced builder. He later became the full-time maintenance man of the Ford Motor Company engineering camp.

Peacock and Texas established themselves at a house on Leatherwood Creek, the best-built and most commodious place they ever had. They called it the White House—and it really was white! There was room for two or three of us at a time to be put up there. The place had an unusually fine well with clean water. The first thing we did, as always in taking possession of temporary quarters, was to put up a sanitary privy. These conveniences we left as souvenirs of our stay. Since they were properly constructed by our regular builders, and located far enough from the water supply for safety, they served as models to whole neighborhoods. Peacock and Texas got along famously with their buildings (one taking one and one the other) but amassed so much nursing that we had to send relief nurses to stay with them before the centers were finished. They organized splendid local committees where we have always had outstanding men, like Mr. Jasper Peters at Brutus, and Mr. Will Gay at Bowlingtown, as chairmen.

239

Bullskin is a delectable creek with broad fertile fields, unusual in our section, creating a green and smiling valley. Our three-acre plot there, high above the creek level, was the gift of Mr. Frank Martin. The land around Bowlingtown is the most open at any of our centers because of the great river bottoms around there, through which the Middle Fork flows. The site for our nursing center was given us by Mr. and Mrs. William Barger, and the right to use a spring, in perpetuity, with its protection from contamination. Our experience with wells had been so dreadful that in accepting gifts of land for our last three nursing centers we insisted on locations that included springs. The ones at Flat Creek and Brutus proved to be adequate for the water tanks set up below them, but the Bowlingtown spring went dry for weeks during the summer months. Years later, Mr. Harper Sibley and his two sisters, the son and daughters of Mrs. Hiram Sibley, gave the Margaret Durbin Harper Center a deep-drilled well, which is indeed a blessing. Up until then, during prolonged spells of dry summer weather, the nurses' cow had to be led morning and evening to the river to be watered.

III

When Brutus and Bowlingtown were finished by the end of 1930, we had added two more lovely places to our holdings. One end of each house, as at all our nursing centers, was devoted to a clinic and waiting room for patients, fitted up with modern appliances and homemade furniture. The clinic bed served not only for examinations but to accommodate a patient whose condition was such that she could not be moved to Hyden Hospital. The nurses had an attractive living room at each place with a rug, curtains at the windows, easy chairs, a desk and a dining table made of solid black walnut by local craftsmen. There were bedrooms for the nurses, guests, and the maid.

A housekeeper-maid, usually a daughter of one of our leading local citizens, was and is an indispensable adjunct to every outpost nursing center. When the nurses came back to the barns, after hours in the saddle, they had to groom and feed their horses. But when they left the barns and walked over to their homes, comfort reigned. They were greeted by a big open fire in the living room, and a hot meal. The kerosene lamps had been cleaned and filled, the candles replaced in the candlesticks, the cow had been watered, fed, and milked, the unused cream had been churned into butter. It would have been physically impossible for the nurse-midwives to carry their districts had they taken time to build fires, clean lamps, water, feed, and milk cows, to say nothing of churning, and preparing meals over a coal range. Remotely rural nurses do not dwell in modern city apartments. Even to feed themselves, they must give more thought and time than are always at their disposal. A garden helps out on this, and the house-keeper-maid adds the canning of vegetables to her other household duties. We put chicken houses and chicken runs at all of our outpost centers, so that the nurses could have their own eggs.

Our patients delight in sharing what they have raised with their nurses. Often, when a hog is killed, a piece of the meat is passed on to them. If a man has a good crop of beans, he will share with his nurse. When a woman pickles beets she remembers the nurses while she provides for her own family. Sometimes a housekeeper presents the nurses with a jar of homemade preserves. Our readers will have gathered that we are so fortunate as to live in a country where manners are still patriarchal. We, in the mountains, all of us, have the same social status, whether we live in large houses on good bottom land, or in cabins on the remoter creeks—leading citizens and poorer citizens alike. We help one another, and work for one another. When a nurse at an outpost center needs a housekeeper-maid, the daughter of one of her best neighbors may come to her. If this young girl is able to carry on with her education, she may herself become one of our nurses, or one of our secretaries.

The thing that the nurses at the outpost centers missed the most through the hot summer months was ice. The fact that there was plenty of it in January didn't help to keep the butter from melting, and the milk from souring in July. We had, of course, the same problem at Wendover. We put the food that could spoil in a rock room built in the mountain behind the Big House, but spoil it often did. Our rapture at Wendover can be imagined when, in 1937, we received from an unknown donor a gift of a refrigerator operated by a kerosene lamp. It was a wonder to me, who had never studied physics, how the lighting of a kerosene lamp generated ice. However, it did, and there was no melted butter or soured milk, no tainted meat or warm drinks at Wendover from the time the lamp-lit refrigerator arrived at our door.

But our six outpost nursing centers continued to have sour milk, melted butter, and warm drinks in hot weather, until Mrs. Henry B. Joy made one of her annual visits to the Frontier Nursing Service in May of 1941. When she first started these visits, she rode horseback down Hurricane Creek to get to us—one of a trio of old Detroit faithfuls, the others being Mrs. Francis C. McMath and Mrs. James T. Shaw. The next time the trio came in, they had to be taken up the river by boat. The third time, they could be eased along in a car. The summer of 1941 was so hot and dry that it was possible to get to all the nursing centers by car, even through the fords of the Middle Fork to Possum Bend. It was then that Mrs. Joy learned the outpost nurses had no ice. This troubled her. It is characteristic of Mrs. Joy that when she is troubled she begins to function. After she had returned to her home at Grosse Pointe, she wrote beseeching letters to a few of her friends asking for money for what she called her Refrigerator Fund. The response was immediate and generous. To all six outpost nursing centers came gifts of lamp-lit refrigerators. Only those who have lived, and worked, through many hot summers without ice can conceive of the comfort that ice brings.

IV

At the beginning of this long chapter I explained why a program which combined bedside nursing and public health with midwifery was peculiarly suited to remotely rural nursing. After more than a quarter-century of experience, it is my conviction that bedside nursing and public health will always yield better results, each in its own field, when they are carried on together. I think now, as I did in 1926, when I wrote the following words to Miss Morgan and Mrs. Dike, in answer to an inquiry from them about my old nursing service in France:

Adaptations are more administrative than anything else. The basic principle of nursing the sick in their homes, and through that human touch creating a spirit of public health to prevent sickness, is peculiar to the people of no one nation. The nurse who tends the sick only, and teaches nothing and prevents nothing, is abortive in her work. On the other hand the nurse who attempts instruction and prevention without combining with them an appreciation of the sickbed, and without meeting its appeal, has failed in the one element which differentiates her profession from all others and out of which it was created.

Chapter 25

I

AFTER the hospital was built and dedicated, and long before its water situation was under control, we began to take in patients. But we did not have our own Medical Director until December of that year. During our first few months Dr. Mildred McKee, wife of a Presbyterian minister who had recently come to Hyden, gave her services to the hospital. These were excellent but restricted because she had a young baby and, before the close of the year, she was so unfortunate as to get a broken back. I had taken up our need for a Medical Director with Dr. McCormack. He knew our situation so well, and worked on it so hard, that within a few months after the hospital was opened he had found, in Dr. Hiram C. Capps of Tennessee, just the physician for us. We worked out an affiliation with the State Board of Health, under which Dr. Capps carried the duties of Public Health Officer, for which the Board paid part of his salary, and those of Medical Director of the Frontier Nursing Service, for which we paid part of his salary. Dr. Capps and his wife, Jean, got hold of a house just below the hospital mountain, with a telephone connection to the hospital, so that we could get him quickly in emergencies. He was also available throughout the year for the emergencies that cropped up on our districts.

Dr. Capps had had a residency in obstetrics. To this special training more than one mother owed her life during the four years he stayed with us. But he was not a surgeon. For our emergency surgery we depended on Dr. R. L. Collins at Hazard, and he never failed us, God bless him. I remember once, not long after the hospital was opened, Dr. Collins riding from Hazard at breakneck speed, reaching the Middle Fork when it was too high to ford, and swimming his horse across the swollen river to reach us. All sorts of legends clustered about his name in Hyden. He is said once to have done an abdominal operation in the jail and once under a shade tree, with an assistant keeping insects out of the open cavity. He never charged us anything for his services, nor would he charge the patients more than he felt they could pay. This he left to us to decide. More than once he said to Mac, "Now, don't let a man sell his cow, or even his only hog, to pay me." His fee for our patients was less than half of what he charged those in Hazard, only $100 for a major operation, but he rarely received more than $10 or $25 in those days. Once when a patient forked up $50 in cash money, and handed it to him before going to the operating table, Mac had to revive him with aromatic spirits of ammonia before he could operate. For nearly a quarter-century this brilliant and humane surgeon met the surgical emergencies of the Frontier Nursing Service, first on horseback and later by car, coming at any hour of the day or night when we called for him. Now Dr. W. F. O'Donnell at Hazard has picked up his mantle, and is carrying on in his tradition.

Not long after the hospital was built, I pulled Ann P. MacKinnon (Mac) from the Beech Fork Nursing Center to be the hospital superintendent. She held this post, except for one year's leave, until 1940 when she went back to the Old Country for the war. She came back to us in 1948 and is the hospital superintendent now. When the hospital began to have enough midwifery to need a hospital head midwife, we put Betty Lester in charge of that. She has a sort of sixth sense that makes her a brilliant midwife. Later, when I made her midwifery supervisor for the whole field of work, she and her horse, "The Old Gray Mare," became familiar sights on every creek and branch of our seven hundred square miles. She, too, went back to the Old Country for the war, returned to us in 1946, and is now in charge of field supervision.

II

What kind of patients did we have in those early days and how were they brought to us? Remotely rural people meet with the ills and accidents of city people, along with others peculiarly theirs. Among the latter, I recall a six-year-old boy with a hemoglobin of only twenty per cent and a skin like parchment, from hookworm. Then there was the four-week-old baby brought to one of our nursing centers from "The Back of the Beyond," and rushed by the nurse, on horseback, to Hyden Hospital, with both eyes so blinded by pus that it was impossible to tell at first whether any sight could be saved at all. After treatment every fifteen minutes for twenty-four hours, the condition began to clear up and the outcome was not total darkness for life.

244

More than one expectant mother came in near the end of her pregnancy, and even in labor, riding sideways, on the rump of the horse, behind the nurse-midwife. "Where else in the world," we often asked ourselves, "would such a woman be brought to a hospital door in such a fashion?" Often a young girl courier rode in from an outpost center holding a sick baby across the pommel of her saddle. Many cases came to us from up or down the river by boat—accident cases, gunshot wounds, appendicitis, women in childbirth, with complications. Many were brought to us by stretcher. If their friends hadn't facilities at hand to make a proper stretcher, as there wouldn't be at a sawmill explosion or a shooting in the woods, they pulled off their coats and ran poles through the sleeves, hastily fashioning a practical stretcher. As the bearers moved forward with the patient, more men left their homes, the fields or the forests, and joined the procession. When a patient had to be carried many miles, he needed at least eighteen bearers, to take turnabout, in relays of six, one at each end of the stretcher and two at each side. Upon two occasions the hospital entertained, unexpectedly, twenty-four stretcher bearers at lunch. These bearers were always volunteers, their services given without charge.

The most tragic of all the patients brought to us were the burned children. These were nearly always little girls. In their domestic duties around home, their skirts would catch in the open fires and in a moment they would be enveloped in flames. We have had as many as six such children at one time in Hyden Hospital. Every winter we have several, even now, although we have reduced their numbers somewhat by getting people to use fire screens and, even more, by encouraging the mothers to put their little girls in overalls. A screen doesn't help to protect an eight-year-old girl when she pulls it aside in order to throw coal on the fire. We estimate that at least a thousand of our little girls are now in overalls in the winter months. Dressed like their brothers, they can tend the fires as safely as the boys do.

From the fringe territory, around the area we cover, with its lack of district nursing, we have always had many dehydrated babies with acute dysenteries. Every summer these babies are brought to Hyden Hospital. Enos and Eva, who were at Wendover during the Mac-Kenzies' visit, were taken over to the hospital later. They came from Polls Creek, where their mother had died of childbed fever when they were two weeks old. We knew nothing about that until their father rode up on muleback with his fifteen-year-old daughter sitting sideways behind him, on the rump of his beast, each of them holding a baby. The father drove a cow in front of them. He told us that his wife had died and his babies were "like to die." He asked us to save them, and to teach their sister how to take care of them. He said he

245

had brought the cow to feed them so they wouldn't be a cost to us. We sent the sister home with him, but said we would have her come back to learn how to care for the babies when they were older and stronger. We knew, the minute we saw them, that the saving of their lives and the restoring of them to health would be a long, hard task. Rarely have I seen two such wasted infants as Enos and Eva were when they came to us. We kept them a year, first at Wendover and then at Hyden Hospital, and when we sent them home, with the sister to look after them, they were magnificent specimens of babyhood. They had six teeth each, both were rosy and brown from sunbaths, and both could stand alone. They had been inoculated against typhoid and diphtheria, and vaccinated for smallpox.

A month after Enos and Eva had been sent back to Polls Creek, Manuel and Nanny came from the same neighborhood, their father driving a cow in front of his mule. Their mother, too, had had child-bed fever. Although she hadn't died, she could not nurse her babies who, at five months, weighed less than seven pounds each. After a hard struggle, especially with Manuel, we sent them home, ready to live and like it. Almost at once a third father rode over from Polls Creek to Hyden Hospital with Moss and Ross. Their mother, too, had lost her milk from childbed fever. Within three years, from that one creek, three sets of twins came to us, each pair arriving on muleback with their father, and each pair bringing their own cow.

Hyden Hospital, as always, needed a vast amount of milk but the local cows we bought in our early years were poor producers. In our *Quarterly Bulletin* for September, 1929, I printed a request for "a fine cow, preferably Holstein, for the babies." This small item caught the eye of Mr. B. H. Kroger of Cincinnati, who at once sent us a generous check. Within ten days a Holstein cow from the Blue Grass was on her way to Hazard by express. After she had been coaxed gently in from the railroad we found to our delight that she continued to give her six gallons of milk a day. She replaced three cows which all combined did not give six gallons, so that not only were our sick babies getting the best possible milk, but we were saving nearly two-thirds of the cost of providing it. We named her after the month in which she came to us—October. None of the many beasts in the service were more widely known than this cow-brute at Hyden Hospital. She and Mac became such buddies that sometimes she followed Mac up the hospital steps to be fed tea cakes. With her sister cow, November, a half-Holstein, October did her bit (and what a generous bit it was!) throughout her life span. Twelve years after Mr. Kroger gave her to us, she died of pneumonia and was accorded honorable burial with the horses.

246

Hyden Hospital needed alcohol, a lot of it, as well as milk. Before the discovery of the sulfa and antibiotic drugs, whisky and brandy were often prescribed for such cases as the pneumonias. We, therefore, had to have alcohol, whisky and brandy. Although those were the days of Federal Prohibition, we had no trouble in getting permits for such alcoholic supplies as the hospital needed, but it was more of a fuss to get them (with more forms to be filled in) than it took to get our narcotics. None of this, though bothersome, was dangerous. It was in getting the stuff to Hyden Hospital that we ran risks. We asked to have it delivered to our wholesale drug house so that it could be shipped to us, along with medicines and cod-liver oil, in conventional packing cases. This the Federal authorities refused to do. They said that alcohol, whisky and brandy must be shipped by themselves, in plainly marked containers, to an express office.

Our nearest express office was at Hazard, a place swarming with bootleggers. These beings, who were linked with a network that spread over the United States, made it their business to encourage illicit distilleries back in the mountains. Some idea of the ramifications of this network was brought home to us after the new motor road, from Hazard to Hyden, had reached the head of Hurricane Creek, thus bringing motor travel to within three and one-half miles of Wendover. One night, Diana was stolen, together with a saddle, bridle, and blanket. Everybody for miles around knew this beautiful mare, and that she belonged to us. After about three days we got word from a man in the White Oak and Wolf Creek section that he had found Diana and was keeping her for us in his barn. Jahugh Morgan rode over after her, along a rough trail of about twelve miles, through a mountain range. She had been ridden so hard, and with such heavy loads, that she was never the same horse again. We learned that the man who had stolen her was a Missouri bootlegger. He had used her to pack whisky from moonshine stills to a truck on the highway, and had then abandoned her. Before this experience, we had never locked anything around our barns, but from that time on we locked up the saddles and bridles every night. We hung halters in our houses to snatch up and carry, in running to save the horses, in the event of a fire at the barns.

It was because of this vast and unscrupulous network of bootleggers that it would have been as much as a teamster's life was worth to drive his mules to the Hazard Express Office and take out a box whose label plainly showed it held government-bonded liquor. Jonah Begley would have done this for us, and shot it out with the bootleggers, but I could not ask it of him. Upon reflection, it seemed clear to me that I could not ask it of anyone. This meant I had to carry the stuff myself. It was just one of those things. I got an official permit which I kept in a jacket pocket of my uniform. I had our allotment of alcohol, whisky and brandy expressed to Dr. Hunt in Lexington, and stored in her attic. There was hardly a trip that I made from Lexington to Hyden that I did not carry with me a pint of whisky, a pint of brandy and a gallon of alcohol. Before I left Lexington I collected the brandy and whisky, and packed a pint in each side of my saddlebags. These never gave me any trouble because they didn't gurgle. I put the metal container with the alcohol in a zipper bag. In my sleeper on the train, I didn't dare leave saddlebags and the zipper bag under my berth, so I slept with them close to my head.

But it was when I got off the train at Hazard, and went around to the stable to get Teddy Bear, that the full embarrassment of my position came over me. Even though I had left my zipper bag within reach, before throwing the saddlebags over the saddle and mounting, a stableman would spring forward to hand it to me. Then the alcohol, which never completely filled the gallon container, made a sound like "glub, glub," thus revealing its presence. As Teddy Bear moved forward with his lithe, swift stride, the alcohol continued to "glub, glub." After we started on the twenty-two-mile trek to Hyden, we often ran into people who were bound our way. If they rode along beside me, I could hardly make conversation because of the "glub, glub, glub"—a horrid sound to me then, and in my memory now. Sometimes a man would ask, "What you got in that thar bag?" and I would answer, "Oh, medicine for the hospital."

When we had traveled a few miles beyond Hazard, I was less uneasy at the risk of discovery because the chances of running into bootleggers were slimmer, and there were friends along my route. But whenever a stranger rode up from behind me, on a lonely stretch of road, my heart thumped with the fear that I might have been followed from Hazard. In view of the coveted freight I carried, my womanhood would have been no protection. Bootleggers were not gentlemen of chivalry. Only a few people knew that I carried government-bonded liquor when I rode from Hazard to Hyden. If I had occasion to mention it in a letter to the hospital superintendent I called it "*frumenti*." Only the "glub, glub" of the alcohol could have betrayed me.

One likes to respect the laws of one's country, even those that one looks upon with distaste, but it is hard to have to risk one's life in order to do it. Sometimes I longed to pack my shipment of Federal bonded liquor into a huge box of old clothes, and ship it to Hazard to be transported in the regular way. However, I did not. Fortified with a permit in my pocket, a permit that would not have protected me for one moment in the presence of a bootlegger, I continued to travel with that horrid "glub, glub" on the pommel of my saddle so long as nothing but horseback miles lay between Hazard and Hyden.

IV

But why should I have minded endangering my life in the Prohibition era when the lives of younger people than I were forfeited every year? Once, as far back as 1923, as I rode through the territory where our Beech Fork Center was built four years later, I passed an old house shortly after Federal agents had fired into it, killing a man and his wife in the presence of their two babies. Whether the young couple were making moonshine or not, they were certainly not making it in the house. Feeling ran so high in the neighborhood, that a man unknown there would have risked his life had he come in at the time. Only a woman, though a stranger, was safe from harm.

One Tuesday in August of 1929, Teddy Bear and I rode over to Hyden Hospital at the edge of dark to have dinner, on our way down to Possum Bend where we were going to take the night. A boy of twenty-one, whom I shall call Bob, had been brought in the night before, shot at his moonshine still, the bullet going into the abdomen and coming out through the lung. Dr. Capps telephoned to Hazard for Dr. Collins, who rode over at once. He found that the bullet had grazed almost every vital organ. Although we expected Bob to recover, he was so badly hurt that he would have to stay sometime in the hospital. The officers said they would not place a guard over their prisoner, but that we must let them know when Bob was ready to be discharged. But I told our Medical Director and Hospital Superintendent that, when this time came, they were to give Bob his clothes around midnight and wish him Godspeed. I would take the rap, if any. There was no rap.

One day, as I sat working at Wendover, I was told that an elderly woman had come "a fur piece" to see me. From her appearance, despite its poverty, I took her for what she was—a woman of good birth and breeding. When she told me her name, I recognized it as a leading one in our part of Kentucky. She sat down and told me her story. She and her husband, who was, she said, going blind from Bright's disease, lived at their own place, about nine miles from Hazard. She had often seen me ride by on my trips home from the railroad. She knew my uniform and she knew who I was. She was in trouble and thought I could help her. Her husband was not able to work any more because of his increasing blindness and generally poor state of health, and they were dependent on the labor of her son-in-law who was not a man from these parts.

249

"Where was he raised?" I asked.

She answered, "He warn't raised, he jest jerked hisself up."

She said he was a hard-working young man with a wife and several children to support as well as the old people to whom the place belonged, and that, though he had had no raising, he was sober and kind. He tended their poor acres of land and, for cash money, hauled railroad ties to Hazard with their team of mules. She told me that one day a strange man rode up to him and asked if he knew where he could get a drink of whisky. Her son-in-law, who lacked the wisdom of the serpent, said he did. The man then asked him if he would take him there. "He tuk him." The stranger then said would he have a drink with him? "He done it." Then the stranger identified himself as a Federal agent and arrested the son-in-law. The tale, as the old woman told it to me, was not unlike others that I heard frequently, and knew to be all too true. She said her son-in-law, who had been taken to jail at Jackson, was to come up before the next session of Federal Court, and would be sent to the Federal penitentiary at Atlanta if convicted. I promised her to do what I could.

Judge A. M. J. Cochran, the United States District Judge for the Eastern District of Kentucky then, presided over the United States District Court under which the boy was to come up for trial. Although I did not know Judge Cochran personally, I knew his reputation in our parts to be that of an upright, stern man who enforced the Federal Prohibition law rigorously. In writing him I thought it more discreet not to tell the story of his agent, as the old woman had told it to me. I did not raise the issue of whether or not her son-in-law had broken the law. But I wrote Judge Cochran that, whatever his offense, it was a first offense, and he had young children, a wife, and her old parents to support. I told him what the mother-in-law had said, about his not having been raised but having had to jerk himself up. For the first time in his life this young man had come in touch with his country's Government, I wrote, of which he had known nothing in his neglected childhood. If this Government showed him a measure of compassion now, we should have the makings of a grateful as well as a good citizen. I added that I would be responsible for his behavior from then on. The upshot of it all was that Judge Cochran released him on probation to me. Some of us stopped off at his house to see him several times a year after that, until the Prohibition Amendment was repealed. I had no fear that this young man would ever again entertain a stranger unawares at a moonshine still!

Although I never met Judge Cochran, I had occasion to write him several letters, and this was not the only case he released on probation to me. The cases in which I failed completely with Judge Cochran were those of second offenders, whoever they were, and whatever the circumstances.

Sometimes the sheriffs and deputy sheriffs in the mountains acted as enforcement officers under state laws which corresponded to the Federal Prohibition laws. In such cases we, who were the nurses and neighbors of the families of the moonshiners, and of those who apprehended them, were sore beset. A shooting affray involving our friends was particularly hard to bear. One night in 1926, when Wendover had not long been opened, there came the hurried tramp of horses' feet at the gate, and hallooing, followed by the loud barking of our dogs. The riders called out that there had been a lot of shooting on Muncy Creek, and that everybody was killed. They did not say "killed dead," so we knew the injured ones were still alive. There was no doctor at Hyden then, and no hospital. The Wendover nurse gathered supplies together, and rode off with the men. She reported to me afterward that she had never seen such a shambles. Three men were wounded in thighs and arms and legs. They lay in pools of blood inside the house and out on the road. Our nurse did such a good job of first aid that, although it was some time before a doctor could arrive, nobody died. But these things were grievous to us. As to moonshine, insofar as our nurses were concerned, I told them they were to see nothing, hear nothing, and say nothing. I dreaded more than words can express to have one of them called to court to bear witness against one of our neighbors, patients, friends. This never happened, because they saw nothing, heard nothing, said nothing.

V

When I spoke in cities, before the repeal of the Prohibition Amendment, and opened the meeting to questions afterward, I was often asked, "What about moonshine?" To this I replied that someone had said there was no such thing as an indiscreet question but to answer it might be indiscreet. Once, however, in a large city (where everything to handle "hard liquor" was about as open as a hospitable front door) I told of two boys at a mountain school who conducted a debate on whether it was better to make moonshine or starve. A well-nourished-looking woman, sitting in one of the front rows, called out in a loud voice, "Better starve!"

Since the repeal of the Eighteenth Amendment, I have been asked several times if conditions as regards illicit distilleries were not now just the same as during the Prohibition era. The answer to that is no, not even in dry territory. It has never been against the code of some of the mountaineers, whose land is too poor for them to eke out a living, to turn their own corn into their own whisky and sell it to the neighbors. When they are apprehended, they take their punishment. But it is not "cruel and unusual punishment," as it was during the Prohibition era. The facts then were as I have described them, and they are not like that now. It is no longer profitable for those suave gentlemen, the bootleggers, to foster the making of the rawest and vilest of whiskies for sale to a thirsty clientele deprived of legitimate sources of supply. Moonshining now is a neighborhood affair that could be handled by local law enforcement, and prevented by a fair means of livelihood for everyone. During the Prohibition era we dreaded the Federal agents, we feared the bootleggers, but not one of us has ever been afraid of a moonshiner, then or now.

In reference to the code of a mountaineer, what he can do with honor and what it would be dishonorable for him to do, I have drawn attention in an earlier chapter to the quality of some of our leading citizens whose conduct, like that of leading citizens everywhere, determines the code to which all aspire. Nowhere in the world do most of us live at the level we expect of our real leaders but we have our codes, and this is true of those mountaineers who have had few advantages in education, and never enough to eat. Something of what I mean was expressed to one of us by a little boy who said proudly, "My daddy's a good citizen. He packs a gun an' has kilt two men, an' he takes his dram, but he hain't never stole even a chicken."

One winter's day, during the Prohibition era, several of us rode up the river to a burial. The wind was piercing. The mountains looked dour. The boughs of the forests were "bare ruin'd choirs, where late the sweet birds sang."

A man, who owned a good piece of bottom land and wore warm clothes, asked this question:

"What does the wind say to you?"

The man who replied came from the head of a hollow where there was almost no bottom land. He wore thin overalls and had no coat.

"Hit says to me, 'I'm a-goin' to split you in two.' "

First man: "Why didn't you work and make money for clothes like I did?"

Second man: "I worked all summer but my children et hit up. There warn't nothin' left for clothes."

Chapter 26

I

WHEN we speak of the early years of the Frontier Nursing Service we do not reckon where these years left off and the middle years began. The middle years, as regards the long future, are probably the ones in which we are living now—part horseback, part jeep—in which many of our problems are still remotely rural and some, like motor accidents, are modern. I think of the early years as extending until the Second World War in 1939, or, more nearly, until 1940 when so many of our old staff left us to go overseas. But I have another classification, for myself, which I call the earliest of the early years. For me these ended late in 1931 when my back was broken. Up until then I lived in the saddle, when I was at home, and no young thing who came to us was called on for harder riding than I did myself.

In going over the mass of stuff—letters, reports, minutes, memoranda —that cover the seven years from 1925 to 1932, I think how wise it was of me not to get a broken back any sooner than I did. By the time this happened, we had completed the organization of the Frontier Nursing Service—inside the mountains and beyond them—except for our Graduate School. Even that had been planned. The Executive Committee minutes show frequent references to the need for it, and to steps taken toward its creation. Therefore, if I write more fully of our first seven years than of the many which followed them, this is not only because of my intense participation in the activity of that period, but because our work reached its maturity then. New and wonderful things lay ahead of us, and many setbacks, but our formation was accomplished in those first seven years. We had committees beyond the mountains in fifteen cities, from which we drew our trustees and the support the work needed. We had a National Medical Council. This grew out of a Medical Advisory Committee in Lexington, formed in 1928, which authorizes the routines under which our nurse-midwives work. We had a National Nursing Council, several of whose members came in to see our work at firsthand, and all of whom believed in its value, helped with their counsel, and, when called on, with their services.

At Wendover, our Central Record System had been set up with a grant from the Carnegie Corporation. The Metropolitan Life Insurance Company, through their great statistician, Dr. Louis I. Dublin, had consented to receive and to evaluate our first thousand maternity cases —a service they continued to render with each successive thousand until the Second World War. The Council of the Alpha Omicron Pi National Sorority had voted to create and support a Social Service Department in the Frontier Nursing Service as its national philan- thropic project, and their 1931 convention endorsed this vote. Our Courier Service was in full swing, and (although we didn't know it then) in some of our couriers we were raising trustees of the future. We had established the custom of giving or getting scholarships for members of our staff to further their postgraduate education. These were in varied fields of work. For example, the Carnegie Corporation gave one to Marion Ross to get a Master's degree in preparation for our Statistical Department. To Bland Morrow we gave one to cover the course at the New York School of Social Work, before she became the A. O. Pi Social Service Secretary, and for Mary B. Willeford (Texas) we got a Fund to help toward her Ph.D. Several American nurses had been sent to England or Scotland for their postgraduate training as midwives. We had the first edition of our *Medical Routine* printed, for the use of the nurses, and a *Record Routine* to guide them in handling their records. Upon the prompting of our auditors, we had taken on, in Lucile Hodges, a full-time, top-notch bookkeeper. Agnes Lewis, who was soon to lift many executive burdens from my shoul- ders, came to us in these earliest of the early years.

While all this was going on, I got hold of our young neighbor from across the river, Grayce Morgan (Taylor Morgan's daughter), who had taken a year of secretarial training at college after she finished high school. She came to us every day, sometimes on horseback, sometimes by boat, and held the job of postal assistant for years. Even as I write these lines she is near us, settled with her husband and children in a house they built on the old place across the river.

With our administrative offices at Wendover where we wanted them, in the heart of our field work, we had to cope with an ever increasing volume of important mail. There was no local post office because there had not been enough local mail to justify one. It took one of us two hours of horseback riding a day to carry our mail to Hyden, and fetch it. I applied for a post office, to be called Wendover, and asked to have Martha Prewitt made the postmaster. This was done. Although ninety-nine per cent of the mail was ours, it was a help to our neighbors farther up the river to have their mail delivered nearly five miles nearer them than had been the case hitherto. When Martha married Clif I thought, this won't do! I could not go through the nuisance of getting young secretaries made postmasters who were likely to marry on me, or off me, at any moment. I therefore asked the Post Office Department in Washington to make Wendover an institutional post office. The postmastership was vested in me, until I became seventy years old in February of 1951. The work was handled by one of our secretaries, who was sworn in as a postal assistant, while the revenues went to the Frontier Nursing Service. At that time they did not begin to equal the cost of maintaining the post office. In our audit for our fiscal year, 1929–30 (the first full year after we became an institutional post office), these revenues amounted to exactly $572.61. Even then mail came to us from all over the world, sometimes with no address but Frontier Nursing Service, Kentucky. One of our nurses received a letter that had been sent in care of the Frontier Nursing Service, Kenya, Africa. Across the envelope had been written, "Try Kentucky, U.S.A."

To sum up, the administrative end of our work was as fully organized by the end of 1931 as was its direction—under our Board of Trustees and Executive Committee.

II

By the end of the first seven years, Hyden Hospital had been running smoothly for four and a half of them and our first Medical Director, Dr. H. C. Capps, had gotten us off to a good start in dependable medical service. The outpost nursing centers were built and the field work, supported by eight local committees of leading citizens, was fully organized. It even included more of the fringe territory beyond ours than we cover now. We extended our nursing in 1930 to include the area at Beverly at the head of Red Bird River. Dr. Harlan S. Heim, the splendid physician living there at the Evangelical Settlement School, was nearer our nursing centers at Flat Creek and Beech Fork—in travel time—than our own Medical Director at Hyden. He promised to give us regular clinics at both these centers, and answer our calls for emergencies, if we would place a nurse-midwife with him to take care of his normal maternity cases. We sent him Ellen Marsh (Marshie Number One). Her district took in the borders of four counties: Leslie, Clay, Bell, and the Stinking Creek section of Knox. Of her value to Dr. Heim, I quote from his letters: "Her services are indispensable. . . . I hardly know what I would do now without her help."

255

One of the tragic things to us about the depression years was that, in reducing our staff, we had to give up this affiliation.

The midwifery part of our work was accepted without question from the day we began it. We did not try to displace the local midwives. Most of them were so old they turned their practices over to us with sighs of relief that we had come. We let nature take her course with the rest. I can only remember one old midwife who made any real trouble for us. She started the rumor that we turned the boy babies into little bears. But when word was passed around from another creek that a boy baby had been born that was not a little bear, this rumor died down. I think that what has kept it alive in my memory was the experience of one outpost nurse-midwife, in that area, who looked so young that the mothers couldn't credit her with having had enough practice to be able to handle maternity cases. When she wrote me that she had trouble getting them to register with her, I wrote back, "Sell your personality." She replied that she had worn out the seat of her pants selling her personality in split-bottomed chairs. No, the old midwives in the main were our fast friends and caused us no anxiety. Where we had problems to face, not only during our first seven years but for a good while afterward, was in giving nursing care to the patients of the men that, in my 1923 investigation, I called pseudo doctors. Although I called these beings pseudo doctors, perhaps the term practical doctors might better explain their status. However, I don't like to see the word "practical" used to describe poorly equipped physicians or nurses, with its implication that people fully qualified in these professions are impractical. We gave bedside nursing care to sick people whether their physicians were our own Medical Director, "brought-on" doctors, or pseudo doctors. Such cases had to be handled by the nurses at their own discretion, but we warned all of them never to give medicine prescribed by a real doctor if a pseudo doctor was giving his own.

Before Hyden Hospital was built we sent many cases to Lexington for medical, surgical, and hospital care that we could look after ourselves once we had our own hospital, medical director, and surgical consultant. We routed them all through Dr. Josephine D. Hunt, who called in such specialists as they needed, all of whom gave their services. One patient was a four-year-old boy who had been terribly burned the year before we found him. His right arm had grown to his side like a wing. This Dr. Fred Rankin released, and grafted skin over the ruined tissues. Dr. Francis Massie saved the injured right hand of an eighteen-year-old boy, which we thought he would lose. Dr. John Harvey worked on a diabetic so successfully that her life was prolonged for years. We made affiliations, first with the Children's Hospital of Louisville and a little later with the Children's Hospital of

Cincinnati, and had started the custom of taking down to them such children as needed special pediatric care, which has always been given free. From the beginning we had been *en rapport* with the Kentucky Crippled Children Commission of which Miss Marian Williamson was the competent and kind director then, as she is now. One of the early patients we sent her, a badly crippled little boy, had gone out in a wagon. Under Dr. Barnett Owen's care, he had been so completely restored to health that he was able to return with me, pickaback on Teddy Bear. As we rode down Hurricane Creek on the last lap of what had been a long journey for a tiny tad, cured though he was, he said to me, "I've most forgot what it feels like to be a-hurtin'."

III

During these seven earliest of the early years, we started the great medical, surgical, and dental clinics through which the finest specialists came to the mountains to serve those who were unable to go to them. The first of these were the trachoma clinics conducted by Dr. Robert Sory of the United States Public Health Service which opened one of its two trachoma hospitals, the Irvine-McDowell, at Richmond, Kentucky. (The other at Rolla, Missouri, was for the Ozarks.) Trachoma was a terrible scourge in the Kentucky mountains in our early days. In 1950, when the United States Public Health Service closed the doors of its hospital at Richmond, we knew that Dr. Sory had trachoma licked at last. In the summer of 1927, he and his nurse, with one of our nurses assigned to help them, spent a week in our section. Following his eye clinics we took eighteen people with severe cases of trachoma down to the Richmond Hospital. In the summer of 1929, Dr. Sory came back again to hold clinics at Hyden, Big Creek, and Confluence. Dr. Capps and the nurses had rounded up hundreds of suspicious-looking eyes. Again, Dr. Sory sorted out the trachoma cases, and again we got the worst ones down to Richmond.

After the first of Dr. Sory's clinics, when we took the eighteen patients to Richmond, we took down three little children nearly blind from congenital cataract, and two with strabismus, to the Children's Hospital in Louisville, where they were operated on with success. All of the twenty-three patients and their nurses traveled on passes from the Louisville and Nashville Railroad. In reckoning up its dividends, did this corporation, I wondered, count in among them the vision restored, the crippled children walking, the sick made whole—all of them, and there were many, transported without charge over its lines? It may be true that corporations have no souls, but our Mr. E. S. Jouett, a Vice-President of this one, had a heart big enough to meet all this vast need.

It must not be thought that we ourselves carried all these patients beyond Lexington, or even always to Lexington. Occasionally one of our own citizens would arrange to go out with ambulatory patients, who did not need nursing care en route. Frequently members of our Blue Grass Committee picked such patients up in Lexington, and took them to Richmond for us. They often entertained in their own homes convalescents while they were waiting for the return trip. Frances McVey, wife of the President of the University of Kentucky, Caroline Carter, Margaret Preston Johnston, were three whose homes were open to almost anyone at almost any time, and Linda Neville, who asked especially for the eye cases. Those that were emergencies she not only took into her own home, but paid for their hospitalization out of a special fund of hers.

When I carried children out myself, it was my custom to take them up to my room at the Lafayette Hotel until one of my friends called for them. I remember one little girl particularly, because of my failure to tell her about the elevator. As the floor of the little room into which I had led her suddenly rose, she gave a sigh of horror that seemed to come from her boots, but she made no other sound. For her, it was a sort of "Pit and the Pendulum" in reverse. The children took with composure things that, though novel, were not startling. One little boy said of the Ohio River, "Awful deep fords folkses have got down here." Two twin girls, Martha and Mary, taken to the Children's Hospital at Cincinnati for cleft palates, were escorted around town by an interne before we sent for them. When they saw the huge city buildings their comment was, "Wouldn't they hold a sight of hay!"

IV

In the summer of 1929, through the State Board of Health, we made an affiliation with the Kentucky State Dental Association, which their voluntary secretary, Dr. J. F. Owen, engineered. That year and again in 1930 and 1931, we had with us Dr. Arthur M. Laird to give dental care to children and expectant mothers. Half of the costs were met by the Kentucky State Dental Association and half by the Frontier Nursing Service. Hundreds of children, and many expectant mothers, had their teeth put in perfect condition under this system, at a small charge. If they couldn't pay in money, they could bring an egg. If they hadn't any eggs, they got free care. One summer Dr. Laird had as an assistant Dr. Philip Blackerby, a son of our friend, Dr. P. E. Blackerby of the State Board of Health. Mrs. Laird, who always came with her husband, was indispensable in helping to operate the dental equipment by hand at the outpost centers, where electrically operated equipment would have been of no use. We moved Dr. Laird's "tricks," as the patients called them, from one center to another in a wagon drawn by mule team. This was an affiliation that we had to give up in the depression days, to our vast regret not only because we liked Dr. and Mrs. Laird but because dental care was terribly needed. There was no dentist in our territory then, and there is none now.

In July of 1930, Dr. Scott Breckinridge gave the first of the gynecological clinics for which he came to Hyden Hospital every year until his last illness. During these years he came to us also for special patients who needed operations between his clinics. That same summer, Dr. F. C. Thomas of our Medical Advisory Committee at Lexington came up in August to give us the first eye clinic, other than trachoma, that had ever been held in our part of the world. For this clinic we did some preliminary testing with charts, but mainly we chose the 103 children and young people for Dr. Thomas to examine on the basis of vision so obviously defective that they could not carry on without treatment of some kind. Dr. Thomas prescribed glasses for 84 of these patients, and these were sold to us at cost ($3.50 a pair) by the American Optical Company. Among the others, some needed special treatment and one an operation. The problem of the eyes of old people does not trouble us. In the early days we used to get quantities of old-age glasses for them, but for years these have been sent us by New Eyes for the Needy at Short Hills, New Jersey. They are just magnifying glasses. The wearing of them means to an old man that he can see to drive a nail again, and to an old woman that she can see to thread a needle. It is otherwise with children and young people. We want to lift the burden of eyestrain from all of them.

For so many years Dr. F. W. Urton of Louisville, with that great anesthetist, Dr. D. M. Dollar, has come up to Hyden Hospital to give us tonsil clinics that it is hard to remember there was a time when he did not come. When we had our first tonsillectomy clinic at Hyden Hospital, in September of 1930, it was Dr. C. B. Kobart of the Kentucky State Board of Health who came to us. He performed 151 operations in two days, all but 19 of them tonsillectomies. The others were for adenoids and polypi. One may well ask how a 12-bed hospital, which was the size of Hyden Hospital then, accommodated 202 patients. (That many were admitted, but some dismissed without operations.) Ann MacKinnon (Mac) still gasps when she talks about that time. In the first place we took over an old frame building in Hyden, called the Blue Hotel, at a cost of fifty cents a room a night. We scrubbed the place and furnished it with our own cots. We had five or six cots to each room, and two children to each cot, lying with their heads at the ends and their feet in the middle. Secondly, we covered the floors of the living room and dining room at Hyden

Hospital with mattresses for the rest of the children, allowing just enough space between mattresses for the nurses to walk.

The children were magnificent in the way they faced these operations. We were careful to explain to them that the needle would hurt, when the doctor stuck it in, but that they wouldn't feel much after that. We also told them that when it was over they could have all the ice cream they could eat. This sounded like a fairy tale to these children, none of whom had ever had any ice cream. In batches of six they sat on a bench outside the clinic where Dr. Kobart operated. After they had gone to him for his hypodermic injections, they had to go back and sit on the bench for about fifteen minutes until they were called in to have instruments, with wires attached, thrust down their throats—followed by the scalpel. Among our little stoics hardly a child uttered a sound, although several of them blinked furiously to keep back the tears. One girl child, with a trickle of blood oozing out of her mouth, said, "Thank you, doctor," before walking out of the room.

V

Worms are the curse of the frontier child. It is not uncommon to find young children with high fever, rapid pulse and respirations, who recover as soon as they have been wormed. It is not unusual for such children to vomit worms as well as pass them in the normal way. Children have been brought to us who have vomited as many as thirty, not one of which was less than six inches long. Among my standard stereopticon slides are two that, in our early years, I used wherever I spoke. One showed a two-year-old child. The other showed the round-worms (pinned against a napkin to be photographed) that had come out of the body of the child. Although these pictures drew shuddering sighs from my audiences, my purpose in showing them had not been that of the Fat Boy in *Pickwick Papers*. I did not want to make their flesh creep. What I wanted to do was to make every grown-up American I could reach worm-conscious, until every American child was worm-free.

With this loathing of worms, it may be imagined with what rapture I greeted the clinics of the helminthologists. This name suggests knights in shining armor and, indeed, they looked like that to my welcoming eyes. They came first in the summer of 1930 to make a direct attack on the worms and, in so doing, try out a new drug, hexylresorcinol, which had been developed during years of patient research at Vanderbilt and Johns Hopkins Universities. They, and the pharmacologists who worked with them, were Doctors Gilbert Otto, Harold Brown, B. H. Robbins—all under the direction of Dr. Paul Lamson.

When the helminthologists asked for volunteers to try out the new drug, we got 820 for them, mostly children from the area around Hyden, whose parents gave their consent. Our couriers undertook to collect the specimens and bring them by horseback to Hyden Hospital. The study made by these helminthologists and pharmacologists took more than a year for its completion. The specimens first collected were to determine the degree of infestation. We found that 80.5% of the 820 people had intestinal parasites—including hookworm, roundworm, whipworm, dwarf tapeworm, and pinworm. After treatment, new specimens were collected by those indefatigable young women, the couriers, in order to discover how effective the hexylresorcinol had been in getting rid of the worms.

Before the next summer, that of 1931, the process of collecting the specimens was repeated, to discover how much new infestation had taken place during the winter months. It was not heavy. But, when the specimens were collected again at the end of the summer, it was found that practically all the patients had been reinfested with a "full burden" of infestation.

The lesson taught by this field laboratory work was clear. Our thousands of children would have to be wormed every autumn, to get rid of the "full burden" of a summer infestation of intestinal parasites. Only so could they grow unhampered. The prevention of intestinal parasites lies in sanitation which, in a rural country, means sanitary privies on every creek and in every neighborhood. We have found this the hardest of all public health measures to put over. During the days of the W.P.A., it helped to have sanitary privies built for the rural schools. These were models in their communities. But, so long as even a few families on a creek have insanitary privies—or none—so long will the barefoot children get hookworm infestation in the summer months, and many children will get infested with roundworms. It is difficult to believe in the invisible. People cannot see the larvae of the hookworm or the eggs of the other worms without a microscope. In my talks to them I have found that although the cycle of the hookworm holds their interest, the story has the unreality of a fairy tale.

In the last quarter-century, we have made some headway in the prevention of intestinal parasites at their source, but it has been one of two health problems over which we have often despaired. The other problem is tuberculosis. That doesn't come into this chapter, because nobody gave us a tuberculosis clinic in the earliest seven of our early years.

Chapter 27

I

RECOLLECTIONS crowd to the forefront of my memory as I draw toward the end of our earliest seven years. All of them could be told in tales because everything we did concerned real people, not theories about people. For example, the clearest way to describe tuberculosis in a remotely rural country is to tell about a family stricken with tuberculosis.

Late one afternoon Teddy Bear and I were riding rapidly to Wendover from Hyden. It had been raining and the river, which was rising, was already so high that we decided not to cross at the regular Muncy ford but to ease off the bank through some bushes, higher upstream, where the river broadened and we could escape the swiftest part of the current. As we neared midstream we heard, above the roar of the rising water, the sound of children crying. I could hardly believe my ears because the sound came from the river itself. There, about two hundred yards below us, were two children standing on a tiny submerged island. Teddy Bear hesitated but an instant before starting towards them, downstream. When we came to the island, I saw two of Black Chester's motherless children, a girl of about seven and a boy of about four years of age. The girl said they had been visiting on yon side of the river, and thought they could wade back over the ford the way they had come. Had they not stopped at the island, they would have been washed away. They had been standing there about an hour, while the water rose nearly to their knees. Even with as powerful a horse as Teddy Bear, I didn't dare take both of them on at once. The boy climbed up the stirrup like a monkey and scrambled into the saddle in front of me. Then Teddy Bear and I turned into the swift current. As soon as we reached the bank, the boy scrambled off and we went back for the girl. Then, with one of them in front of me and one behind, we rode rapidly down the river road to Black Chester's home at the mouth of Short Creek. There I gave the children to their grandmother to warm and dry and feed.

Black Chester was called black to distinguish him from a relation of the same name who, a blonde, was called White Chester. Although Black Chester had a lawless reputation in our part of the world, I liked him. Furthermore, I trusted him because I had never known him to do a mean or an underhanded thing. He was a good husband, a good son, and a good father, but he was too ready with the trigger and sometimes ran afoul of the law. His wife, a superior woman in mind and character, had died of tuberculosis not long after I built Wendover, leaving a family which included four young children, two girls and two boys. Black Chester's old mother took care of the children and of his house.

The condition of this family troubled us because of the massive exposure they had all had to tuberculosis. We had no X-ray machine at Hyden Hospital then, but we succeeded in getting a chest X-ray on Black Chester out Hazard way. He had incipient tuberculosis. About the time that we learned this, and shortly before Teddy Bear and I picked up the children out of the river, Black Chester killed a man and was sentenced to the penitentiary at Frankfort for two years. He didn't want to serve his sentence, so he cleared out. I had written the physician in charge of the hospital at the State penitentiary to ask if he would personally look out for Black Chester, give him hospital care and rest, and get his tuberculosis cured when he went down there. The physician wrote me back a kind letter in which he said he would do everything he could. This information I gave to the old grandmother and told her to tell Black Chester, from me, to come back and surrender to the law and get his disease cured. She seemed to be in touch with him because she told me some days later that she had sent him the message but that he didn't aim to go to Frankfort. I saw the old lady again, and again urged her to get Black Chester to come back and surrender so that his tuberculosis could be cleared up. Her reply was, "He don't aim to do hit." That was the only reply I could get out of her, as the weeks passed: "He don't aim to do hit." Then one day I got a letter from Black Chester himself in which he told me that he was going far away, where nobody could find him, and he didn't know when he would come back. He asked me to look out for his children and wrote, "Don't let my little girls be destroyed."

Black Chester, a proud man who had been a good provider, did not ask for financial help for his family. What his little ones needed was parental care. Two of them had nearly lost their lives for the lack of it. They also needed, desperately, to be built up in some way to create resistance against the tuberculosis to which they had been so terribly exposed, and there we were up against it. Whenever we ran into tuberculosis, which was constantly, I felt like Dante, when he wrote over the gates of the Inferno, "Abandon hope all ye who enter here." The only state sanatorium for this disease had a waiting list so long that it was hopeless to apply for any but the pay beds. The counties where the Frontier Nursing Service worked did not have the welfare funds, and could not have raised them by taxation, to pay for months of care for their tuberculous patients. Our own funds were so limited that we could not often send a case there, and few were the families who could afford it. We did the best we could for our tuberculous patients with screened porches for them in the summer, separate beds and dishes, sputum cups, warm clothing, extra food. More than once a cow, and its feed, was given a tuberculous family by friends of ours. But it is only as this book is written that the State of Kentucky has put into operation regional sanatoria for tuberculosis cases. In the Laurel County one, a few free beds are available for patients from our section.

Hard as it was to get a bed for an acute case of tuberculosis, it was an even harder task to find a preventorium that would take a pre-tuberculous mountain child. We longed to build our own. In our early years I even chose a site where we could put up a row of little wooden huts in which the children could stay inexpensively during the summer months—a place with room for a garden and chickens and a bit of pasture for cows. But we have never had the money even to buy the site and build the huts, let alone run the place afterward. What could I do for Black Chester's children? After much searching about, I found a small preventorium in the mountains of Virginia, under the auspices of the Episcopal Church, which consented to take the two little girls at a reasonable rate. For the little boys I found nothing.

Three years passed. Then one day I heard again from Black Chester. He wrote me that he was so homesick for his children he had decided to come back and go to the penitentiary. As soon as he had surrendered and been taken to Frankfort, I wrote the prison doctor. To my amazement I learned from him that Black Chester had indeed had tuberculosis but that the lesions had been newly healed and, with care, he should stay well. I, who had thought of him as knocking around the world at hard labor and without proper food, could not figure out how he had been cured. I had to wait until his release from the penitentiary to learn about this. A pardon petition was circulated in behalf of him. This I refused to sign but I wrote a personal letter to the governor, to send with the petition, in which I told him I knew nothing of the rights and wrongs of the sentence but that I did know that the prisoner was a good father and his children needed him.

Soon after Black Chester was pardoned, I stopped off at his house to chat with him. I told him how puzzled I was that his tuberculosis

264

had been cured while he was away. I asked him if he would be willing to tell me what he had done during those three years. He told me something then that I did not divulge to anyone during his lifetime. He had enlisted, under an assumed name, in the United States Army, and had been sent to the Philippines. When his tuberculosis had been discovered out there, he had been put in an Army hospital where he had stayed until he was cured. Then he had been given an honorable discharge, under his assumed name. So all the time that I had troubled about him knocking about the world under extreme hardships, he had been reclining in one of Uncle Sam's beds under the best possible conditions to effect a cure. That was my last conversation with Black Chester. He got into another shooting affray. Neighbors found him and his enemy—both shot dead.

II

It was after Teddy Bear and I picked Black Chester's children out of the river that the Frontier Nursing Service received a gift of money from the late Mrs. William Monroe Wright to buy a cottage and forty-nine acres of land on the Wendover side of the river at Muncy ford. Because most of this land was cleared, and could be put into pasture, we called it The Clearing. We installed Lewis Morgan, and his wife Mrs. Becky Jane, down there as caretakers.

Not long after we had bought The Clearing, Teddy Bear and I came back from rounds of the outpost centers. We were both tired. I had him turned into the pasture for rest, but his lively inclinations led him on a tour of exploration instead. With the ease of a great cat he climbed up to the top of a cliff. There he slipped on the moss and fell about twenty feet onto his back. When he failed to come down to the gate at the edge of dark, Lewis took a lantern and went in search of him. He found him wedged between the base of the cliff and a tree. He and Jahugh got hold of four other men. They cut down the tree, built a runway of smooth lumber, eased it under Teddy Bear, lassoed his four legs with a rope, and hauled him out. Although he was able to walk up to the Wendover barn, his injuries were terrible. During the following week I did his dressings myself, and they took about an hour each day. I recklessly tore up my sheets to cover his bruised back, and used slings over the head and an injured eye. I hired a fifteen-year-old girl to come by the day and mind him. Wherever there was a bit of grass in the Wendover boundary she led him to it and stayed by him so that, in his partial blindness, he wouldn't fall off the slopes in which all mountain grass terminates.

For a while I thought that Teddy Bear might recover but, on the evening of the eighth day, he lay down not to rise again. Just before he died, he lifted his head and thrust his muzzle between my hands. As I sat there by him, Brooke came over to me, put his young arms around me and said, "Don't grieve, Aunt Matron. Ah, don't grieve." I could not help but grieve. Teddy Bear had been my sole companion over thousands of miles of lonely trails. I remembered the time when my girth broke on the edge of a precipice, my saddle turned and I fell under him, and how he stopped stock still to look down at me until I picked myself and the saddle up. I remembered his brief hesitations on the brinks of swollen or icy river fords, and then the proud toss of his head and the swift stride forward. Recollections of all his endearing ways came back to me, like his nuzzling at my uniform pockets for apples. Several horses have I loved in my lifetime but none had ever come so close to me as Teddy Bear and none, I knew, ever would again. I could not help but grieve.

III

Not even in the war-devastated areas of northern France have I known greater poverty than we had in the Kentucky Mountains in our early days, at a time when living conditions beyond the mountains were good. It just wasn't possible for a man to raise enough to feed his family on steep land, utterly unsuited for any kind of a crop but timber. Families without bottom land, and they were the most in number, went hungry and ill-clad. Although there was no aid for dependent children in those days, the neighborhood ties were so binding that, if a man met with misfortune, everybody who had a surplus pitched in to help feed his children. But few people had a surplus. I recall a seven-year-old girl, brought to Hyden Hospital with pneumonia, who had on her body nothing but a worn dress and an old red sweater that belonged to her father. Her twin brother had given her his shoes and stockings to make the trip in on muleback, because she had none of her own.

We call the shipments of clothing that people send down to us "grab" because, in our early years, the nurses grabbed the warm things for those of their families that were destitute. Our method has always been to give the new things to children, the old people, the sick. Ever since we have had a Social Service Department, to whom the nurses could report needy cases, much of the used stuff, or grab, is distributed through that department. The rest of the used things are sent to our various nursing centers to be disposed of in what we call "grab sales." These enable people who are too proud to take anything as a gift to buy what they need at a nominal price. For example, we sell a warm overcoat for fifty cents and a stout pair of shoes for a quarter. It is amazing to me what a thrifty mother can make out of the most unusual garments. Someone sent us once a great many leather gaiters. One young mother got them all for a dime, took the buttons off, sewed them together and made a really warm coat for one of her children. The Bennett Junior College, up at Milbrook in New York, once sent us a number of old-fashioned riding skirts of heavy black broadcloth. All of these were turned into pants for little boys. One mother made a coat for her daughter out of a pair of white flannel trousers. She had no pattern but it was a good coat.

Our friends beyond the mountains have been magnificent, over the years, in sending us grab as well as many new garments but we have always run short of shoes. Where there wasn't enough money in a family to buy shoes for everyone, the father had to have a pair to get out and plow his land or to cut the timber from which came his only cash money. As soon as a boy and girl were old enough to work, then they too had to have shoes. The younger children often did without. Sometimes their feet were tied up in feed sacks. Sometimes they had an old pair of the father's shoes—monstrous on their little feet. It was not until the Christmas of 1929 that all of our children were shod. It happened like this. The chairman of our St. Louis Committee, Mr. Harry French Knight, came down to spend Thanksgiving with us. We have always tried, as a staff, to get together on Thanksgiving Day. Although it is never possible for all to be at this reunion, as many come as can. It was nothing for the outpost nurses to ride eighteen miles in to Hyden or Wendover, and back the same evening, in order to attend our Thanksgiving Day dinner. Mr. Knight asked the assembled crowd what they would like for Christmas. In a full-throated chorus everybody called out, "Shoes!"

At that time only four of our six outpost centers were built, but in those neighborhoods, and around Hyden and Wendover, we had 3,123 children. The district nurse-midwives had checked up on them and found that 203—about 6.5 per cent—had no shoes. It was impossible for these children to go to school with rough sacking as the only protection for their feet. Mr. Knight promised to give us 203 pairs of the best quality of sport shoes if we could arrange for them to fit. That part was easy. Each district nurse outlined on paper the right foot of each of her barefoot children. Across each outline she wrote the child's name, and her name. These drawings were sent to Mr. Knight at St. Louis. He took them to the Brown Shoe Company, which assigned a clerk to the job of choosing shoes to fit each child. Then the drawings were stuffed into the corresponding shoes. The shoes fitted perfectly, with a wee margin for growth. It was our fifth Christmas in the mountains and our happiest. No little feet were blue with cold that year.

267

Only those who lived through the great drought of 1930 can grasp, even in imagination, the magnitude of that disaster. Arkansas, Oklahoma, and Kentucky were the states with the most severely stricken areas. When we, in the Kentucky mountains, had gone through the winter and spring of 1930 with almost no snow or rain and therefore no subsoil water, and entered upon the scorched summer months, we knew that we were headed for famine. The Frontier Nursing Service, with its passion for facts, determined to find out exactly what the food situation would be from the fall of 1930 until the next harvest in the fall of 1931. We engaged Mr. Lee Morgan, one of our neighbors with a superior education as well as an intimate knowledge of crops, to start a series of surveys for us in September, in order to ascertain the exact number of bushels of corn each family would have in the year ahead. The corn crop, which is fed on the ear to cows and mules, is ground into meal for breadstuff for the population. By the end of January, Lee had made 11 surveys covering 1,175 families with a total population of 6,584 people. His figures were tabulated by the statistician in the Wendover office. His estimates for the spring months, made from figures collected in the fall months, were found to fall short of the actual conditions by only 2 per cent. From his study of the drought-stricken cornfields we figured that by January 17 per cent of our families would be entirely without food, that 55 per cent would be without food in March, and nearly 70 per cent by the first of June. Over 92 per cent would be without corn before the next harvest.

Early in October, when Lee had completed his study of the first 115 families and their crops, I took his data to the American Red Cross in Washington. It was a small sampling but enough, I felt, to show them that they would have to plan for disaster relief on a vast scale. They took over the crisis in January of 1931. By then one-fifth of our people had no food. They had been carried for four months, unaided, by a population of which less than 8 per cent had a surplus sufficient to last until the next harvest. It was a record characteristic of a proud and independent people, and it would have been hard to match it in the world's history.

The situation in the Kentucky mountains was rendered even more difficult because of the hundreds of men who came back from the cities after the market crash. Where a mountain farm could only support the old people and one or two sons and their families, the other sons had gone out to work in places like Hamilton (Ohio), Detroit, Cincinnati, or they had been loaders at the mines or hands employed by the railroads. They were hard-working men who earned good pay and supported their families. But the industries, the railroads, the mines, which had taken this labor away from the mountains, no longer needed it and now cast it out. So these men came back to the little farms which would have had hard work feeding them in normal times and, during the great drought, could not feed them anything. We employed what men we could that summer, in building our last two outpost centers, and in doing repairs on our properties when we could get funds—but our own subscriptions had been cut following the market crash. In a single day at Wendover forty men came to me clamoring for work, work of any kind, anywhere. In an article I wrote for *The Survey*, August, 1930, I called the men who had poured back from the cities, "The Corn-Bread Line." Almost all of them were heads of families, decent, independent people who had never begged in their lives, and begged now only for work.

The final tragedy of the great drought lay in the total loss of the only cash crop of the people, which was timber. All through those winter months in which there was almost no snow or rain, everybody had gotten busy making the rafts to take down on the first spring tide. But there were no spring tides. The rafts lay in the deep pools of the river, or along its dried bed on the bars and shoals. Tied up in them was the only money which could have come that year in this section of the mountains.

All through that dreadful summer of 1930 we nurses carried on a battle royal against disease. Fortunately nearly all of our people were inoculated against typhoid fever, but some of the shots had to be repeated that year and we went into all the fringe territories that called on us for help. Between June and September, when the wells and springs were drying up, dysentery and the skin diseases flourished. There was a scarcity of water for bathing when sometimes the nearest wet well lay half a mile away. There was an increase of miscarriages among the pregnant women. This, Dr. Arthur McCormack told me, was known to be characteristic of famine periods.

The only thing that kept our people alive was the American Red Cross. Mr. Mitch Begley took the chairmanship of a splendid local committee at Hyden, giving almost his entire time to this work. The two Red Cross representatives in our section, Mrs. Connolly and Mr. Goodacre, were indefatigable in their effort to get extra allotments of food for pregnant women, for families with tuberculosis. By March they had even succeeded in getting small allowances of fodder for such of the cows as had survived. The Red Cross method, which was one of giving grants for food on the nearest local merchants, was admirable because it kept the merchants going. They had to haul the food in from the railroads and this meant they had to be able to make enough to feed their mules in order to carry on. However, the Red Cross allowance of $2.50 per person per month, with a maximum of $20.00 for even the largest families, was not enough to do more than stave off actual starvation. "Brought-on" flour and meal were more expensive than the home-ground meal had been, and much less nourishing. There was no margin to give a man working calories, to provide growth for children, to enable an expectant or a nursing mother to take care of her baby, or to prevent the ravaging effects of pellagra and tuberculosis. No provision was made for milk for the young children and nearly half of ours were entirely without milk of any kind.

We set out to raise a special milk fund. Mrs. Ballard's brother, Credo Harris, was in charge of WHAS, the Louisville *Courier-Journal* radio station, in those days. He offered me fifteen minutes of the best evening time and allowed me to make a direct appeal. I asked for money for canned milk and also to replace the cows the people had slaughtered, when it would be possible to feed cows again. I took as my slogan: "Give a cow now. If you can't give a cow, give a can." A lot of money came in as a result of that talk and we spent it all on canned milk, except for a few cows bought later. We were able to give four quarts of milk a week, for months, to several thousand children. We also gave quantities of cod-liver oil. We supplied shoes to more than three hundred children whose families could have bought them in normal times.

From one of my letters to our National Chairman, Mrs. S. Thruston Ballard, written in March of 1931, I quote a few paragraphs:

The hardest thing is to see the level of our people at such low ebb. Over 60 per cent are now on Red Cross relief, and of course the margin is just enough to sustain them. The allowance is $2.50 in Leslie County and $2.00 in Clay, per month, with a few exceptions where there is tuberculosis or pregnancy. The Borden Milk Company have given us 1,000 pounds of dried milk, and the Pet Milk Corporation have given 6 dozen cases of evaporated milk; Mrs. Douglas has given us $1,000 for milk, and others have given us smaller sums for this purpose. We are now giving milk to something like 2,000 children, whose families are on Red Cross relief. . . . But, they have to be found, they really don't know how to ask for things.

Yesterday, when I was in Mr. Mitch Begley's office, a pale, lean, hungry, tired-looking man, with one arm, came in. I remembered him. His arm was blown up by a shotgun and he was operated on at our hospital about a year ago, and nearly went crazy because he didn't know how he could make a living. He said, slowly and quietly, "Mitch, do you reckon you can increase the allowance a little bit? We can't make out." Mr. Mitch said, "I will see what I can do." Then the one-armed man said, "My fodder is give out for the mule. Can I have a little fodder for the mule?" Mr. Mitch replied that the Red Cross wasn't feeding mules.

Nobody is feeding the mules. The Government wouldn't. The Red Cross claim that feeding the mules is beyond their scope. The poor creatures are starved and how they can plow the spring crops is beyond my comprehension. Many of them have had nothing but the wintry forest for weeks. . . .

It may be remembered that during the period of this disaster, a storm raged in Washington and, indeed, all over the country, as to whether or not the Federal Government should release large stocks of grain that it had on hand, to feed the mules and the cows in the drought-stricken areas. I felt that we could learn from Pharaoh, who released the grain Joseph had hoarded in preparation for the great Egyptian drought. Another storm that swept the country concerned the question of direct Federal relief to supplement the inadequate sum of money the Red Cross had raised from voluntary donations. About this, *The New Yorker* wrote: "A simple way to break the deadlock in Washington would be to call that relief fund a little item in national defense. Children who starve this winter will be of no use whatever in the next war." My own opinion was that the Federal Government should make a grant in aid to the American Red Cross to enable it to double the subsistence allotments given to people, to provide fodder for every cow and every mule, but should leave the direction of the relief program in the hands of the voluntary agency.

V

It was not until early April in 1931 that enough rain fell to bring our first tide in two years. When all up and down the rivers word was passed that the waters were rising, the excitement was like the return of troops from war. In a few hours the rivers rose ten feet, then fifteen, and the great rafts, which had lain so long at their moorings, swung out to midstream. The moorings were severed and on a mighty rush of current the rafts started down. As the first ones passed, the men on them began cheering, these quiet highlanders, and the people on shore cheered back and waved at them. Then more rafts followed, over two hundred on the Middle Fork alone, and for forty miles down the river the cheering men were answered by the people on the shores. Women dropped their hoes, men stood at the plows waving their hats. Like a triumphant army the rafts swept on. The drought was broken, the heavens had opened, the harvest was to come. We felt as George Herbert did in the early seventeenth century when he wrote:

I once more smell the dew and *rain,*
And relish versing: O, my onely Light,
It cannot be
That I am he
On whom Thy tempests fell all night.

271

Chapter 28

I

THERE is no subject about which we are asked more questions than our Courier Service. It is made up of girls, nineteen years and over, who first come to us as juniors for periods of from six weeks to two months throughout the year. Those who return, called seniors, stay as long as they wish and can. All are under the direction of a Resident Courier and all are volunteers. The idea of such a service, as I wrote elsewhere, was the outcome of my experience with the Card Motor Corps in France, staffed by girl chauffeurs. Transport was the backbone of the work in the American Committee for Devastated France, even as it is in the work of the Frontier Nursing Service. And such transport! Kentucky mountain transport, depending as it did in its early days entirely on horses and mules, called for girls who had more than horsemanship to offer—although that had to be good enough for them to travel icy trails, swim swollen rivers, carry sick babies on the pommels of saddles, escort nervous guests.

Our FNS couriers had to know as much about their mounts as our Card chauffeurs knew about their camions. They had to know what a given horse could do and what would be too much to expect of him. Upon the couriers still falls the decision of which mounts to give to which nurses, and that means they must know the horsemanship—or lack of it—of each individual nurse. Responsibility for all the horses, placed at all our stations over a seven hundred-square-mile area, rests upon them. All barn equipment is checked by the couriers; theirs to see that no saddle girth breaks on the steep descent of a mountain. We now have only twenty-two horses, instead of thirty-five to forty, but the couriers must carry responsibility for a motor fleet of twelve jeeps, a station wagon–ambulance, and a three-quarter-ton truck, as well as for beasts.

Just as the chauffeurs in the American Committee for Devastated France worked under the direction of a chief from their own ranks, so do the couriers in the Frontier Nursing Service. For many years their chief has been Jean Hollins from New York. After she had served as junior and senior courier she volunteered, in 1936, to take a course in animal husbandry at the University of Kentucky in order to be of more use to us. Dr. W. W. Dimock, who was then Director of the University's Department of Animal Pathology and who is now Director Emeritus, gave her all the opportunities at his disposal to learn everything she could about horses and cows. Jean has remained with us since then, with the title of Resident Courier. When she goes off to visit her family another top courier takes over her job. Helen Stone (Pebble) of New York, and Fanny McIlvain of Philadelphia, did this for years before we entered the war. Then Fanny had to take over a man's job in running her country place, while Pebble turned her hobby of flying into the service of her country when she joined the WAAFS in which she rose to the rank of Flight Commander. She could not get back to the Frontier Nursing Service for five years. To Jean fell the direction of all our transport service throughout the war years. Whenever her family, whose consideration of her responsibilities is regal, just naturally had to see something of her, then Fredericka Holdship (Freddy) came down from Sewickley, Pennsylvania, as relief. She and Jean both took the Red Cross training as nurse's aides in order to help out at Hyden Hospital and on the districts during the war, when we were desperately short of nurses. When we have been for short periods without a Social Service Secretary, couriers have relieved in that job too.

Couriers even ran the administration of Hyden Hospital during an epidemic of influenza early in 1941, when Vanda Summers, the Hospital Superintendent, all of the nursing staff but Davey, the clinic nurse, and five of the six maids had come down with the flu. This epidemic was so widespread in the staff, as well as on the districts, that twenty-two out of forty-one succumbed to it. My Assistant Director, Dorothy Buck, managed to keep one well nurse-midwife at the Hospital, and one at each outpost center, as though by sleight of hand. When Marion Shouse and Mary Wilson in Washington, D.C., learned of this crisis, they came down at once and pitched in.

Under Jean's direction, the couriers buy the remounts to replace horses that have been put to sleep because of accidents or old age. They also have the care of all sick and injured animals—take their temperatures, drench them, poultice and bandage them. About this one young thing said to me, "Horses are as much trouble to nurse as babies, and a lot more unhandy shape." Horses as well as people suffer from epidemics. In the days when periodic ophthalmia was considered a communicable disease, we had an outbreak of it among our horses. Our trustee, Dr. Charles E. Hagyard, came up from Lexington to study the situation and give his advice and help. But this was not his first visit. Seventeen years ago he first came to us with a veterinarian officer of the United States Army to hold a horse clinic, at which he covered the preventive as well as the curative aspects of a horse's care.

It is due to preventive care (by isolating new horses for two weeks) that we have not had a severe epidemic of horse distemper since 1937. This one was introduced by Puck, a new horse who had come by truck from Lexington, and was met at the head of Hurricane Creek by Jean Hollins on Lady Ellen. She led Puck the three and one-half miles along the trail to Wendover. In a couple of days he fell sick with a bad cough and a yellow discharge from his nostrils. With appalling rapidity the distemper spread through the Wendover barns and to Brutus, where Lady Ellen had been sent the day after Puck's arrival. Twelve of our animals came down with it. Some of them were desperately ill with complications like laryngeal abscesses and pneumonia and with temperatures as high as 106 degrees. (The normal temperature of a horse is about 100 degrees, taken rectally of course.) Dr. Hagyard, who could not come himself, sent one of his assistants—at no cost to us—to diagnose the disease and prescribe remedies. The couriers slept on hay in the stalls of the sick horses, so as to keep up their treatments during the night. So well did they handle this epidemic that only one of the horses died.

In our records are many testimonies to the grief we all have felt over the loss of the beloved horses who have so gallantly shared with us our work and its dangers. A Philadelphia courier wrote this about Tramp on the morning he was put to sleep: "Last night I was playing with him and he pulled the St. Christopher charm off my bracelet and ate it. I have a feeling it will see him through to a happy land beyond, where he will see all his old friends, and be able to eat grass, roll and buck—forever if he wants to."

Reminiscent of earlier times is the custom among the old people in the Kentucky mountains of referring to their stock as property. A man will say that he is going to the barn to "feed the property" by which he means his cows, horses, mules, hogs. Our property is worthy of the best quality of feed, and they get it. To cut costs, we skip not only the retailer but the wholesaler and order our hay in carload lots through a brokerage firm called the Cincinnati Grain and Hay Corporation. The brokerage firm refers to its hay and grain as though they were living entities. For example, "The new oats are moving now, and they are very bright."

But there is a lot to do for property besides feed it, as all our couriers know. Two of them from Cincinnati gave accounts, heart-rending and comical, of the time they took a cow and her calf from one outpost center to another. We felt that all that could be said about such a trip had been said until a Cleveland courier went through the same experience with Pebble and later wrote it up as "something to haunt the dreams of all couriers, new and old." Only those who have ridden in front of or behind cows, with calves cavorting around their horses' legs, can form an idea of the tediousness of such travel. The couriers have found it easier to take sick patients to the hospital by any transport available from horses to trucks than to coax, drive, or lead the property.

Our couriers often go out with the nurse-midwives on their sick calls and their deliveries, where they are of real help. Some eighteen years ago a Chicago courier spent twenty-four hours with the Wendover nurse-midwife, in a one-room cabin—as poor a house as any on our districts—where gusts of wind blew the snow in from a hole in the roof. A broody hen sat in a dark corner. A lard can, turned upside down, served as a third chair. The courier prepared food for the patient, brought in wood for the fire, swept the floor, and bumped her head on a great hunk of pork suspended from the ceiling. A courier from Minneapolis kept a diary while she was with us in 1940, in the form of letters to her mother. In these she describes not only her work with and for the horses but the many times she went out on district calls with the nurses at the centers. She wrote that on a postpartum visit near Bowlingtown, she combed and braided the mama's hair while the nurse-midwife, Eva Gilbert, washed the baby. With Minnie Meeke at Brutus she attended a delivery, as many couriers have done before and since, and was awed to note that the mother "never uttered a sound during the whole thing."

We have another group of letters, written in 1947 for the Lexington, Kentucky, Junior League, by a Blue Grass courier. They are as filled with nursing duties as with courier work because she had been a member of the Red Cross Volunteer Nurse's Aide Corps during the war. She spent some time at the Beech Fork Nursing Center where she went on two deliveries with Chappy, the senior nurse-midwife in charge. To one case she rode with Chappy in a borrowed logging truck. Since Chappy was not satisfied with the patient's condition, she picked her up, put her in the cab of the truck, and they all drove to Hyden Hospital—Chappy in the cab with her patient and the courier on the snow-covered bed of the truck with the delivery bags. Of the second delivery, she wrote that it was a first baby with father and mother deeply anxious when she and Chappy arrived. What awed her was the way in which Chappy completely, and quite placidly, absorbed all their fears and transformed them into confidence.

Only three of our couriers have written fully about their doings in the FNS, although more than two hundred of these young things have seen service with us during the past quarter-century, some of them several times. In naming them, I have had to limit myself to those whose frequent visits led to the assumption of administrative duties, and those who took photographs of professional rank. These girls, in their generation, impress me as being a step ahead of the generation of my own girlhood. They have more initiative than we had; they are less evasive and, in their frankness, they tend to see things whole. Although I would not say that their courage is greater than ours, it has been tested in ways that lay beyond our remotest dreams. Some of the couriers served all over the world in war. Others, who saw their husbands off to the Second World War and to Korea, stayed at home to bear the babies, to hold their little families together in the almost servantless households of their day. As my thoughts linger with our couriers—those of the long ago, those with us now—I realize that even if they had written up their adventures in the Frontier Nursing Service, ". . . time would fail me to tell of Gideon and of Barak" and the rest who, although they did not stop the mouths of lions and were not sawn asunder in our service, did throw into the work they gave us the generous abandonment of their youth.

The greater part of the couriers continue to work for their old Service after they leave—on our committees, or alone if they live where we have no committees. Their special skills are often used in our behalf. From them have come two out of our three best photographers and one out of our best three cartoonists. Marvin Breckinridge's photographs were taken in our early years. Nancy Dammann of Chicago has come back more than once in the foulest weather in order to get the snow scenes that professional photographers cannot take, because they won't travel in foul weather. (Our third truly great photographer was Edith Anderson—Andy—a member of the Alpha Omicron Pi Sorority and their Social Service Secretary in the Frontier Nursing Service for several years.) As to cartoons, few in the newspapers and magazines are better done than those Barbara Whipple drew for our *Quarterly Bulletins*—cartoons in which the horses, couriers, even the geese come alive.

We are often asked where the couriers come from, and how they happen to volunteer for work with the Frontier Nursing Service. They have come from "out of the everywhere into the here"—from as far south as Texas, as far north as Maine; from England, from California. The early ones were young things from the households of our personal friends. Mrs. E. A. Codman, our second Boston chairman, had been my friend before the Frontier Nursing Service existed and had a Boston Committee. In our early days she sent us her niece. The mother of our first St. Louis courier had been a Kentuckian and was a family friend. Many of the early couriers, and some later ones, have come through members of our Board of Trustees, and our committees, in a number of American cities. Other couriers became interested in us as the result of my talks with colored slides at girls' schools or at general meetings. Since we have had courier chairmen attached to our committees, many couriers come through these chairmen. All of them are interviewed by the chairmen who vouch for their horsemanship, their driving, their character, their stamina. Undoubtedly more couriers come to us now through old couriers than in any other way. Some of them apply because other members of their family have served with us. We have had three sisters of early couriers, three nieces, and seven sets of cousins. Kate Ireland of Cleveland, a younger sister of an early courier, has relieved Jean in the post of Resident as this book draws to its close. Until now we have had only one daughter of a courier, Betty Dabney, whose mother—one of our first and best—died in Betty's babyhood.

So many girls now go to college that we have a long waiting list of couriers who apply for the summer months, but we sometimes run short of enough couriers to handle the work in the fall and spring. During the winter we depend on Bennington College whose students may take their practical field work with FNS. Many of the old couriers register their girl babies with the Service as soon as they are born, sometimes by telegram. Enough of these couriers-to-be are registered with us now to make it hard for an applicant, without ancestry in the Frontier Nursing Service, to get in during the sixties and seventies of this century.

II

The Forgotten Frontier is the name of our motion picture to the making of which Marvin Breckinridge gave the better part of a year of her girlhood. First, she took lessons from professionals. Then she came down to the mountains several times to shoot her pictures, so as to take them at all seasons of the year. The result was a gift to the Frontier Nursing Service of five reels of dramatic pictures as good, professional men tell us, as the best of the silent moving picture period. Insofar as we know, *The Forgotten Frontier* is the only motion picture of its kind, unique in its portrayal of an early American way of life that has, even in the Kentucky mountains, largely receded into the past. The pictures were acted from real events by our own people—amateurs and volunteers all. There is a shooting scene between two men in a forest, produced like one that had occurred not long before, with the injured man, accompanied by a Frontier nurse, carried to Hyden Hospital by his neighbors on a stretcher made of saplings run through the sleeves of their coats. There is a good logging and raft picture. In another reel, one nurse is shown crossing a swollen river ford, and a second nurse is shown swimming the river on horseback when it is too deep for fording. There is a childbirth scene with the actual birth blacked out but showing our saddlebag setup and Texas handing the baby to its mother afterward.

Whenever Marvin had people lined up for her to shoot a scene, she met the appointment herself no matter what the weather. One night she and I stayed at Hyden Hospital because the river was a little too high to get back to Wendover without swimming. She had arranged for a group of men to meet her the next morning across the river from the Hyden ford. While she sat at breakfast, wondering how she could get herself and her great camera over there intact, Dr. Capps dropped in. With his rather charming drawl he said, "Miss Marvin, you can't cross the regular ford but I got over the river at Skimmer Jim's. If you sit on your laigs, and hold the reins in your teeth and lift the camera up with your hands, you can get across at Skimmer's." That is about as Marvin did it. Dr. Capps himself took part in these pictures. With his mare, Lady Jean, he re-enacted Dr. Collins' swimming the river to reach us for an emergency operation.

When *The Forgotten Frontier* was finished, we decided to have its premiere in New York City and to make the event a profitable one for the Frontier Nursing Service. We engaged Mecca Hall for the evening of January 15, 1931. Mrs. Langdon Marvin of our New York Committee, who had come down to Kentucky to see our work at firsthand, consented to act as chairman of a subcommittee to meet weekly and handle the details. The New York Committee opened a one-room office and engaged in Anne Winslow, Vassar graduate, a most capable executive secretary.

We had a diorama of the Frontier Nurse at work in winter designed and executed by Dwight Franklin, whose exhibits in the Museum of Natural History are famous. Anne placed this exhibit, rent free, in a window on Fifth Avenue. The seal of the Frontier Nursing Service, now so widely known, was comparatively new then because the young artist, David Shoemaker, had drawn it for us only the year before. Anne had posters printed with this seal and a notice of the entertainment. These she placed in hotels, clubs, restaurants, museums, professional offices, Fifth Avenue busses, and the Grand Central and Pennsylvania Railroad Stations. Her enthusiastic assistants in all these enterprises were the New York couriers of that era. Our benefit was a huge success. Miss Ruth Draper gave herself to us that evening and was at her glorious best. The great hall was full, except for a few top balcony seats, and fifteen debutantes, who acted as ushers, were run off their feet. *The Forgotten Frontier*, with Mr. Tertius Noble at the organ, drew a stupendous applause. It must be remembered that those were the days of the silent motion pictures and that few films were better or more dramatic than ours.

We showed *The Forgotten Frontier* hundreds of times after its premiere in New York, sometimes to drawing room groups (in 16 mm. size) and sometimes (in 35 mm. size) at regular motion picture theaters and in large halls. Insofar as I recall, it was last shown in April, 1939, at a command performance at Government House in Ottawa, where Marvin Breckinridge took it at the request of Lady Tweedsmuir. Marvin told me that Lady Tweedsmuir was eager to see a system analogous to that of the Frontier Nursing Service introduced into parts of Canada. The diorama that Dwight Franklin made for us has been exhibited as recently as the spring of 1950 when our Assistant Director, Helen E. Browne (Brownie) took it to New York for the International and Fourth American Congress on Obstetrics and Gynecology. It gets free storage, between exhibitions, in the basement of the Security Trust Company at Lexington, Kentucky.

III

The financial success of our New York venture brought us the knowledge that we could make money to supplement the gifts of our friends. This seemed frightfully important to us in the early thirties because so many of our friends were having to cut their gifts and we, at least until the effects of the drought were over, needed more and not less money. We decided to see what we could do with a cruise. We approached the International Mercantile Marine with the request that we be allowed to sell tickets on the *M. V. Britannic* of the White Star Line for a West Indies cruise in February and March of 1932 on a commission basis. They agreed, and offered us twenty-five per cent of every ticket we sold. It seemed to our Executive Committee that a task of this magnitude would need offices in Boston and Chicago, with full-time executive secretaries. Accordingly we opened offices in both places. We gave the post at the Boston office to Zaydee DeJonge, a delightful New England woman, whom I had known as one of the volunteer chauffeurs in the American Committee for Devastated France. In the Chicago office we placed Mrs. John C. Gardner, a Wellesley graduate and friend of mine. She not only did a bang-up job of selling tickets in and around Chicago but came down to the Kentucky mountains, with her four children, to spend the summer months in a small rented house, while she steeped herself in the doings of the Frontier Nursing Service and of her mountain neighbors. Fleming H. Revell had asked us for a book about our work. Caroline Gardner, with a delightful narrative style and some success in selling

279

short stories to magazines, was the person we chose to write this book. She called it *Clever Country*. This was the first of the books to be written about us.

The advantage in having a cruise as a benefit was that all of our committees everywhere could co-operate on it. We had volunteer sales agents in Baltimore, Cincinnati, Cleveland, Detroit, Hartford, Lexington, Louisville, Philadelphia, Pittsburgh, Rochester, St. Louis, and Washington. Wherever these agents were men, like our St. Louis Chairman, Mr. Harry French Knight, and our Cincinnati Chairman, Mr. James M. Hutton, their offices handled the sales for us.

At midnight, February 26, 1932, the *Britannic* sailed from New York to the West Indies. She made the usual stops but we had arranged unusual things for the enjoyment of the FNS passengers. At Port-au-Prince, airplanes of the U. S. Marines circled over the ship before it was boarded by my cousin, Colonel Jeter Horton, with a contingent of Marines who had arranged special things to give our people a good time. At Colon, a cluster of seaplanes came flying over the canal to circle above the ship. Later, my cousin, Major General Preston Brown, in command of the Canal Zone, came aboard with his aides to pay a courtesy call on the *Britannic's* captain and to invite him and the passengers to a reception at Balboa that afternoon. General and Mrs. Brown received their guests on the broad verandas of their house at Quarry Heights. They had invited to meet them representatives of the Diplomatic Corps, Army and Navy, the Public Health Service. Bands played while refreshments were passed; there was dancing on the tennis courts for the young people from the ship with plenty of officers to cut in. At the very last, as the sun was setting, just before we started back on our return journey across the Isthmus from Balboa to Colon, came the lowering of the flag at headquarters and the salute to the colors. All day we had watched our flag flying over an achievement for which Americans may be thankful as well as proud. Our thoughts were of General Goethals, working for eleven years with no other financial reward than the pay of a Major General, and of General Gorgas working in the same measure against mosquitoes more terrible than jungle beasts. Our concept of patriotism was deepened by the memory of these two old patriots.

After two days in Havana we returned to New York and our first cruise to the West Indies was over. Although we had cleared less than $6,000, because of the difficult financial winter, with boat rates reduced to fit the times, we felt that our first venture into the nautical field had justified itself. This decided our Executive Committee to keep open its offices in New York, Boston, and Chicago and undertake another Caribbean cruise in the spring of 1933. We again made our arrangements with the International Mercantile Marine but this time we chartered a whole ship—the *S. S. Belgenland* of the Red Star Line, a famous cruise ship in those days—at a cost of $60,000 for fifteen days.

From our experience in taking a large group of people on the *Britannic*, we had learned that many things could be arranged for the pleasure of the passengers that were overlooked on even the best commercial cruises. We took a teacher of contract bridge as our guest on the *Belgenland*, with the proviso that she give free bridge lessons in one of the lounges every day that the ship was at sea. We booked previews of the best moving pictures, which were shown at night. We enlisted the services of six "Dean's List" students from Yale, Harvard and Princeton. These young men, who were sons of people we knew, were given the cruise with the understanding that they help the agents of the American Express Company on the shore trips. This was the service they were there to render but naturally they liked to dance in the evenings with the girls, whose mothers much preferred them to "gigolos." We had in mind to build up a reservoir of good will. We expected at that time to stay in the cruise business and to make our annual cruise a benefit on a national scale.

The Frontier Nursing Service geared all its winter's work beyond the mountains toward the promotion of the *Belgenland* cruise and, in spite of the deepening depression, the situation about three weeks before the ship was due to sail indicated a profit to the Service of approximately $20,000. Then came the "Michigan moratorium," and the cancellations exceeded the bookings. We had a cruise cancellation clause in our contract, that we could have put into effect two weeks before the ship was due to sail, but the International Mercantile Marine, whose dealings with us were always courteous and fair, volunteered to go on with the cruise at their own risk. They did not lose. We had enough passengers to pay the $60,000 in full, but we made no profit whatever. The *Belgenland* sailed at the period of the breaking down of the entire American banking system. But there never were better sports than its passengers. We visited the Panama Canal again, where General and Mrs. Preston Brown entertained us as before. Again we stood at attention for the lowering of the flag at sunset.

After our *Belgenland* cruise, shipping companies besieged us to charter one of their ships for February-March, 1934. We had behind us several hundred old cruising friends, each an ardent salesman in our behalf. With only a little capital we could have swung into a successful cruise the following year and, until the Second World War, could have met my dream and our budget with one great annual event in which all of our committees shared. But we were dead broke. So ended our attempt to float our budget by means of a floating ship.

IV

This is the place in which to say something of Will Rogers and of what he meant to the Frontier Nursing Service. He had spoken enthusiastically about us to my brother Carson whom he met out in Peking. This emboldened me to ask him if he would take part in our *Belgenland* cruise. He wrote me this letter that, because it was personal, I did not use in the cruise publicity:

Well if it aint Mary Breckinridge:

I have read more about you than I have Mahatma Gandhi. I got the book and I can ride those mountains blindfolded. I can't be a midwife but I can sure hold the nurse's horse. Now about this pilgrimage you are making to the West Indies in behalf of better babies in Kentucky. That's a kind of a round about way to deliver babies, but it sounds mighty sound and practical. And they say you can live cheaper on one of these trips that you can at home. Lots of folks are making em just to dodge their daily mail from creditors.

Now I can't go. You can't do nothing when you are in the movies but just stay home and make faces at the world.

I would sure take you up on the thing, but it would be mighty slow traveling. I can and have made that same trip between breakfast and "supper." But its good for you "old folks" that are in no hurry.

The trip I want to make is right out in that virgin baby country of yours. I can talk to those people that are breeding these babies. So when I get some time off I am heading for this incubator country of yours. You can't beat old Kentucky for a breeding ground. Its the limestone in the soil, and the corn in the jug that does it.

What become of the Chinese Breckinridge? There is another good breeding ground is that China. He had just been made a "General" when I saw him in Peking. So there is liable to be Breckinridges all through those Mongolian Mountains too.

Well anyhow good luck to you on your trip. I am going to see if I can't write something about the trip in a Sunday article drawing folks attention to it and the cause it is for.

So save me a good mule and a good nurse and I am ready to go into the mountains and see "How Life Begins."

Good luck to you and your fine cause.

(*Signed*) WILL ROGERS

Mr. Rogers was as good as his word. He gave his entire article of Sunday, February 19, 1933 to the *Belgenland* cruise. He continued to take an interest in the Frontier Nursing Service until his death. The last thing I had from him was a telegram on New Year's Day of 1935 saying, "HAPPY NEW YEAR AND BEST WISHES TO A GREAT WORK."

Chapter 29

I

I T was while we were knee-deep in preparations for our *Britannic* cruise that I had my back broken. After Teddy Bear's death, I did not get another horse of my own. I started the custom of riding the new horses we bought before turning them over to members of the staff. In this way I became familiar with several of our mounts but never kept one long enough to form an attachment for him. More than two years after Teddy Bear's death we got on trial, from the Blue Grass, a fine new animal with the erect ears and the markings of the famous Peavine Kentucky saddle strain, and also with the immense wind, endurance and the shoulder formation of the thoroughbred. It is not uncommon in Kentucky to cross saddle stock with a thoroughbred and some such pedigree lay behind Traveller. He did not in the least resemble General Lee's famous gray for whom he was named.

While Traveller was on trial I had been riding him and had taken a liking to him. He was so nervous an animal, with such a tender mouth, that I used a light bit on him and guided him with a light hand on the reins. Everything in the mountains appalled him. He had a way of springing and starting into a run at the sight of a pig wallowing, at the sound of dried cucumber tree leaves rustling. He forded the rivers in a series of bounds. Through all of this he seemed easy to control and I had no fear of him. Our annual Thanksgiving reunion was at Hyden Hospital in 1931. When we had finished dinner Betty Lester got up and, on behalf of the staff, told me they had bought Traveller to present to me for my very own. Although I don't like for my associates to give me things, their joy in this gift was such that I could not refuse it.

Between Thanksgiving and Christmas I had a string of engagements lined up beyond the mountains, at which I was speaking in behalf of the *Britannic* cruise. On Sunday afternoon, November 29, I left Wendover to ride the three and a half miles up Hurricane Creek. Two people rode with me, one to take the horses back to Wendover and the other Dorothy Clark, a junior courier who was returning to her home in New York. It was drizzling, so I wore over my uniform the Service raincoat of those days, modeled after that used by the Royal Canadian Mounted Police. It had a huge cape to shed snow and rain. Since I had not worn it before when riding Traveller, this was his first experience with a cape-coat.

Dot and I rode down to the river and turned our horses in to drink. My cape was not buttoned. As Traveller raised his head, a puff of wind blew it wide open. Traveller gave one terrified bound before he started to run. Even then I could have saved the situation by turning him into the river. But I did not realize he was running away, so I turned him towards the trail up Hurricane Creek. In a moment I knew that he was out of control, but it was too late to turn him then. A sheer wall of mountain rose on my right and a precipice of some ninety feet dropped down to the creek on my left. The only thing that could stop Traveller would be to get rid of the raincoat but I was in it and sitting on it. My effort to throw it back and off terrified him the more. He seemed to skim through the air. We cleared three miles of up and down trail—mostly up—in less than fifteen minutes. I knew I could keep my seat as long as I kept a grip with my knees, but I was sure that my knees would not outlast Traveller. I had plenty of time in which to decide how to take the fall. I had no intention of being thrown over his head, and I didn't want to go off to the left and roll down the precipice. Near the head of Hurricane, when I lost all sensation in my knees, I threw myself forward on Traveller's neck, dropped the reins, cleared the stirrups, and rolled over to the right. We were going at such terrific speed that I hit the rocky ground with force. I had the sense to keep my head up, as I went over, so that I retained consciousness.

Up near the head of Hurricane there is a group of houses where nice people have always lived. Since it was Sunday afternoon, several men were sitting out on their porches who ran down to the trail when they heard Traveller coming. I heard one of them exclaim, when they saw the uniform, "It's one of our nurses." I told them how to carry me and they took me to the nearest house and laid me on a bed. Then some of them went after Traveller who, rid of the raincoat, had run only several hundred yards before stopping to wait for what would happen next. When in the course of time Dot Clark caught up with me, she helped the men to make a stretcher. She walked beside them as they carried me to the highway. When the men had placed me on the back seat of the car, Dot knelt on the floor to steady me while we drove to Hyden. News of my accident traveled ahead, as such things always do in the mountains. Dr. Capps met me with the hospital stretcher at the end of the new highway. The road had not been built up to our hospital then, but a host of Hyden friends were on hand to carry me up the mountain. When I told the doctor that my injury seemed to be in the back, he put me on a table instead of in a bed. Then I heard him say to Mac, "Give her a fourth of morphine." This was a relief, because I had some shock, as well as pain, but the greatest relief to me was that I no longer had to put up a front. While I lay on stretchers carried by mountain men who, however terrible their injuries, never let on by a sound that they are in pain, I felt that the honor of the Service demanded the same stoicism from me. So I joked with them, telling them I would have dieted had I known they were going to carry me. It was wonderful to be able to drop that front and no longer pretend that nothing much was the matter.

That evening Dr. James E. Hagan, the fine orthopedic surgeon at Hazard, sped over to Hyden to see me. He made arrangements for me to stop at the Hazard Hospital for X-rays on my way down to Lexington. There was no ambulance in our part of the world then and it was not until later that Mr. Edsel Ford gave us our own station wagon-ambulance. We got hold of an old-fashioned hearse from Hazard. The morning after my injury a group of Hyden friends came up the mountain to carry me down to the hearse. Dr. Capps went with me as far as Hazard where he and Dr. Hagan took the pictures to go with me to Lexington. Mac went all the way with me as did my secretary, Wilma Duvall, to handle a lot of telephoning. I arranged to be carried to the Lafayette Hotel. I thought I could work better at a hotel than in a hospital, and I knew the Lexington doctors would not be likely to move me once I got there. A motor road had recently been cut from Hazard to Lexington. Although the contractors were still working on it, my hearse got through safely.

As soon as she heard I had reached the Lafayette, Dr. Hunt came around bringing with her Lexington's famous orthopedic surgeon, Dr. W. Marmaduke Brown. By this time the X-rays were dry and could be clearly read. Duke, as all of his friends call Dr. Brown, took the X-rays over to a strong light, then said, with a frank courtesy that showed more respect for me than I rated, "Your back is broken, crushed second lumbar vertebra." In a moment there flashed before me the *Britannic* cruise, with all the engagements I had lined up ahead in preparation for it, and our dreadful need of the money we expected to make out of it. I said to Duke, "You will have to fix me up some way so that I can start out in a few days." He replied somewhat as follows: "You will need eight weeks on a Bradford frame, and then a metal brace. It will be months before you can travel." Still dazed with the shock of the news, my only reply was that I had to get going and that he would have to fix me up so that I could start out in a few days.

With a sort of grave gentleness Duke repeated his verdict and left me.

I lay for about an hour too dazed to think or plan, with a breakdown of morale like that of a shell-shocked soldier. Josie Hunt, Mac and Wilma came over to me with sympathy so quiet and understanding that it should have brought me around, but it didn't. Then I remembered Adeline, the anchoress in England, who had started me on the inside-out way from childishness toward childlikeness. I knew that Adeline's courage could be offered to God in behalf of my cowardice. I told Wilma to cable Adeline what had happened, and to ask her to stand by. Within a few hours a cable came back: "INDEED I AM WITH YOU. LITTLE ONE. MAY HE HOLD YOU IN HIS HEALING HANDS."

From the time that I turned to Adeline, I began to come out of my slump, which was just as well because I had quite a lot of work to do. A press dispatch about my injury had gone out from Hazard. One effect of that was bad. News reached my brother Carson in China before he had time to get a letter and caused him great distress of mind. The other effect was good. Telegrams with offers of help poured in upon me from our committee members and trustees. Two of them took on my first engagements. The day after I reached Lexington I settled down at the telephone (with Wilma to hold the receiver) and called up the other people at whose houses I was to speak, to ask them if they wanted to cancel the meetings or take substitute speakers. The first person I called was Mrs. Henry Ford at Dearborn, because a meeting at her house was my next engagement. She was, as always, understanding. After she had expressed her sympathy, she said she preferred to put off the meeting until the next year when I could take it myself. In one way or another, Wilma and I disposed of my itinerary.

Meanwhile, the members of our Executive Committee were leaping into the breach. Our National Chairman, Mrs. S. Thruston Ballard in Louisville, sent me the following telegram:

TERRIBLY DISTRESSED AT YOUR NEWS I KNOW YOU NEVER CONSIDER YOURSELF BUT FOR THE SAKE OF OUR GREAT CAUSE FOR MY SAKE AND FOR THE THOUSANDS WHO LOVE YOU MUST ABSOLUTELY FOLLOW THE DOCTORS INSTRUCTIONS THEREFORE AS NATIONAL CHAIRMAN I ORDER YOU TO MAKE NO PLANS UNTIL I SEE YOU ON FRIDAY I WILL ARRIVE LEXINGTON IN FORENOON GREATEST LOVE

She came into my room at the Lafayette all smiles and encouragement. We were laughing together when Desha Breckinridge popped in. He said: "I entered this room in distress, troubled about Mary and fearing I had missed Sunshine (Mrs. Ballard). Mary is laughing, and Sunshine is found." With that, he carried her off to lunch.

Mr. Manning came to my room, sat down beside me and read a

letter he had written and mailed to all the subscribers of the Frontier Nursing Service. In his own inimitable language, he told of my accident before asking our friends to give to a fund to make up for my loss of time, and to relieve the burden on my mind. He, Mrs. Ballard and Mrs. A. J. A. Alexander, Alex's widow, had signed the letter which said they had each given $5,000 to start the fund. Our thousands of patients—the sick, the children, the expectant mothers—we were not going to let them down. My heart welled over with thankfulness. It was thus, through gratitude to God, that I took my first step back on the way I had lost, the childlike way that leads to His kingdom. He is kind to the unthankful, as Christ said.

II

Upon reflection, and I had time for reflection, there seemed to be no reason why I should spend my eight weeks on a Bradford frame down in Lexington when I could go by ambulance to our own hospital at Hyden. I took this up with my kinsmen and my friends, who were in and out of my room constantly, and with Dr. Brown. He said that as we had a competent physician at Hyden, I could go back, and return to Lexington in late January to be fitted for a steel brace before giving up the Bradford frame. Mac took me back in Mr. Clarence Kerr's ambulance. We particularly wanted Mr. Kerr to go up to the mountains because he, like so many Blue Grass people, is a horseman and we wanted a horseman's diagnosis on Traveller. After Mr. Kerr had ridden him, he said that he was not an "outlaw." He had run away only because he was frightened by the cape on my raincoat. It was Mr. Kerr's opinion that when Traveller had become mountain-wise he would make us a serviceable horse.

As I lay on my Bradford frame in Mac's room at Hyden Hospital, it diverted me to make plans to gentle Traveller. My first concern was to get him accustomed to the blue-gray cape-coat that was part of the uniform of the Frontier Nursing Service. A horse does not forget. I knew he would run away again if anyone attempted to ride him a second time in the raincoat. I had a letter from General Preston Brown at the Canal Zone in which he said: "Do permit a relative to reproach you mildly for riding a nervous throughbred attired in a cape of any description. They always flap and are certain to cause a nervous horse to be quite unmanageable."

Dr. Capps volunteered to get Traveller "adjusted" to the raincoat. He found, however, that Traveller wouldn't even let him approach, whether he wore the coat or carried it over his arm. So we adopted other tactics. The cape-coat was hung in his stall at Wendover. He snorted and reared but he couldn't get away from it. Then the Wend-over barn man, who fed him and cleaned his stall, began wearing the coat while he performed these duties. Before long Traveller formed new associations, pleasant ones, which linked the cape-coat with his oats. When he had come to look upon the coat favorably, he allowed the barn man to mount him in the once terrifying costume. After that the better riders in the Frontier Nursing Service could give him the exercise he needed.

I thought of another thing to do to quiet Traveller's highly sensitive nervous system. In the early days of racing in England, when the thoroughbred stock was inbred to develop its endurance and swiftness, it was found that a goat around the racing stables exercised a quieting influence upon the horses. Some horses had their own goats and became much attached to them. From this comes the expression "to get his goat," because unscrupulous people sometimes stole a horse's goat the night before he was to race. This would so upset the horse's equi-librium that he couldn't do his best on the tracks the next day. We bought a nanny goat for Traveller.

Nanny's first effect upon Traveller was happy in the extreme. She became as deeply attached to him as he to her, slept in his stall at night, and trotted down to the river to water with him in the morning. Unfortunately, however, we hadn't figured that a goat, as well as a horse, might have a nervous system. One day when a strange dog frightened Nanny she tore up the mountainside. Traveller bolted after her. Although Nanny followed Traveller everywhere he went on land, she refused to cross the river nor would Traveller, devoted as he was to her, allow her to be carried on the pommel of his rider's saddle. This meant that when anyone rode Traveller from Wendover to Hyden, someone else had to ride as far as Muncy ford to carry his goat across the river for him, and then meet him on the return trip to take his goat back over the water. When all of this was reported to me, I agreed that we must dispose of Nanny. She had been brought to see me in my room where I took a liking to her. But there was no doubt about it, she had to go. Her departure upset Traveller so much, emotionally, that for about a week he was off his feed. I am sure he would have known her after an absence of years, but we sent her too far away for him to see her again.

III

I did not go back to Lexington until January 25, 1932. Despite a few ups and downs—figuratively speaking, since I lay on the Bradford frame with the middle of my body higher than my head and shoulders —I had a happy time. Wilma and I had enough correspondence with our cruise secretaries and volunteer agents to take up part of each day. In the remaining hours I had lots of fun. I gave a dinner party for the men who had carried me by stretcher up and down, and again up, the hospital mountain. They all came to my room after dinner and joked with me. Sergeant Will Sandlin, who was one of these men, brought me a poke filled with his own apples. The patients who were able to walk, especially the prenatals, came in and sat by my open fire. My Hyden and Wendover friends visited me as did our staff from the outpost centers, when they could take the time off duty. The girls at Wendover brought Wendy, my bull terrier dog, to keep me company from time to time. But she was so domineering with the hospital dogs that I couldn't let her stay.

Hyden Hospital was seething with Christmas preparations not only for the patients and the Hyden children, but for all the outpost centers to which the supplies would be taken by wagon team. We had then, in Cynthia Beatty, the first of a long line of volunteer Christmas secretaries. As she unloaded the shipments from outside friends, she brought me squeaky toys for amusement. Now and then the neighborhood children came to see me and, on Christmas Eve, the older ones sang carols under my window.

To add to my happiness, I had a visit from a friend of my Rosemont school days, Mrs. Arthur Bray, who stopped off in Kentucky on her way from England to visit friends in Australia. When Judge Lew Lewis met her he said, "I am more British than you are." This puzzled Evelyn who was of pure English stock—in fact, an Englishwoman. But I knew what Judge Lew meant. Evelyn was English only, whereas he was of English, Scotch, and Welsh descent; therefore he was more *British* than she. Evelyn and Mac and all our staff from everywhere thought of amusing things to give me on Christmas Day. From Mac came a wooden plaque that hangs in my room at Wendover now. Burned into it are these words: "JUST ABOUT THE TIME YOU THINK YOU CAN MAKE BOTH ENDS MEET, SOMEONE MOVES THE ENDS."

Aside from my custom of always spending Christmas holidays in the mountains, there were two special reasons why I had made plans, long before my accident, to be at home. The first reason was that we were changing medical directors with the New Year. I had known for months that Dr. Capps would be leaving us for postgraduate work and, after that, to settle at his home town in Tennessee in private practice. Months before he left I had decided on the man I wanted as his successor. Through Dr. Graeme Mitchell of the Children's Hospital in Cincinnati, we had secured the services of Dr. John H. Kooser the previous summer for pediatric clinics. He spent five weeks with us, as a volunteer, and examined nearly one thousand children who had suffered most from hardships caused by the drought. His work was so thorough, and we liked him so well, that we asked him to become our Medical Director as of January 1, 1932, and he accepted the post.

Although Dr. Kooser had taken some graduate training in obstetrics, he did not feel he had had enough experience to be responsible for that part of our work. I appealed to Dr. Benjamin P. Watson, a member of our National Medical Council and Director of Sloane Hospital at the Presbyterian Medical Center in New York, who consented to take Dr. Kooser on as a special resident during the autumn months. So it came about that we had the joy of this competent physician and fine friend for an unbroken period of more than eleven years, until he left us in the summer of 1943 to volunteer for the Medical Corps of the U.S. Navy.

When Dr. Kooser entered upon his engagement with us, our affiliation with the Kentucky State Board of Health was severed by mutual consent. Dr. McCormack agreed with me that our work had become too big for one man to combine with it the duties of a public health officer. During the years that Dr. Capps acted as health officer, and the State Board of Health paid part of his salary, he could receive no fees from his patients. He answered the emergency calls of sick or injured men and women, but he encouraged such patients to get a private physician for complaints that were not emergencies, whenever they could afford the fees. Often they could not, for the fees sometimes ran as high as fifty dollars for one visit—because of mileage charges and the time it took a physician to reach his patient on horseback.

Under our new arrangement, with a Medical Director who was not a public health officer, we could ask our grown-up patients to pay for medical care. But, so poor was our section following the drought, and with hundreds of unemployed men back from the industrial centers, that at the end of our first full fiscal year, 1932–33, under the pay system for adults we had only received $247.15 in medical fees. This included the sale of such of our drugs as Dr. Kooser prescribed, at their cost to us. It was not until the end of our fiscal year 1936–37 that the medical fees, including the sales of drugs and supplies at cost, rose from less than $800 annually to more than $1,600.

IV

The second reason why I needed to be at home over the Christmas holiday season had to do with the Federal farm loans. During the spring of 1931, following the drought of 1929–30, the Department of Agriculture had loaned money to the farmers in the drought areas to buy seed and fertilizer. It was essential for people who had no other credit to take advantage of these loans in order to plant their crops. The loans, which ran for only a few months, fell due in the autumn of 1931 and the early winter of 1932. Meanwhile the crops, which had been mortgaged to the Government as security for the loans, shared in the market collapse. Men who repaid their loans had to sell two or three bushels of corn to get the price one bushel brought before the market collapse. Not five per cent of the borrowers in our section were able to do this. To take away so large a part of their crops would have caused another famine. They asked to have their loans renewed for a year, or until corn got back to what it had been worth in the spring when the loans were made. Not only was this not done, but the Department of Agriculture put such pressure to bear on the borrowers that many of them sold their hogs to meet its claims. I had a list of the names and addresses of people I knew whose livestock had been sold. There were enough of them to fill a legal-size sheet of paper. This I had mimeographed and sent to the Department of Agriculture. No results.

After I had been taken down to Lexington again I saw Desha Breckinridge. He felt, as I did, that a nation which could give financial assistance to banks, railroads and insurance companies, through the newly created Reconstruction Finance Corporation, could afford to extend credit relief to its drought-stricken farmers and tenants. Desha took the matter up with Senator Alben W. Barkley and Representative Virgil Chapman, who introduced bills in both Houses of the Congress to extend the Federal farm loans for one year. This did bring results. The Department of Agriculture sent their representative from St. Louis to Lexington to see us. He, Desha and I had a conference on and around my Bradford frame.

I told the St. Louis man that unless the Department of Agriculture changed its policy, not only in Kentucky but in Arkansas and Oklahoma as well, I would go to Washington by ambulance and appear on my Bradford frame before committees of both the Senate and the House, to speak in behalf of the farmers and tenants. I knew that my father would not approve of my doing this sensational thing. Nevertheless, I said I would do it, and Desha told the St. Louis man that I meant what I said. The St. Louis man, startled, but courteous and sympathetic, said he would make recommendations. This conference brought real results. The Department of Agriculture changed its policy and our harried people were left in peace.

As for me, Dr. Brown's skill and care had restored me to my work not so handicapped but that I could make a go of it. Late in February, after I had learned to walk in my new steel brace, I went on to New

York with Wilma to take the *Britannic* cruise as Cousin Lily Beattie's guest. The International Mercantile Marine, in a kind gesture, invited Texas to go along as their guest so that I would have a nurse with me. I lived in the steel contraption and felt about it as the old lady felt about her feet when she said, "Cold feet are not pleasant, either by night or by day."

Chapter 30

I

IN April, 1932, after the *Britannic* cruise, I came back to the mountains—to Wendover. Since I was not allowed to ride horseback I made the three and a half miles down Hurricane Creek sitting on an air cushion tied to the horse's saddle, with a man leading the horse, while Wendy and the other Wendover dogs formed part of my enthusiastic escort. It was not until the next April, seventeen months after my back was broken, that I received Dr. Brown's permission to make rounds of our outpost centers—over eighty miles of horseback travel—during a period of eight days. I had begun to ride again (wearing the steel contraption) but this was to be my first tour of the outpost centers since my accident, my first meetings with our local committees, my first visits to the outpost nurses.

It was "Dogwood Winter" when I set out, with Pebble Stone as my escort, to Hyden Hospital where I stayed the night. Three cases of acute appendicitis had been brought in during the past few days, two by stretcher and one by boat from twelve miles up the river. The boat patient, Bige, was a boy of ten. When Dr. Kooser took me to see him I gave him a trick box that he said would pleasure him always. One of my mountain friends was expecting her baby that night. She told me she wanted to name it Mary, but about nine o'clock Betty Lester, in white from head to foot, her face wreathed in smiles, looked in to whisper, "Not Mary but Marius has come."

It rained all through the night. In the morning it was reported that the fords in the Middle Fork of the Kentucky River were too deep to cross without swimming. Several are too rocky to swim. Texas was now my escort. We decided to ride over Thousandsticks Mountain to Bull Creek, ride down it four miles, cross the gap over the next mountain to Hell-for-Certain Creek and ride down Hell-for-Certain to the river, and then along its banks to the Possum Bend Nursing Center. I rode Carminettie, a steady pony, but slight for deep or swift fords.

We made what we mountaineers call a "soon start" and Lassie and Carminettie traveled well through the angry waters of Bull Creek and Hell-for-Certain. Near the mouth of the second creek, before we came down to the swollen backwater of the Middle Fork River, we saw through the mist and gathering dusk the blue-gray uniform of the Frontier Nursing Service, worn by one of our outpost nurses, Dunny, who came plowing upstream to meet us. She guided us around the quicksands and then, by a narrow trail, to the road that led to Possum Bend Nursing Center. There all was warmth and welcome. Edith Marsh (Marshie Number Two) and Pepper, the bull terrier, ran out to help unsaddle the horses and take us in to the living room fire and the supper, for which the men and women of our Confluence Committee joined us.

The rains stopped in the night and the river eased down a bit. Soon after breakfast one of the couriers, "Frenny" Rousmaniere, rode in from over Shoal Mountain with a six-year-old boy on the pommel of her saddle. He had stuffed dried peas in his ears and she had gone down to Bowlingtown to get him and take him to Dr. Kooser at Hyden to have the peas removed. She reported that Shoal ford, between Confluence and the Margaret Durbin Harper Memorial Center at Bowlingtown, was passable. So Texas and I started out on a trail that led first up and over my favorite mountain, now garlanded in dogwood and redbud and the tender green of young leaves. Through a sort of watery sunshine we could see "a fur piece" the windings of the river way below and the little homes nestled here and there. Then we came down on Elkhorn Creek and rode to where it emptied into the river above Shoal ford.

The river was angry, its big rocks concealed by dark waters. Here again we saw the blue-gray uniform of the Frontier Nursing Service. Dorothy Buck (Bucket) had come to meet us and see us safely across. We exchanged greetings, with the water up to the horses' bellies, and then Bucket led the way on Dixie. We traveled about five hundred yards near the bank, before Bucket turned and slowly started across the ford. The horses hardly seemed to move. They picked their way step by step in the rocky bed. I thought of Frenny with the six-year-old boy on the pommel of her saddle and wondered again how often our guardian angels saw us through.

At Bowlingtown we stayed over an extra day to give my back a rest and to attend a dinner-committee meeting. Bucket's housekeeper dished up a wonderful feed with guinea hens from off the place as the *pièce de résistance*. When I said we had to push on next day the men at the meeting asked me how I planned to get over the Barger ford, the deepest on the river but with a sandy bottom and no snarling rocks. I said that our horses would have to swim if the water hadn't gone

294

down. With that Will Gay, our chairman, looked at me sternly and said, "We won't have our Director swimming that river." When Texas and I rode down to the Barger ford the next morning we found three of our friends there with a boat. Our chairman sprang on Lassie, a second friend mounted Carminettie and a third put Texas, me and our saddlebags in the boat. We reached the shore dry but the men were wringing wet to the waist from their swim.

Across the river, we met the Barger family, who invited us to a wedding at eleven o'clock. The rambling old Barger house, surrounded by trees and shrubs, lies near the river in rich bottom land. In one of its large rooms, a girl and her fourth cousin (of the same name) were sitting side by side in front of a minister. The family and friends gathered around them and the ceremony began. "Stand on your feet and join your hands," said the minister. The young girl, rosy-cheeked, and the young man with a shock of yellow hair arose and clasped hands. "Will you take her and cleave to her and cherish her as long as you both live?" asked the minister. "I will," answered the boy. Then the minister turned to the girl. "Will you take him and cleave to him and cherish him as long as you live?" "I will," she answered. After that he pronounced them man and wife. At the splendid dinner which followed, a lot of fun passed around at the expense of the bride's older unmarried sister. "She will have to dance in a hog trough," they said, as that was the custom when a girl let her younger sister marry ahead of her.

Later in the day, Texas and I rode up Leatherwood Creek, across a mountain gap and down Panco Creek to Bullskin—a stretch of about eleven miles. At the Brutus Nursing Center, on Bullskin, Lois and Jean, followed by their dogs, came running out to meet us in a way that reminded me of a line in my favorite mountain ballad, "We will all go out to meet her when she comes." Again we had our committee members to dinner before gathering around the fireplace, above which hangs a picture of Belle Barrett Hughitt in her youth. I saw the Florence Williams Memorial Library, given Brutus since my last visit, with its records of how constantly the books are borrowed, and how carefully they are returned, by old and young.

Early the next morning, Texas and I rode away to continue our rounds which were to take us to the Red Bird, the Flat Creek, and the Beech Fork Nursing Centers. At all of these places there would be the same glad welcomes from nurses, dogs, patients, committee friends. The trails we were to follow would be as lovely as those we had ridden, and nearly all of them as rough.

Between Brutus and Red Bird we got into territory unknown to us. We had been warned not to take our usual route down Jack's Creek to Red Bird River because the river ford, at the mouth of the creek, would be impassable. So we turned up a fork of Little Jack's Creek to cross a mountain where we had never been before. What was our delight to find in a cabin at the head of the fork one of our former patients, brought to Hyden Hospital two months before for the removal of a six-pound cyst, and returned to her remote abode on a stretcher. Her husband came in from the steep hillside he was plowing to greet us. They pressed us "to take the night" but when we had to decline, their daughter, ruddy-cheeked and in overalls, volunteered to act as our guide across the gap to the head of the next branch. We wound up and up through glorious country, white with the bloom of dogwood, sprinkled with great yellow patches of mustard in seed, the air heavy with the odor of wild plum. Sometimes we heard the note of the thrush or saw the cardinal and his mate.

Near an abandoned site, where a cabin had burned, we came to an old apple orchard, hoary but still lovely, near the ruined chimney. In such a sequestered spot could an anchoress, like Adeline, have found the quiet for contemplative prayer. Springs gushed out of the mountainside and tore down to the branch. The branch was racing to Little Jack's Creek, Little Jack's rushing in its turn to Red Bird River. Red Bird meets Goose Creek at Oneida to become the South Fork; the South Fork, eighty odd miles farther on, joins with the Middle Fork and the North Fork to form the Kentucky River. The Kentucky, gathering in all these Appalachian waters, moves towards the Ohio, and then the Ohio sweeps on to join the Mississippi in its majestic march to the sea. These springs, this tiny branch, were tributaries of that mighty river on whose banks I had spent the happiest hours of my girlhood in the long ago. The continuity—the unity—the swift passing. We felt a part of it as we reined in for a moment where the springs came out of the mountainside, near the old apple orchard by the ruined chimney.

II

The description I have given of a part of my first rounds after a break of seventeen months, will have shown a little, but only a little, of the spirit of our nurse-midwives. There is an *esprit de corps* in the staff of the Frontier Nursing Service that has been commented on by many of our guests in words that are treasured in my heart. Perhaps the most significant thing said about our crowd, because it was said by an expert in human relations, came from the late Dr. Charles E. Kiely, a neuropsychiatrist of Cincinnati. After he, with our surgical friend, Dr. John A. Caldwell, had stayed overnight at several of our stations, he told me that ours was the best integrated group, the sanest, the most wholesome, of any with which he had come in contact during his professional life. Much the same thing is said by those members of our Board of Trustees who visit us often. When the late Roger K. Rogan of Cincinnati, a Vice-Chairman of this Board, made his first visit to us with his wife, Margaret, he commented on the happy faces, the pleasant manners of everyone he met, and said that utilitarian things seemed to be done with spiritual insight.

It is true that those who stay with the Frontier Nursing Service for any length of time (and some are in it for life) need and have a deeper motive than a search for adventure, although heaven knows a willingness to accept misadventure must be a part of their mental equipment. It would take research through endless records of the Service to list all the broken arms and other injuries the staff have suffered in horseback accidents, but I think the honor of the first broken arm goes to Mac. As to near deaths, there have been many times when the life of a nurse was in jeopardy. My Marine Corps brother, who came in to see us several times, gave our nurses his highest title for courage when he called them Marines. What I feel about them is well put in the description of little dog Rags in *Timothy's Quest:* "Ready for death if need be, but very much in hopes of something better."

III

When Dorothy Buck (Bucket) first came to us in the fall of 1928 she got off the train at Krypton in mountains so snowbound that the man who was to take her on muleback to the nearest nursing center, Possum Bend at Confluence, did not feel his animals should make the trip. Bucket walked off alone, following directions until, to her relief, she caught sight of a girl in a uniform like hers, coming to meet her. It was Billy Williams, one of the Possum Bend nurses then. Bucket stayed with the Possum Bend nurses a week, going out on foot to visit their patients with them, before the welcome news arrived that the mail had gotten through at last and the mail rider had brought her horse. (In those days we sometimes sent our horses by parcel post.) Bucket's horse was a coal-black animal named Remus. He had a frightening way of baring his teeth at strangers and plunging the length of his bridle, but he was the most sure-footed horse in the Service and, therefore, given to new nurses.

With Billy Williams as escort, Bucket set off on Remus and rode for "miles and miles and miles—and miles!" stopping every now and then to knock the snowballs from the horses' hoofs. Finally Billy took a short cut that led up Thousandsticks Mountain on the far side from Hyden Hospital. There they met up with our old friend, Mr. Hence Stidham who, always the kindest of men, came to Bucket's rescue. He led Remus, Billy led her own horse, and they all walked. Bucket said that her legs, unaccustomed to hours around a saddle, now wobbled; her feet, accustomed to city pavements, stumbled; her heart thudded; her breath left her; she stopped to gasp. The two figures walking steadily ahead with the horses called to ask if she was all right. She said that she thought of the chubby babies, the wide-eyed children, and the friendly mothers she had seen during the past week. She thought of them, and tried not to think of Remus, "waiting for his first bite of nurse." Then she called reassurance to the others and staggered on upward—up over Thousandsticks towards Hyden Hospital.

Many of the early nurses told me that nothing they had to face after they began work with the Frontier Nursing Service was harder than their first trip in. Mac says she arrived in the buckboard on its maiden voyage to test it out in advance of bringing in Sir Leslie and Lady MacKenzie and Mrs. Ballard. It was Mac who went down to Krypton to meet Nora K. Kelly when she first descended at that way station at 4:45 on a cold morning. Kelly noticed that Mac paid special attention to the stirrups and girths of their mounts, for which she was to be thankful later. As they rode up the bed of a rocky creek to the top of a mountain that lay between them and Confluence, and then down the mountain in the bed of the creek called Trace, Kelly said brightly to Mac, "Are we hitting the road soon?" The reply dashed her, "Why, this is the road; it is the main road, and a good one too." Finally they came out on the river at Confluence where a deep ford lay between them and the nursing center of Possum Bend. To Kelly's amazement Mac struck right across the river, deeper and deeper in the horrible yellow current. The water rose to their knees and then, just when Kelly expected it to go over her head, it became shallow and she reached the other side. After a stop for food and rest at Possum Bend, Kelly faced twelve more miles of riding with several more crossings of the river—faced them like the seasoned trooper she had already become. When they reached Hyden Hospital, she wrote, "As for myself, now that the trip in was over, nothing seemed impossible."

They still do almost impossible things, these nurses of ours, when they work with Nature in her savage moods—what Galsworthy calls "nature with a small 'n,' " which is not the Nature of the poets and the artists. We are often asked if our people appreciate the difficulties the nurse-midwives sometimes face in answering their calls. Those who share these difficulties understand them as no others could and their appreciation is the measure of their understanding. This letter came to us in the winter of 1948 from Deep Ford Fork:

I do know it was cold, snow, and frozen on the night on the Sunday, Feb. 2nd at 2:30 when I call the nurses—and how willing they was to cross that snow Hill for sake of my wife when my baby Hubert was born about 9:20 Monday morning. I sure thank the kindness and willingness of two nice nurses while in my home, Miss Reid and Miss Lenschow.

(Signed) RUFUS FELTNER

Our most terrible horseback accident happened in early December of 1949 when Anna May January's horse plunged in soft mud and slid over a bank. When she fell, and the horse with her, the pommel of the saddle struck her abdomen, causing the gravest internal injuries. Since she was on the district of the Possum Bend outpost center, it was hours before she could be gotten to Hyden Hospital. Dr. Maurice O. Barney, our Medical Director then, with one of our nurses, carried her down to St. Joseph Hospital in Lexington by ambulance. Several of our surgical friends had gone off to a convention but one of them, Dr. Eugene Todd, was there and he operated. His operation, the blood transfusion and the new antibiotic drugs (which kept the peritonitis at a minimum) saved Anna May's gallant life. She rides again.

IV

I wish this book might be long enough for me to give a sketch of each nurse whose service has been of significance in our success, but that would mean sketches of so many as to fill the book. Their names so throng my memory, as I write, that I find it almost unbearably hard not to put all of them down on these pages. One of the early ones, who seemed to have a predilection for misadventure, was Mary Harry. Her history even before she came to us from Nova Scotia, where she traveled on dogsleds, was lively enough. She had served on a British hospital ship during the First World War. Just after the ship had landed some patients, a Zeppelin dropped its bombs on the huts. This killed many of the patients and some of the doctors and nurses. Our Harry had five pieces of shrapnel taken out of her side. After she came to the Frontier Nursing Service she had two emergency operations due to bits of the intestines getting caught in old adhesions. As if all of that wasn't enough, her horse ran away with her and she was thrown over his neck and fractured her skull. The last straw was when a copperhead snake reached through a chink in the log barn, against which she was leaning to loosen her horse's girth, and bit her on the shoulder.

The first of our nurses to die in action was Nancy O'Driscoll. She was not with us long because she did not live long, but none who ever came to us made so deep an impress on our people in so short a time. It is hard to convey to those who did not know her the gaiety of that charming personality. One evening, when Mac was playing Harry Lauder's songs on the gramophone, she announced that she would have

299

only Scotch tunes played in Heaven. Said Nancy, "But you'll play the Irish airs for me, Mac." One Tuesday morning Nancy rode across the river to a mother who needed her care. She became ill, with an acute pain, on her district but did not return until her work was done. When she got back to Hyden Hospital her appendix was ruptured. This was before the days of penicillin, but everything else that could be done was done for her. When she died, on the fifth day after her operation, her casket was carried down the winding road from Hyden Hospital by eighteen of the men who honored her. Raven, her black mare, followed the casket with stirrups reversed. It was said of Nancy that she had left "the memory of loving deeds." Wherever Nancy went, happiness, trust and hope sprang up around her in the saddest lives.

It was seventeen years before another nurse died on duty. Florence Samson (Sammy) carried the general nursing on the Hyden district for nearly seven years and with it the respect and affection of her patients. When in the course of time the riding and jeep driving, the exposure to weather, proved bad for her arthritis, Bucket (now First Assistant Director) transferred her to the hospital. On days when the wards were not busy, Sammy could be found sitting in a wooden rocking chair with one of the fretful children in her arms. One Tuesday morning she died suddenly, without struggle and without pain. Again there was an outpouring of friendship and farewell from the community, and members of the Hyden High School ball team were Sammy's pallbearers.

V

It was during the years of what has rightly been called the depression that my young associates in the Frontier Nursing Service met a financial crisis as gallantly as they meet "nature with a small 'n.'" Up until then we had been able to pay salaries at what was considered a high level twenty-odd years ago, and income taxes then were low. Our staff were able to set aside enough money to take the long vacations they needed during the six weeks, annually, that we have always allowed for vacations. They were able to set aside money for their old age. But when hard times came "a-knocking at the door" the Frontier Nursing Service shared in the common disaster. Nearly all our subscribers stood by us but most of them had to reduce their subscriptions drastically. In one case that I recall, a trustee who had been able to give a thousand dollars a year could only give twenty-five. Fortunately, our people had recovered from the drought so that we no longer needed to meet costs of things like milk and shoes on a vast scale. The Alpha Omicron Pi National Sorority, through its Social Service Secretary, continued its financial assistance. This enabled us to handle cases of acute distress, so that we were not haunted by people poorer than we were for whom there was no relief. But we could not carry on as we had done.

It was during the depression that we cut our field of work, closing out our fine affiliation with Beverly and reducing the staff to one nurse at each of the six outpost centers where there had been two. This meant lopping off territory and patients carried from these centers. This was heartbreaking. In the course of time, and in the following order, we put a second nurse back at Possum Bend, Brutus, and Beechfork. But Red Bird, Flat Creek and Bowlingtown each have only one nurse even now and, in consequence, a heavy fringe territory to handle as best they can. We cut the administrative end of our work to the bone, placing a mighty load of work on the few who remained. As for Hyden Hospital, so many hospital nurses were unemployed that we could take care of our sick patients by engaging nurses, in rotation, for little more than their maintenance, and letting them go when they got employment outside. More than once we had the help of a nurse who came as a volunteer, just because she knew we were up against it and she had the means, not only to give her service, but to pay her own travel expenses. One volunteer nurse of this period, Betty Washburn, came all the way from Minneapolis to help us, has been a supporter of our work since then, and is one of its trustees.

As I have said elsewhere, we closed our outside offices after the bank failures, because of which our *Belgenland* cruise made no money. We were heavily indebted to several of the wholesale firms with which we dealt, to some of our trustees, to banks, and to our staff. As to the wholesale firms, some of them let their bills ride for more than a year while they continued to give us credit. After we got back to a monthly payment basis of our accounts, our loyalty to these old firms could never be shaken. As to the trustees, they gave the money they had lent. As to bank loans, these we repaid, but some of them we had to renew. We still carry one bank loan as a sort of scar from our depression wounds. As to the staff, theirs is a tale of heroism.

When our salaries had fallen badly in arrears and we were cutting down everything we could short of folding altogether, with some prospect even of that, we told our nurses and secretaries that if they remained with us it would have to be on the basis of two-thirds of their salaries with no assurance that they would receive even that. However, our Executive Committee assumed legal responsibility for the payment of salaries on a two-thirds basis, and this was eventually done. Our National Chairman, Mrs. Ballard, wanted each member of the staff to be financially free to accept or reject these terms. She said she would give all salary in arrears, and a month's salary in advance, to any who rejected them. This she did at a cost to her of ten thousand dollars. Those who stayed on with the Frontier Nursing Service elected to share its chances of success or failure at a time when failure seemed nearer than success. We were so young a philanthropy then that we had the barest start on an endowment, and no reserves. So many more of our staff chose to remain with us than chose to leave that we had to send some away who wanted to see the thing through. There lie, imbedded in the minutes of the Executive Committee, excerpts from some of the letters I received from my young associates at that time, of which this is one:

I could no more dream of giving up the Frontier Nursing Service than I could expect to fly by flapping my arms. As I wrote you when I asked to come down here two years ago, I feel that it is the most real bit of work in the country and we can do the greatest good by our services here in the mountains.

This letter, given in full, was written by the young secretary who came to Wendover every day—on horseback or by boat—from across the river:

My desire to remain with the Frontier Nursing Service is twofold: My interest in the Service as an organization, and the welfare of the mountain people.

Watching the growth of the Frontier Nursing Service has not been without interest from the dawn of a lovely July morning, which brought you to us on Teddy Bear, to the present time.

I remember too well the difficulties and tragedy we faced without proper medical attention before you came to the mountains.

My willingness to stay with the Service through the crisis is unbounded. Please let me thank you for giving me this opportunity to try to express my appreciation to you, the Executive Committee and the Service, for the marvelous work that has been done for the people here, which are, truthfully speaking, my own.

Chapter 31

I

IT would have been impossible to launch the Frontier Nursing Service, with its use for the first time in America of the nurse as a midwife, without the co-operation of many leaders in nursing fields. That there would be some opposition in this country to the idea of midwifery for nurses was to be expected. There are always people to look askance upon any development with which they are not familiar and which they do not understand. What surprised me was not that a few should disapprove of us, but that so many could, by a reach of the imagination, appreciate what we had set out to do. The help these leaders of nursing gave the Frontier Nursing Service took a practical turn whenever there was a practical outlet for their sympathetic interest. A quarter century ago, Florence Johnson and Mary Magoun Brown of the New York Chapter of the American Red Cross Nursing Service started the custom of meeting our English and Scots nurses on their ships at the docks. Since they were in uniform, and well known, their presence sped the routines of landing as much as their welcoming smiles gladdened the day for new arrivals on a strange shore.

Nurses will understand how much the counsel of the seasoned old war horses in our profession meant to me not only in the blending of district work with midwifery but in difficult problems of administration. Even before we had our fine committee at Providence I made a special trip there for a conference with Miss Mary Gardner. I sought out Miss Annie Goodrich, to tap her well-stored mind, and Miss Lillian D. Wald down at Henry Street. Miss Mary Roberts, distinguished editor of the *American Journal of Nursing* until her retirement in 1949, not only stood foursquare behind the Frontier Nursing Service as a friend but gave the endorsement of the *Journal* to our venture, in her editorials as well as in the stories the *Journal* accepted about our work. In other nursing leaders, who had helped me to prepare for my nursing work long before, the Frontier Nursing Service had staunch allies.

Several leading nurses have come to observe our work at first hand and none has left us without saying or doing something useful. In 1928, when Miss Winifred Rand, outstanding specialist in the care of young children, came to the mountains to advise us in that supremely important aspect of our work, and we were going over our general Medical Routine together, she said to me, "Why don't you have all of this bound into a book?" Up to that time our Medical Routine was loose-leaf, poorly assorted, with no index. An early visit from Miss Hazel Corbin, Director of the Maternity Center Association in New York, brought her sympathetic understanding to bear upon our maternity problems. Following this visit the Maternity Center Association organized the Association for the Promotion and Standardization of Midwifery, Inc., to which Dr. Ralph W. Lobenstine gave his obstetrical prestige and the warmth of his generous heart. When I was asked to go on the board of this Association, I looked forward to years of further co-operation with Dr. Lobenstine. His untimely death in 1931 set the clock back in the development of the American nurse as a midwife. Despite his loss, the Maternity Center Association carried through such of the plans he had fostered as were possible without him and opened, in 1932, under the name of the Lobenstine Clinic, the first postgraduate school for midwifery on the American Continent. Since I like to be of use to any board on which I serve, it was a joy to me that the Frontier Nursing Service could provide, in Rose Mc-Naught, the first supervisor for this school. She was one of our early American nurses, the quality of whose work was so fine that we had sent her on a scholarship to London for her midwifery training. One of the first American nurses to be taught midwifery at the Lobenstine Clinic was Della Int-Hout (our Inty). She has spent the greater part of her nursing life since then in the Frontier Nursing Service, leaving friendships and flowers (for she is a born gardener) on every district she has served.

No more inspiring nurse ever came to see us than the late Major Julia C. Stimson (later Colonel), Head of the Army Nurse Corps. After a horseback tour of our outpost nursing centers she wrote an article for the subscribers to our *Bulletin*, from which I give the following paragraph:

If out in the world one met a nurse who could deliver babies, superintend primitive carpenter work and well-digging, dose and care for horses, advise about farming, teach untrained girls cooking, live cheerfully by candlelight and with enamel basin and pitcher bathing facilities, keep well and full of humor and common sense, one would think the combination of all these qualities was worthy of comment. And down there in that Nursing Service seventeen or eighteen nurses were doing all these things—and each one thought her particular center and her particular work and her particular patients were the very best.

A special way in which leading nurses on both sides of the Atlantic have helped us lies in the interest they pass on to younger nurses to come and serve with us. Except during and immediately after the war we have never run short of nurse applicants for our work. The wish that lies in the heart of every true nurse to give her service to those who need it most, coupled with the desire in many young women for adventure and hardship, brings nurses of a fine caliber to us when, in the world beyond the mountains, they could get double and treble the salaries we are able to pay. Thus, all of our staff are volunteers in part through the measure of their financial sacrifice. My own longing for adventure and hardship when I was young, my own choice of nursing as the field in which I felt I could give the most service, enable me to understand the motives that lead most of my young associates to the Frontier Nursing Service for at least two or three years of their buoyant lives. It will be sad if the time ever comes when such aspirations of the ardent young heart find no answering echo from the leaders of nursing.

II

The American Association of Nurse-Midwives was started as a Kentucky association in October of 1928. The sixteen charter members, all on the staff of the Frontier Nursing Service, were the only nurse-midwives in the United States then. A year later, with the legal advice of my cousin, George Hunt of Lexington, we incorporated under the laws of Kentucky and adopted a seal. This shows the Kentucky cardinal on the bough of a small fruit tree with his mate below him on her nest and the legend, "LIFE IS THE GIFT OF GOD." In our articles of incorporation we stated that our object was "to foster, encourage and, in the qualifications for its own membership, to maintain a high standard of midwifery with special reference to rugged, difficult and economically poor areas."

Our sixteen charter members were working in a rugged, difficult and economically poor area so we knew what it was all about. We have today a membership of 164 scattered from the Belgian Congo to Siam. Such of us as are in the United States, and can do so, get together for an annual meeting in the fall as the guests of the Frontier Nursing Service at Wendover, where a distinguished obstetrician comes to give us an address on the use and the value of the nurse, as a midwife, in obstetrics. Helen E. Browne (Brownie) has held the post of Secretary of the American Association of Nurse-Midwives for years.

"Rugged, difficult and economically poor areas"—in the "regions roadless and mountainous," of which Sir Leslie MacKenzie wrote so long ago. What does it mean to be a nurse-midwife in such country as this?

For May Green, on Red Bird River, it meant an anxious mind when she recognized a shoulder presentation of the baby soon after she reached the cabin where the mother lay in labor. She sent the husband on her horse back to the Clara Ford Nursing Center with a note to be telephoned to Dr. Kooser at Hyden Hospital. It would be two hours before he and Dorothy Buck, Midwifery Supervisor then, could reach the cabin, hours where the minutes seemed like years to Green, whose responsibility might force her to act before they could come. At last she heard hoofbeats, the welcome hoofbeats of the doctor's horse. As soon as Dr. Kooser entered the cabin he started to scrub up while Bucket and Green prepared for him. There came the moment when all stood ready: Bucket by the patient's head with a mask and a can of ether, two neighbors to support the patient's legs, Dr. Kooser—scrubbed, capped, gowned—with Green as his assistant holding a flashlight. Then the open fire was extinguished, the chimneyless lamp put out, the flashlight snapped on; a minute more and the patient was sleeping. The baby was pushed up, turned and brought out and the delivery was completed; all by the light of one small flashlight.

The need for putting out the open fire and the lamps in a cabin home before using such an inflammable thing as ether will be plain to all who read these pages, but it will take a stretch of the imagination to grasp how quickly a physician must work to safeguard the general health of his patient if the night is cold. Mercifully, the fire can quickly be rebuilt again when the baby is born and there are always willing hands to do it. One story more, chosen from among many, will show the differences between a frontier and a city technique.

When Nora Kelly was the nurse in charge of the Caroline Butler Atwood Memorial Center at Flat Creek she was called out on what she expected to be a routine midwifery case. She had made her rounds for the day, had dismissed a class of twenty-seven girls she was teaching to knit, and was enjoying a cup of tea and reading her mail when the call came. The patient, who was expecting her first baby, had received good prenatal care. Kelly anticipated rather a long labor but one with the usual normal outcome.

In the Frontier Nursing Service, once a woman is in labor we never leave her, not even for a moment. After Kelly had been some twenty hours with this patient, Louise Mowbray arrived from the next nearest nursing center, sent by the midwifery supervisor to relieve Kelly or to help her, as seemed indicated. About seven o'clock the second evening, Kelly left the patient with her colleague and went back to the Flat Creek Center to telephone a report on the case to Dr. Kooser. He said he would start at once on the eighteen-mile horseback ride that lay between them. It was after midnight before the two nurse-midwives heard Traveller's hoofs in the distance. Again everything was set up. After the lamp had been extinguished and the fire put out, Dr. Kooser delivered a nine-pound girl, with forceps, by the light of a two-cell flashlight. Nora Kelly had delivered more than two hundred maternity cases with the Frontier Nursing Service when this event took place. This was but the second case that called for forceps.

The complication that we dread the most in our section is hemorrhage. (A hemorrhage is the loss of a pint or more of blood.) We have had hundreds of postpartum hemorrhages in somewhat less than nine thousand maternity cases. Of these we have lost three mothers. The nurse who is a midwife is trained to act quickly in a postpartum hemorrhage. If the hemorrhage comes before the delivery of the placenta (afterbirth), the nurse-midwife has to slip on a fresh sterile glove and go after it. This is called a manual removal. Until the delivery of the placenta, the third stage of labor is not complete. If, or when, it has been delivered, her hypodermics are at hand to restore the patient. More than once these have not been enough, but when that happens the nurse-midwife knows what she must do.

I remember a patient in the neighborhood of Possum Bend who, the third stage of labor completed, had suddenly a gush of blood. Almost at once her face became a terrifying white, her skin cold and clammy. She lost an estimated three or more pints of blood. After rubbing up the uterus to stimulate contractions, and driving in the hypodermics, without a moment's hesitation, Gwladys Doubleday, the nurse-midwife, slipped on a clean rubber glove and so compressed the bleeding points of the uterus between her hands that no further blood could escape. (This procedure is called a bimanual compression of the uterus.) She then dictated a note to a member of the family who could write. This was taken to the nursing center and telephoned through to Dr. Kooser at Hyden Hospital by May Green, the other nurse-midwife at Possum Bend at that time. Green hastened to the bedside of the patient. Doubleday did not dare to relax her hold on the uterus so it was left to Green, with the help of a neighbor woman, to warm blankets and wrap up the exhausted mother, surrounding her with irons heated in the open fire and fruit jars full of hot water, to bandage the arms and legs (to keep the remaining blood near more vital organs), and to give rectal salines to replace some of the lost fluid. At last, after nearly three hours from the time of the hemorrhage, the nurse-midwives heard Traveller's hoofbeats outside, bringing Dr. Kooser to take over. In such cases the physician always brings his supplies, and a setup for giving fluid intravenously in the cabin. Some four days after all this had happened I rode by this patient's cabin, dismounted and went in to see her. She was nursing her baby.

It will be seen from these reports how vital a part the physician plays in the life of a nurse-midwife in a remotely rural area. Some of the graduates of the Frontier Nursing Service School of Midwifery have been sent by their mission boards to jungles in South America and Africa with no physician nearer than two or three days of travel time. From our own early experience we know that these women will save many lives which the nurse who is not a midwife would lose, but our hearts ache when we think of the anguish of these remote nurse-midwives when they know, as no nurse without their training could know, exactly what is wrong and exactly when they should have a doctor—and then cannot get one.

III

Not only does a frontier nurse-midwife sometimes have to hold the fort until the Medical Director can reach her, but she often has to take final responsibility in the knowledge that he cannot reach her in time. This has been true with us in the case of hundreds of postpartum hemorrhages. In the late thirties, Bucket went with the Wendover nurse to attend a midwifery case about which they were both anxious. This patient began to hemorrhage severely after her baby was born but before the placenta was delivered. Quick as a flash Bucket slipped on a fresh glove and went up into the uterus after the placenta. She acted so quickly, and the patient responded afterward to restoratives so well, that a mother, who would have died before the doctor could reach her, made an uneventful recovery.

Another type of case where the nurse-midwife had to intervene occurred also in the thirties, in the Bull Creek district with Helen Browne (Brownie) in charge. Dr. Kooser had seen this mother and he and Brownie both knew that she was expecting twins, and that the first twin lay in a normal position to be born without difficulty. It was otherwise with the second twin which presented a prolapsed arm. With no telephone connection, with hours of delay before the messenger on Brownie's horse could reach the doctor, and the doctor could come, with the mother's pains such that a ruptured uterus was not unlikely, Brownie had to go in after the second twin and turn it (what is called an internal version), bring it down and out. The mother and both babies are alive to this day. Brownie remembers this case as one with the added horror of flies. It was summertime; the patient lived in a small open cabin with no screens. Brownie found it hard, in slipping on a clean glove, to keep off the flies.

For the best results in frontier work there must be outpost centers to which patients may be moved when they cannot be carried as far as a hospital and, finally, the rural hospital to which cases may be relayed from all over a vast area. Of the use of outpost nursing centers as temporary hospitals for patients who cannot be moved farther, I could give many examples but I shall choose only those of the winter of 1936. This was one of those terrible mountain winters when the trails were blocked with snow and ice. Even our hardy horses had trouble pushing through some of the drifts. One of the maternity patients in the Beech Fork neighborhood had heart complications diagnosed as "mitral insufficiency, hypertrophy and dilatation, broken compensation with fibrillation, partial heart block." Friendly neighbors, superintended by Dr. Kooser, carried her through a blizzard to the Jessie Preston Draper Nursing Center. We sent up an extra nurse under escort to special this patient because the Beech Fork nurses were frightfully busy with five more babies due to come. Our couriers shared as always in the hard riding. Jean Hollins, on Lassie, covered the sixteen icy miles from Hyden to the Center, carrying digitalis, brandy, supplies for glucose infusions.

While all of this was going on at Beech Fork, Dr. Kooser got word from one of our Brutus nurses that a young mother under her care had developed a severe respiratory infection. So, Dr. Kooser rode the forty-five miles from Beech Fork to Brutus, over several rough mountains, and went with the nurse to her patient's home. He found the patient had lobar pneumonia. Here, as at Beech Fork, neighbors carried the mother, and her three-day-old baby, by stretcher through the driving snow to the Belle Barrett Hughitt Nursing Center. Since five more babies were expected in that area too, an extra nurse rode over the mountains to special the pneumonia. Night had fallen by the time she got there, but a man with a lantern had gone to meet her on the trail and escort her the last few miles.

A few days later, another young mother in the Brutus area went into convulsions after the birth of the baby, without any warning symptoms before labor or during labor. She had twenty-one convulsions and during that time she was stretchered, in the very heart of the blizzard, along Bullskin Creek to the Center. In a period of less than a week Dr. Kooser, going back and forth between the Beech Fork and Brutus Nursing Centers, traveled nearly 150 miles on horseback over trails so icy that often he and Traveller had to slide down them. The Midwifery Supervisor, Bucket, rode with him to the patient with convulsions. They spent the day in the saddle in the storm, that night and a second day and night working over the patient, and the following day again in the saddle in the storm. The woman lived, but her baby was dead. In the next room to hers in the Belle Barrett Hughitt Nursing Center at Brutus, the woman with pneumonia died, leaving a week-old baby. It is terrible to fight for lives against such appalling odds as "nature with a small 'n'" can stack against you in a frontier country, and then to lose one of those lives.

Although our medical directors have done complicated obstetrical procedures in mountain cabins and at outpost centers, we naturally prefer to move our abnormal cases to Hyden Hospital when their condition and the weather permit. Many are the expectant mothers who have ridden into the Hospital on horseback, not only through the thirties but the forties as well. Two recent cases have come, the one from Elkhorn Creek and the other from the headwaters of Hell-for-Certain, over the range of mountains that leads to Thousandsticks. One had her baby, a fine boy, within eight hours after her arrival. The other got off her mule, sat down on a bench in the waiting room and announced calmly to the clinic nurse that she thought she was already in labor. She was! While Betty Lester was Midwifery Supervisor she brought a patient to Hyden Hospital from Leatherwood Creek over three mountain ranges in three counties, a distance of eighteen horseback miles. Six hours later, Herman and Hannah, lusty twins, arrived safe and sound.

One bitterly cold afternoon late in a February, Peggy Tinline was called to a case on Sally Sizemore's Branch. She found the patient bleeding from an obstetrical complication known as a central placenta previa. It was about six o'clock in the evening before Dr. Kooser, on horseback, could get there. He prepared the patient for removal to Hyden Hospital, took a blood specimen from her, and then rode on ahead to get everything ready for a Caesarian section. Meanwhile the woman's husband had gone up and down the branch to get stretcher bearers. They drifted into the cabin by ones and twos, shaking the snow off their caps and shoulders as they entered. When sixteen men had turned up, the patient, warmly wrapped, was put on a stretcher made from two husky saplings with several cross slats. Four men carried the stretcher on their shoulders while others carried lanterns, and led horses and mules, between taking turns with the stretcher. It was a terrible trail, down Sally Sizemore's Branch, up Bull Creek, up Jones's Branch, then over a ghastly mountain to Asher's Branch and over Thousandsticks Mountain to Hyden Hospital and salvation. Travel was at the rate of about a mile an hour. In the pitch dark and the bitter cold the stretcher bearers struggled on, through the icy creeks—the water reaching often above their knees—and over the mountain ridges. The overalls on their legs froze and rattled as they walked. Peggy walked beside her patient.

After Dr. Kooser had telephoned Dr. Collins at Hazard that we needed him, and had typed the specimen of the patient's blood, he telephoned Dr. D. D. Turner, Health Officer in Leslie County then, to ask if he would come to the Hospital and match the patient's blood specimen. Our hospital staff volunteered the blood. Then Dr. Kooser left Mac to prepare for the operation, and rode off to meet the procession. He saw their lights (lanterns and pine flares) even before he heard the men's voices and the crunch of their feet. As soon as the stretcher bearers with their precious freight reached Hyden Hospital, Dr. Collins did a Caesarian section. Little five-pound-fourteen-ounce Jane and her mother were none the worse for their dreadful night.

The obstetrical complication that we in the Frontier Nursing Service consider the most worrisome is a miscarriage, whether an early or a late one. Even though these patients sometimes make a normal recovery in their homes, they are always in immediate need of medical care. Whenever possible we get them to Hyden Hospital, or at least to the nearest outpost nursing center. The question of intravenous fluids to be given them must be handled as best one can. Dr. Kooser recalls how he improvised supplies for one such patient. The Ford Motor Company owned a small distilling apparatus at their place on Red Bird River, only a mile from the Clara Ford Center to which the patient had been stretchered. They sent Dr. Kooser several quarts of distilled water. This was thrice boiled on the kitchen stove and thrice filtered. With the salt tablets already at the Center, a new enamel can, and new rubber tubing, Dr. Kooser had all he needed to make his own normal saline solution for the intravenous.

Maternity patients with badly damaged hearts trouble us because childbirth is for them a terrible risk. Although our Medical Director gives planned parenthood instruction to such of our healthy women as want it and can make use of it, we do not consider this technique safe enough to protect women with badly damaged hearts. We advise sterilization for such women. Rarely have we failed to get their consent, and that of their husbands, for this operation. My cousin, Dr. Scott Breckinridge, at his annual surgical clinics, and Dr. Francis Massie, who has given us the clinics since Scott's death, have safeguarded in this manner a number of women who would probably have died as the result of childbirth.

IV

From the time that our work began until the close of our fiscal year in 1951, we had delivered 8,596 registered midwifery patients. Of these, 6,533 were delivered in their homes—primitive homes most of them. Our records seem to show that the technique we developed in the Frontier Nursing Service is as safe as a city technique even when put through such severe testing as I have outlined in this chapter. We had ten maternal deaths of which two were heart cases. Although Dr. Louis I. Dublin of the Metropolitan Life Insurance Company did not assign these deaths to puerperal causes, in his tabulations of our maternity cases, we have always counted them among our maternal deaths because both women died within a month after delivery. Two deaths from pneumonia, with pleural effusions, were classified by Dr. Dublin as puerperal deaths under "joint cause procedure," because both patients had colds before they went into labor. These patients could probably be saved today with the new antibiotic drugs. The following figures will give our maternal death rate with, and without, the heart cases:

Gross Maternal Death Rate—1.2 per thousand

Puerperal Death Rate—.93 per thousand

Over the years, one is struck by how many women one can carry through the most desperate situations without losing any, and saddened by the fact that one does lose others whose conditions are hardly more desperate. We lost two women in our first thousand deliveries but none in the second thousand. In our sixth and seventh thousand deliveries we lost no women—not one among two thousand patients— but in our eighth thousand deliveries we lost four. Back in 1932 when the national maternal death rate was still deplorably high, and Dr. Dublin sent us his tabulation on our first thousand maternity cases, he wrote us as follows:

The study shows conclusively what has in fact been demonstrated before, that the type of service rendered by the Frontier Nurses safeguards the life of mother and babe. If such service were available to the women of the country generally, there would be a saving of 10,000 mothers' lives a year in the United States, there would be 30,000 less stillbirths and 30,000 more children alive at the end of the first month of life.

The study demonstrates that the first need today is to train a large body of nurse-midwives, competent to carry out the routines which have been established both in the Frontier Nursing Service and in other places where good obstetrical care is available.

The Metropolitan Life Insurance Company was so generous as to tabulate each one of our first four thousand maternity cases, as each series was completed, and their detailed findings are of immense scientific value. Early in the Second World War, Dr. Dublin wrote me that the Metropolitan was losing so many statisticians that they couldn't continue these tabulations for us until times were normal again. That many facts on each later series of thousands are available is due to the competence of our statisticians. We hope someday to have the later series as carefully tabulated as the first four thousands. From the time that the Carnegie Corporation first set up our statistical system, with Marion Ross as statistician, until the time of this book, we have kept the most careful records of our midwifery patients and their babies from the prenatal date of registration until one month after delivery. Then the mothers cease to be midwifery patients and go back to their family folders as general patients; the infants cease to be neonatals and become babies.

In 1928, at the request of Dr. George W. Kosmak, brilliant editor of the *American Journal of Obstetrics and Gynecology*, I wrote an article for the *Journal* about our first 130 deliveries, which I concluded in the following words—so true then:

We know we have only just begun in our attack on a problem where the totals are staggering. Our merit is to have made that beginning. In Kentucky we have a race horse named Fair Play. In those who differ with our methods we invoke that spirit. . . . The mothers we are helping . . . bore their babies on lonely gaps and creeks unattended but by neighbors. Small wonder we have lost more women in childbirth in America than men in war.

Chapter 32

I

INSOFAR as we can learn, the Frontier Nursing Service has accumulated the only considerable body of obstetrical facts available in the United States on our native rural population. We will have nine thousand complete case studies at about the time this book is published. These are not only of scientific value, but to those Americans who are descended from the old British stock they depict the obstetrical history of their own great-great-grandmothers. The most significant thing to me in these case studies is that more than ninety-nine per cent of our mothers have borne their babies without the help of forceps. The preceding chapter will have shown that such obstetrical complications as hemorrhages, toxemias, malpresentations, and the rest, occur in our native population as they do everywhere else, but on less than one per cent of these patients have forceps been applied. The figure varies in the different series so that it takes thousands to get an average that is reliable. In our third series of one thousand deliveries, there was only one case of low forceps; in our seventh-thousand series. there were only two cases. In our fourth-thousand series, on the other hand, there were thirteen cases of low forceps, and six in our eighth series. In the 8,596 maternity cases delivered by the Frontier Nursing Service at the close of its fiscal year, April 30, 1951, there had been fifty forceps cases, or six-tenths of one per cent. The number of women delivered by Caesarian section was even smaller—forty in all. Of these only nineteen had Caesarian sections because of a contracted pelvis.

The question that will arise in every thoughtful mind is why there should be this discrepancy between the Kentucky mountain woman and her city sister, whose babies are so often taken from her. Doubtless there is too much deliberate obstetrical interference in city hospitals but not so much, I am convinced, as many people think. In the Outer Hebrides I found that a physician was as rarely needed by the nurse-midwives for a forceps delivery as he is by us. I learned that in the city of Glasgow, on the other hand, forceps deliveries ran much higher although normal childbirth was encouraged and nurse-midwives were widely used. What do the Hebrides and the Kentucky mountains have in common to enable the women in both areas to deliver their babies themselves? Three reasons may be inferred from known facts. At the time that I made my study of the Hebrides, and started our work in the Kentucky mountains, I found not a single woman of child-bearing age in either area who had not been a breast-fed baby, because the bottle-fed babies had died. A flattened pelvis, due to rickets, and giving trouble in childbirth, was a rare phenomenon among mothers who had been breast-fed. A diet of herring in the Hebrides, days of sunshine in the Kentucky mountains, had put plenty of Vitamin D in the breast milk, while phosphorus and lime would come from the milk and eggs available to some extent in both regions. Thus one reason for natural childbirth was the almost total absence of the flattened pelvis so often found in cities, especially in the days before bottle babies were scientifically fed and their mothers taught by visiting nurses to prepare formulas.

A second thing that the Hebridean and Kentucky mountain women had in common was a complete lack of ancestral obstetrical care—a lack going back to the dawn of time. City women of recent generations, in Europe and America—lots of them—had had the help of obstetricians when they could not deliver their babies themselves. But in remotely rural areas like those of the Outer Hebrides and the Kentucky mountains there had been no such help for women. By a severe process of natural selection, their descendants inherited a pelvis through which a baby could pass unaided. A woman with a contracted or a misshapen pelvis did not transmit this type of pelvis to a daughter because she had died with her first baby.

The third reason, and I think the most significant, why the Kentucky and Hebridean mothers can deliver their babies themselves is because both belong in a homogeneous population. In such a population the baby's head is racially designed to go through the mother's pelvis. In a port city like Glasgow, as in many modern American cities, so many marriages have taken place between people of so many different racial stocks that obstetricians are called upon to pull a Mediterranean head through a Nordic pelvis. Such a head was not designed to go through such a pelvis. Why should we expect a heterogeneous population to bear children with the ease of a homogeneous one?

II

No questions interest me more profoundly than those concerning populations, about which endless theories are spun and about which there are available so few facts. The argument of Malthus, that without war and disease we should multiply beyond our capacity to feed ourselves, is used even today, and as often refuted, without throwing fresh light on the realities of population trends. It is in the study of Nature, and the history of human nature, or so it seems to me, that one finds the key to the study of populations. Many years ago I saw a cartoon in which a Mr. Germ was sitting on a sofa courting Miss Microbe. Little microbes were playing on the floor. "Whose children are those?" he asked, and she replied, "My sister's. She was married this morning." In primordial creatures like fishes, we find millions of young with almost no infancy. In the higher orders of mammals, there are few offspring and the infancy of the young extends to a year or more. In the coming of man on this planet, we got a prolongation of childhood but, until recent times, it terminated with marriage in adolescence not only among the poor but in families of gentle and even of royal birth. Isabelle of Angoulême was married at fifteen to King John of England. Poor darling, what a time she had! At thirteen, in Russia, I read Miss Strickland's *Life* of her and was shocked. Our own great-great-grandmothers were usually married in their teens. Nowadays almost all parents who can compass it, and whose children have normal or superior minds, send their girls as well as their boys through the high schools and often through the colleges. With this prolongation of childhood, this deferment of marriage through the fertile age of adolescence, we get smaller families. That this should result is consistent with what we can observe of Nature's laws, which embrace man as well as the lower orders of life. But in man we find a range beyond the reach of the lower orders. Among primitive peoples there seem to be few who can transmute the stuff on Nature's loom from physical to mental fertility, and, in civilized communities, none of those with low intelligence quotients could go through college no matter how far their childhood was prolonged. These mental children seem, to a district nurse-midwife like me, to have an amazing physical fertility for which they cannot be taught methods of control, and of not one of them could it be said, as Macaulay wrote of Hastings, "a mind as fertile as his."

In 1931, when I first began seriously to think in terms of populations, I wrote an article on the subject which I sent to *Harper's Magazine*. It came out in July of that year. Unfortunately, the editors substituted a controversial title for mine and this led to angry letters, mostly from people who had not read the article itself. I was gladdened, however, by one letter from an English scientist who said that he thought I was on the right track. I still think, as I wrote twenty years ago, that there is a unity in Nature and that on the loom of creation is woven but one stuff. If it is used in the development of the mind, there is less of it for physical fertility. It seems plain to me that the reason why women in history have created so little in comparison with men is because most women until recent times have exhausted themselves in giving the creative forces of life to the race. So often where one finds a great man, one discovers that his mother had a mind as keen as his. She produced him and he produced the statecraft, the strategy, or the art which reached him through her creative sacrifice. If a normal girl in any walk of life marries in her teens, she marries at Nature's most productive age, and she will probably be fertile. If the same girl puts her adolescent fertility into studies, or some form of creative work, and marries in her twenties, she will be relatively infertile. We can all cite exceptions. An occasional woman does achieve creative work and a large family. She is endowed beyond the common run.

In my article of 1931 I suggested a feasible piece of research to determine how much the prolongation of childhood and the higher mental activities of women were responsible for the decrease in the birth rate of intelligent people. I suggested that a foundation endow, upon their marriage, one thousand or more college-bred young couples in their twenties—selecting only those who were using the mental skills they had acquired—with the stipulation that they agree not to limit their families for ten years; that the foundation sponsoring this research give financial support to the parents for each child born during the ten years, and scholarships to carry it through the schools and universities. In this way we could learn from facts, which is the only way we ever learn anything, whether my hypothesis is true or not. As a law, I would express it thus: The fertility of the race is in inverse ratio to its intelligence, plus the prolongation of the period of education past the adolescent age. This conforms to what we may observe in Nature from microbes to man, but Nature, including human nature and its history, cannot be comprehended in a law so simply stated. We know that those who live close to her are more fertile than city dwellers, that physical causes of infertility, some of them remedial, exist in both men and women, that excessive luxury may inhibit breeding even in animals—variations and exceptions world without end.

Even the spiritual growth of man is stuff woven on Nature's creative loom, when he comes into conscious relationship with his Creator. We are accustomed to the sneers of those spiritual defectives who talk about the suppressed sex life of a spiritual genius. Would it be possible for any other love to live in the consuming religious fires of a Saint Paul, a Lady Julian, a Saint Francis? The family begotten of such ardor is as wide as the human race. The great lovers of God, and of their kind, in history were often single men and women.

As man develops mental powers, and grows in spiritual perception, he looks forward to a time when he can raise the economic level of the world, when epidemics will no longer decimate populations. He dreams of the day when arbitration is substituted for war. Need he lose to famine then the freedom he will have won from pestilence and battle? Not according to my thinking. When the economic level of a population rises, its fecundity decreases. Why? I think this is because more girls as well as boys defer marriage, and those who have the mental capacity to do so carry their education beyond the adolescent age. The mental and spiritual stuff, which must gain ascendancy in man for his dreams to come true, will have automatically set limits to his reproduction. It is not because men can grow more food to the acre than once they could that we shall avoid famine, but because vaster numbers of men and women will have minds and hearts so enlarged that there needs must be fewer people.

III

So much nonsense has been written about the size of mountain families, always on the basis of theories and usually with a sensational end in view, that the Frontier Nursing Service, with its liking for facts, has made available in its *Quarterly Bulletin* family statistics covering a period of twenty years. We have always carried our patients on a family basis and for this reason our average population per family is factual to the fraction of a point. Since our work covers a mountain area of some seven hundred square miles, and since nearly ten thousand people in this area are on our records, our figures are indicative of the size of mountain families. It is generally known that rural families are larger than city families. The Bureau of the Census in Washington has estimated the average number of related persons in urban households in 1930 as 3.62 persons and in rural-farm households as 4.45. The same unrounded estimates for 1940 are given as 3.32 related persons in urban households, and 4.14 related persons in rural-farm households. The number of related persons includes the head of the household and all other persons in the household related to him by blood, marriage, or adoption.

Mr. Howard G. Brunsman, Chief of the Population and Housing Division of the Bureau of the Census, wrote me that a valid comparison could be made between the Bureau's rural-farm household figures and the average number of related persons in Frontier Nursing Service households. At the close of our fiscal year in 1930 we had cared for 1,345 families with a population of 6,972, which represented an average population per family of 5.18—including "the head of the household and all other persons in it related to him by blood, marriage, or adoption." In 1940 our comparable figures were 1,712 families with a population of 8,517 people and an average population per family of 4.97. Our figures for 1950 were 2,155 families with a population of 9,753 and an average population per family of 4.53. Comparable national figures for 1950 have not been released by the Bureau of the Census as this is written.

Two things may be noted from these facts. First, the average mountain population per family in the area we cover has, over a period of years, been only a fraction of one point above the comparable national average. Figures for other rural areas must also have been a fraction of a point above, as well as below, the national average—or there could not be an average. Second, there has been what Mr. Brunsman calls a substantial decline in the average population in the families we carry. This is what I would have expected to happen with a rise in the economic level of our people, which has enabled them to send more girls as well as boys through high school and college, and thus to defer many marriages beyond the fertile age of adolescence.

In one of his seventeenth-century sermons, John Donne spoke of "that seminal power which we call Nature." We in the Frontier Nursing Service find that our research seems to germinate in the work we do. It was because Mary B. Willeford (Texas) lived and worked among people whose income and health she knew that she could write the thesis for her Ph.D., *Income and Health in Remote Rural Areas.* Dr. Kooser's studies on pellagra, which were so good that Dr. M. A. Blankenhorn of the University of Cincinnati collaborated with him on them, and which were published in the *Journal of the American Medical Association,* could not have been made without clinical studies of hundreds of people who co-operated with him because he was one of themselves and not a "brought-on" man. Pellagra, a dietary disease, came alive to us when a child of five, called Nora, was brought to us from beyond our territory with the sore tongue and mouth, the nervousness, the diarrhea, the rash, characteristic of pellagra. It took six months of food, care, and treatment at Hyden Hospital to restore Nora to as normal a condition of health as so stricken a child can reach. Only then could the real child, with its personal desires, come alive in what had been a blasted body. Placed with admirable foster parents on Camp Creek, Nora found that, like the young Queen Victoria, she wanted a bed to herself. With what she could save out of her allowance of ten cents a week, with Alpha Omicron Pi Social Service funds, and with the help of her foster parents, Nora got her bed.

The seminal power that causes research to germinate in our work is nowhere more evident than in a study by Dr. Kooser, in which Dorothy Buck participated, printed in the *American Journal of Obstetrics and Gynecology,* a study on the possible relationship of diet to the late toxemia of pregnancy. This study showed that there appeared to be, among the registered maternity patients cared for by the Frontier Nursing Service—all of whom had had prenatal care—a direct relationship between seasonal incidence of toxemia and the seasonal scarcity of food. Among country dwellers the food supply gets low in the late winter and spring. The stored potatoes, the dried beans, the pickled beets, the canned tomatoes, have given out by then. For reasons I have never been able to fathom, the cow is allowed to go dry at the same time. With this seasonal scarcity of food, which continues until the gardens come into production, Dr. Kooser found a seasonal rise in toxemia among our mothers.

Dr. Ella Woodyard, our Research Director, has nearly completed a study of the effect of thiamin on a child's intelligence and bodily vigor, when taken by the mother before it is born and during the nursing period—a study that was possible because expectant mothers registered with us every day. I have already written that our children, tested in their fourth year, have an average intelligence that runs several points above the norm. We will find it hard to cope with our babies if they become any more vigorous mentally and physically than many of them are now. Not so long ago a woman with an eighteen-month-old boy came to our out-patient clinic at Hyden Hospital and sat down to nurse him. The Medical Director said to her, "Don't you think it is time to wean your baby?" "Yes I know, Doc," she replied, "I know, but every time I try to, he throws rocks at me."

IV

We have been amazed, although perhaps we should not have been, whenever one of our scientific articles has caught the attention of the lay press. Dozens of small-town papers from places as far apart as Sumter, South Carolina, and Monroe, Michigan, reported on *Pellagra and the Public Health* while several metropolitan papers—the Cincinnati *Enquirer* in particular—discussed it in detail. I think that American newspapers do try to give their readers as full an account as possible of what goes on outside their city limits, and that some of them consider serious work and its results as reportable as murder. To the Frontier Nursing Service the American press has been uniformly kind. The space they have given us would, if thrown together, fill a book larger than this one and would include the personal touch of such people as the late John Finley of the *New York Times*, Mrs. Ogden Reid of the *Herald Tribune*, and others in the top ranks of the newspaper world. But where the press has helped us most has been in printing the names and often the pictures of such of their own local citizens as sponsor our meetings and our benefits. Publicity of this kind is way and beyond all other in its value to us because it ties our work in with the communities which lend it their support.

Although we are sometimes grieved by a sensational piece about our people and us, such a story is rarely written by a city or a society reporter. They take us on as just another assignment and, in talking with them, I find they often have more assignments in a day than anyone could possibly cover adequately. We meet on equal ground. When I am making a tour beyond the mountains I, too, have more assignments than I can carry without strain. Despite the added drudgery it must mean to these men and women to cover our meetings, I have met only with courtesy and consideration at their hands, and my gratitude to them is coupled with respect. Occasionally a bewildered reporter messes things up, as when one wrote that we had developed a cure for hookworm to be given hypodermically! Once in a while a misstatement will travel, uncorrected, all over the United States as did an item under the caption of "Modern Women" which said, "Carrying the sick six mules on stretchers through blizzards is all part of the day's work with Mrs. Mary Breckinridge." In writing about Dr. Dublin's reports on our maternity cases, one paper said, and others repeated, "Two men had died from causes not connected with childbirth."

Many feature stories and magazine articles have been written about the Frontier Nursing Service, but they have been of little value to us. Not five hundred dollars in money for the support of our work has come to us from all the countless people who read them, and not a single person, equipped to help us in any department of our work, has joined us because of them. On the nuisance side, we get letters every time an article appears—from old men who want to correspond, from young women who ask me to be their mother. Since one could not have a religious faith which did not carry with it a searching for God's will in all approaches, such letters cause me much anguish of spirit. We consider magazine articles and feature stories a real burden upon our limited time and strength, even when they are not sensational and carry nothing that is detrimental to the Frontier Nursing Service and its people. We do try, however, to the extent that our busy lives permit, to co-operate with story writers who are ladies and gentlemen upon whose integrity we may depend.

There is another breed of writer with whom I make short shrift when I can. Sometimes he comes as a deceiver, whose sensational intent is masked by economic or scientific inquiries. Sometimes he is just a bully, and of such it is easier to dispose. A being in one of our large cities once wrote me that he was coming in to do a feature photographic article on our work. I replied courteously, but firmly, that we didn't want it. He wrote, "And if I choose to come and take photographs of your nurses, what are you going to do about it?" Our trustee, Mr. Rex Farmer, was sheriff of Leslie County at that time. When I reported the circumstance to him, he said, "Don't let it trouble you, Mrs. Breckinridge. We will take care of him." Fortunately for this photographic feature writer, he did not come. We are not a group of helpless women to be bullied by such creatures. Our men will protect us always. There are far too many people whose response to the challenge of a philanthropy like ours is, "How can I cash in on this? What is there in this for me?" In contrast to them, I rest my mind with memories of the newspaper reporters—men and women—who have done their jobs as well as they could, and with invariable courtesy. The publicity they have given us has sold thousands of tickets to our benefits, has brought hundreds of people to hear me speak. Without them, we could not have financed the Frontier Nursing Service. I wish I could have every one of them to a chicken dinner right now.

When Frederick Maurice was at King's College, London, his lectures were so factual that his students jibed, "The seventeenth century was followed by the eighteenth, and that, gentlemen, is a fact." This chapter has concerned itself mainly with a few facts and the mootable questions raised by these facts. Such things matter not only to the Frontier Nursing Service but to all those aware of their import for the human race. One day I received a note from a charming gentleman who wrote that he didn't see the wisdom of encouraging the perpetuation of the "so-called human race." He added kindly, "If it must continue, let us have Kentuckians." This reminded me of an indignant gentleman who, in denouncing some scandal of sixty years ago, referred bitterly to "this so-called nineteenth century." Now, if one is given a peach pie to eat and, upon taking a bite, discovers it to be filled with prunes, one has a right to be outraged and exclaim, "This so-called peach pie!" But the human race is a fact, and we belong to it. We travel, all of us together, on one of the lesser planets, "in this small course which birth draws out to death."

> The lyf so short,
> The craft so long to lerne,
> Th' assay so hard,
> So sharp the conquering.

Chapter 33

I

THE Second World War determined the future course of the Frontier Nursing Service two years before the United States entered it, when—on September 3, 1939—"the blind Fury with th'ab-horréd shears" slit the thin spun life of peace. To Great Britain we owed not only the system of nurse-midwifery, which we were the first to import to the American Continent—just as the Nightingale system of nursing had been imported decades before—but on Great Britain we had depended for the postgraduate training in midwifery of the Frontier Nurses. Our long-deferred plan for the Frontier Graduate School of Midwifery had to be reshaped and put into operation at once. It was my fault that it had been so long deferred. Despite my liking for small beginnings, I wanted the school to start on an established basis, in Lexington, affiliated with the University of Kentucky. Dr. McVey, President of the University then, endorsed this idea as Dr. Donovan, his successor, would now. The physicians on our Medical Advisory Committee wanted it so much that they were willing to work for the indispensable hospital connections. Our plan called for the graduate nurse students to get most of their field work with the Frontier Nursing Service in the mountains. A University school in Lexington did not come about because I failed, after several attempts, to get it financed.

We had already made use of the Frontier Nursing Service field when, in 1935, at the request of the National Society of the Colonial Dames of America in Pennsylvania, we took two Indian girls (trained as nurses in Philadelphia) for a year's postgraduate work. The Colonial Dames in Kentucky gave a full scholarship for Adaline Clark, while Virginia Miller's scholarship was met by the National Society of the Colonial Dames in Massachusetts, Maine, and Michigan. Mr. John Collier, the Commissioner of Indian Affairs, and his nursing staff were eager to have these two fine nurses prepared to work on reservations in Wyoming and Nevada, to which they were sent when their year with us was over. It lay in the thought of the Indian Bureau at that time that the nurse-midwife might find her niche in its medical and nursing services. At Commissioner Collier's request we sent Mary B. Willeford and Bland Morrow, with a letter from him, to study the possibilities of nurse-midwifery on such Indian reservations in the Southwest as the Osage, the Pawnee, the Pueblo, the Navaho, the Hopi, and report back to him. To Adaline and Virginia we had taught not only midwifery but our frontier technique in district bedside nursing and public health.

From our experience in teaching the two Indian nurses we learned that our burdened supervisory staff could not add the training of graduate nurses in midwifery to their regular duties. When, in the fall of 1939, we were faced with an emergency there was nothing for it but to start the Frontier Graduate School at Hyden Hospital, with a staff to handle it, at once. This brooked no delay because a number of our British nurse-midwives wanted to return to their homes as early in 1940 as we could release them. To the Frontier Nursing Service, with its Anglo-American staff working as one family, the parting from such of our British sisters as went over was hard to bear. Our last months together were spent in readjusting the field for a curtailed staff and in getting the School of Midwifery organized.

We started on November 1, 1939, with a class of only two students, who were detached from the hospital staff and assigned to the School, under the supervision of Nora K. Kelly. To make even this modest beginning I had first to get the permission of many people. Our Executive Committee, who had long ago approved the idea of a Graduate School, met at the call of its chairman, Mr. Jouett, to endorse this one. Dr. McCormack, Health Commissioner for the Commonwealth of Kentucky, who had never failed us and did not fail us then, authorized the creation of the School, told me to run it like those in Great Britain, and said that he would arrange for impartial examinations similar to those conducted by the Central Midwives Boards in England and Scotland. The late Dr. Charles B. Crittenden, who at that time was head of the Division of Maternal and Child Welfare in the State Board of Health, took responsibility for the examinations, oral, written, and practical. This Division has held these examinations for each six-months class since then, while the State Board of Health, under its successive commissioners, has followed the custom begun by Dr. McCormack of giving a certificate licensing the graduates of the School to practice midwifery in Kentucky, with the title of Certified Midwife. It is only when these examinations have been successfully passed by our students that they receive the diploma of the School.

The third group whose permission we needed and received was our

Medical Advisory Committee in Lexington, of which Scott Breckinridge was the obstetrical member then, as Dr. A. J. Whitehouse has been since Scott died. During the following months I was to see a number of the great obstetricians on our National Medical Council, and to get advice and help from them. A fourth group whose endorsement was essential, not only to the plan's success but to its inauguration, was that of our Hyden Committee. Lastly, I wanted the widespread endorsement of our people. I therefore arranged to make rounds that fall in all of our outpost areas.

Fortunately for the task I had undertaken, I was able to ride horseback again after a lapse of more than a year. Although my readers are probably as tired of my broken back as I am myself, one last reference to it belongs here. During the thirties I had ridden long stretches (twenty to twenty-five miles) whenever I wanted to go direct to one of the more distant outpost centers. Soon I noticed that if I said I was going somewhere one of my young associates—nurse, secretary, courier —had business in the same direction. I no longer had occasion to saddle a horse, to tighten or loosen a girth. Other things lessened the strain of riding for me. My back had the protection of an aluminum brace, which was lighter and gave better support than the old steel one. After trying out several horses, I had found in Babbette, a gray mare Pebble gave us, a mount that was spirited and swift but did not shy and jar my back. Babbette did more for me than that. My back had a way of giving out after three hours in the saddle. Whenever this happened I had only to say to Babbette, "The back has crashed, take it easy." At once she would drop to a gentle walk. Despite these amenities in riding, my back gave more and more pain as the years passed.

Early in 1938 we had a large luncheon meeting in Boston at which Mrs. Codman asked Dr. Jason Mixter to introduce me. As we chatted during lunch, he was so kind as to say that he would like to take some new X-rays and do a lumbar puncture if I could spare him a week end. I did. He called Dr. William Rogers, orthopedic surgeon, in consultation. They told me I would be a bedridden invalid unless I had a spinal fusion within a few months, and that they would be enchanted to do the operation for me at the Baker Memorial of the Massachusetts General Hospital in June. They did. My brother Carson turned up for the operation, as did Mac, who was on a holiday in the East. Then I lay for something like three months in plaster shells. To make a short story out of what was a long one, I went about after that in a plastic contraption that I called by the French peasant name of "Suson." The only thing that reconciled me to living day and night for months with Suson was Dr. Rogers telling me that she was an experiment. Doctors and nurses adore being used in experiments.

All this is why my rounds in the fall of 1939 were the first I had made in more than a year. Everywhere along the trails over which Babbette and I rode, the wild Michaelmas daisy, called "farewell summer" by the mountaineers, was blooming in clusters of purple and white. Our local committees for the six outpost nursing centers had asked the citizens on every creek and branch to bring box lunches to a rally to meet me. In this way I was able to explain the plan for the Frontier Graduate School of Midwifery to some two thousand people. After each talk, when I called for a discussion from the floor (the ground really!) not only did members of our committees express themselves, but a number of our old patients as well. At one of these rallies a man, whose wife we had carried safely through a terrible postpartum hemorrhage, stood up and said, in the clear English of the mountaineer, "We'll do anything she wants—the blessed old gray-haired critter." Not long after that I spoke beyond the mountains to one of the state associations of women's clubs. A local newspaper wrote of me next day as "an aluminum-haired, dynamic sexagenarian"!

II

When we started the Frontier Graduate School of Midwifery we had everything we needed to make a beginning, except money. To our joy, but not to our surprise, because we always expect the best to happen and often it does, six of our trustees in Detroit, Pittsburgh, Louisville, and Cincinnati gave us the money for equipment, including a life-size manikin, and scholarships to take care of the students in the first three classes. In order to enlarge the classes, we needed a house. The money for this was given through the efforts of one of our New England couriers, and Mardi Cottage (Midwives Quarters) held its housewarming on the day we learned of Pearl Harbor.

Before Nora Kelly returned to England in the fall of 1940—the eleventh British nurse-midwife to go back during that year—I had asked Eva Gilbert if she would take the post of instructor in the School. She consented at once, although it meant a wrench for her to leave the Margaret Durbin Harper Center which she had carried with devotion for five years. Eva, like Bucket, was a college graduate with a Master's degree. Like Bucket, and like Texas (who won her doctorate in 1932), Eva had gone at her own expense to Great Britain to take postgraduate training in midwifery. Like Texas and Bucket, she was given the experience, for which there is no substitute, of using her skills as a district nurse-midwife.

Dorothy Farrar Buck was Dean of our School from its inception until her death in 1949, when Eva Gilbert succeeded her as Dean. When Eva left us for family reasons, she was succeeded as Dean by a graduate of the School, Helen Marie Fedde (Hem), who had taken a Master's degree at the University of Kentucky in preparation for this post. In setting up the curriculum of the Frontier Graduate School of Midwifery, we based it on the six-months course for graduate nurses given by the British schools at that time. The course includes medical lectures, classroom instruction, visits to expectant and postpartum mothers on the districts, attendance at large prenatal clinics, and a minimum of twenty normal maternity cases delivered by each student under the supervision of her instructors. Of these cases, five must be in the hospital and five on the districts, as was required by the British Central Midwives Boards. Our students assist the medical director on his abnormal deliveries. We have been able, since Mrs. Belknap gave us our fine X-ray machine, to take X-rays of the expectant mothers. Any that puzzle our Medical Director are read for him, as a courtesy, by Dr. Harold G. Reineke of Cincinnati, a great roentgenologist. This is not the place to go further into the course, which meets its purpose of training nurses in midwifery.

Although the majority of our normal maternity cases are taken care of in their homes, we do take a certain number of such cases in Hyden Hospital, especially those from our fringe territories. We hospitalize normal cases for ten days after delivery, or longer if we know they have a stretch of horseback riding to do before they reach their homes. Their babies lie in bassinets immediately next the beds of the mothers, except at night when they are moved into a night nursery to keep them at a warmer temperature than we like in the mothers' wards, and to keep the wards quieter so that the mothers can sleep. Any one of our mothers, during her waking hours, can reach over to the bassinet, pick up her baby and hug it, if she wants to. This is not the same system as the one called "rooming in" now in use in several metropolitan hospitals. Our mothers do not have the care of their babies, or the responsibility for them. During the first six days after delivery, a mother at Hyden Hospital has nothing to do for her baby but nurse him and enjoy him. She has nothing to do for herself but take prescribed exercises in bed. After the mothers get up, and before they go home, they learn how to take care of their babies, unless they have had babies with us before. Maternity is a happy time for our women at Hyden Hospital. After childbirth, they need physical and mental rest and they get it.

The natural tendency of a normal woman is to nurse her baby and it is usually her desire. Almost universally our babies are breast-fed. If one of our older babies gets sick and is admitted to the hospital as a patient, we bring the mother in too so as not to interrupt the breast feeding. If a nursing mother comes to one of our surgical clinics for an operation, her baby comes with her so that it can continue to get

327

its breast milk. At our last surgical clinic we had seven guest babies, all under eight months old.

III

The tie between the Second World War and the Frontier Nursing Service is symbolized for me in the name of a hostelry that used to be in Paris, called "The Hotel of the Universe and Portugal United." As the war sucked ever more and more of our irreplaceable staff into its dreadful maw, we struggled to keep the Frontier Nursing Service on an even keel. We could not spare one of the few nurse-midwives who stayed with us to run Hyden Hospital so I asked Miss Lyda Anderson, whom I first knew in the Southwest and saw much of in France, if she would come to us as Hospital Superintendent. She consented at once, although it meant leaving her well-earned retirement and, in June, 1940, she took over when Ann MacKinnon went overseas. She ran the hospital superbly until near the end of the year when she slipped on Thousandsticks Mountain and broke her arm. By that time we could spare Vanda Summers from the Clara Ford Nursing Center on Red Bird River, so she became the Hospital Superintendent.

The position of hospital head midwife has always been of supreme importance in the Frontier Nursing Service because upon her falls the delivery of normal hospital maternity cases and responsibility, under the Medical Director, for abnormalities, as well as for mothers and newborn babies. With the creation of the Frontier Graduate School of Midwifery, the hospital head midwife has had to be a teacher, on top of everything else. The most brilliant teacher we have ever had, the most lucid in imparting knowledge, is Helen E. Browne, now an Assistant Director. Like all the people to reach top positions in our Service, Brownie had first proved herself for years as a district nurse-midwife. We pulled her in from the Flat Creek Nursing Center, late in 1940, to fill the post of hospital head midwife. She then became responsible for the hospital experience of the students in the Graduate School. This includes prenatal examinations and the treatment of such prenatal abnormalities as toxemia, antepartum hemorrhages, abnormal presentations, as well as the management of normal childbirth. Brownie and I had both been trained as midwives at the British in the Woolwich dockyard section of London, but Brownie remained there afterward as a teacher of student-midwives. Brownie carried through class after class of nurse-students of midwifery at Hyden Hospital, and then ran the hospital itself as its superintendent, until I brought her to Wendover (when we knew Bucket would die) to be broken into the post she holds now. She, more than I, is now responsible for the

328

administration of the Frontier Nursing Service, where she fosters the fair and friendly spirit we have cherished over the years.

During the war we could not always keep two nurse-midwives at the three outpost centers where the work was heaviest, but none of the six centers was left even for a day without one in charge. A few of those who stayed on were seasoned veterans in the Service, like Cherry (Rose Evans) at Possum Bend. As assistants to our nurse-midwives we often had non-midwife nurses, during the war, but occasionally we used couriers who had taken training as nurse's aides. Sometimes the second nurse was a cadet.

In the spring of 1944 Miss Anna D. Wolf, Director of the School of Nursing at the Johns Hopkins Hospital, asked us if we would take four of her senior year students, under the terms of the Bolton Act passed by the Congress, for five or six months' training in rural district nursing and public health. The first four cadets were followed by two more from Johns Hopkins and others from Michigan, Ohio, and Lexington, Kentucky. Except for a brief period of approximately six weeks spent at Hyden Hospital, in order to learn the relationship between a remotely rural hospital and its districts, the cadets were placed with the nurse-midwives at the outpost centers, and at Wendover, for purely district experience. Dorothy Farrar Buck took personal charge of their assignments, their papers, their rating. They were a fine group of young nurses, several of whom afterward entered the Frontier Nursing Service, after taking their training as midwives at the Graduate School. Under the Bolton Act we also took into the School nurses sent by us a number of states, and Puerto Rico, to be placed afterward in the rural areas of their own states where there was a shortage of physicians. It was not until the end of the war that we took members of the Army Nurse Corps Reserves into the School, under the Veterans Administration, which paid their fees.

After the United States entered the war we lost Dr. John H. Kooser, the Medical Director who had been with us for nearly twelve years. Although the Office for Emergency Management of the War Manpower Commission listed the employees of the Frontier Nursing Service as "essential within the meaning of the National List and Index of Essential Activities," we never claimed exemption for anyone. So, when Dr. Kooser told us he wanted to go into the Navy Medical Reserve Corps, we signed his release and sent him off with a smile when our hearts were heavy. The effort to locate another Medical Director involved me in correspondence a foot high with people all over the United States. Dr. Frederick C. Irving of the Boston Lying-In wrote me, "I would send you someone on my staff, but I have no staff except a few elderly men." Dr. McCormack told me that even the refugees were scarce. It began to look as though we could say of civilian doctors what Oliver Herford said of the Dodo: "This pleasing bird, I grieve to own, is now extinct." But we had to have a Medical Director. One physician for a hospital, and ten thousand rural people, did not seem an excessive supply even during a war. At last we discovered Dr. James Malcolm Fraser, who was with the Indian Bureau, which consented to release him to us. A big welcome awaited him, his wife and baby. When a second baby came, after they joined us, Joy House rang again with the music of young children, as it had done before Dr. Kooser took his family away.

We had a high priority rating for supplies during the war and ran really short of but two things: horseshoes and diapers. In 1942 we got a horrid shock when the wholesale houses told us that their supplies of horseshoes were exhausted and they could get no more. Without horseshoes we were sunk because more than eighty per cent of our district travel was on horseback, and in this rocky country horses must be reshod every four weeks. Agnes Lewis had several kegs of horseshoes on hand. Dr. Charles E. Hagyard succeeded in getting us two more kegs in Lexington to add to this reserve. But for thirty-six horses, this added up to only a few months' supply. We were forced to take this crisis up at the highest levels in Washington, where it was hard to convince officials that horseshoes were essential to childbirth. It was even hard to convince them that horseshoes were essential to horses! One War Production Board official wrote a Virginia farmer that wear and tear on horseshoes might be minimized if the shoes were taken off the horses outside of working hours. He also suggested that "unessential styles" in horseshoes should be eliminated! Representative John Flannagan came to the rescue of the horses and their owners by asking, on the floor of the House, if we were to have zipper horseshoes. After the newspapers had cut in on the laughter, we were notified, early in 1943, that horseshoes had been taken off the priority list, and a factory was authorized to make them.

Shoes must be turned, by a farrier, to fit a horse's feet, and put on expertly. Our local blacksmiths vanished during the war—most of them to return no more. From then on we have had to keep our own blacksmith, who goes every four weeks to the outpost centers to shoe the horses. In between he does other suitable and useful things.

As regards diapers, in 1943 we ran desperately short of them. The layettes people sent us came with apologies instead of diapers. The mail order houses would send few or none. Only once could we get a dozen dozen, on our written statement that they were not intended for the same baby! Through the *Quarterly Bulletin* we appealed to our friends who responded nobly, as always. Many of them went from shop to shop in their home towns, sending us anything from a few yards of bird's-eye to a dozen diapers. They sent us their old linen too,

330

with which we diapered the hospital babies. It had to be washed carefully to keep it from falling to pieces, so it wasn't much use to the district babies.

On July 7, 1943, Representative Frances Bolton of Ohio rose on the floor of the House and asked for one minute in which to present the national problem of diapers. She wrote us privately that she had a tough time. In the newspapers we read how one member of Congress had gotten up to reply that, in earlier times, "millions of babies had been born without these conveniences." We wondered how he happened not to have heard of swaddling clothes, which took a great deal more yardage than diapers. The reason given for the inexcusable crisis was that looms used for making bird's-eye had taken to making burlap, a war necessity. Yet other looms continued to turn out material for the clothes of men and women, even party dresses, in such quantities that the shops had a surplus of them. War is war—but why take it out on the babies?

IV

This chapter began with the departure for war of eleven of the British nurses on our Anglo-American staff. We did not expect all of them to come through unscathed, what with the perils of ocean crossing, the bombings on land. Two who returned to us when the war was over, Betty Lester in 1946 and Mac in 1948, had miraculously escaped destruction. It was disturbing that rumors arose about Betty in our territory, no one knew how, and spread—first, that her ship had been torpedoed, and then that she had been killed by a bomb in London. When she returned to Kentucky, several of her old friends asked her why she was not dead. No such rumors spread about any of the other nurses so that our uneasiness tended to focus on Betty. She was a Sister (head nurse) at a London hospital during most of the war. A buzz bomb did strike the house where the nurses lived, one night in 1944, killing several nurses and wrecking Betty's room and bed. But Betty had volunteered to relieve for a night Sister on the wards and had not gone to bed. One of her shoes was dug out of the debris five weeks later, and a week later its mate. When she turned up in New York, where I saw her, she stood in those selfsame shoes, good prewar leather. Mac, during most of the war, was in charge of a hospital train, a train so immaculately kept that after a tour of inspection Lady Mountbatten told her it was as clean as her husband's ship. When this train got blitzed, Mac was rather badly injured. However, she too turned up in Kentucky to become the Hyden Hospital Superintendent again and is, as everyone who loves her says, the same old Mac.

Yes, we thought it not unlikely that some of the British members of our staff would be killed. What none of us knew then was that the next two who were to die would be Americans, Texas and Bucket. Texas had left us to get outside experience she thought would be of use to us when she returned, as she expected to do. She became Public Health Nursing Consultant with the Federal Children's Bureau, where she worked to within twelve days of her death on Christmas Eve, 1941. Twice during the preceding summer she had come down to see us. Four days before she died she wrote from a hospital, "May you all have the very merriest of Christmases and I will be with you at Wendover, even though I am in New York." On Christmas Eve, after the telegram about her had come, a few of us who loved her were sitting together when we had a sense of her presence. Then we knew that she had awakened from the sleep of death to come back and spend Christmas with us at Wendover. When a beloved and useful person dies in what is called the prime of life, heads are shaken sadly and lips murmur, "What a pity!" It is as though we thought of this life as all the life there is, as though there were no usefulness, no affection, anywhere but here. Birth and death—the coming on to this little planet and the leaving of it for wider neighborhoods—what does it matter? A finely edged tool, forged and sharpened, is of supreme usefulness, there as here.

Bucket's death was caused by the same insidious disease that had taken Texas, but it was not until two years after Dr. Massie's first operation on her, in February, 1947, in Lexington, that she died. When he talked over her condition with her, before we brought her back to the mountains, she said, "Thank you for telling me." She turned her convalescence at Wendover into a glorious springtime adventure, giving herself wholly to the sights and scents of April and May. Before the end of the summer she had taken back all of her regular duties. In May of 1948 she had her second operation at our own Hyden Hospital. When she came from under the anesthesia, Dr. Massie sat down beside her and told her it would now be only a matter of months. Again she returned to Wendover, where she began to turn her administrative responsibilities over to Brownie. She worked with Brownie until she grew too weak to make the daily walk to her office in the Garden House. On Thanksgiving Day she was not able to go to the living room in the Big House for the celebration but she had all of the Hyden and outpost nurses visit her in her cabin bedroom. She had smiles and humorous greetings for everyone. For her old friends in the Frontier Nursing Service she left special notes and gifts. The card she wrote Mac is typical of the personal touch in each: "From an old nurse who is leaving, to an old nurse who has come back."

"To gain experience one must have suffering," wrote Sir Oliver Lodge. The question was whether we made it worth while. All Bucket's twenty-one years with the Frontier Nursing Service were constructive. The last months of her life were creative. She did indeed make her suffering worth while. It was as though she threw the base metal of her dying body into a crucible from which came out pure gold.

Bucket said again and again, and wanted it known, that dying from cancer was not too bad. She did not think that people should dread it as they do. She believed that when, as in her case, surgery had been promptly sought and yet was too late—she believed that reasonable people should be told the truth. She said, "I thought I would have been afraid but I am not afraid." She drank the wine of life as a sacrament and she was willing to drink it to its dregs. One of the last things she said to me in her conscious moments was, "I have such a feeling of peace." She repeated, "Deep peace."

On a bend of the Kentucky mountains in the Wendover holdings, overlooking the winding river, we set aside a plot for a staff burying ground. To this Bucket's body was carried by men who had been her neighbors and friends. But she, the real Bucket, had passed beyond the boundaries of "this bank and shoal of time." We know that her spirit is nearer to us than the grave we tend, because to us she gave the steadfast affection of her loyal heart.

Chapter 34

I

KENTUCKY mountaineers with ancestral ties going back to Great Britain felt the war profoundly even before the time came when they poured out their lives in behalf of their own country, as they have done in all our wars. When Mrs. Arthur Bray made her last visit to Wendover in 1937, she went walking one day up Hurricane Creek. Here she met an old man who asked if she were lost. When she answered that she was just taking a walk with the dogs, this conversation took place:

"Are you from Mrs. Breckinridge's?"

"Yes. Mrs. Breckinridge and I are old friends."

"Where did you come from?"

"From England," she answered, "I'm English." With that his old face lit up as he told her that his forbears had come from England, that his grandfather used to tell him tales of England, passed down in the family, and that he himself had always wanted to see England more than he wanted anything else in the world. He then asked her, "And how is the Old Country now?"

The fall of France affected those of us who had known her agonies of the First World War and her incredible gallantry in the face of them, like the death of a beloved person, and when Britain stood alone, those of us whose people had come from the Old Country stood right beside her in our hearts. It was during this year that our Executive Committee empowered me to ask four British friends of the Frontier Nursing Service, who had all stayed with us in the Kentucky mountains—Mrs. Arthur Bray, Lady MacKenzie, the Honorable Arthur Villiers, Mrs. Frederic Watson—to become members of our Board of Trustees. We felt that in this gesture we clasped their hands.

Meanwhile, the lava of war flowed on to Pearl Harbor, and beyond. That the Frontier Nursing Service, in its eighteenth fiscal year, had sons of military age came home to us early in 1943 when Taylor Morgan's grandson, Maurice—aged seventeen—volunteered with the Navy and was sent to the Pacific. Our first grandchild (Richard Charles Hoskins) was born at about that time, on January 8, 1943, in the Beech Fork District. It was Texas who had brought his mother, a Bowling baby called Nell, into this world. The babies of our early days were growing up. By 1944 many of the boys we had delivered were eighteen; they, as well as hundreds of others we had nursed through early childhood, were now scattered all over the planet. Some of these young soldiers and sailors, stationed within reach of some of our old staff overseas, sought them out.

It was staggering to reflect upon the battles in which our young things were engaged and the places where they went, boys who had rarely left the neighborhoods in which they were born. We saw letters to their families from India, New Zealand, Holland, Germany, France, Belgium, North Africa, Jerusalem, Sicily, and more Pacific Islands than we had known the names of before. One boy wrote his people from Germany: "To you in this letter I am sending a small fragment of myself." Another from India: "Please don't worry, and may God bless you and keep you for I love you." Still another wrote from the Holy Land: "I saw the tomb where Jesus was buried . . . the manger he laid in when he was a baby. I saw the rock he prayed on . . . and, Mother, I even saw the River Jordan and the Dead Sea. . . . Just received the Purple Heart. It sure is a pretty medal."

We set aside a room in one of the log cabins for a Victory Shrine Chapel. Roger and Margaret Rogan gave us a cross to stand on a table. Later, another trustee gave an altar. On the retable is carved:

1941   TO THE MEMORY OF THOSE WHO DID NOT RETURN   1945

In this log chapel we hung our service flag, changing the number under the blue star as more and more of our children went off to war. As the nurses sent their names in from the districts we typed them on the loose-leaf pages of a book with the creeks they came from, the branch of the military service they entered, their decorations, and their deaths. On the last pages of the book we put the names of the men in our own families who were in military service, our staff, our couriers, but we did not include these in the numbers below the stars. When the war was over the number under the blue star was 1,040. Under the gold star it was 42. We had known that all of our children could not return from that dreadful holocaust. My mind often reverted then, as it has since the fighting started in Korea, to the Scottish lines:

> Mony a heart will break in twa,
> Should he no come back again.

335

II

That the Nazi propaganda had its dragnets everywhere was never made so clear to us as when it pitched into the Frontier Nursing Service. Vanda Summers' brother, a parson in the Church of England, wrote her late in 1942 that he had been listening to a German station transmitting propaganda—chiefly abuse—in English. Two women were boasting of Nazi social services when suddenly one of them ripped into the Frontier Nursing Service and concluded by saying, "It only serves to show the dreadful state of social services in America." We held steadfastly to our work, so despised by Goebels, for the young children and their mothers, including the preparation of more Frontier nurse-midwives to serve yet more people.

The scarcity of men made everything harder than it had been, a scarcity we began to feel as early as 1941, when many had enlisted or left the mountains to work in the defense plants. Just before the dawn of the first Christmas Day after Pearl Harbor, Cherry ushered a little Carol into the world to add her chant to the universal chorus of Christmas morning. Cherry was alone in the house, except for a kind neighbor woman—no man within call—when the newspapers which papered the ceiling of Carol's birthplace burst into flames. Cherry and the neighbor woman dashed for water, climbed up on beds and chairs and heaved the water above their heads, tearing the paper down where they could reach it. In this heroic manner they saved Carol's home. But nothing could save our administration building, the Garden House, when it caught fire in bitter weather two weeks later while everybody was at lunch in the Big House. We don't know the cause, unless the little furnace in the log building had been overheated to cope with the zero temperature outdoors. Although we still had employees, and they hauled out the great fire hose to throw its stream of water on the flames, it was to no avail. So, they turned the water on the big horse barn and saved that.

At the first alarm of fire from a passer-by who came running up, the couriers grabbed halters and rushed to the barn. Jean had the help of two juniors on that bleak January day—Celia Coit, Pat Ferneding. The three of them soothed the frightened horses as they led them down to the river. Meanwhile, the rest of our crowd made heroic efforts to save what they could reach in two of the offices that the flames had started to lick but had not consumed. Our bookkeeper, Lucile Hodges, crawled on her hands and knees to the FNS books and ledgers and dropped them out of a window before making good her own escape. When nothing more could be rescued, Andy started taking photographs of the conflagration. These, and the letters about the fire sent me in the East, came out in our next *Bulletin* and quad-

336

rupled the outpouring of assistance that reached us from all sides. Those of our crowd, like Agnes Lewis and Jean Hollins, whose bedrooms were above the offices in the Garden House, had lost all their clothes but the ones they wore and, in Aggie's case, irreplaceable personal possessions. Clothes from people in Lexington were brought up at once by Mrs. Waring Wilson on a special trip, and came later in the mails from other places. At so many times in the life of the Frontier Nursing Service we had pitched in with the other neighbors to clothe those who had been burned out that it seemed natural enough to have people pitch in to clothe us. What astounded me at the time, and still does, was that hundreds of people from all over the United States sent in so much money to rebuild the Garden House, and refurnish it, that we never had to make an appeal to anyone. More than twenty thousand dollars came to us spontaneously—some of it in checks of from one to several thousand dollars, some in gifts of three or four dollars. But nothing came through solicitation because nobody was solicited. With the insurance of five thousand dollars (all the insurance companies had let us take out on the Garden House), these gifts built a new Garden House, larger than the old one, and furnished the offices downstairs and the bedrooms upstairs.

The burden of building, the coping with priorities, the locating of scarce supplies, all that was carried by Agnes Lewis, Executive Secretary, who, in the twenty-one years since she came to the Frontier Nursing Service, has shifted every strain she could assume from my shoulders to hers. She, Lucile, and Bucket, unknown to me, suggested to the old staff—nurses, secretaries, couriers—that the gifts they were sending in following the fire be used to create a memorial to my brother, General Breckinridge, the Marine. For this the current staff joined with the old. The $963 they gave was used for the Wendover dispensary in the new Garden House—its doors, windows, and inside walls, as well as its furnishings. It is thus that my brother's name became linked with the work of those whom he had likened to Marines.

III

This is the place for my narrative to swing again beyond the mountains, in order to tell something of what the Frontier Nursing Service owes the membership of its committees in faraway cities, and its subscribers, who have lent their support to a charity which most of them have never seen. It is because they believed in us, trusted us, liked us, that we have grown from our infant beginnings into a national philanthropy, grown like the banian tree we envisioned long ago with branches "yielding shade and fruit to wide neighborhoods of men."

337

And just as I cannot name all the hundreds of our couriers, nurses, secretaries—not even some young things who worked directly with me, not even some of the very best of them—so I cannot name all the hundreds of people who have served the Frontier Nursing Service on its committees beyond the mountains, or the thousands whose donations have kept it going. These friends have carried us through thick and thin, with more thin than thick. Not once during the first twenty-five years of our existence did we have money in the bank to meet our obligations three months ahead of when they were due. Rarely have we had money even one month ahead, but I always knew that our friends would never let us fall into the dregs of dissolution. And they never did.

The year in which this book has been written is the only stretch of time when the Frontier Nursing Service has walked by sight as well as in faith. This came about because Mrs. Morris B. Belknap, our National Chairman, wrote all our trustees (except those in England) to ask if they could give or raise $50,000 in honor of our quarter-century of unbroken service, and to set me free to write this book. It was the first appeal ever made to our Board of Trustees, as a Board, and they responded so generously in their own gifts, and through those they solicited, that Mrs. Belknap turned $55,617.93 over to our Treasurer, besides stock that added $15,000 to our endowment fund. It is because nearly the whole life span of the Frontier Nursing Service has been spent in periods of depression, war, inflation, war again, that we have achieved only half our early goal of a million-dollar endowment. Unlike many philanthropies, we do not wail over small returns from endowment funds but thank God when they are paid in every quarter that some income is assured us. This income of not much more than twenty thousand dollars, the small fees from patients (which have never met ten per cent of our budget), the small revenue from the Wendover Post Office, the fees that the nurse-students pay to the Frontier Graduate School of Midwifery, supplemented by a grant from the Daughters of the Society of Colonial Wars, the drive for local donations put over annually by our Hyden Chairman, Mr. Emmett Elam—all these together fall short of meeting our budget by more than one hundred thousand dollars every year. That the budget is met, including the costs of repair and upkeep on our vast rural properties, is due to the more than four thousand people who subscribe to us annually, and to the committees who work like hound dogs in our behalf.

There could not be loyalty greater than that of subscribers to the FNS. Those who take us up rarely drop us while they live, and when an old subscriber dies it is not unusual for his gift to be taken on by a member of his family and carried in his name. This happens sometimes

338

among our large as well as small subscribers. The Edith Harkness Nurse is a living memorial to one who loved and served us well. The Helen Draper Ayer Nurse is supported by a cousin in memory of the woman who gave us the Beech Fork Center. Some of our subscribers, large and small, arrange to have their gifts sent monthly by their banks. One has done this for twenty-two years. But most of them respond to our little "Waiting Horse" card reminders. The new subscribers, without whom we would be sunk, because of the thinning ranks of the old, mostly come as a result of my talks.

Our policy with our committees has been to give them the most complete autonomy possible, with the result that no two of them run their affairs quite alike. The only thing we ask of them all is that they keep to the standards in fund-raising set by the National Information Bureau. Some of our committees give annual benefits, some occasional benefits, some send out appeals. Some are extremely active and some, especially when they lack a chairman, are inactive for a long time. All of the active ones are good about lining up meetings for me to report on the doings of the Frontier Nursing Service.

Each committee works out its own method of organization. Here are a few examples, taken from among many. Rochester has a small committee with a long list of sponsors attached, rather like the tail to a comet. Its only chairman, from its inception until the last few months, was Helen Rochester Rogers, who has been succeeded by the wife of a great obstetrician. Chicago, on the other hand, has always had a large committee and has had several chairmen, each an outstanding woman and my friend. Our Minneapolis Committee has few members but each one of them is personally devoted to the FNS, and its chairman has come down to the mountains to inspect its work at firsthand. Some of our committees represent the real interest of small communities, like those at Princeton and Hazard. One, the Blue Grass Committee, was organized by Mrs. George Hunt to include in its membership people from several towns and counties. The Detroit Committee has always had a man as a chairman, as had the Cincinnati Committee until the death of Roger Rogan. The Baltimore Committee is exceptional in that its chairmen have been medical men. Since the death of Dr. Welch, it is the only committee to have an obstetrician at its head. The New York Committee chairmen have been many—all fine—with an old friend of my Card days holding the post now. A number of our larger committees have volunteer secretaries. New York and Boston each have a treasurer. Mrs. H. F. Stone (Pebble's mother) and Mr. Charles Jackson have held these offices on their respective committees for an unbroken period of more than twenty years.

Our New York Committee is unique in that its executive group and officers meet monthly and work hard throughout the month at the

339

Bargain Box—a thrift shop in which the Frontier Nursing Service is associated with several other charities. Since 1940 this has brought us in a steady income of thousands of dollars a year. Friends send rummage to be sold there, not only from all around New York City, but from as far west as Wisconsin, as far south as Kentucky. The Philadelphia Committee collaborates on the Bargain Box. Their rummage is deposited at the garage of one of the members, and carried to New York in the station wagon of another. The proceeds from its sale are credited to Philadelphia. The Bargain Box more nearly meets my idea of co-operation in fund-raising—like our Caribbean cruises—than any other one thing our committees do because it does include the participation of more than one group. But our *Britannic* and *Belgenland* cruises united all of our committees everywhere in a common effort. Even now I cannot think of a better way to do this.

When Mrs. Lawrence Groner was its chairman, our Washington Committee first engaged John Mason Brown to give his only annual lecture at the nation's capital, in the ballroom of the Mayflower Hotel, as a benefit for the Frontier Nursing Service. Mr. Brown has done this every year since then, except when he was with the United States Navy in the Second World War. Washington is unlike any other city where we have a committee in that there we get the luster of national and international names as sponsors for our benefits. While Mrs. Roosevelt was in the White House she started a custom, to which Mrs. Truman has adhered, of leading the list of patronesses for our annual benefits. The wives of three successive Chief Justices of the Supreme Court have been patronesses of these benefits. When Lord Halifax was the Ambassador to the United States from His Majesty's Government, Lady Halifax was one of our patronesses. The wives of some of the members of the Cabinet, the Senate and the House, and high-ranking Army and Navy officers, are among our patronesses, as are a few ladies of the Diplomatic Corps. Shortly before the Second World War the wife of one European diplomat said that she hesitated to allow her name to be associated with an organization that called itself Frontier Nursing Service, because there had been so much talk about the rectification of frontiers. Poor darling! Her country's frontiers were indeed rectified by one dictator, and are rectified now by another.

Mrs. Roosevelt not only led the list of sponsors for our Washington benefits but more than once she introduced me when I spoke at the George Hewitt Myers Textile Museum. She invited me several times to attend luncheons and dinners at the White House, and once to a family dinner with her and the President. When President Roosevelt was a young man, he had ridden through parts of our Kentucky mountains. His and Mrs. Roosevelt's knowledge of our problems was as profound as it was sympathetic. A Washington friendship that I count among the most worth while of my whole life was that of the late Mr. Justice Brandeis. The first time Mrs. Brandeis invited me to have tea with them was because the Justice and I held Kentucky in common. After that, every year when I went to Washington, Mrs. Brandeis telephoned me to come for an hour's conversation with the Justice. He always saw me alone and, as we talked, his vast and humane intellect ranged all over the world. Punctually at the end of one hour, Mrs. Brandeis came into the room to serve us tea.

Throughout the years since our work began I have gone to our committees beyond the mountains whenever they wanted me, to speak to whatever crowds they could line up to hear me. I met engagements also with as many other groups as wanted me—schools, churches, hospitals, women's clubs, men's luncheon clubs, conferences and conventions—when I could fit them into my tours. Always I have tried to make special talks to the chapters of the Alpha Omicron Pi Sorority, which maintains our Social Service Department. It is twenty years since I met with four members of the Chicago North Shore Alumnae Chapter—Mrs. Edgard C. Franco-Ferreira, whom I had known in France when she was one of our Card chauffeurs, Mrs. Warren C. Drummond, Mrs. Kenneth S. Cole, and Miss Cora Jane Stroheker. These four women proposed to the A. O. Pi Council that they create and support a Social Service Department in the Frontier Nursing Service as their national philanthropic project. The tales I have told of early social service cases will have shown that social work is as indispensable in rural areas as in cities. The quality of our social work has been fine because of the interest as well as the support of the A. O. Pi Alumnae, many of whom have visited us, and because we have had Social Service Secretaries who were tops.

I speak to as many thousands of people as are willing to let me tell them the story of the Frontier Nursing Service. Among my records I find that on one brief tour, from October 17 to November 13, I spoke twenty-six times in fourteen cities. On my last Midwestern tour before this book, I took to the air as the only way of getting around quickly enough, but even then I had side trips on local trains and by car. To the churches and schools I speak without pay but I ask a professional fee from the women's clubs, made payable to the Frontier Nursing Service. In this way I have tried to meet my own railroad and hotel expenses; for years the fees I turned in more than met them. I raised my fee, as I got older and wearier, so as to have fewer engagements. I thought, rather naïvely, that I could make the same amount of money with half the amount of work but not half as many people wanted me at the larger sum.

Although I spoke often over the radio in early years I have never liked to do it, and I do it now only on local stations at the request of our committees, to whom I refuse nothing that it lies in my power to give. I have gotten out of many radio engagements by asking bigger fees for the Frontier Nursing Service than the sponsors of networks are willing to pay. None of my radio talks have inspired people to send money to the Frontier Nursing Service, with the sole exception of the one I made in Louisville during the drought, when I was allowed to ask for milk funds. What these talks do bring to us is an almost unbearable amount of mail.

IV

That I have had money for personal expenses in all of my journeyings from place to place, all of my talks to thousands and thousands of people, is odd because I made hay of my little fortune years ago. It will be remembered that, in 1925, I promised to underwrite the work I had started. To refresh my mind on this, I have run through an old correspondence with my mother's chief executor, the late Mr. John C. Gardner, who used every argument in his power, backed by the strongest family friendship, to induce me to stop selling securities. In one letter he quoted a clause about me in my mother's will which reads as follows:

In all my former wills the one-fourth interest devised above has been bequeathed and devised to some Trustee for a definite period for the use and benefit of my said daughter. . . . After mature deliberation I have decided to make the above bequest and devise to my said daughter absolutely. It is my earnest request to her, however, that she use only the income derived from said bequest.

The clause went on to state that it was my mother's wish that the principal she had left might remain in the hands of her executors, but that this expression of her wish was not to be construed as creating a trust. I was the only one of her four children whose funds she had put into the hands of a Trustee in her former wills, and the only one of the four to have a clause about the bequest inserted in her last will!

My mother tried to understand her children, each so different and all so migratory. I don't know why she had thought I needed special protection, because no one knows oneself as one is known in the heart of a good mother. But this last will, written after Breckie's death, showed her comprehension of the stupendous emotional strain that follows in the wake of the death of an only son. I knew, from my last conversations with her, that she had understood how much this tension would need always to be channeled to some purpose, and that no concern for my financial welfare should block that channel. So she set me free, with a human mother's longing for me to be sheltered and an almost divine understanding of my deeper needs. This explanation is made lest people think that in giving up an income ample for my wants, I was responding to a call from God. It wasn't that way at all. To Mr. Gardner I wrote, in part,

I quite agree with you that the use I have made of my funds is utterly without sense or judgment from any point of view that takes into account primarily my own span of life—and it is a use I could not have made had I dependents. But I know, as you cannot, that I could not have gotten my work under way without so using my funds . . . and when it [the money] isn't there any more I will take a living wage for my services like other workers. Perhaps it will be better so. I like to feel that I can give what I do in memory of my children, but that is personal, and perhaps it stands in the way—then let it go too. . . . I can't tell you how hard it has been to write this. But at least I am sure you will believe in my sincerity, even when you hold my sanity in small esteem!

After receiving this letter, Mr. Gardner asked if I had thought that I might live to an enfeebled old age, in which I could not work, and might become dependent on my people. In reply I told him I had thought of that too. I promised to keep enough to pay for a room in a really nice home for old ladies to which I could go when my working days were over! I wrote:

Remember that when we talk of my giving up my money in pushing this enterprise, I don't want to do it any more than you want me to. There is nothing heroic about it. I just had to push the enterprise, and if it took the money, why so much the worse. I had rather have the money, much. But there isn't scope to make a primary thing out of it.

The greater part of my money did not go into overdrafts, only $8,015 by 1930, when my underwriting of the Frontier Nursing Service came to an end. The money I lent the FNS without interest, paid back to me over the years without interest, meant a complete loss of that much principal, but I could have done without it. The building of Wendover took lots more of my capital than that. But, until we had a hospital, there just had to be some place where the sick could be taken, where we could receive people interested in our work, whose right it was to come in and see it at firsthand. However, I could have built Wendover and still have gotten by.

The thing that proved to be my financial undoing was the upkeep of Wendover, and the running of it both as a cottage hospital and as a guest house, for a period of nearly five years. From my records, which are not complete, I find that I entertained 328 guests at Wendover, who stayed a total of 2,184 days. More than half of these guests were patients—people with pneumonia, marasmic infants, women who were having babies, and children, most of them sick, who just had to be sheltered. There didn't seem to be any way out of my having to carry the cost of all this because the Frontier Nursing Service, during its early years, never met its budget. No Executive Committee would have been willing to add a place like Wendover to a budget already cumbered with overdrafts. It was not until 1930 that the Frontier Nursing Service was able to take over the running of Wendover, and its upkeep. Later in the thirties, I deeded the place to the FNS with no strings attached. My money didn't give out until sometime in 1938. Then I took "a living wage like other workers," namely, our own workers of whom the highest paid then (except the Medical Director) received $125 a month. The minutes of the Executive Committee show that I asked to be given the same salary as the others, and I have stayed since then in the same category as those who have been with us five years or more. I still have the residue of my principal that I promised Mr. Gardner to keep, and its income meets my personal expenses when I am on a tour. I have the joy of entertaining personally the people I ask to lunch or dine with me, at restaurants and clubs, and of doing other things myself that are as essential as that to one of my hospitable traditions.

When I wrote that my mother, by removing all restraints from my capital, had set me free, I meant just that. Not only was I free to channel the tension of my grief into the service of young children and their families, unimpeded by a shortage of immediate funds, but the impetus of this drive freed me from lesser constraints. An old lady once said she did not like to hear the Ten Commandments read out in church because they put ideas in people's heads. One idea they could never put into mine is that of coveting my neighbor's goods. I do so ardently not want anything that is his. Even in shops, my feeling is one of deep gratitude that the things displayed there cannot be pushed off onto me. I can buy the pair of shoes I need, with thankfulness that none of the other things will ever be mine. To travel light has always been my natural inclination, intensified a thousandfold as my travels near their end. I cling, with an affection Christ will forgive me, for He too was human, to a few beloved objects that are symbols of my dead. Aside from them, my luggage is light and I am free.

Chapter 35

I

THE thoughtful readers of this book will have been asking:
"Now what about the economic future of these Kentucky mountaineers? You have said nothing about how anybody makes a living, since rafts went down the river and men rode horseback to public works at the railroad. What about it?"

Even while the rafts were going down the rivers, and men strove to earn cash money at the railroads, even as far back as that, a better economic future for our people was our deepest concern. Any plan for the health of young children, and their mothers, will fail if their fathers can't make a living. Our region had two undeveloped economic assets, timber and coal. We will come to coal later. Our thought then was in terms of timber. My father believed that a region like ours could become not only self-sustaining but comfortably well off if it were developed as mountains should be, and not as agricultural land. From his knowledge of the great forests of Europe, he often discussed with me the difference between forestry—where timber is cultivated like an asparagus bed and yields crops for centuries—and what in America often goes by the same name but is really the reforestation of denuded areas. He and I both remembered the floods on the Mississippi, that had increased in magnitude with the destruction of the forests which once protected the headwaters of its tributary streams. From that mighty river, away on up to the Middle Fork of the Kentucky, on whose banks we were living, he saw but one picture and he saw it whole. The tributary streams of the Mississippi—to the east and to the west—which begin as tiny rivulets susceptible of restraint, swell in volume at each confluence until they become the Ohio, the Missouri, and other rivers second only to these. When the forests are destroyed on the mountain gaps and slopes where the rivulets arise, there is nothing left to hold back the melting snows of winter, the torrential rains of spring. Then these waters rush unimpeded down out of the

345

mountains in flood tides, to become the swollen rivers that overflow their banks, destroy the wealth of cities, and inundate the bottom lands on which America depends for much of its food.

That part of his native state where my father spent his last years, and where he died, is a vast watershed, with the gaps of the mountains protected in his time by virgin timber—a fifty per cent stand of white oak that it will take two hundred years to replace, a good stand of yellow poplar, the most valuable of the softwoods hereabouts, that it will take one hundred and fifty years to restore. My father felt it to be wasteful and costly to allow such timber to be ruthlessly destroyed. He knew that before these forests could be replanted, the uncontrolled waters would rush to the Ohio and the Mississippi, carrying our top-soil with them, and flooding lowland cities and farms. Before my father's death at Wendover on December 3, 1932, he talked this over with me and with other Kentuckians who were our friends. We decided, among us, that a National Forest Purchase Unit should be created, under the Weeks Law, by the National Forest Reservation Commission, to be administered by the Forest Service, and that this should include much of the heavily timbered land in the eleven counties of eastern Kentucky in which lie the headwaters of the Cumberland River and the three forks of the Kentucky River.

The advantage of forest conservation in these eleven counties would not all lie in the protection this would give the lowlands from disastrous floods. Development of the forests in perpetuity, as a crop, would give employment to about a fourth of the rural population. The opening up of highways, the protection of fish and game, and other attractions to draw tourists, would provide a natural economic outlet for this area. The bottom lands could continue to be planted in gardens and corn, the gentler slopes in fruit, with such legumes and grasses as soy beans and lespedeza, which hold the soil. The pay given for employment in a national forest, the tourist trade that would come with high-ways to mountains which kept their scenic beauty, would yield a steady revenue in money. We even thought it possible that small woodwork-ing industries might be developed, to use the by-products of the forests and give employment during the winter months. All of this was woven into our plans, but the initial step was to get a National Forest Purchase Unit before the forests were destroyed.

It was in Washington in the summer of 1933, not many months after my father's death, that I made my first approach to the National Forest Reservation Commission. I had discovered, to my surprise, that the chairmanship of this Commission was vested in the Secretary of War with the title of President! The Secretaries of the Interior and of Agriculture and four members of the Congress comprised the rest of the Commission. I asked Senator Alben Barkley for an introduction to

Mr. George H. Dern, the Secretary of War at that time. Senator Barkley pulled the telephone over, called Mr. Dern, and said, "A charming lady from Kentucky is here, who wants to see you." I could imagine the courteously suppressed groan at the other end of the line, so I said, "Tell him ten minutes." As a matter of fact, I took only eight minutes of the Secretary's time because I knew exactly what I wanted to say. I had made it my business to gather and digest all the facts available to me on the U.S. Forest Service from the time of President Theodore Roosevelt, when Gifford Pinchot was Forester. (This was the simple title by which the Chief of the Forest Service was then known.) As far back as 1907, Mr. Pinchot had engaged an expert lumberman to study and report on Eastern lands suitable for National Forest purposes. Among the areas he recommended was that in which the Frontier Nursing Service is now located. In 1914, one of the National Forest Examiners made a reconnaissance of land which included our section and strongly recommended that it be set aside as a purchase area. His report says, "There is no section of Kentucky so bountifully supplied with streams as is the part of this area north of Pine Mountain which embraces the entire headwaters of Middle Fork." In 1921, another Forest Examiner reported that physical conditions had not changed since 1914, but that large financial interests, organized as coal and timber companies, were holding the key tracts and purchase was doubtful until the coal was worked out.

These and many other facts about the Forest Service were known to me, but of course I didn't bring them to the attention of Secretary Dern! I only asked him for permission to confer with the Forester, the late Major R. Y. Stuart, and with the Secretaries of the Interior and of Agriculture, who were Mr. Harold Ickes and Mr. Henry Wallace at that time. Secretary Dern readily granted this, and asked me for a memorandum embodying my ideas about a purchase unit. Secretary Wallace said, very properly, that in the matter of forests he would follow the advice of the Forest Service, a bureau in the Department of Agriculture. Secretary Ickes told me that he welcomed plans for forest conservation. From Major Stuart (who died not long after I met him), from Mr. F. A. Silcox, his successor as Forester, and from their associates, our project received thorough and courteous consideration.

I had already lined up the data for Secretary Dern's memorandum, in the hope that he would ask me for one. Mr. Walter Hoskins, our indefatigable trustee at Hyden, had worked up a list for me of eighty-seven companies and individuals holding considerable tracts of timber-land in the three of the eleven counties with which we were most concerned, the fee acreage of each tract and its valuation, and the names and addresses of representatives of the companies. When I had this list mimeographed it covered a page just under two feet long, just over one foot wide. Many of the holders of these timberlands in the Kentucky mountains lived as far away as Pennsylvania, Michigan, Ohio, Georgia, Massachusetts, Tennessee, Arkansas, New York, Virginia, West Virginia. Some were Kentuckians, but very little of the timber lay in the hands of the original mountain owners. With this list as an appendix, I prepared a comprehensive five-page memorandum covering the area under consideration, and offering the hospitality and horses of the Frontier Nursing Service to visiting foresters. I sent seven copies of all this to the Secretary of War, for himself and the six members of his Commission, as well as copies to the Forester.

A period of two years ensued, during which the Frontier Nursing Service was in close touch with the U.S. Forest Service. Mr. Silcox sent several of his associates down to see us, to study forest tracts on and near the area of our work. A memorable visit was that of Chief Land Examiner, Mr. W. E. Hedges, who came in May of 1935. His sense of the value of the human beings living in and near the forests was as profound as was his knowledge of trees. He saw the picture whole, as my father had seen it, namely—that flood control for the Mississippi Valley must start with the protection of the forest cover on the watersheds, that a National Forest was the only way to ensure this protection, and that this National Forest would help support the economy of the rural people living in and around it. I know that Mr. Hedges gave a report favorable to the plan for a National Forest Purchase Unit for our watersheds. That the plan fell through was not due to lack of eagerness on the part of the Forest Service, nor was there a lack of cooperation on the part of our local citizens, who at numerous meetings where I spoke gave the idea vigorous applause.

Our failure to get the National Forest Reservation, with all that it would have meant to Americans from the sources of the Middle Fork to the Mississippi Delta, was total—and in a few years there will be no forests as we once knew them. The reason for this failure seems to have lain in the mineral that underlies the forests, which could not be bought by the Forest Service, or sidestepped in the purchase of surface rights. Our Regional Forester wrote me from Washington, "This is the same condition which we have found to exist elsewhere in Kentucky, West Virginia and Virginia, where the bulk of the value, present and prospective, is in minerals, especially coal." Only recently Mr. Hedges wrote me of his

keen disappointment over the failure to extend the national forest system into that great headwaters section. . . . I firmly believe that a national forest would have supported the local economy, without prohibitive public expense. . . . In fact, as I look around at the continued uninterrupted destruction of our forests I see as great a need for extension of public ownership, or public regulation of lumbering operations, as there existed during Pinchot's time.

For this destruction one should not place full blame on the lumber companies. The tax laws of many states, including Kentucky, discourage forestry and favor lumbering. No tax concessions are given companies to conserve trees of small girth for later harvesting; no penalties are laid on them for the destruction of such trees. The fault for this lies partly with us, an apathetic citizenry. Meanwhile, the floods in here, and in the lowlands, are bigger and more frequent as the forest cover disappears, and terrible forest fires start in the cut-over lands, strewn with dead branches, to destroy such of the soil as had not already been washed away by erosion. Meanwhile, the cities on the Ohio River build more and better flood walls. If a man from Mars were to drop in upon the planet Earth, he might find it perplexing to understand why money, including Federal money, is paid out in the construction of flood walls to protect the cities in the lowland valleys, when the same money, spent in the conservation of the highland forests, would have controlled the floods. Some of those who travel through here see the operations of the lumber companies—including outside companies who take out of the region the wealth they glean from it—and think that an economic outlet has been assured our people through them. This is transient. It will soon pass away. But the desolation left by the destruction of the forests will remain for generations to come.

II

There are few things for which we have worked harder than for roads. That thousands of Kentuckians should be isolated from the twentieth century by the lack of modern highways was an intolerable anachronism. The Frontier Nursing Service, an incorporated philanthropy, completely nonpolitical, has never attempted to influence legislation, and it would be an act of gross impropriety for it to do so. However, when legislation to provide road funds has been passed, we can and do agitate to get some of this money for our section. Soon after Route 80, a modern road, was constructed from Hazard in Perry County to Hyden in Leslie County, we began to push for road funds to extend this highway thirty-odd miles farther on to Manchester in Clay County. We were instrumental, in 1932, in persuading the State Highway Commission to make appropriations to continue Route 80, and to get the work started—but it took years for it to be finished, with its surface of black top. The stretch of Route 421 between Harlan and Hyden was pushed to completion during the war to gain access to thousands of acres of timber. These highways now bisect the seven hundred square miles of FNS country through the middle and, in our Middle Fork section, lengthwise almost from end to end. Route 80 has

349

concrete bridges over the Middle Fork and over Red Bird River—but we still have to cross the rivers afoot, on swinging bridges, in the greater part of our territory.

I have referred several times in this narrative to swinging bridges. The one at Wendover is an example of what can be done by neighborhood co-operation. Before we had this bridge, the people hereabouts were forced to cross the Middle Fork by boat whenever the river was up. In October of 1939, we called for a rally at Wendover Big House which was attended by some forty men. Each pledged himself to do something toward the construction of a swinging bridge over the river. Leslie County donated the two great cables upon which the bridge is suspended. The Frontier Nursing Service gave the hardware—nails, spikes, and woven-wire handrails. Some of the men at the rally pledged the heavy timber to support the land ends of the bridge, some the planks to floor the bridge, some the use of their mule teams for hauling, and the others promised their labor. A model swinging bridge was constructed through this co-operation, with its land supports so high above the flood mark that the biggest of our recent floods did not reach them. The bridge itself was bashed to pieces in this flood, by the debris swirling down with the swollen waters, but its supports on the banks were not undermined. These supports held the cables taut, so that it took only a few days to get the bridge restored.

It is the custom in the Kentucky mountains to hold "workings," as they are called, in which the men give their labor. Some of these workings are held for a common enterprise, as were those that built the Wendover swinging bridge; some are the acts of Good Samaritans to neighbors in distress. If a man's house burns down it is not unusual for a whole neighborhood to donate several days at workings to help him put up another house. Many workings have been sponsored by our local committees at all of our stations, to clear overgrown trails for the nurses' horses, to repair roads leading to the nursing centers, to replace broken fences. The Hyden citizens have held innumerable workings on the winding road that leads up the mountain to Hyden Hospital, to keep it passable for the hospital patients and the nurse-midwives. Through these voluntary efforts our people often got us out of the mire, but could effect no permanent improvement in this road because it had not been surveyed and it had no drainage. My father used to say there were three principles in mountain road building—the first was drainage, the second was drainage, and the third was drainage. Before the chestnut in our forests had been destroyed by a blight we used it to make culverts under the Wendover road, after digging ditches on the inner side. These culverts served to take the wet weather streams out of the road and to carry them under it. Years later, the Rural Highways division of the State Highway Department replaced them with proper culverts.

The work of the Civilian Conservation Corps and the Works Progress Administration in the thirties did wonders for our native trails. The picturesque road the CCC built along Red Bird River can be used by cars and trucks today, because it was well surveyed and has adequate drainage. We asked the WPA if they would build a proper road leading up to Hyden Hospital on Thousandsticks Mountain. They agreed to do this with two provisos. The first was that the FNS, and other people through whose land the road passed, must give the county a permanent right of way. Everybody was glad to do this. The second proviso was that the FNS must tear down its barn, through the middle of which the old trail passed on its way to Hyden Hospital. Mrs. Henry Alvah Strong gave us a new barn, nearly twice the size of the old one, which Oscar Bowling built on a gentle slope in the pasture, where it stands out with the majesty of a battleship. At Mrs. Strong's request, we called it Aunt Hattie's Barn. The road the WPA built in the middle thirties to Hyden Hospital was black-topped in the late forties by the Rural Highways.

In the late thirties, after Route 80 was completed, and the CCC had finished the winding road up Red Bird River, we knew the time had come to get a motor vehicle of some kind for Vanda Summers, who was the nurse-midwife then at the Clara Ford Center in that section. But a modern, low-slung car would have been of little use to her except on Route 80 itself. We asked Mr. Edsel Ford of our Detroit Committee if he had a Model A Ford car he could turn over to us, for use at his mother's nursing center. Mr. Ford, who took a personal interest in everything he did for us, had a Model A car completely reconditioned before he sent it down to us, and equipped it with new tires and batteries and a set of tools. Henrietta, as we named her, stood up to the wear and tear of a heavy district for seven years. Then Mrs. Henry Ford replaced her with a jeep, which we called Henrietta II. But she was not our first jeep. Jane, our first, was lent us by Mrs. Henry Ford while the war was on, to be used between Wendover and Hyden. Jane had been a model used by the Ford Motor Company in making military jeeps and, until the war was ended, Mrs. Ford was not allowed to give us title to her.

At the beginning of this chapter I said that when we first began our work our region had two undeveloped economic assets, timber and coal. Local coal mines in here have been worked for generations, but no considerable headway was made in shipping coal to outside markets until after the end of the Second World War. Then a number of the mines around Hyden began to truck their coal over Route 80 to the railroads at Hazard and Manchester. This has given employment to hundreds of young veterans, many of whom live on their own land where they have gardens. It has greatly improved the standard of living of all those who are engaged in mining—whether as miners, truck drivers, landowners who get royalties on the coal that is mined, or the operators themselves.

Years ago I attended a conference, held under the auspices of the University of Kentucky at Quicksand, where it was stated that in one of our mountain counties only five per cent of the total acreage was under cultivation. The speaker, one of the University men, went on to say that the density of the population in this five per cent of the county was equal to the density of Belgium. In mountainous country such as ours almost all of the people dwell in the valleys. The cultivation of these narrow bottom lands cannot afford a living to so many people. The mountainsides themselves must sustain the economy, as ours might have done through scientific forestry, as ours now do through the development of coal.

III

With the coming of the highways has come also the great blessing of electricity, not everywhere as yet, but to the homes along the rivers and even to some of those along the creeks. After the Rural Electrification Administration had run its lines through our Red Bird River section, in the forties, our three outpost centers at Red Bird, Flat Creek and Brutus connected with them. The Kentucky–West Virginia Power Company, which first came to Hyden in 1935, extended its lines up the Middle Fork more than a decade later, and our Beech Fork Center connected with them. It now has lines running to parts of the lower Middle Fork, with which our centers at Confluence and Bowlingtown are connected. In 1948, the Kentucky–West Virginia Power Company agreed to run a branch line across the river to Wendover, and to our neighbors a few miles beyond, if we would have the Wendover property wired for electricity. There were so many buildings in our boundary, and the cost of wiring them in rigid conduit was so great, that this would have been impossible had not Mrs. Roger Rogan offered to do it as a memorial to her husband.

The work on the connections had started, and had just linked up with the living room in the Big House, when Mrs. Rogan came with the Reverend Francis John Moore to Wendover, to dedicate the lights. Members of the staff of the Frontier Nursing Service from all our stations, with a little group of neighbors, gathered for the ceremony at the edge of dark, as we mountaineers call the twilight. The shadowy living room of the old log house was lit by candles and an oil lamp as Dr. Moore, in his robes, began to read the service of dedication. When in his reading, Dr. Moore came to the words

In joyful Thanksgiving, we dedicate, at the edge of dark, these lights, to the Glory of God, to the dear memory of Roger Kemper Rogan, and to the service of this Nursing Community . . .

those who stood near the candles and the oil lamp extinguished them—those who stood by the first two electric lamps ever to shine in this remote forest turned on their greater light.

Telephones are another blessing of civilization but, oddly enough, we had more of them before the highways came in than we have had since, although the ones along the highways have been greatly improved. In the early thirties the Rangers of the State Forest Service—like all foresters, a splendid body of men—installed their own telephone lines from their headquarters on Red Bird River through the timber lands up and down the river. To these they connected our nursing centers at Flat Creek and Red Bird. A private telephone line ran along the Middle Fork River, with which Beech Fork, Wendover, Hyden Hospital, Confluence and Bowlingtown were connected. The only place where we had no telephone in those days was Brutus on Bullskin Creek.

At meetings of our Bowlingtown and Brutus Committees, I asked the men if they would construct a telephone line between those two points—a distance of some ten miles along a rough trail—if the Frontier Nursing Service bought the telephone wire and the insulators. Our men gave their services without charge. After they had cut poles from the forests, dragged them over to the line and set them up, we bought the wire and they strung it. When a Brutus nurse had a message for the Medical Director at Hyden Hospital in those days, she could telephone it to the exchange at Bowlingtown, which telephoned it to Confluence, which telephoned it to the Hyden exchange, which connected it with the doctor. These messages were often messed up in transmission—rather like those in that whispering game, where people sit in a circle and pass a sentence from one member of the circle to the next. For example, this message from Brutus reached Hyden Hospital: "The milk of Blinkie is paltry." Blinkie was the Brutus cow. Dr. Kooser, not feeling that information about her lay in his department, transmitted it to Jean Hollins at Wendover. Jean, knowing that Blinkie was fresh, asked to have the message repeated. The second time it came through like this: "The wife of Bill Couch has palsy."

It proved impossible to keep our telephone line between Bowlingtown and Brutus in repair. The oddest things happened to it. One man borrowed a piece of it for a clothesline for his wife. He returned it with many apologies, but the line had to be strung up again. Another man, who had imbibed too freely, shot a lot of the glass insulators off the poles, under the impression they were targets. After the Brutus line was abandoned, we did not have a connection there until the Forest Rangers installed one in 1950, over the mountain range from Red Bird River to Bullskin. The line from Confluence to Bowlingtown was abandoned years ago by the private company which had built it, because of the expense of its upkeep in a region where few people used it.

After the great flood in June, 1947, we had no telephone lines anywhere in our territory because they had all been washed away. Wendover's line to Hyden was repaired fairly soon. Although the Forest Rangers had lost nearly a hundred poles, they reset their line within a few months. Our Beech Fork Nursing Center did not get a telephone again for three years, and the telephone at Confluence has not been reinstalled even now. This means that two of our outpost nursing centers, Possum Bend and the Margaret Durbin Harper at Bowlingtown, have now no telephone connections.

IV

It cannot be amiss for the Frontier Nursing Service to list its own presence in this section of the Kentucky mountains as a factor in sustaining the local economy. Not only have we taken no wealth out of our region but wealth from beyond the mountains comes to it through us. Nearly a million dollars of outside money has been spent on our vast properties, in buildings and other improvements, and on their annual maintenance. Except in the case of supplies and workmen not obtainable in our section, we have used local materials whenever possible and local labor. Our annual payroll, in salaries and wages, is all paid out right in here in our own section because our offices as well as our work are here. One way, then, in which the economy of a rural area can be strengthened is through the location of work like ours in such an area, where a hospital, administrative headquarters, and numerous outpost centers bring money as well as health to rural citizens.

But the health of a population is in itself an essential factor in upholding an economy, and both public and private measures need to be taken to assure it. There is confusion in the minds of professional as well as lay people as to wherein lies the difference between public and private measures, between, for example, the work of a district nurse-midwife like ours and that of a county public health nurse. The position of a county nurse, working in a county health unit, is analogous to that of a nurse in a city health department. In a rural county where the milk comes from a thousand separate cows, many of them with Bang's disease, where the water supply comes from a thousand wells and springs, many of them infected, and where there is almost no sanitary disposal of excreta—in such a county a health department, with at least one county nurse attached to it, is as needed as is a health department in a city. A county nurse, attached to a health unit, is a useful person but with no time to spend in the homes of her citizens as a bedside nurse, a midwife, or a health teacher on a family basis.

In all American cities of any size there are not only city health departments, with nurses working under them, but Visiting Nurse Associations as well. The nurses working with them, under voluntary boards and supported largely by voluntary funds, do for their patients all of the things that the nurses in a city health department could not and do not handle. But in truly rural areas, where the need for such nurses is as acute as in cities, the charitable citizens haven't the wealth to support Visiting Nurse Associations. This chapter has stressed the economic problems of such rural areas as are mountainous, but no rural areas are centers of vast wealth. To take two extremes, land worth ten dollars an acre does not yield the revenue of land worth ten thousand dollars a square foot. I know of no district nurse in any truly rural area who is not supported by outside philanthropic or church funds. This fact poses a problem. The states give financial help to the health units of rural counties, or there could be no health units, and to help them do this the states receive Federal aid. This policy is in the *public* interest. Should the Federal and State Governments set up Visiting Nurse Associations for rural areas? Not according to my thinking. If we let government control the nursing and medical care we receive as *private* citizens, then government will become so paternalistic that we may expect officials to drop down from the heavens by parachute to tuck us in bed and hear our prayers.

Visiting Nurse Associations in rural areas, as in cities, should be supported and controlled by private enterprise in philanthropy, as the occasional district nurse is now—as is the Frontier Nursing Service. Philanthropy could carry this load with some such tax exemption as that suggested by Robert W. King in *Harper's Magazine* (October, 1948) namely, by the deduction of contributions for philanthropic purposes not from one's taxable income, but *from one's tax itself*, up to an allowed per cent of one's income. It is more grown-up for Americans to keep this money, through action taken by their elected representatives, and to carry their responsibilities themselves, than to tell Daddy to take the money and do it for them.

355

V

The value of any nursing program, whether rural or urban, lies in the quality of those who take up nursing and in the preparation they receive for this career. Since I first worked as a district nurse, a lifetime ago, I have had hundreds of nurses pass through my hands in France and in Kentucky, all of whom received their basic training in the schools of nursing of Europe and America. The foundation for what they accomplished as district nurses was laid in their training schools and, with most of them, it was well laid. The demand for nurses today in new and ever widening fields of work is so great that many despair of meeting it. All sorts of experiments are carried out in the nursing field but most of them do not lead to a greater number of qualified nurses, or even to a desire on the part of more young women to become nurses. The programs devised for attracting young women into the nursing field do not stress the care of the sick, although this is an attraction greater than all others to generous-minded girls. We have not abolished birth and death. All we have done is to lengthen the span which lies between, and this span is still filled with illnesses, injuries, operations, and the wounds of war.

Our first nursing need in America today is for more nurses to take care of the patients in hospitals and in homes, in cities and in rural areas, alike. My suggestion for meeting this need is to try out again the two-year course of training for nurses which gave us our early leaders. Only applicants with high school diplomas, or an equivalent in private tutoring, should be accepted for this two-year course. After they had completed it, they should be well qualified to nurse patients in hospitals and in homes, rural and urban. I suggest that they then take Part One of their state examinations and be given the title of G.N.—for Graduate Nurse. If they needed money to continue with their nursing studies they could earn it, and at the same time meet a desperate national need, before taking a third year of training which should lead to Part Two of their state examinations and the title of R.N.—for Registered Nurse. In this third year they could gain an insight into such specializations as mental hygiene, public health, district nursing, communicable disease, et cetera—which now take up approximately a year of the three-year course of training. During both the two-year period and the third-year period their lectures, laboratory work, classroom instruction, should all be at the college level, so that those Registered Nurses who wished to do so could take a fourth year, in affiliation with a university, and earn a Bachelor's degree. Such a plan might be tried out experimentally in one or two states, to discover whether it were workable or not. Its advantages should be: First, more girls, undoubtedly, would be attracted to nursing. Second, the need of more nurses to take care of patients could be met in two years. Third, small hospital schools, many of which give excellent basic training to nurses, could carry the two-year course, leaving the third year to larger institutions. Fourth, the system is one suited to a democracy in that no door is closed to anyone. Any nurse could move on, at her own pace and as her financial circumstances allowed, up the scale. No secondary class of attendants is created to whom all future doors are closed.

I watch with interest another experiment in the training of nurses—that of the four-year consecutive course, leading to a college degree as well as to a diploma in nursing, with emphasis on the college affiliation. This experiment, like all others, must stand or fall by its results. These will be poor if the young women who take this course have not spent enough time in caring for patients to get to know the feel, the look, the smell of disease. Until a nurse gets to know a pulse so that the bare touch of it tells her something, until she is so familiar with sickness that the least movement of a patient conveys a meaning to her, she is not, in the real meaning of the words, a trained nurse. The techniques of nursing can be mastered with far more ease than can this profound knowledge of patients.

In the course of this story I have reported on the effort we in the Frontier Nursing Service have made to help members of our staff get college degrees, and more advanced degrees when they qualified for them. I have so much respect for these things that Texas, with her doctorate, and Bucket, with her Master's degree, often teased me about it. When the first of four honorary degrees of LL.D. was conferred upon me, they called it a consolation prize given me only because I couldn't earn a real one! I don't think I shall be misunderstood when I say that college degrees should not lead automatically to positions where nurses direct or teach other nurses, unless those who hold these degrees are better trained and more experienced *in nursing* than those they teach and direct. The collegiate schools require their students to spend less time with patients than is required of students in the hospital schools. A number of leaders in the nursing world of today give support to the theory that hours spent in college lecture rooms and laboratories may be substituted for hours spent in close contact with patients. But in this matter, as in everything else, facts and not theories are all that count. Enough facts are not yet available to indicate whether a higher proportion of the graduates of the collegiate schools are better *as nurses,* or less good, than those who have gone through three years in nursing at the great hospital schools. Insofar as the Frontier Nursing Service is concerned, everyone who rises to top positions has come up from the ranks, and none teach or direct the work of others who have not first proved themselves on the common battlefield.

357

Chapter 36

I

THOSE of my readers, thousands of them, who have a deep-rooted affection for the Frontier Nursing Service will want to know something about our plans for the future. But when I think of us in a future, even that of next week, I am reminded of a cartoon I saw years ago in a London paper. A bewildered man sat in a baby Austin car right under the nose of a gigantic bus, with traffic snarled in all directions. Leaning out over the bewildered man, the bus driver said, "May I ask, sir, what are your plans?" If one looked at things only from the outside, there would seem to be not much use in making plans while wars, cold and hot, keep their stranglehold on the future. But those of us who travel within, as well as without, know that we are not helpless; that there is no reason why yet another civilization, ours, should move inexorably toward its doom. Such being so, we in the Frontier Nursing Service make plans.

We have come a long way since our work began, since we first started to build our hospital and depended on mule teams to haul its cement and plaster from the railroad. We hitched our wagon to a star then, and when we traded wagons for trucks, we held on to the star. The heart of our work has lain in its start with things as they were and its acceptance of the laws of growth. In planning for future growth the Frontier Nursing Service still adheres to the principles that gave it being.

There will never come a time, in no matter how remote a future, when man will not enter the world through birth and leave it by death; when the young of the race will not need protection; when the broken, the sick and the old will not need the kind of care we in the Frontier Nursing Service are trained to give. There is no future foreseeable to our generation in which there will not be people who work on the land and, in so doing, provide the essentials of life to those who work in cities.

For more than a quarter century, the Frontier Nursing Service has gathered facts about the birth and death, the childhood, the sickness and accidents of those who live on the land—mountainous land with more timber and coal than food. The readers of this book know that the system we developed did not originate with us. We were reminded of this as recently as 1938, after we had a visit from Dr. Harley Williams of England, when he wrote an account of our work that was printed on a leader page of the London *Times*. In this he spoke of our descent in tradition from the Highlands and Islands Medical and Nursing Service, and said, "The daughter service has in some respects and in a miniature scale surpassed the parent."

Our aim has always been to see ourselves surpassed, and on a larger scale. From the time they could reach us without too much effort, doctors, nurse-midwives, nurses, social workers, have traveled into the Kentucky mountains to study our methods at first hand. They come through the World Health Organization, and other international agencies, and from Europe, Africa, Asia, the Americas, and the islands of the seven seas. At the bedside of one mother in labor on one of our creeks—a mother who was eager to be of help to others—there were present an American supervisor, a French nurse-student from our Graduate School, a British nurse-midwife (who had just joined us) and, as guests, a Hindu physician and a Finnish nurse.

The needs of the young child and his mother will always bring together in a common interest the peoples of diverse tongues and nations. In a mutual exchange of ideas and experiences, we in the Frontier Nursing Service gain as much from our overseas guests as we give, and sometimes more. One of our plans, then, for the future is to continue to receive professional people from other rural areas for on-the-spot study of our work.

A second plan, which we want to bring about soon, is to start a course in rural district nursing analogous to the course in midwifery which we have successfully carried for years at our Graduate School. Charitable agencies and churches are willing to support visiting nurses in country areas of this continent and the FNS, like the Queen's Institute of District Nursing in Great Britain, should prepare nurses for rural visiting nurse associations. We have to teach our frontier techniques to our own nurse-midwives. We taught them to the Indian nurses when they were with us years ago. After the second of our twentieth-century planetary wars, we brought over on a fellowship a gifted young French nurse, Odette Prunet. A graduate of the Bordeaux School, she worked all through the German occupation in the French nursing service of the Aisne that I organized so many years ago. We trained Odette in rural district nursing and public health before we allowed her, at her own request, to take her training as a midwife at our Graduate School. To the extent that it could be done with undergraduates, we taught the same system, during the war, to the cadets who came to us under the Bolton Act.

For the past several years we have often taken on a larger staff at Hyden Hospital than we needed to run it, in order to give the young nurses who come to us an insight into district nursing. They serve in rotation on the wards of the hospital, in its huge outpatient clinics, and on the districts around Hyden—in all branches of our work except midwifery—under the supervision of the fine nurses responsible for this work. Whenever enough nurses come to us, we place some of them at the outpost centers, and at Wendover, to give them a wider field experience. Through this rotation service, these young nurses learn the interrelationship between a rural hospital, its clinics, and the districts from which its patients come. Thus they get an integrated picture of rural work. It is this rotation system that we intend to develop into a school in order to prepare nurses for rural visiting nurse associations.

For more than a year we have had a third plan. On June 5, 1950, the late Dr. Paul Titus, Secretary of the American Board of Obstetrics and Gynecology, wrote me a letter of which this is a part:

It is a great pleasure to report to you that at the recent annual meeting of the American Board of Obstetrics and Gynecology action was taken of direct concern to the Frontier Nursing Service. . . .

In spite of the fact that the Medical Director of the Frontier Nursing Service cannot rigidly limit his work to obstetrics-gynecology, the Board voted to make that position the sole existing exception to the rule requiring two years of post-training practice in the specialty.

This is further evidence of the high regard in which the Service is held by obstetricians-gynecologists of this country. You would be gratified if you could have heard the comments during the discussion of this proposal.

Under this ruling you may publicly state when seeking to fill the position of Medical Director, that your applicants should be men who have completed the formal residency training for Board certification, that the Board accepts work in this position as fulfilling the requirements for post-training practice in the specialty. . . .

When I wrote Dr. Titus that we wanted a permanent Medical Director equipped in both surgery and obstetrics, I asked him if his Board would be willing to allow their men to work for one or two years as assistants to such a physician. His reply was favorable. Through this plan we hope not only to provide ourselves with qualified medical assistants, but to imbue young physicians with our love of rural areas and their people, so that some of them will be willing to settle in country districts even at a financial sacrifice.

It has been our experience that almost the only doctors trained to handle surgery and obstetrics, along with medicine, are the medical missionaries. Our first inkling of what such a doctor could bring to the Frontier Nursing Service came in 1945 when Dr. Henry S. Waters threw his lot in with ours, after he had been released from internment in the Philippines. During the six months this skilled surgeon stayed with us, we learned what it meant to our patients to have their surgical emergencies quickly met. From the time that Dr. Waters went back to the Philippines, we have sought to find another medical missionary, qualified as he was, willing to stay in America with the Frontier Nursing Service. This came about with the arrival from the Middle East of our present Medical Director, Dr. F. William den Dulk. Men with the qualifications called for by the American Board of Obstetrics and Gynecology, who assist Dr. den Dulk in rotation for a year or two, will not only meet the requirements of the Board but will have added a cubit to their stature.

Our fourth plan involves the writing of textbooks. Our work has been referred to in the nurses' *Handbook of Obstetrics* by Louise Zabriskie, R.N., Director, Maternity Consultation Service, New York City, and Nicholson J. Eastman, M.D., Professor of Obstetrics, Johns Hopkins University. Several writers of textbooks for physicians, among them Dr. Eastman and Dr. Titus, have made kindly references to the Frontier Nursing Service in their well-known books. But books on obstetrical nursing are not suited to the teaching of midwives, and books written for students of obstetrics are too advanced for them. We have a number of excellent British textbooks for use in the Frontier Graduate School of Midwifery. There should be an American textbook, designed to prepare American students of midwifery for work in areas such as ours. Our Medical Director and Assistant Directors are qualified to write it. One of our plans is to arrange for them the time in which to do it. When we get our rotation system developed into a School of Visiting Nursing for rural areas, we shall need also to write our own textbook for that.

Our fifth plan naturally concerns itself with more space and money to do the things we have outlined in the first four plans. Our hospital plant needs another building to double its beds and provide more room for its huge outpatient clinics and for such modern equipment as an electrocardiograph. This plant is the focus for all our educational plans as well as for the better care we seek increasingly to give our patients. Medical science has taken many strides from the days when doctors drew blood away from pale people, on down to these modern days when they give new blood to such people. No rural hospital seeks to become, or could become, a medical center, but there is legitimate expansion possible for country hospitals as well as for those in cities. At our Hyden Hospital, for over twenty years, we have blown a bugle for meals instead of ringing a bell. To us this bugle call brings its challenge for more than the food we need.

In the new wing for Hyden Hospital, whenever it is constructed, we shall build St. Christopher's Chapel. For this we have a glorious fifteenth-century French stained glass window of St. Christopher and the Christ Child, when he carried Him over a ford like ours. Many years ago my cousin, the late Preston Satterwhite, had this window in his New York entrance hall. I used to stand before it and tell Preston that if the Frontier Nursing Service had a patron saint it could not be other than St. Christopher, on whose help we counted when we carried children on the pommels of our saddles through treacherous fords.

The legend of St. Christopher arose in the mists of the earliest Christian times but was not recorded until, in the thirteenth century, Jacobus de Voragine included it in his *Legenda Aurea*. This legend, in a sixteenth-century English translation, I read aloud every Christmas Eve at Wendover and every Christmas Day at Hyden Hospital. Then I read Laurence Housman's poem on the death of St. Christopher. In the poem the Saint has finished his work. During all the long years that followed the time when he carried the Christ Child, and with Him the weight of the world, he has used his great strength and stature to help travelers across his ford. One glad day he lay down to die. It was then that he heard the voice of a passer-by calling to him for help through the deep waters. At this summons, he prayed for strength as he forced himself to get up.

> When he reached the ford at length,
>   Spake the Voice of all his bliss,
> Saying, "Christ shall give thee strength!"

The glorious window at Preston's place, before which I used to stand, is ours because Preston gave it to me. He had stained glass experts take it apart and pack it for shipment to us. It stays just as the experts left it until we build the new wing to Hyden Hospital. Then St. Christopher's Chapel will be built too and the window, high up on Thousandsticks Mountain, will glow in the light of the morning sun.

II

The thing that we most want—more than all our plans—is to better the work we do now in the years to come. Which of you has not felt,

362

as we so often do, the bafflement that comes from having really tried to do better and failed? We sometimes feel as though we were rusty tools from which is expected the precision of fine instruments. But in our hearts we know that the rustiest tools are of more use, if they yield themselves to the hands of the master Craftsman, than shining instruments untouched by His hands.

Since the first aim of the Frontier Nursing Service is to help children, we struggle continually to improve our techniques in their behalf. In common with all who study the loss of infants at birth, we know that some of these deaths need not be, and perhaps one field in which we can make real progress in the years to come lies in the prevention of some of this waste of human life.

We have never done enough for children, even though the emphasis of all our years of work has lain with them. We must find a way in which we can help to bring about a normal emotional life for more of them, during those tender years when wounds are made which leave scars forever.

The secret of helping children is to understand them. My brother, General Breckinridge, the Marine, told me once that you could not work out a strategy to meet your enemy unless first you put yourself into his mind and heart. Children can be helped to grow up into childlike, instead of childish, persons only by those who will enter into their minds and hearts *at each stage of their growth*. Men will continue to cherish grudges against each other, nation will continue to fight nation, until enough children have been understood to bring about a new generation of men. This means, according to my thinking, that the people who have it in their power to bring peace between man and man, between nation and nation, are those who have the training of young children, and are willing to learn how to do it right.

For more than forty years I have brooded over that saying of the Christ about the little children He took in His arms, "Their angels do always behold the face of my Father which is in heaven." What did He mean? What did He really say? He spoke in Aramaic. The only records we have of His words are in Greek, copied from copies, three hundred years after they were spoken. Only once is He recorded as having written anything Himself, when He stooped to write on the ground. And the winds blew the dust of those immortal words away. In the agrapha of Christ, gleaned from the works of the early Christian Fathers, and elsewhere, I found an agraphon that helps me to a meaning in St. Matthew's record: "I was among you with the children, and ye knew me not." He is still among us with the children, and we know Him not.

Earlier I mentioned that in man, alone among mammals, there is a prolongation of childhood, which allows for mental and spiritual growth. But in the first six years of childhood, man's emotional patterns for the rest of his life are largely determined. If he grows up beset by fears, looking for scapegoats, holding grudges, seeking self-protection, then he will be too blinded emotionally to enter into alien minds and hearts and forestall their will to war. War is preventable, but not by nations made up largely of childish men. As for Nature, "To sacrifice she prompts her best." In every war, the first to pick up the gauntlet are those of our young men who are childlike enough to see straight ahead of them, and discount the cost.

> Not see? because of the night perhaps?—why, day
>   Came back again for that! before it left,
>   The dying sunset kindled through a cleft:
> The hills, like giants at a hunting, lay,
> Chin upon hand, to see the game at bay,—
>   "Now stab and end the creature—to the heft!"
>
> Not hear? when noise was everywhere! it tolled
>   Increasing like a bell. Names in my ears
>   Of all the lost adventurers my peers,—
> How such a one was strong, and such was bold,
> And such was fortunate, yet each of old
>   Lost, lost! one moment knelled the woe of years.
>
> There they stood, ranged along the hill-sides, met
>   To view the last of me, a living frame
>   For one more picture! in a sheet of flame
> I saw them and I knew them all. And yet
> Dauntless the slug-horn to my lips I set,
>   And blew. *"Childe Roland to the Dark Tower came."*

III

I have written of my first meeting with Adeline Cashmore, in England at York. "The great man is the transforming man." This describes a spiritual genius. I don't know what methods Adeline used in helping others, but she pointed to the childlike way for me. She wrote, "In Christ, the Creator and the creature meet." She used creature in its old meaning of a created thing. Among the logia of Christ, found in an early Greek papyrus in the sands of Egypt, is this, "Raise the stone and there thou shalt find me, cleave the wood and there am I." To Adeline, the heart of Christ, in whom "the Creator and the creature meet," shares in the travail of creation:

Also, for all things perishing, He saith,
"My grief, My pain, My death."

The reason I have told about Adeline in this book is because her part in the Frontier Nursing Service has been the most significant of all. She knew, as only a spiritual genius can know, that I had been sent to her so that she could carry the Frontier Nursing Service in her prayer. That my heart was, to use a mountain expression, "pure wastings and sweepings" didn't matter, so long as I could be taught to surrender it. Adeline carried into her prayer the "pure wastings and sweepings" of all this piteous world. She loved God, as she knew Him in Christ, so utterly that when she lifted causes and people up to Him and held them there, a channel was opened through which God's love could pour unimpeded. "And that is a precious gift of working," said Lady Julian, that other anchoress of the fourteenth century, "in which we love God, for Himself; and that which God loveth, for God." Such "working" is the task of divinely gifted ones like Julian and Adeline, but it requires courage of a high order. They do for us what we cannot do for ourselves. "Can ye drink of my cup?" asked the Christ. They drain His cup.

Since Adeline's death on April 15, 1945, I have been more conscious of her, and therefore more understanding of the things she wrote me, than I was before she died. Her body is lying near those of a few missionaries and seventeen R.A.F. boys, in a bit of consecrated ground in South India. The R.A.F. boys were gallant people, but Adeline was the bravest of them all.

IV

I laid aside these pages as the last lines were written, to mount Babbette and ride up the river, and then on up Camp Creek, to meet with neighbors gathered around a log fire in the open. Someday I shall have taken my last ride, but I shan't know at the time that it is my last one. Nor do I remember my first one, because I took it in early childhood. The adventure I longed for when I was young was to become mine, although not in the form in which I longed for it then.

But it is not of horses so much as of people that I am thinking as I end this book. Old friends will say, "Why didn't you tell about that?" I expect I did. "Why didn't you write more of the men and women who shared adventure with you?" I know I did. And, in the need to get a balance, their names, with some thirty thousand other words, were swept away. There is no one who has been a friend to the Frontier Nursing Service but has entered into the making of this book.

I have drawn help from memories of many friends in a life blessed by friendships. And I drew help from more people than these. "The great Intelligences fair that range above our mortal state"—with whom I live in the writings they left, or the books others wrote about them—those men and women of the long ago, have helped me more than I have the power to tell.

> . . . to what majesty of stars I hold
> My little candle of experience.

AFTERWORD

By Dale Deaton

The Frontier Nursing Service has more than doubled in age since Mary Breckinridge began writing *Wide Neighborhoods* in 1950. Yet, remarkably, its purpose, philosophy, and structure have remained constant since 1925. Progress in its educational program, its support of research efforts, and its interest in promoting the FNS method of health care have enhanced developments within the Service and have increased its importance as a model.

Wide Neighborhoods itself initiated a major change within the organization. Mary Breckinridge dedicated two years to research and writing. To direct the activities of FNS during this period, she appointed Helen E. Browne as assistant director, with responsibility for administrative functions. Betty Lester became field supervisor, and Agnes Lewis, the executive secretary, supervised most nonmedical activities.

Although Mrs. Breckinridge kept informed of everything happening within the Service, for the first time in twenty-five years she no longer directly supervised either administrative or field services. After *Wide Neighborhoods* was published she directed the FNS mainly through staff meetings and never resumed direct contact with daily activities to the extent that she did prior to 1950. It was with confidence and probably also relief that she left these duties to Brownie, the General, and Miss Agnes. Two days after Mrs. Breckinridge's death on May 16, 1965, Helen Browne was elected director.

The loss of Mary Breckinridge was a personal tragedy to her staff, family, and friends, but her death had little adverse effect on the field operations of the FNS, for she left the organization in excellent hands. Yet so strong was her personal relationship with the people of the area that, at a meeting with local committee members shortly after her death, staff members felt they should ask if the people wanted FNS to continue without her. The reaction was bewilderment as to why the question was raised. The FNS remained and the question has not come up again.

Helen Browne, who remained director until her retirement in 1975, and her successors, Dr. W.B. Rogers Beasley, director until June 1980, and Elaine Pendleton, present director, have had to deal with a host of problems and circumstances never encountered by Mary Breckinridge. The world of health care has changed drastically, beginning in the 1960s with the Johnson administration's War on Poverty, especially the Medicare and Medicaid programs of the federal and state governments.

Hyden Hospital and the Home Health Agency were certified for reimbursement by Medicare/Medicaid in 1966, the first time FNS received extensive governmental support; the aid received during World War II was microscopic by comparison. Increases in funds and programs have resulted in an expansion of services which neither the organization nor its patients could otherwise afford. As in the past, every patient is treated regardless of financial circumstances, but philanthropic support has played a decreasing role in meeting operating expenses in the past fifteen years. Private support must increase its percentage of yearly budgets, however, if FNS is to avoid limiting services to those covered by insurance and government reimbursement.

Home Health Agency nurses are now responsible for providing care for home-bound patients, and district nurses no longer visit in homes. This change, primarily a result of financial strains and government regulations, has restricted preventive health care education to clinical or classroom settings. It has also prevented home visits by the nurse-midwives. Home deliveries are now rare exceptions because of reimbursement restrictions. Other nursing duties traditionally performed by nurse-midwives are now performed by family nurse practitioners.

In June 1970 the family nurse practitioner training was combined with the Frontier Graduate School of Midwifery. This change gave official academic sanction to the course in rural district nursing listed in the last chapter as one of Mrs. Breckinridge's five practical plans. In essence, a degree is now offered for what FNS nurse-midwives have done for years. Since 1939, the school has trained 376 nurse-midwives, 3 family nurse associates, 68 family nurses, and 135 family nurse-midwives, a total of 582 graduates. The faculty has varied from three to nine nursing professionals and one to four physicians, who also treat patients. Training and practice in family nursing and nurse-midwifery have been observed by thousands of visiting professionals, and graduates of FNS, students, and staff have practiced throughout the United States and in many foreign countries. By these means the FNS methods have been promoted continuously in rural and developing areas.

Research has been a part of FNS since the beginning, although financial restraints and the emphasis on clinical service have limited the research program. Nevertheless, FNS has often participated in studies by making itself available to professionals from outside its ranks. One such researcher was Dr. John Rock, who directed a clinical study, beginning in 1958, in the development of the first oral contraceptive. FNS provided a perfect setting for two reasons. First, detailed medical records were available on all patients. In fact, the FNS area was the only location in the United States possessing the medical histories of an entire indigenous population, an almost necessary condition for obtaining conclusive results from the research. Second, some contraceptive efforts were already being made, so that FNS nurse-midwives and doctors had a good relationship with patients regarding birth control measures. By the early 1960s the "Pill" was being introduced around the world, with far-reaching impact. In Leslie County itself, the birth rate has decreased from one of the highest in the nation in 1952 to about the national average in 1978.

Many other changes have taken place in the organization since the early 1950s. The new FNS facilities bear little resemblance to those of thirty years ago. In 1975 the Mary Breckinridge Hospital replaced the Hyden Hospital and Health Center opened in 1928. New district nursing centers are now located at Oneida, Wooton, Big Creek, and Pine Mountain, all opening within the last five years. The Pine Mountain Clinic expanded FNS health care into Harlan County in 1979. The oldest center, that at Beech Fork, is still in use, but a new building is under construction at this writing. All buildings are modern. The hospital is equipped as a forty-bed acute care facility, and includes a pharmacy, laboratory, physical and respiratory therapy programs, delivery, operating, and emergency rooms. It is also the location of the Frontier School of Midwifery and Family Nursing, and the Primary Care Clinic. The district centers are licensed as Primary Care Extensions and Rural Health Clinics. In 1979–1980, the staff of fifty-two nurses and nine physicians handled more than 60,000 patient visits. Nearly 23,000 of these were to the district nursing centers and over 7,000 were home visits by Home Health Agency nurses.

Each district nursing center has a committee made up of community members. For fifty years these bodies served in conjunction with a committee of interested citizens in Hyden as the organization's link to the community. In 1975 a Local Advisory Committee was formed, composed of representatives from each center committee and members from the area at large. The committee's purpose is to evaluate the FNS and to keep the organization informed of changing community needs and attitudes.

The area served by FNS—Leslie, Clay, Perry, and Harlan counties—has experienced many changes, educational, social, cultural, and economic, particularly within the past decade. Increased demand for coal has generated many jobs, and the number of high school and college graduates now remaining in the area is very encouraging. New school buildings have been constructed throughout the area and residents have made tremendous improvements to their homes. Although the region retains many of its distinctive characteristics, the residents are no longer an isolated population unaware of outside events and untouched by outside influences. Libraries, civic groups, shopping centers, and designer jeans are now a part of everyday life, although progress for mountain people does not necessarily mean a simulation of conditions elsewhere. But, while the people's pride in themselves and their homeland seems to be experiencing a rejuvenation, they continue to have little influence on their own economy and future development. Economic booms and busts are still determined by fluctuations in the need for coal.

The Frontier Nursing Service, too, is increasingly influenced by outside forces. The concepts of nurse-midwifery and family nursing practice have spread throughout America in the past fifteen years, and colleges of nursing around the country have added these programs to their curricula. The present trend is toward university settings for all nursing education. If this trend continues, nurse-midwives and family nurse practitioners will soon be operating in every area of the United States, and FNS will prove to have had a greater influence on the future of health care methods than any other philanthropic organization. But the opposition of some in the medical profession must be recognized. If the opposing forces succeed in holding down the number of nurse practitioners, the role of the FNS as a model will be lessened.

Ultimately, public preference and governmental policy will determine the future not only of the Frontier Nursing Service but of the method and philosophy it represents. When Mary Breckinridge said of FNS, "The glorious thing about it is that it has worked," she was speaking quite accurately of the period before Medicare/Medicaid and the current volumes of governmental regulations existed, when there was only a handful of nurse practitioner programs in the United States, when these practitioners posed no threat to other professionals, when their patients had few alternatives, and when the public attitude toward all health care professions was one of unquestioning obedience. All of these factors have changed greatly since the publication of *Wide Neighborhoods.*

Still, the Frontier Nursing Service works today. Any serious consideration of the role of nurse practitioners must include a detailed scrutiny of the FNS. The organization's design should be tested and demonstrated in other rural areas, in developing countries, in urban and metropolitan locations. The immediate concern of everyone wanting to see primary health care made available to all areas of the world must be to inform the public, to let each of us know that we have the right to choose the method of health care we prefer. Our individual preferences will play a part in the ultimate outcome. Each of us can influence governmental policies as well by making legislators aware of our wishes. As we—professionals and laymen alike—strive to bring adequate health care to all, to know that we have a model demonstration of how it can be done is our greatest assurance of success.

Dale Deaton, a historian by training, is Director of Development for the Frontier Nursing Service.